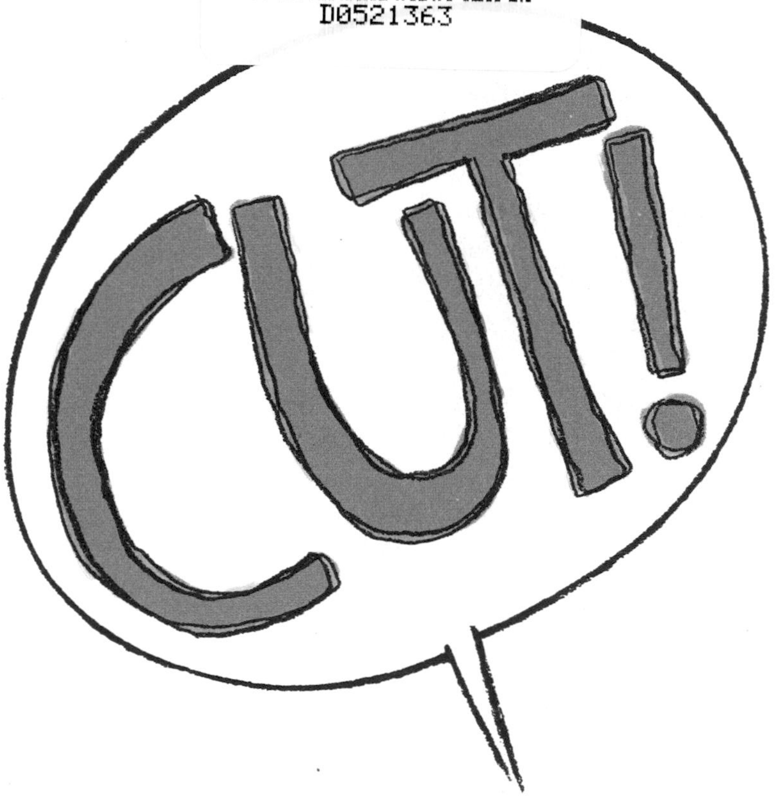
CUT!

Other *Baby Blues*® Books from Andrews McMeel Publishing

Guess Who Didn't Take a Nap?
I Thought Labor Ended When the Baby Was Born
We Are Experiencing Parental Difficulties . . . Please Stand By
Night of the Living Dad
I Saw Elvis in My Ultrasound
One More and We're Outnumbered!
Check, Please . . .
threats, bribes & videotape
If I'm a Stay-at-Home Mom, Why Am I Always in the Car?
Lift and Separate
I Shouldn't Have to Scream More Than Once!
Motherhood Is Not for Wimps
Baby Blues®: Unplugged
Dad to the Bone
Never a Dry Moment
Two Plus One Is Enough
Playdate: Category 5
Our Server Is Down
Something Chocolate This Way Comes
Briefcase Full of Baby Blues®
Night Shift
The Day Phonics Kicked In
My Space
The Natural Disorder of Things
We Were Here First
Ambushed! In the Family Room

Treasuries
The Super-Absorbent Biodegradable Family-Size Baby Blues®
Baby Blues®: Ten Years and Still in Diapers
Butt-Naked Baby Blues®
Wall-to-Wall Baby Blues®
Driving Under the Influence of Children
Framed!
X-Treme Parenting

Gift Books
It's a Boy
It's a Girl

BABY BLUES® 27 SCRAPBOOK

By Rick Kirkman
& Jerry Scott

Andrews McMeel
Publishing, LLC

Kansas City · Sydney · London

Andrews McMeel Publishing, LLC
an Andrews McMeel Universal company
1130 Walnut Street, Kansas City, Missouri 64106

www.andrewsmcmeel.com

11 12 13 14 15 RR2 10 9 8 7 6 5 4 3 2 1

ISBN: 978-1-4494-0182-5

Library of Congress Control Number: 2010910476

Find *Baby Blues*® on the Web at
www.babyblues.com.

——— **ATTENTION: SCHOOLS AND BUSINESSES** ———

Andrews McMeel books are available at quantity discounts with bulk purchase for educational, business, or sales promotional use. For information, please e-mail the Andrews McMeel Publishing Special Sales Department: specialsales@amuniversal.com

BABY BLUES®
BY
RICK KIRKMAN / JERRY SCOTT
ICK!

DO WE HAVE A DEAL?
OKAAY...
©2009, BABY BLUES PARTNERSHIP DIST. BY KING FEATURES SYNDICATE
SIGH!
www.babyblues.com
FROM NOW ON WE SAVE THE RICE KRISPY TREATS FOR DESSERT.
KIRKMAN & SCOTT 9.20

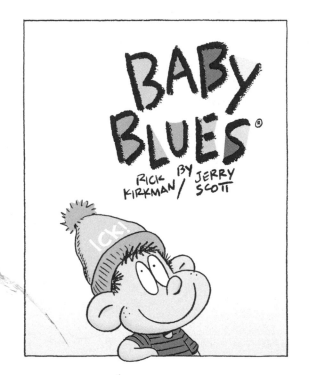

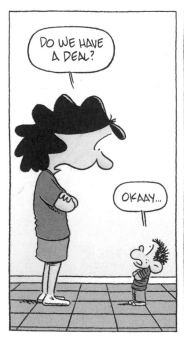

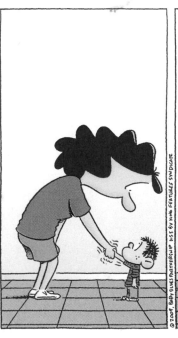

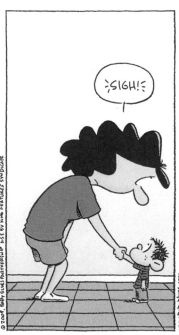

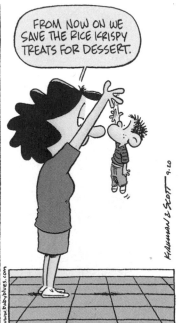

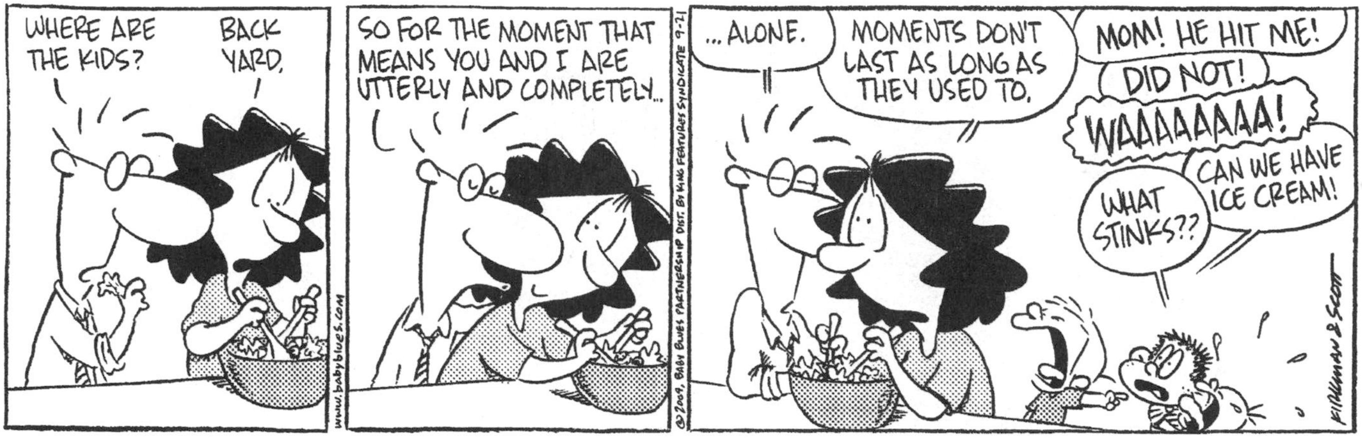
WHERE ARE THE KIDS?
BACK YARD.
SO FOR THE MOMENT THAT MEANS YOU AND I ARE UTTERLY AND COMPLETELY...
...ALONE.
MOMENTS DON'T LAST AS LONG AS THEY USED TO.
MOM! HE HIT ME!
DID NOT!
WAAAAAAAA!
CAN WE HAVE ICE CREAM!
WHAT STINKS??
www.babyblues.com
© 2009, BABY BLUES PARTNERSHIP DIST. BY KING FEATURES SYNDICATE 9-21
KIRKMAN & SCOTT

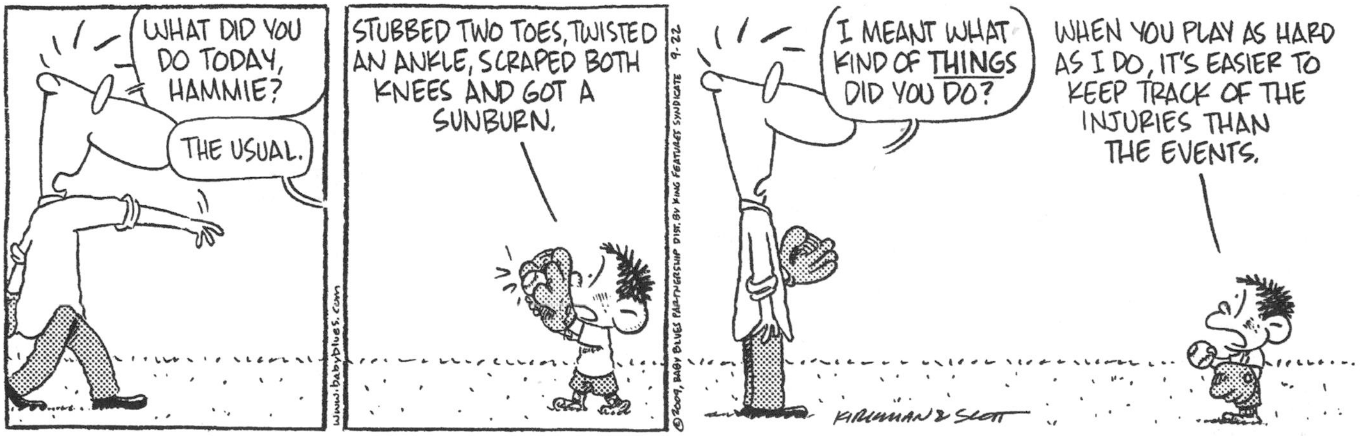
WHAT DID YOU DO TODAY, HAMMIE?
THE USUAL.
STUBBED TWO TOES, TWISTED AN ANKLE, SCRAPED BOTH KNEES AND GOT A SUNBURN.
I MEANT WHAT KIND OF THINGS DID YOU DO?
WHEN YOU PLAY AS HARD AS I DO, IT'S EASIER TO KEEP TRACK OF THE INJURIES THAN THE EVENTS.
www.babyblues.com
© 2009, BABY BLUES PARTNERSHIP DIST. BY KING FEATURES SYNDICATE 9-22
KIRKMAN & SCOTT

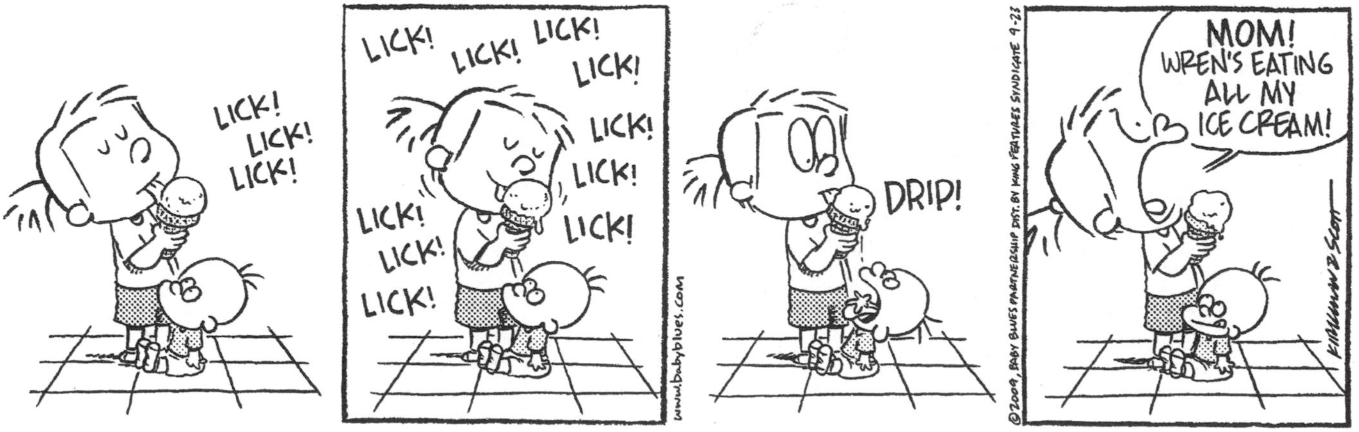
LICK! LICK! LICK!
LICK! LICK! LICK! LICK! LICK! LICK! LICK! LICK! LICK! LICK!
DRIP!
MOM! WREN'S EATING ALL MY ICE CREAM!
www.babyblues.com
© 2009, BABY BLUES PARTNERSHIP DIST. BY KING FEATURES SYNDICATE 9-23
KIRKMAN & SCOTT

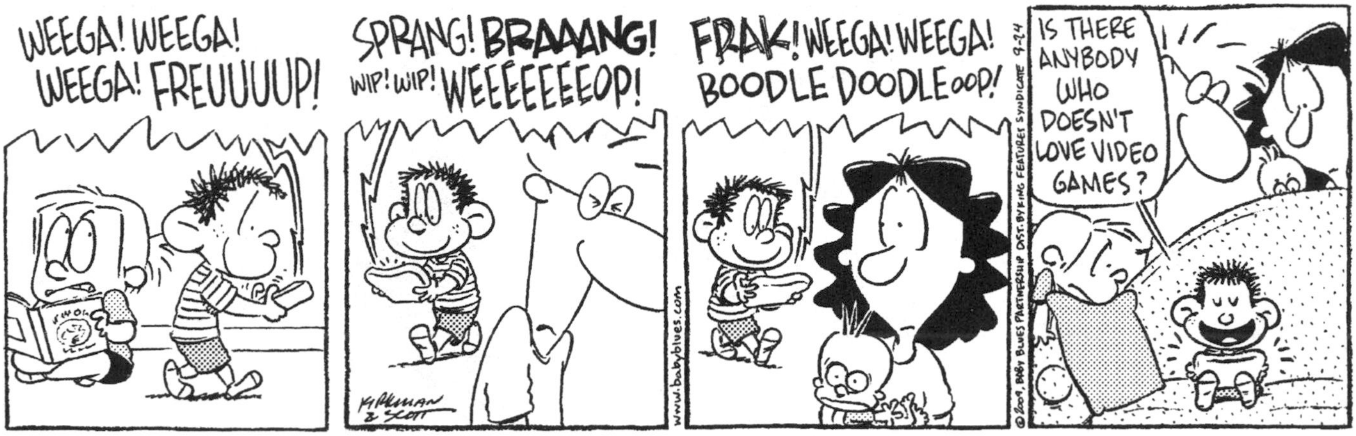
WEEGA! WEEGA! WEEGA! FREUUUUP!
SPRANG! BRAAANG! WIP! WIP! WEEEEEEEOP!
KIRKMAN & SCOTT
www.babyblues.com
FRAK! WEEGA! WEEGA! BOODLE DOODLE OOP!
©2009, BABY BLUES PARTNERSHIP DIST. BY KING FEATURES SYNDICATE 9-24
IS THERE ANYBODY WHO DOESN'T LOVE VIDEO GAMES?

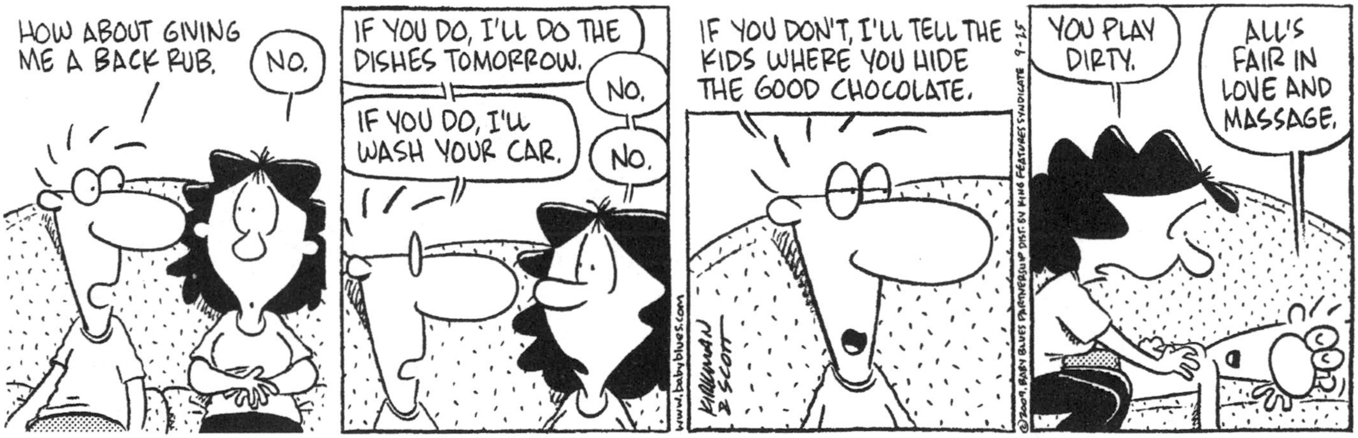
HOW ABOUT GIVING ME A BACK RUB.
NO.
IF YOU DO, I'LL DO THE DISHES TOMORROW.
NO.
IF YOU DO, I'LL WASH YOUR CAR.
NO.
www.babyblues.com
KIRKMAN & SCOTT
IF YOU DON'T, I'LL TELL THE KIDS WHERE YOU HIDE THE GOOD CHOCOLATE.
©2009, BABY BLUES PARTNERSHIP DIST. BY KING FEATURES SYNDICATE 9-25
YOU PLAY DIRTY.
ALL'S FAIR IN LOVE AND MASSAGE.

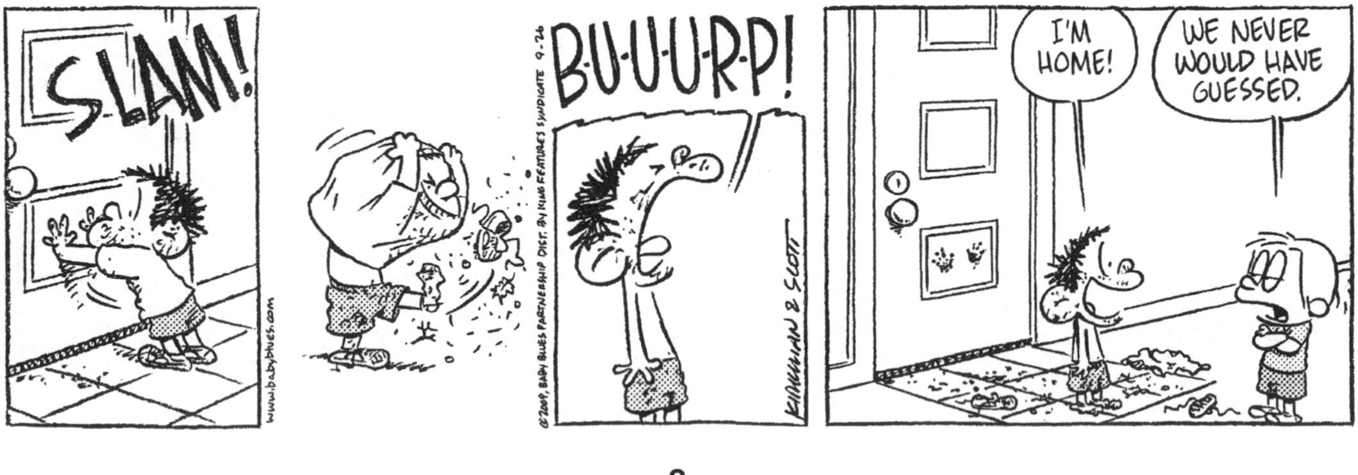
SLAM!
www.babyblues.com
©2009, BABY BLUES PARTNERSHIP DIST. BY KING FEATURES SYNDICATE 9-26
B-U-U-U-R-P!
KIRKMAN & SCOTT
I'M HOME!
WE NEVER WOULD HAVE GUESSED.

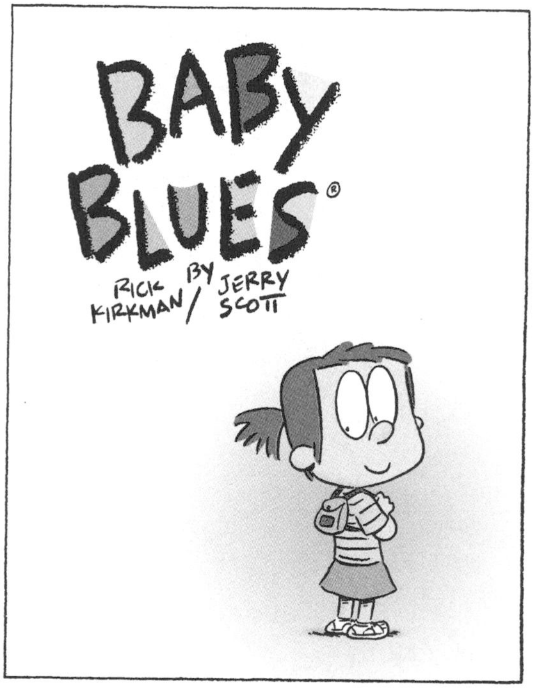
BABY BLUES®
BY RICK KIRKMAN / JERRY SCOTT

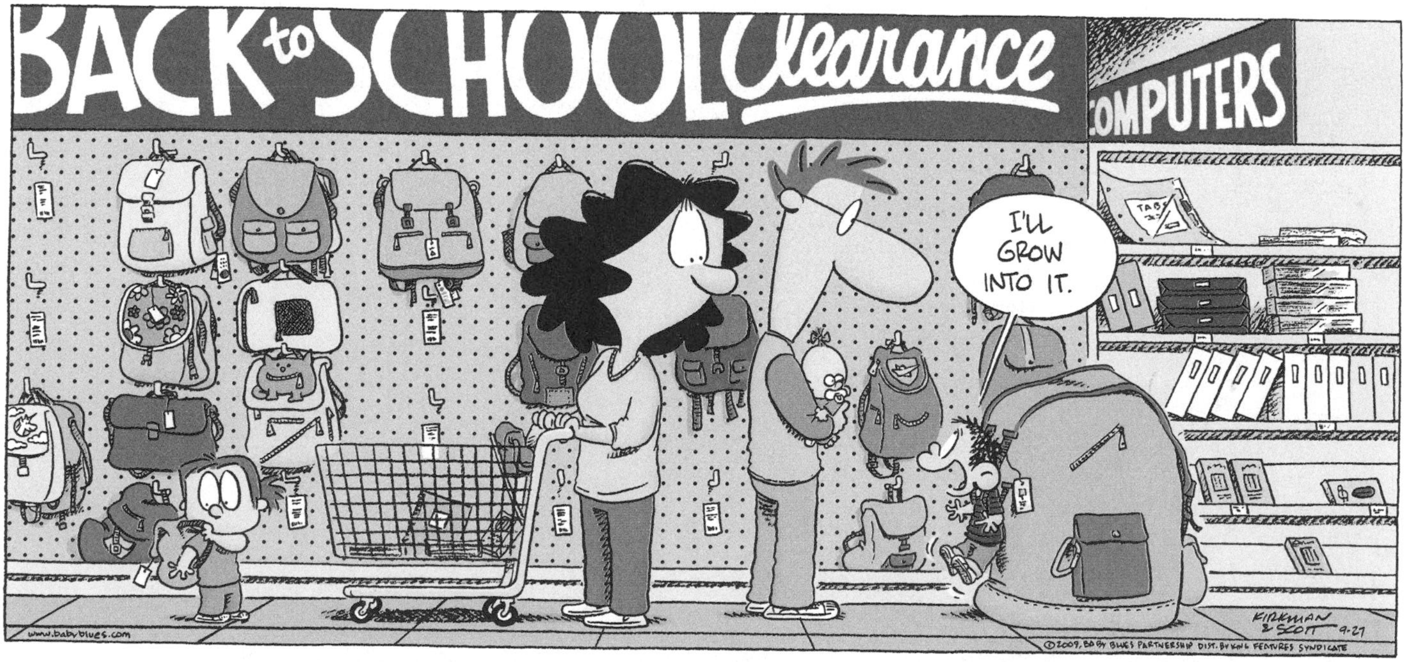
BACK to SCHOOL Clearance
COMPUTERS
I'LL GROW INTO IT.
www.babyblues.com
KIRKMAN & SCOTT 9-27
©2009, BABY BLUES PARTNERSHIP DIST. BY KING FEATURES SYNDICATE

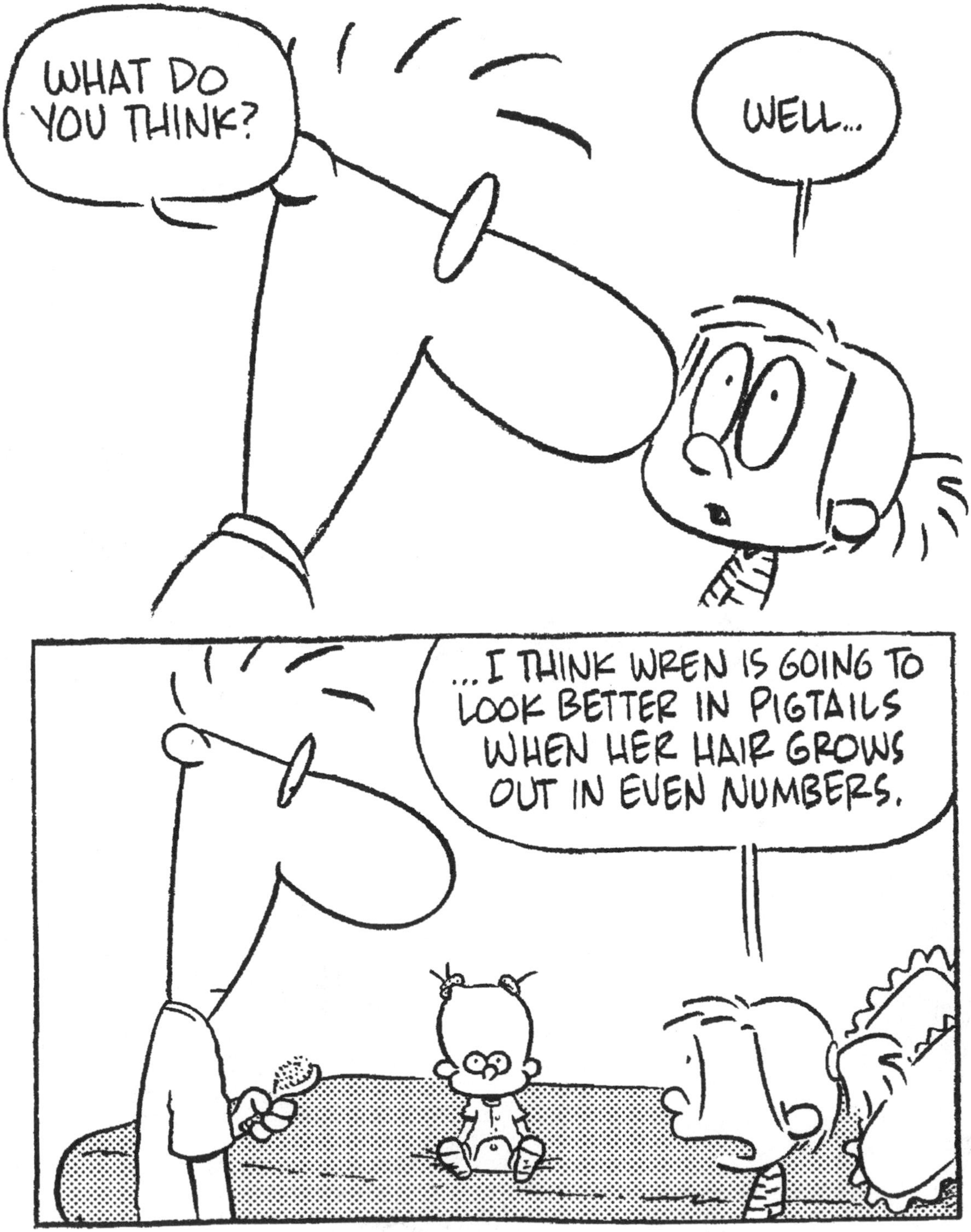
WHAT DO YOU THINK?
WELL...
...I THINK WREN IS GOING TO LOOK BETTER IN PIGTAILS WHEN HER HAIR GROWS OUT IN EVEN NUMBERS.

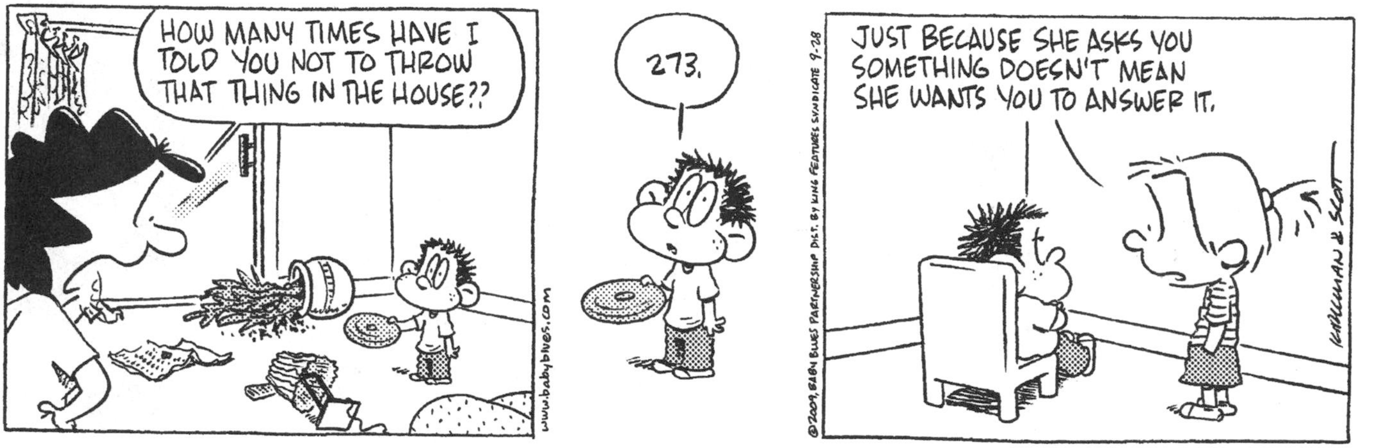
HOW MANY TIMES HAVE I TOLD YOU NOT TO THROW THAT THING IN THE HOUSE??
273.
JUST BECAUSE SHE ASKS YOU SOMETHING DOESN'T MEAN SHE WANTS YOU TO ANSWER IT.
www.babyblues.com
©2009, BABY BLUES PARTNERSHIP DIST. BY KING FEATURES SYNDICATE 9-28
KIRKMAN & SCOTT

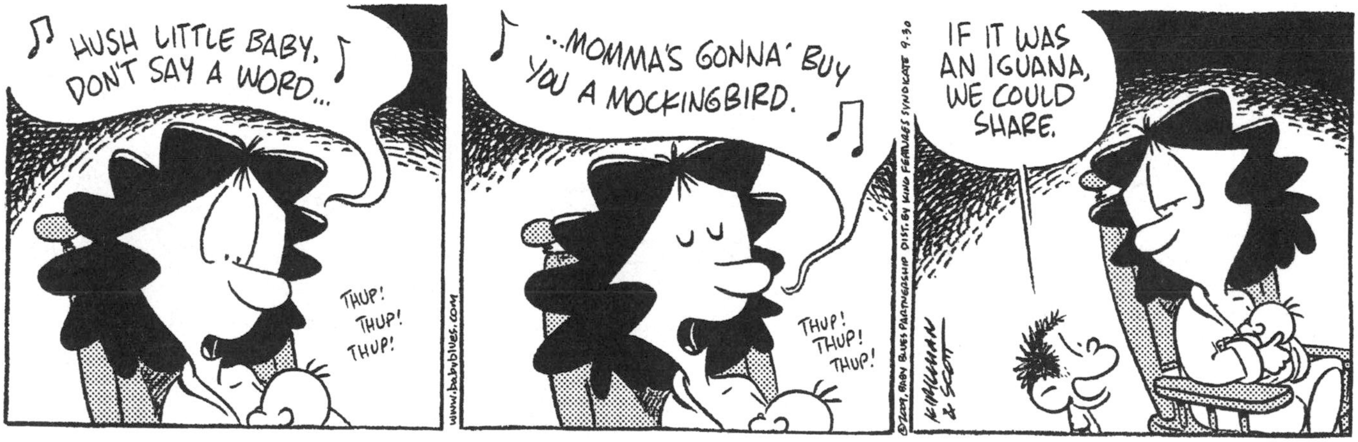
HUSH LITTLE BABY, DON'T SAY A WORD...
THUP! THUP! THUP!
...MOMMA'S GONNA' BUY YOU A MOCKINGBIRD.
THUP! THUP! THUP!
IF IT WAS AN IGUANA, WE COULD SHARE.
www.babyblues.com
©2009, BABY BLUES PARTNERSHIP DIST. BY KING FEATURES SYNDICATE 9-30
KIRKMAN & SCOTT

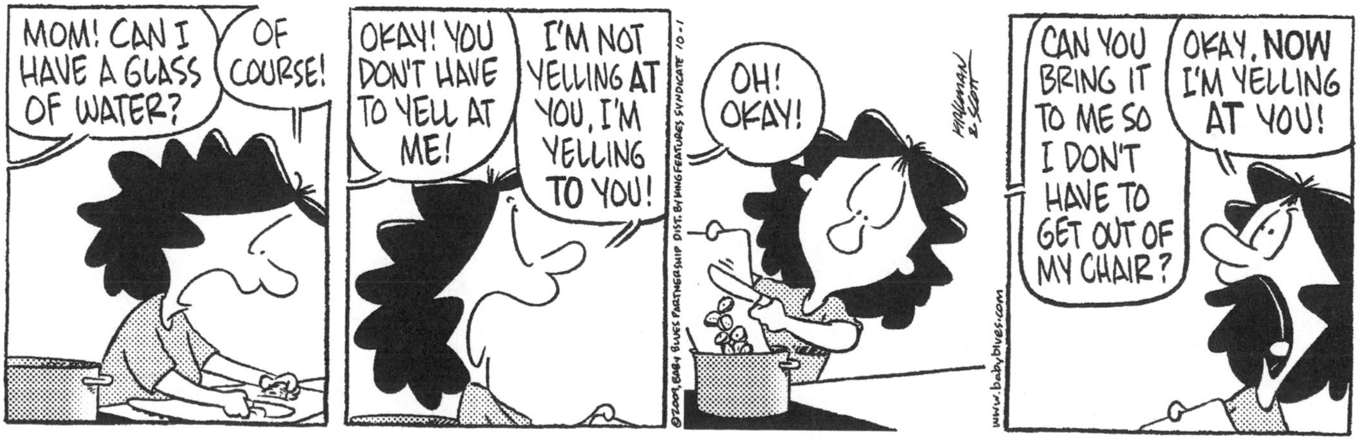
MOM! CAN I HAVE A GLASS OF WATER?
OF COURSE!
OKAY! YOU DON'T HAVE TO YELL AT ME!
I'M NOT YELLING AT YOU, I'M YELLING TO YOU!
OH! OKAY!
CAN YOU BRING IT TO ME SO I DON'T HAVE TO GET OUT OF MY CHAIR?
OKAY, NOW I'M YELLING AT YOU!
©2009, BABY BLUES PARTNERSHIP DIST. BY KING FEATURES SYNDICATE 10-1
KIRKMAN & SCOTT
www.babyblues.com

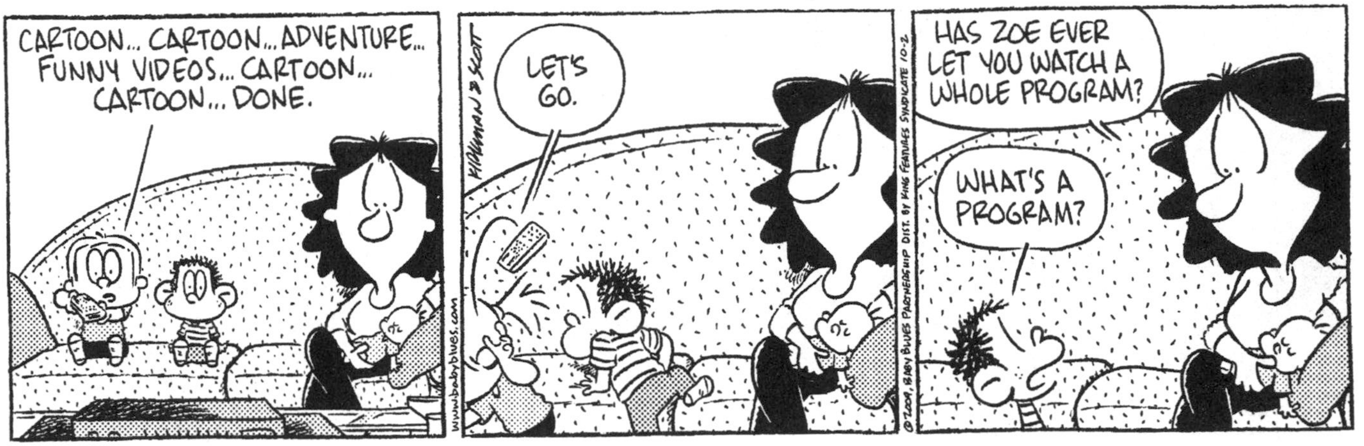
CARTOON... CARTOON... ADVENTURE... FUNNY VIDEOS... CARTOON... CARTOON... DONE.
LET'S GO.
KIRKMAN & SCOTT
www.babyblues.com
HAS ZOE EVER LET YOU WATCH A WHOLE PROGRAM?
WHAT'S A PROGRAM?
©2009, BABY BLUES PARTNERSHIP DIST. BY KING FEATURES SYNDICATE 10-2

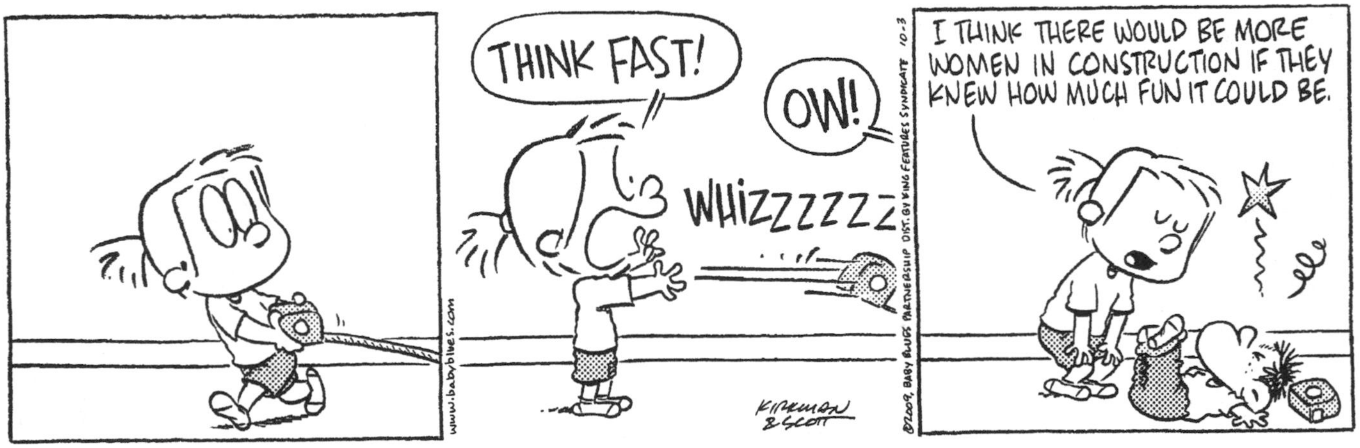
THINK FAST!
WHIZZZZZZ
OW!
www.babyblues.com
KIRKMAN & SCOTT
©2009, BABY BLUES PARTNERSHIP DIST. BY KING FEATURES SYNDICATE 10-3
I THINK THERE WOULD BE MORE WOMEN IN CONSTRUCTION IF THEY KNEW HOW MUCH FUN IT COULD BE.

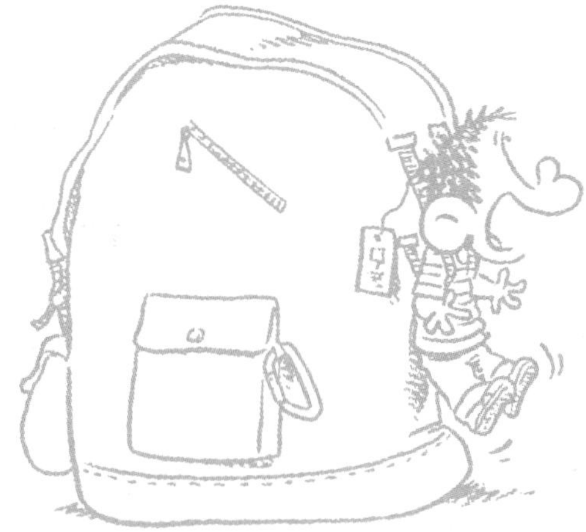

BABY BLUES®
BY
RICK KIRKMAN / JERRY SCOTT

WHAT DO YOU THINK?
IT LOOKS LIKE A PIG-NOSED, FLOP-EARED SPACE MUTANT WITH BAD BREATH AND HAIR PLUGS.
HA! DAD RECOGNIZED YOU RIGHT AWAY.
DA-AAD!
www.babyblues.com
10-4
© 2009, BABY BLUES PARTNERSHIP DIST. BY KING FEATURES SYNDICATE
KIRKMAN & SCOTT

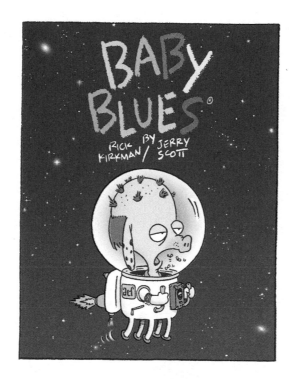

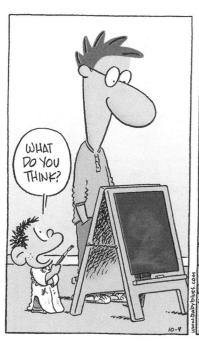

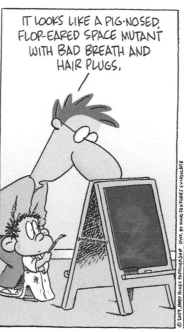

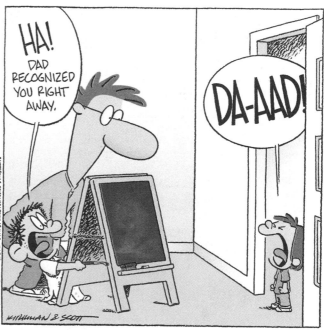

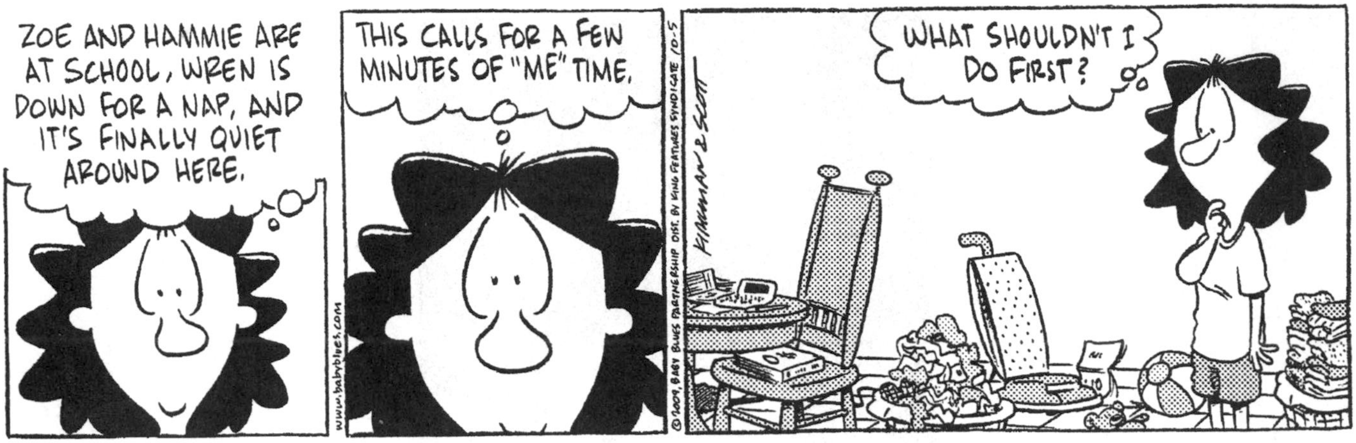
ZOE AND HAMMIE ARE AT SCHOOL, WREN IS DOWN FOR A NAP, AND IT'S FINALLY QUIET AROUND HERE.
THIS CALLS FOR A FEW MINUTES OF "ME" TIME.
WHAT SHOULDN'T I DO FIRST?
www.babyblues.com
© 2009, BABY BLUES PARTNERSHIP DIST. BY KING FEATURES SYNDICATE 10-5
KIRKMAN & SCOTT

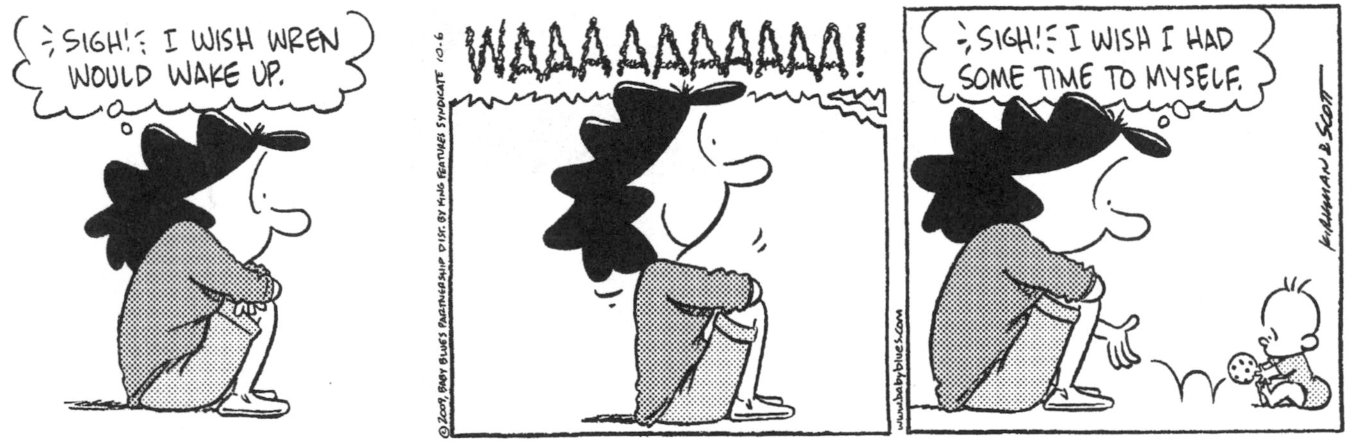
SIGH! I WISH WREN WOULD WAKE UP.
WAAAAAAAAAA!
SIGH! I WISH I HAD SOME TIME TO MYSELF.
© 2009, BABY BLUES PARTNERSHIP DIST. BY KING FEATURES SYNDICATE 10-6
www.babyblues.com
KIRKMAN & SCOTT

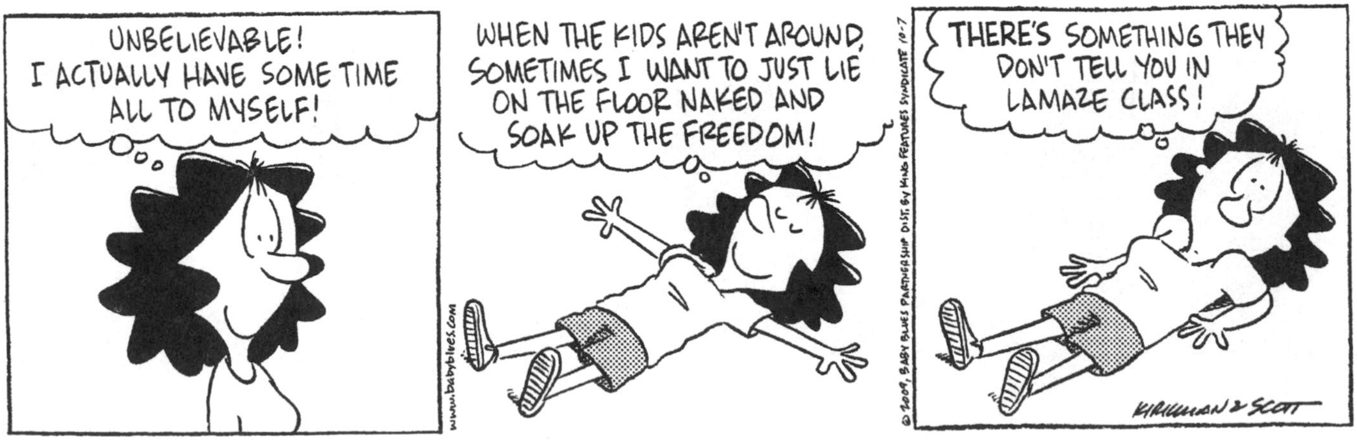
UNBELIEVABLE! I ACTUALLY HAVE SOME TIME ALL TO MYSELF!
WHEN THE KIDS AREN'T AROUND, SOMETIMES I WANT TO JUST LIE ON THE FLOOR NAKED AND SOAK UP THE FREEDOM!
THERE'S SOMETHING THEY DON'T TELL YOU IN LAMAZE CLASS!
www.babyblues.com
© 2009, BABY BLUES PARTNERSHIP DIST. BY KING FEATURES SYNDICATE 10-7
KIRKMAN & SCOTT

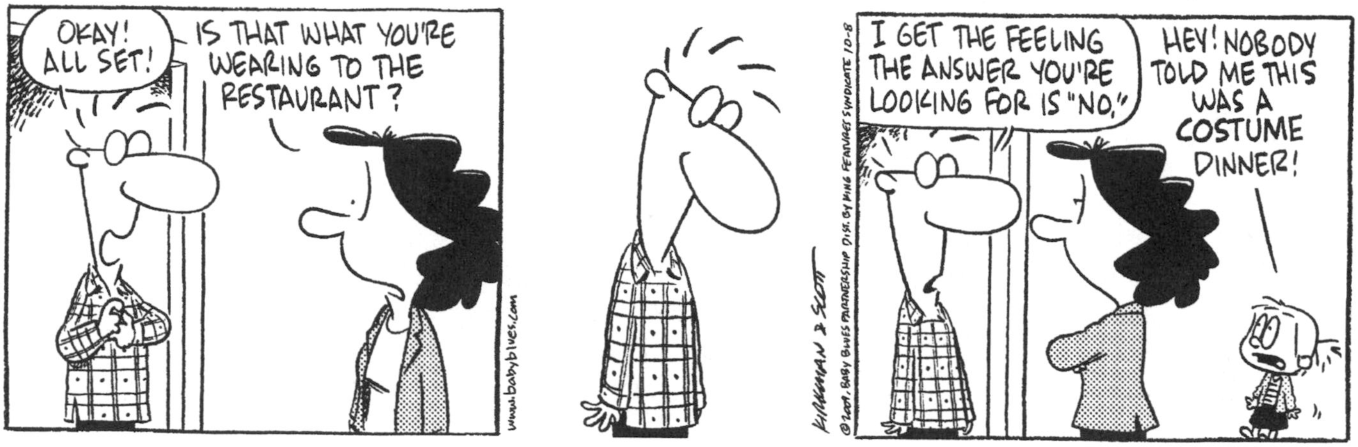
OKAY! ALL SET!
IS THAT WHAT YOU'RE WEARING TO THE RESTAURANT?
I GET THE FEELING THE ANSWER YOU'RE LOOKING FOR IS "NO."
HEY! NOBODY TOLD ME THIS WAS A COSTUME DINNER!

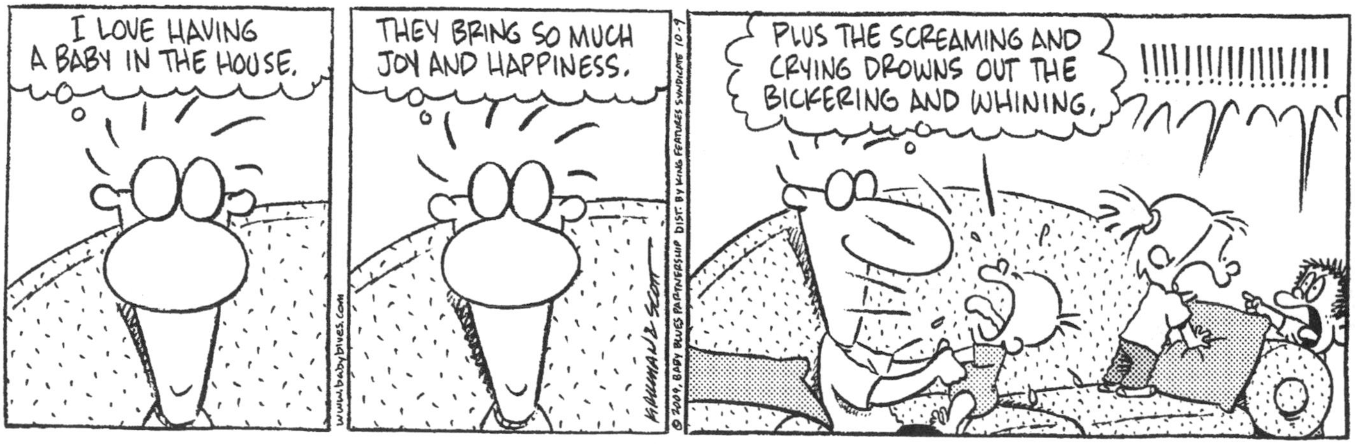
I LOVE HAVING A BABY IN THE HOUSE.
THEY BRING SO MUCH JOY AND HAPPINESS.
PLUS THE SCREAMING AND CRYING DROWNS OUT THE BICKERING AND WHINING.
!!!!!!!!!!!!!!!!

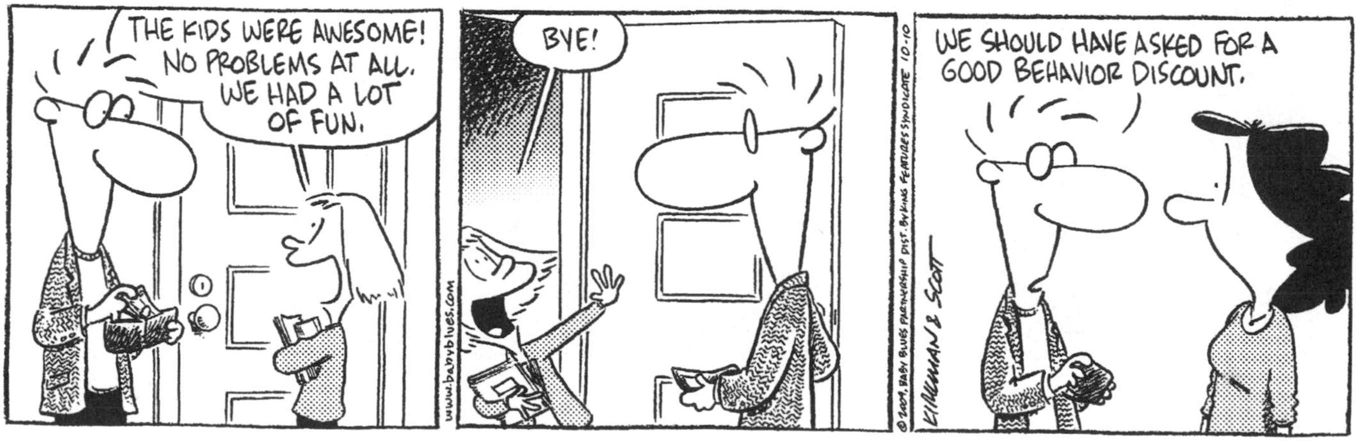
THE KIDS WERE AWESOME! NO PROBLEMS AT ALL. WE HAD A LOT OF FUN.
BYE!
WE SHOULD HAVE ASKED FOR A GOOD BEHAVIOR DISCOUNT.

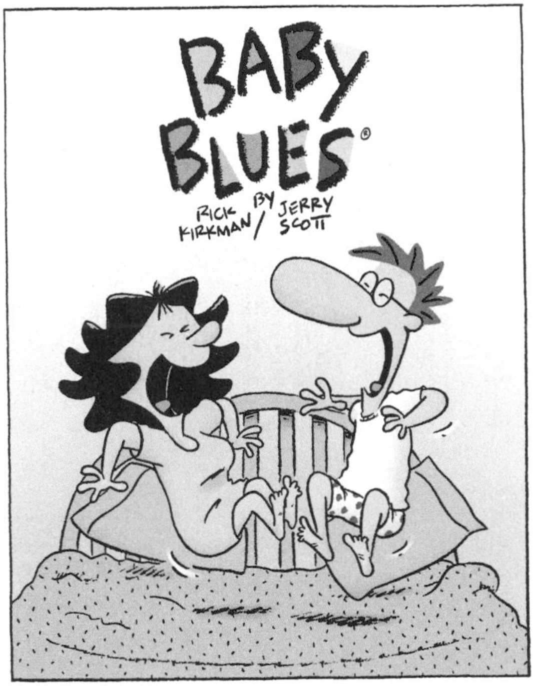
BABY BLUES®
BY RICK KIRKMAN / JERRY SCOTT

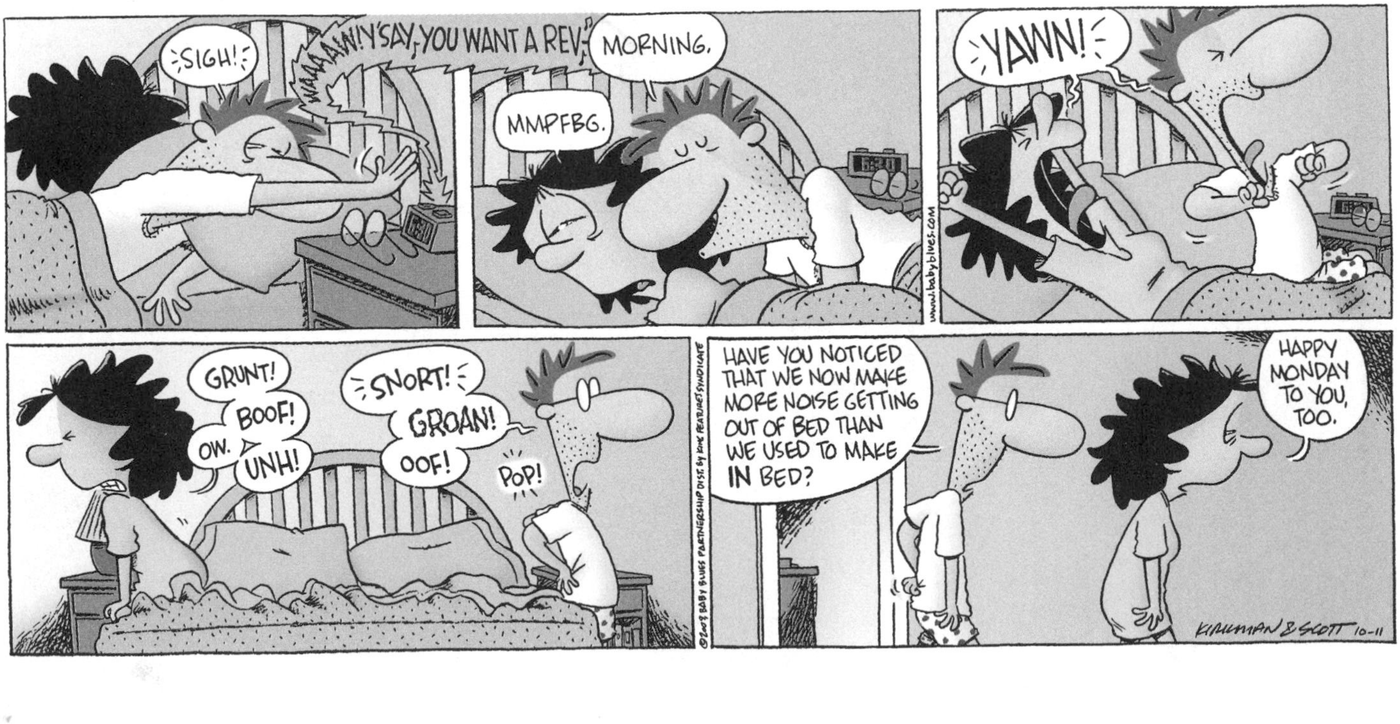
SIGH!
WAAAAAW! Y'SAY, YOU WANT A REV
MORNING.
MMPFBG.
YAWN!
www.babyblues.com
GRUNT!
BOOF!
OW.
UNH!
SNORT!
GROAN!
OOF!
POP!
©2008 BABY BLUES PARTNERSHIP DIST. BY KING FEATURES SYNDICATE
HAVE YOU NOTICED THAT WE NOW MAKE MORE NOISE GETTING OUT OF BED THAN WE USED TO MAKE IN BED?
HAPPY MONDAY TO YOU, TOO.
KIRKMAN & SCOTT 10-11

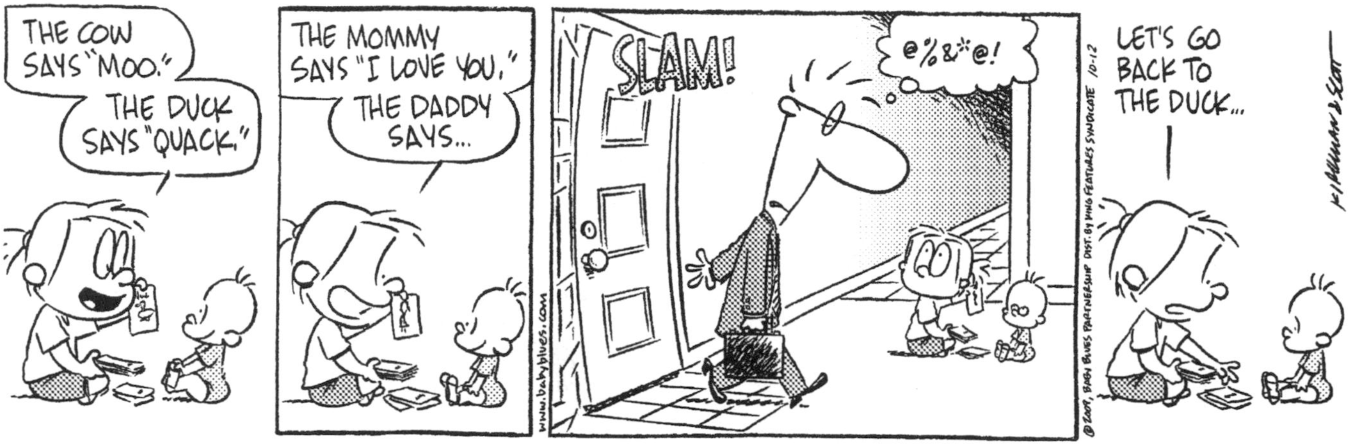
THE COW SAYS "MOO."
THE DUCK SAYS "QUACK."
THE MOMMY SAYS "I LOVE YOU."
THE DADDY SAYS...
www.babyblues.com
SLAM!
@%&*@!
© 2009, BABY BLUES PARTNERSHIP DIST. BY KING FEATURES SYNDICATE 10-12
LET'S GO BACK TO THE DUCK...
KIRKMAN & SCOTT

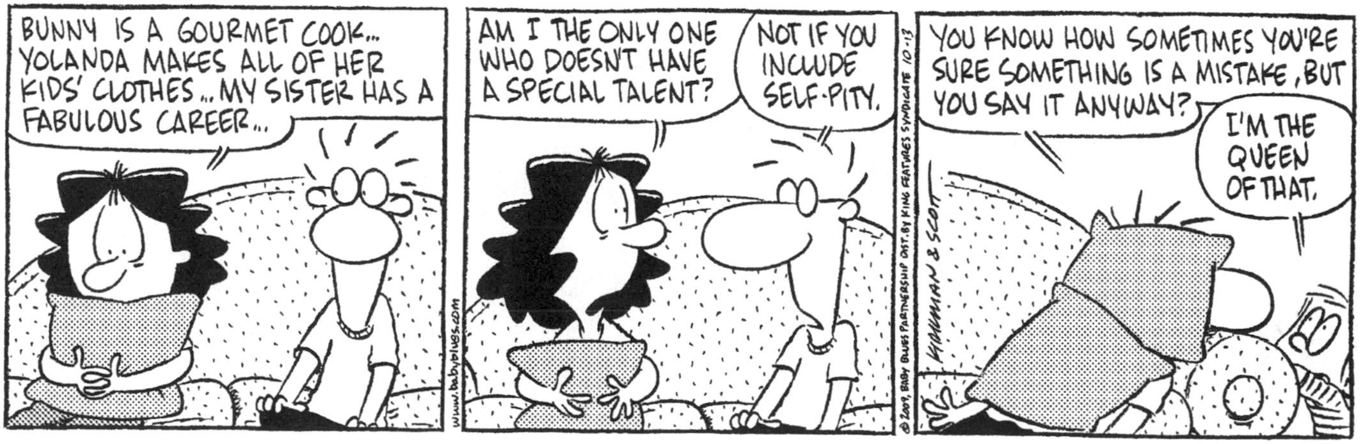
BUNNY IS A GOURMET COOK... YOLANDA MAKES ALL OF HER KIDS' CLOTHES... MY SISTER HAS A FABULOUS CAREER...
www.babyblues.com
AM I THE ONLY ONE WHO DOESN'T HAVE A SPECIAL TALENT?
NOT IF YOU INCLUDE SELF-PITY.
© 2009, BABY BLUES PARTNERSHIP DIST. BY KING FEATURES SYNDICATE 10-13
KIRKMAN & SCOTT
YOU KNOW HOW SOMETIMES YOU'RE SURE SOMETHING IS A MISTAKE, BUT YOU SAY IT ANYWAY?
I'M THE QUEEN OF THAT.

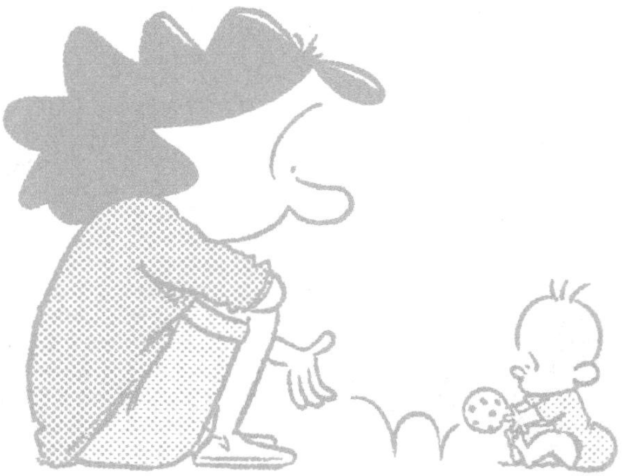

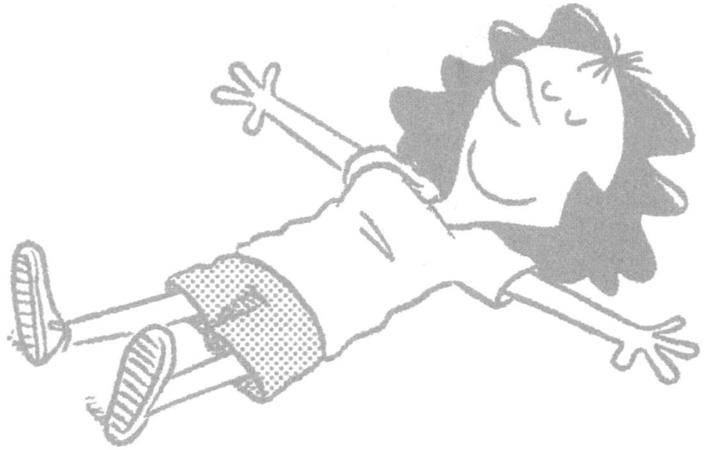

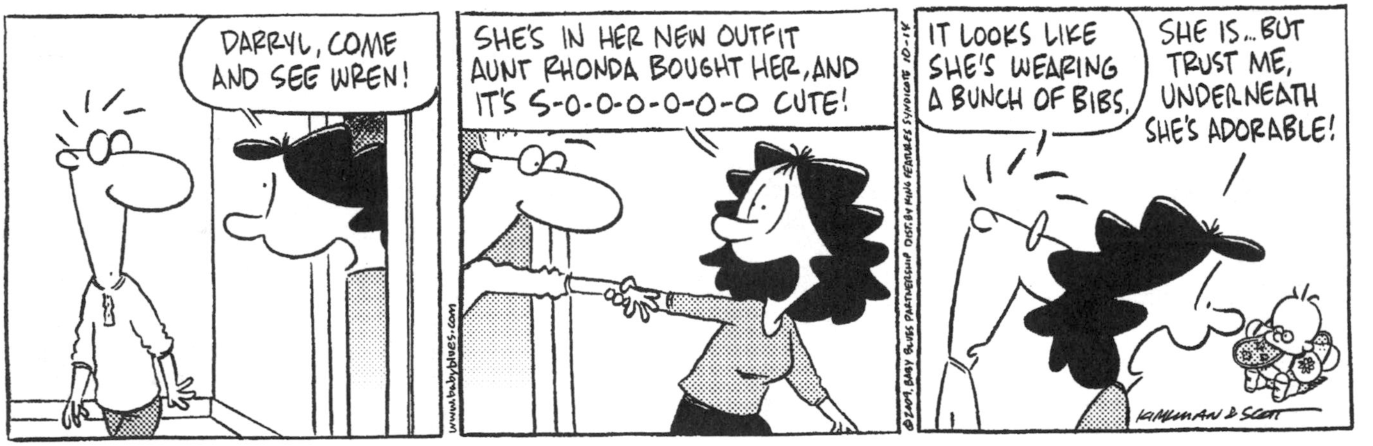

DARRYL, COME AND SEE WREN!
SHE'S IN HER NEW OUTFIT AUNT RHONDA BOUGHT HER, AND IT'S S-O-O-O-O-O-O CUTE!
IT LOOKS LIKE SHE'S WEARING A BUNCH OF BIBS.
SHE IS... BUT TRUST ME, UNDERNEATH SHE'S ADORABLE!
KIRKMAN & SCOTT

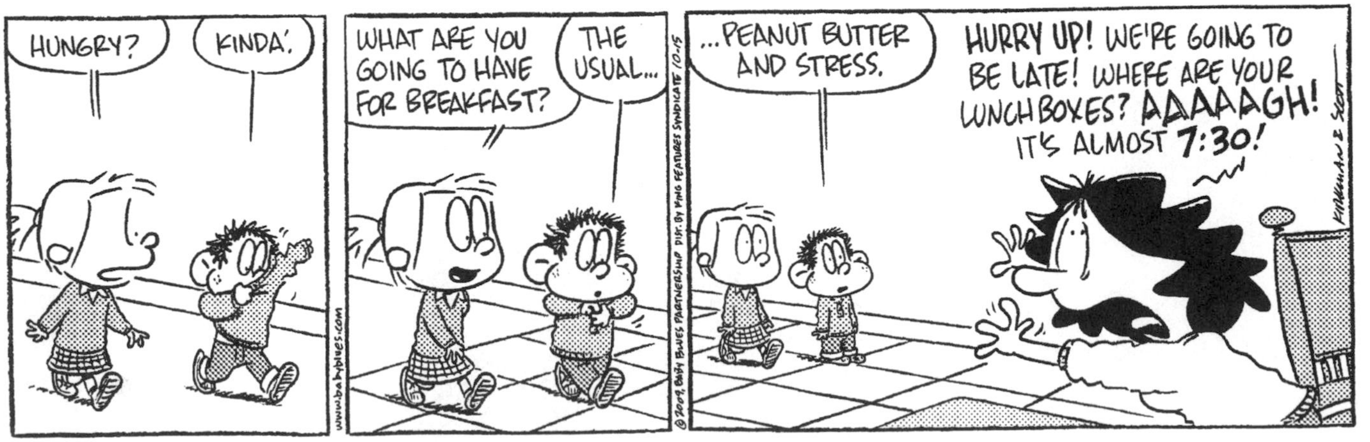

HUNGRY?
KINDA'.
WHAT ARE YOU GOING TO HAVE FOR BREAKFAST?
THE USUAL...
...PEANUT BUTTER AND STRESS.
HURRY UP! WE'RE GOING TO BE LATE! WHERE ARE YOUR LUNCHBOXES? AAAAAGH! IT'S ALMOST 7:30!
KIRKMAN & SCOTT

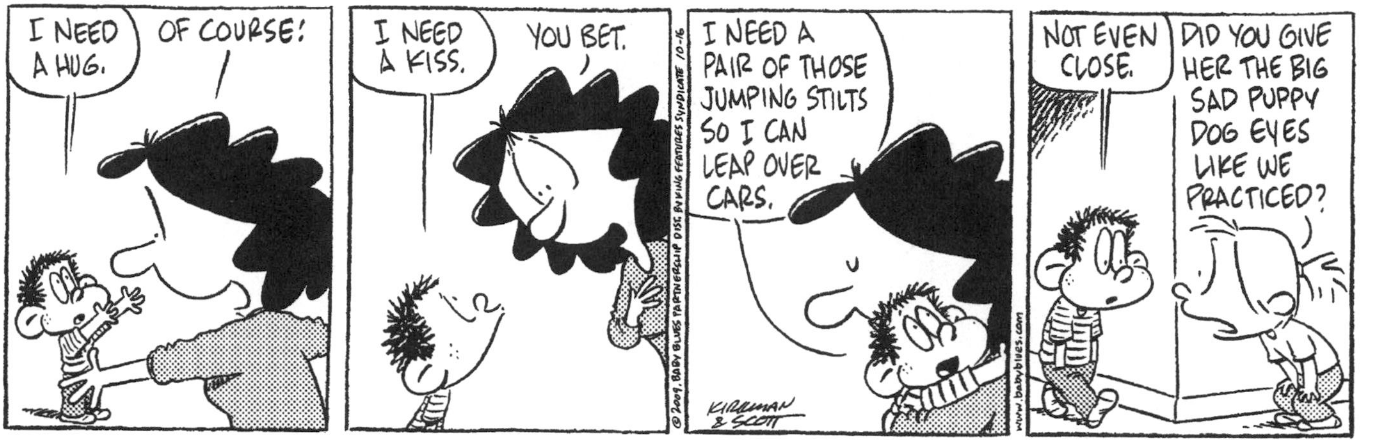
I NEED A HUG.
OF COURSE!
I NEED A KISS.
YOU BET.
I NEED A PAIR OF THOSE JUMPING STILTS SO I CAN LEAP OVER CARS.
KIRKMAN & SCOTT
NOT EVEN CLOSE.
DID YOU GIVE HER THE BIG SAD PUPPY DOG EYES LIKE WE PRACTICED?

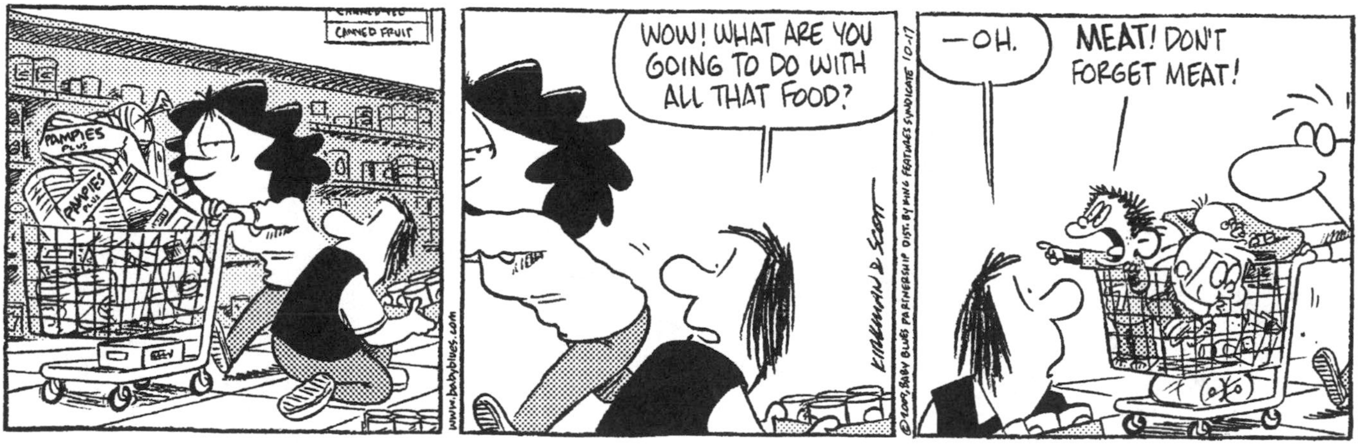
CANNED FRUIT
WOW! WHAT ARE YOU GOING TO DO WITH ALL THAT FOOD?
KIRKMAN & SCOTT
—OH.
MEAT! DON'T FORGET MEAT!

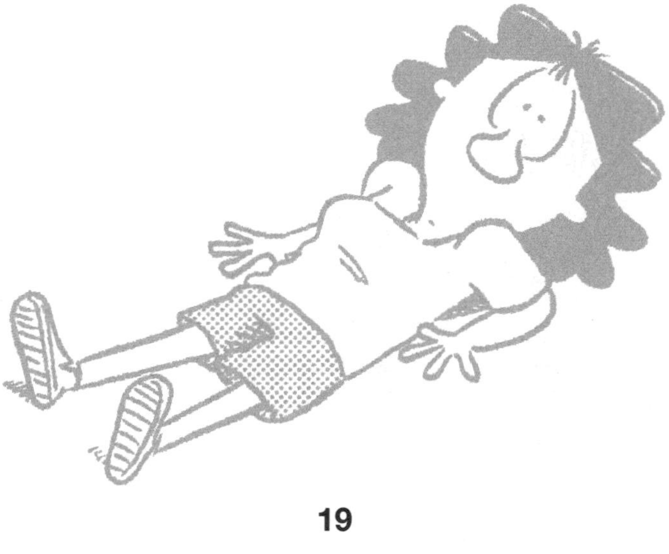

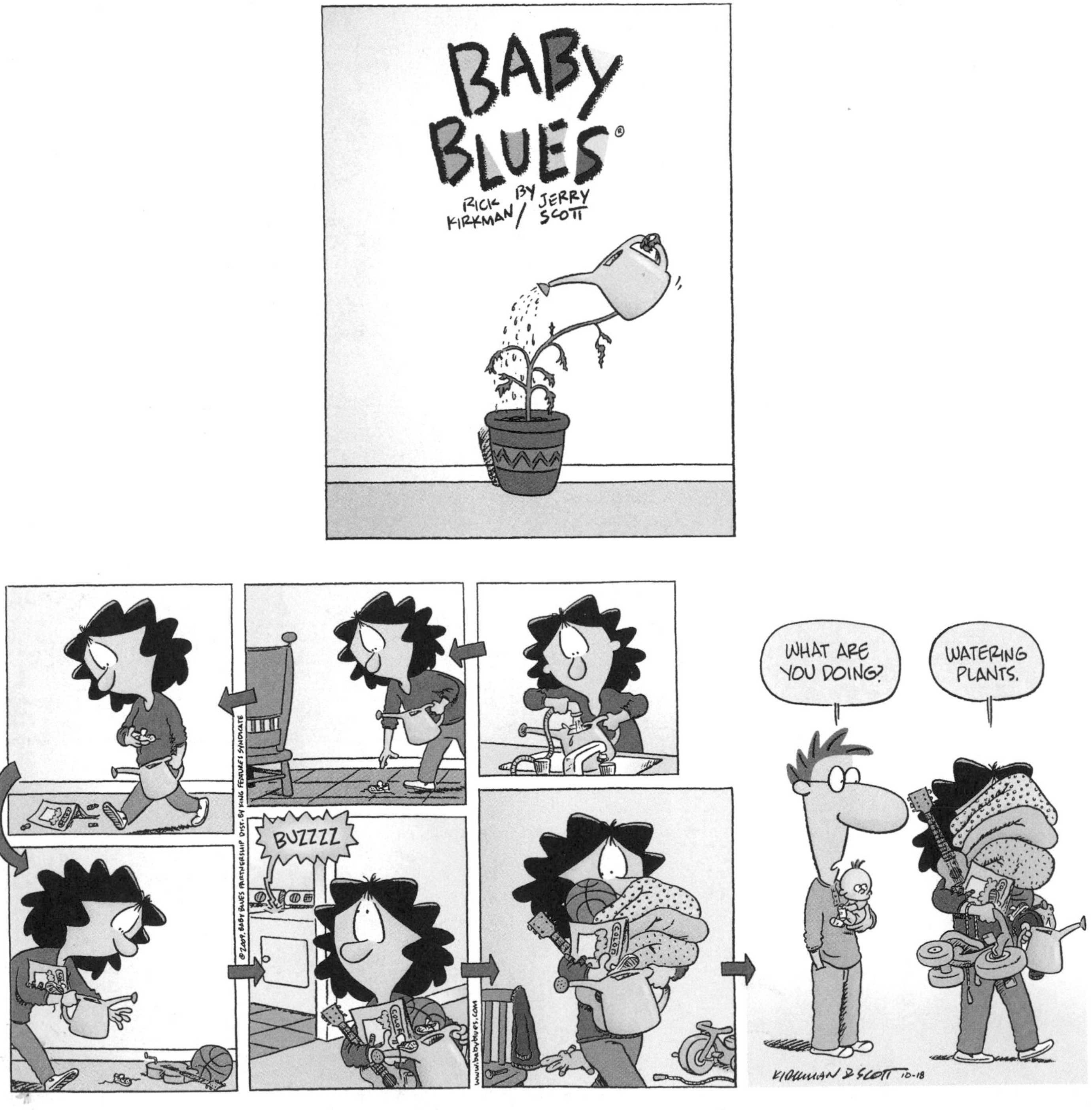
BABY BLUES®
BY RICK KIRKMAN / JERRY SCOTT
©2009, BABY BLUES PARTNERSHIP DIST. BY KING FEATURES SYNDICATE
BUZZZZ
www.babyblues.com
WHAT ARE YOU DOING?
WATERING PLANTS.
KIRKMAN & SCOTT 10-18

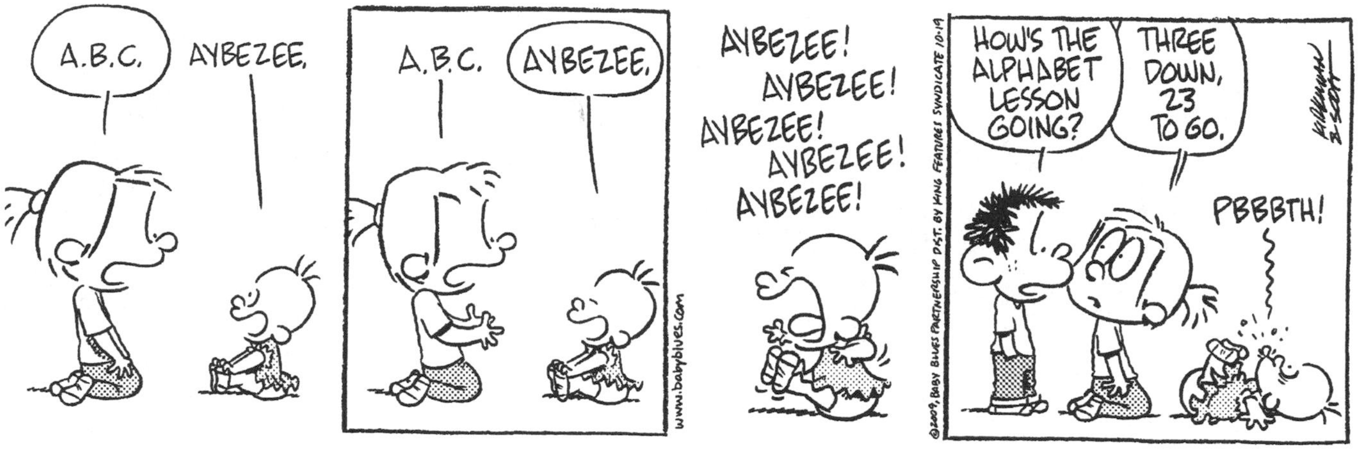
A.B.C.
AYBEZEE.
A.B.C.
AYBEZEE.
www.babyblues.com
AYBEZEE! AYBEZEE! AYBEZEE! AYBEZEE! AYBEZEE!
©2009, BABY BLUES PARTNERSHIP DIST. BY KING FEATURES SYNDICATE 10-19
HOW'S THE ALPHABET LESSON GOING?
THREE DOWN, 23 TO GO.
PBBBTH!
KIRKMAN & SCOTT

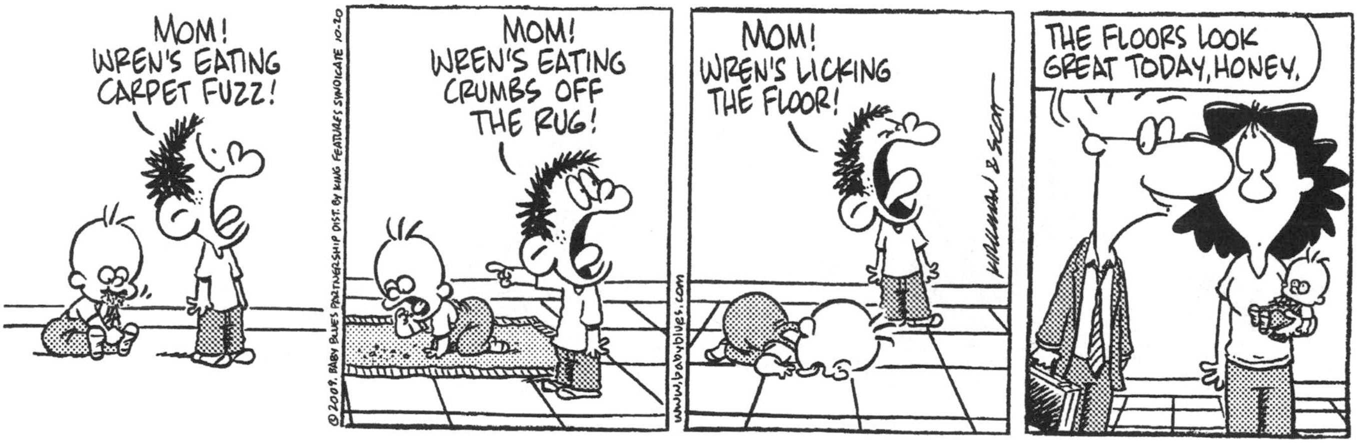
MOM! WREN'S EATING CARPET FUZZ!
©2009, BABY BLUES PARTNERSHIP DIST. BY KING FEATURES SYNDICATE 10-20
MOM! WREN'S EATING CRUMBS OFF THE RUG!
www.babyblues.com
MOM! WREN'S LICKING THE FLOOR!
KIRKMAN & SCOTT
THE FLOORS LOOK GREAT TODAY, HONEY.

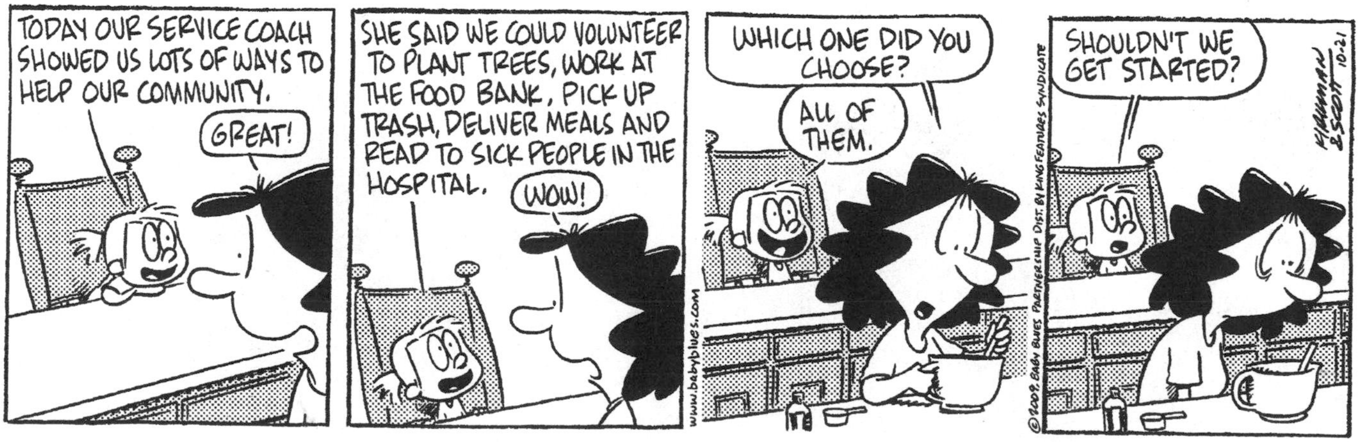
TODAY OUR SERVICE COACH SHOWED US LOTS OF WAYS TO HELP OUR COMMUNITY.
GREAT!
SHE SAID WE COULD VOLUNTEER TO PLANT TREES, WORK AT THE FOOD BANK, PICK UP TRASH, DELIVER MEALS AND READ TO SICK PEOPLE IN THE HOSPITAL.
WOW!
www.babyblues.com
WHICH ONE DID YOU CHOOSE?
ALL OF THEM.
©2009, BABY BLUES PARTNERSHIP DIST. BY KING FEATURES SYNDICATE
SHOULDN'T WE GET STARTED?
KIRKMAN & SCOTT 10-21

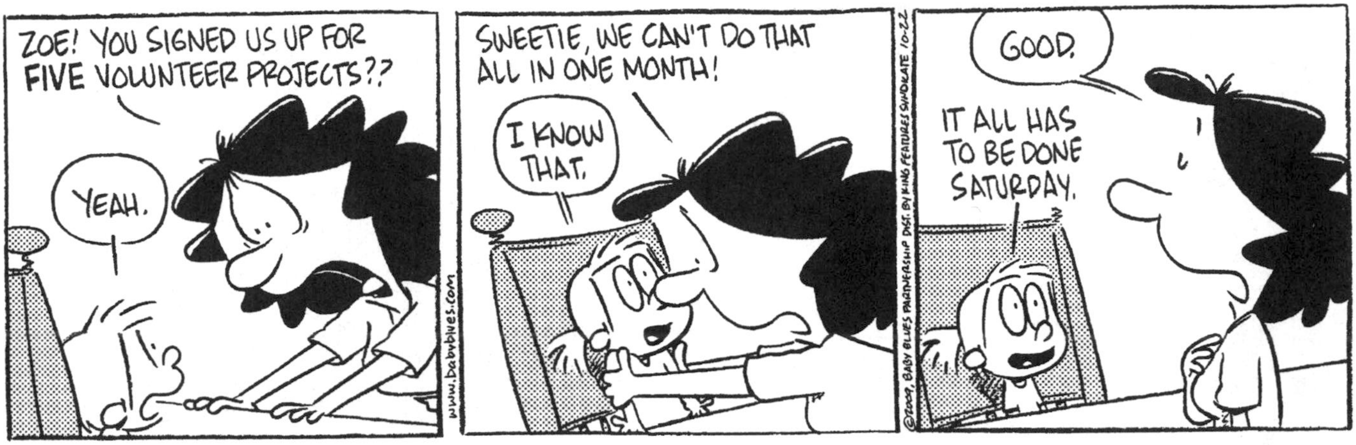
ZOE! YOU SIGNED US UP FOR **FIVE** VOLUNTEER PROJECTS??
YEAH.
www.babyblues.com
SWEETIE, WE CAN'T DO THAT ALL IN ONE MONTH!
I KNOW THAT.
©2009, BABY BLUES PARTNERSHIP DIST. BY KING FEATURES SYNDICATE 10-22
GOOD.
IT ALL HAS TO BE DONE SATURDAY.

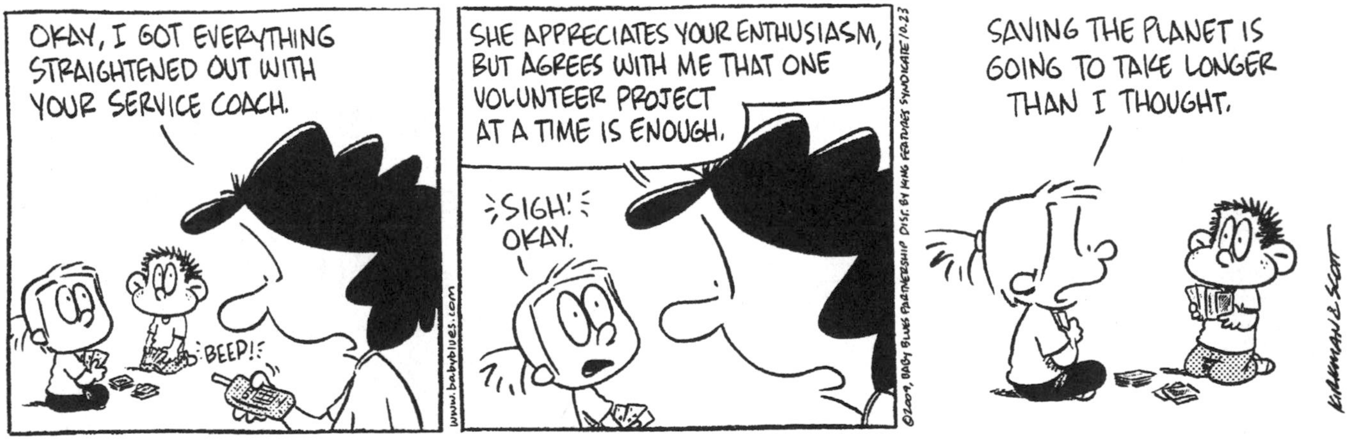
OKAY, I GOT EVERYTHING STRAIGHTENED OUT WITH YOUR SERVICE COACH.
BEEP!
www.babyblues.com
SHE APPRECIATES YOUR ENTHUSIASM, BUT AGREES WITH ME THAT ONE VOLUNTEER PROJECT AT A TIME IS ENOUGH.
SIGH! OKAY.
©2009, BABY BLUES PARTNERSHIP DIST. BY KING FEATURES SYNDICATE 10-23
SAVING THE PLANET IS GOING TO TAKE LONGER THAN I THOUGHT.
KIRKMAN & SCOTT

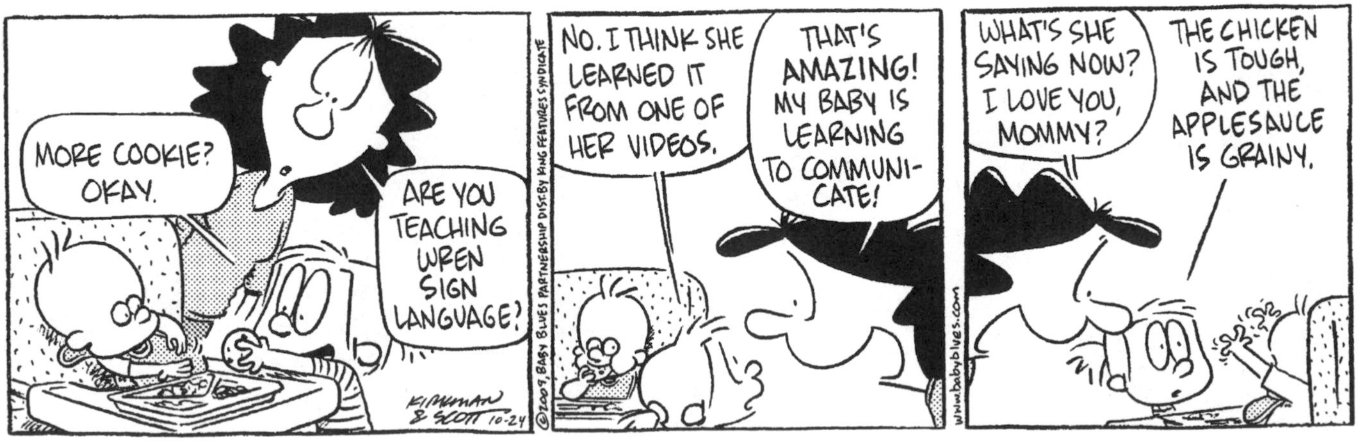
MORE COOKIE? OKAY.
ARE YOU TEACHING WREN SIGN LANGUAGE?
KIRKMAN & SCOTT 10-24
©2009, BABY BLUES PARTNERSHIP DIST. BY KING FEATURES SYNDICATE
NO. I THINK SHE LEARNED IT FROM ONE OF HER VIDEOS.
THAT'S AMAZING! MY BABY IS LEARNING TO COMMUNICATE!
www.babyblues.com
WHAT'S SHE SAYING NOW? I LOVE YOU, MOMMY?
THE CHICKEN IS TOUGH, AND THE APPLESAUCE IS GRAINY.

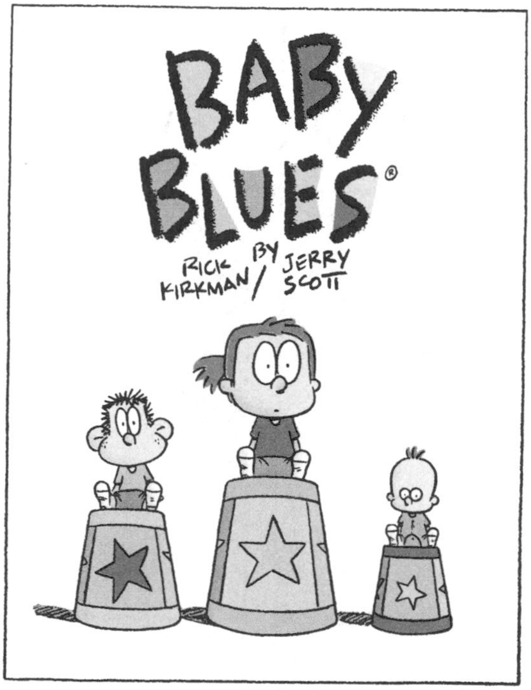
BABY BLUES®
BY RICK KIRKMAN/ JERRY SCOTT

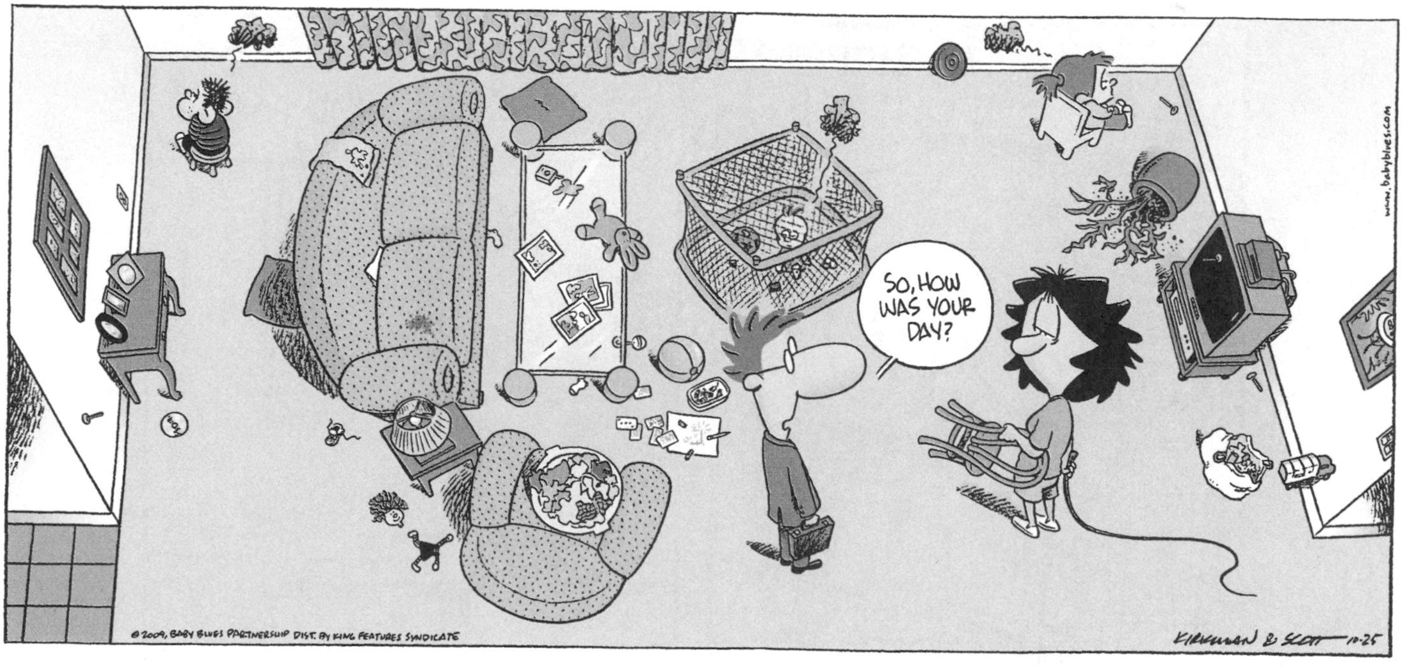
SO, HOW WAS YOUR DAY?
www.babyblues.com
©2009, BABY BLUES PARTNERSHIP DIST. BY KING FEATURES SYNDICATE
KIRKMAN & SCOTT 10-25

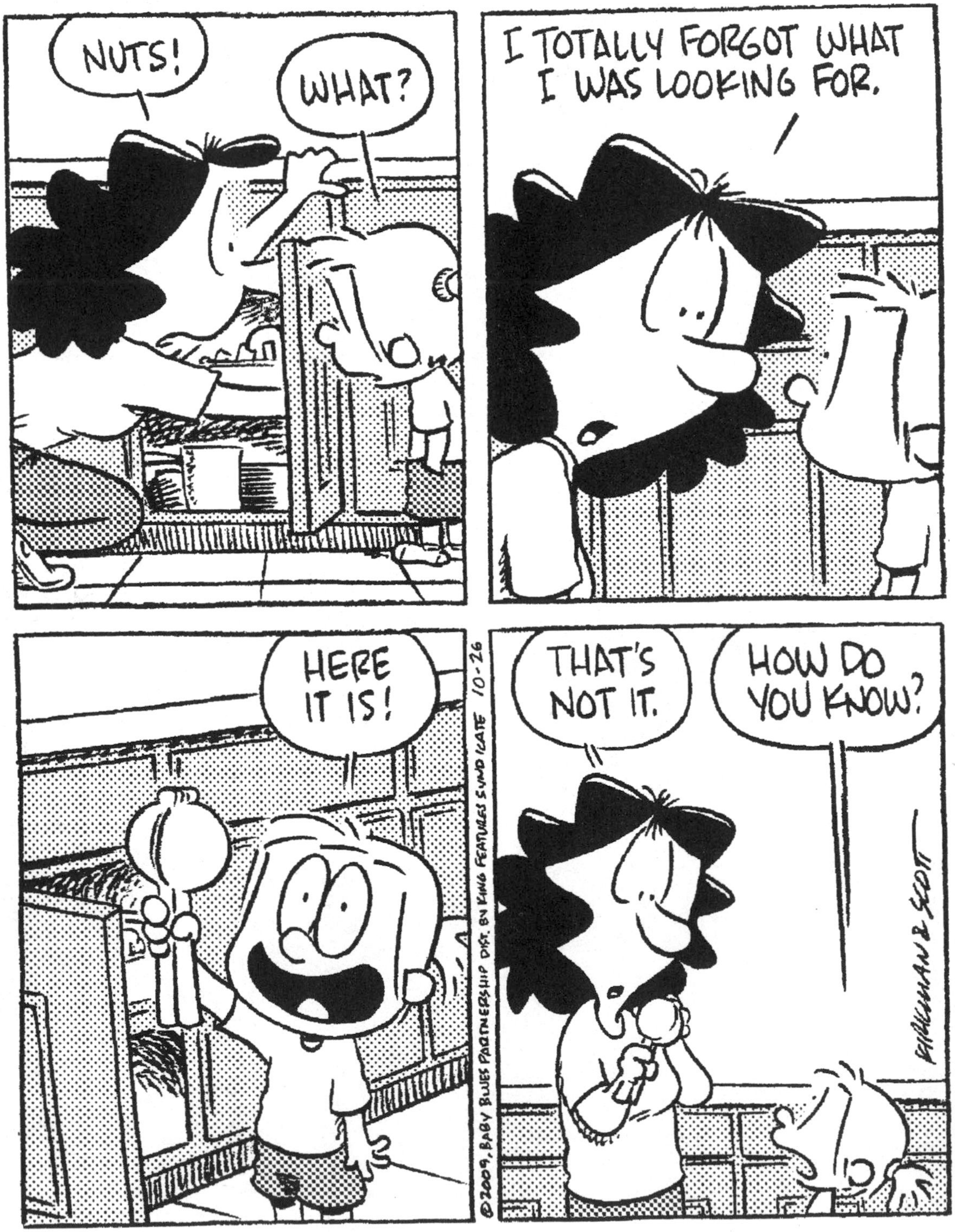
NUTS!
WHAT?
I TOTALLY FORGOT WHAT I WAS LOOKING FOR.
HERE IT IS!
THAT'S NOT IT.
HOW DO YOU KNOW?
©2009, BABY BLUES PARTNERSHIP DIST. BY KING FEATURES SYNDICATE 10-26
KIRKMAN & SCOTT

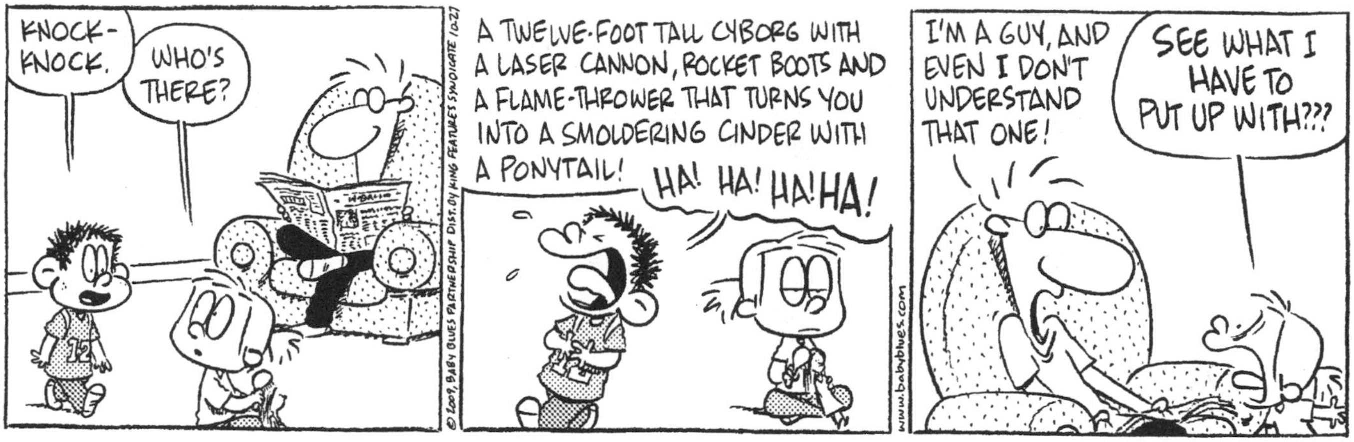
KNOCK-KNOCK.
WHO'S THERE?
A TWELVE-FOOT TALL CYBORG WITH A LASER CANNON, ROCKET BOOTS AND A FLAME-THROWER THAT TURNS YOU INTO A SMOLDERING CINDER WITH A PONYTAIL!
HA! HA! HA! HA!
I'M A GUY, AND EVEN I DON'T UNDERSTAND THAT ONE!
SEE WHAT I HAVE TO PUT UP WITH???
© 2009, BABY BLUES PARTNERSHIP DIST. BY KING FEATURES SYNDICATE 10-27
www.babyblues.com

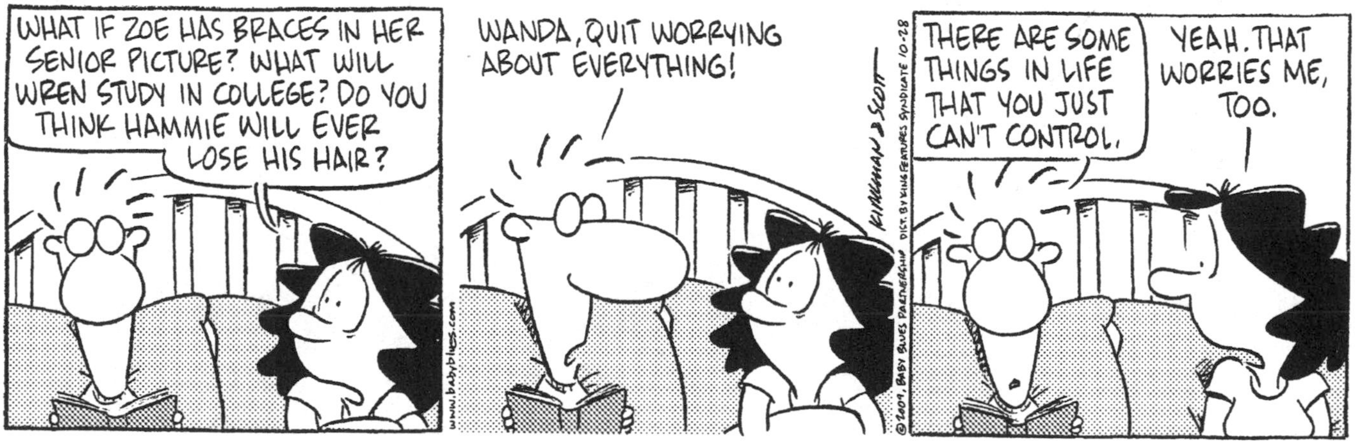
WHAT IF ZOE HAS BRACES IN HER SENIOR PICTURE? WHAT WILL WREN STUDY IN COLLEGE? DO YOU THINK HAMMIE WILL EVER LOSE HIS HAIR?
WANDA, QUIT WORRYING ABOUT EVERYTHING!
THERE ARE SOME THINGS IN LIFE THAT YOU JUST CAN'T CONTROL.
YEAH. THAT WORRIES ME, TOO.
www.babyblues.com
KIRKMAN & SCOTT
© 2009, BABY BLUES PARTNERSHIP DIST. BY KING FEATURES SYNDICATE 10-28

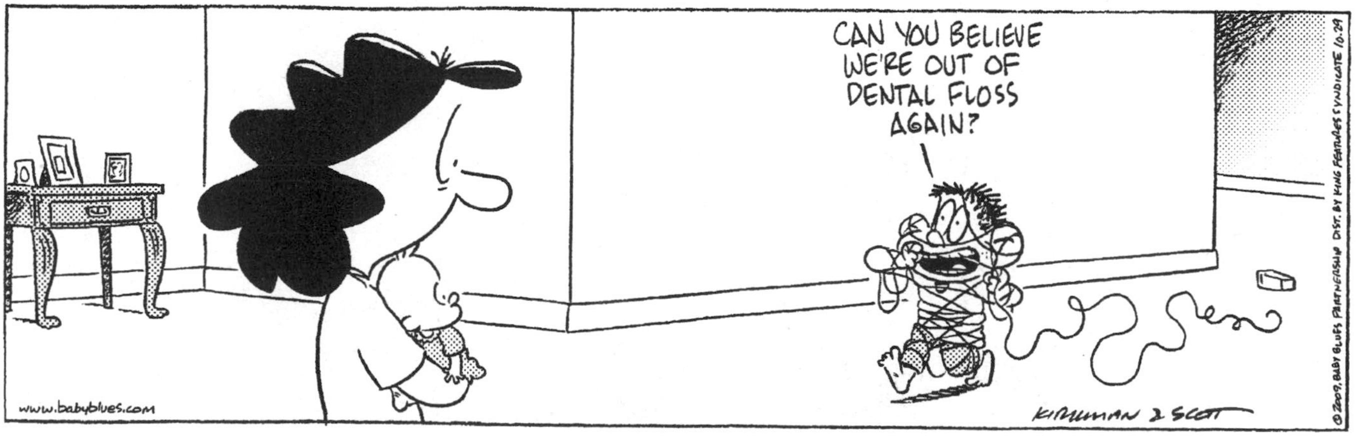
CAN YOU BELIEVE WE'RE OUT OF DENTAL FLOSS AGAIN?
www.babyblues.com
KIRKMAN & SCOTT
© 2009, BABY BLUES PARTNERSHIP DIST. BY KING FEATURES SYNDICATE 10-29

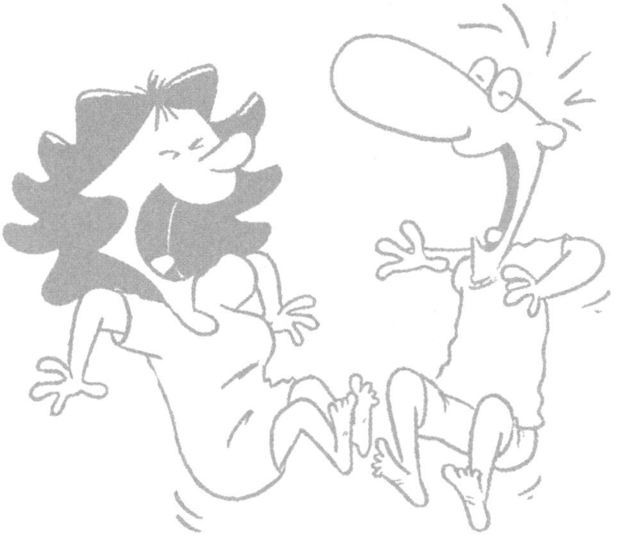

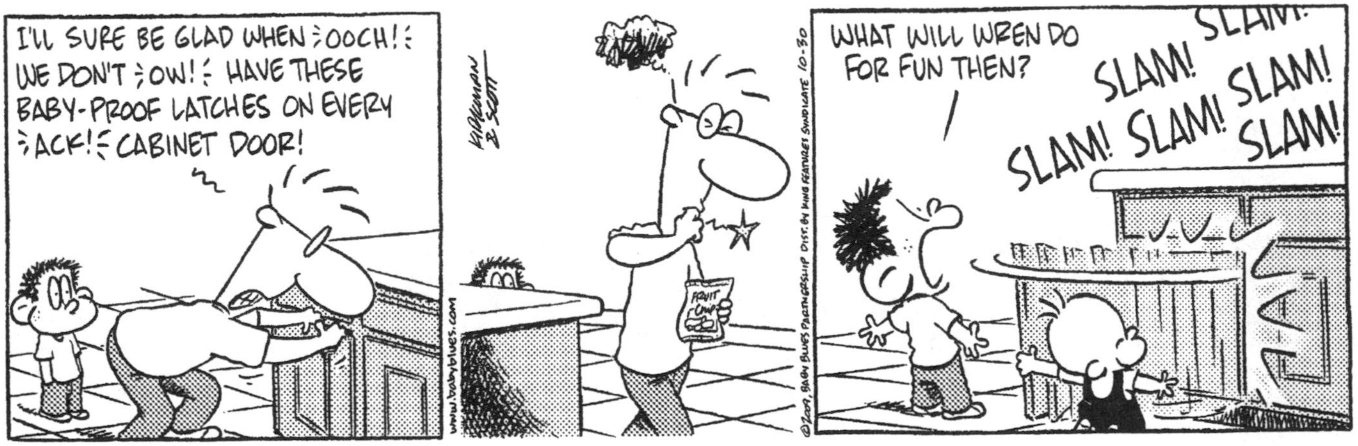
I'LL SURE BE GLAD WHEN ;OOCH!; WE DON'T ;OW!; HAVE THESE BABY-PROOF LATCHES ON EVERY ;ACK!; CABINET DOOR!
WHAT WILL WREN DO FOR FUN THEN?
SLAM! SLAM! SLAM! SLAM! SLAM!

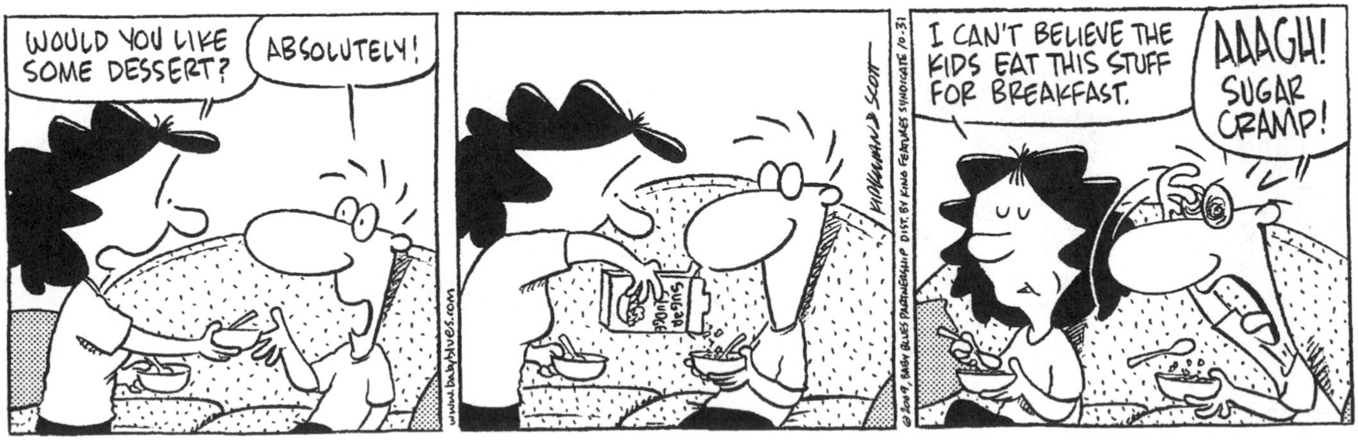
WOULD YOU LIKE SOME DESSERT?
ABSOLUTELY!
I CAN'T BELIEVE THE KIDS EAT THIS STUFF FOR BREAKFAST.
AAAGH! SUGAR CRAMP!

BABY BLUES®
BY RICK KIRKMAN / JERRY SCOTT

YOU KNOW WHAT WOULD BE COOL?
IF I COULD TURN INVISIBLE AND FLY!
BUT IT WOULD BE EVEN COOLER IF I COULD TURN INVISIBLE, FLY, AND ONE OF MY FISTS WAS A FROZEN YOGURT DISPENSER!
—A FROZEN YOGURT DISPENSER THAT ALSO FIRES LASERS!
BZZZZZAP!
POW!
THAT WAY I COULD SNEAK UP ON BAD GUYS, ZAP THEM WITH MY LASER BEAMS, AND THEN ENJOY A TASTY TREAT.
HEY! IF YOU FILLED A UTILITY BELT WITH VARIOUS TOPPINGS, YOU COULD BE MY SIDEKICK!
I THINK I NEED TO GO SPEND TIME AMONG FEMALES.

KIRKMAN & SCOTT 11-1 www.babyblues.com

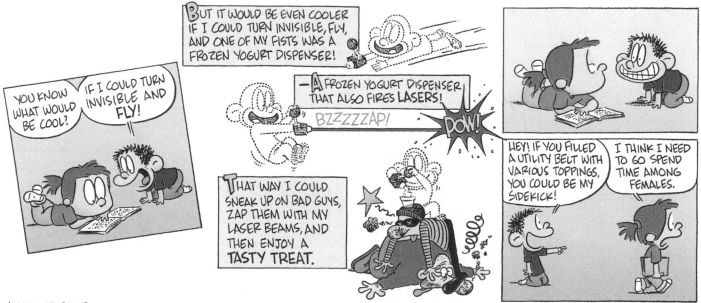

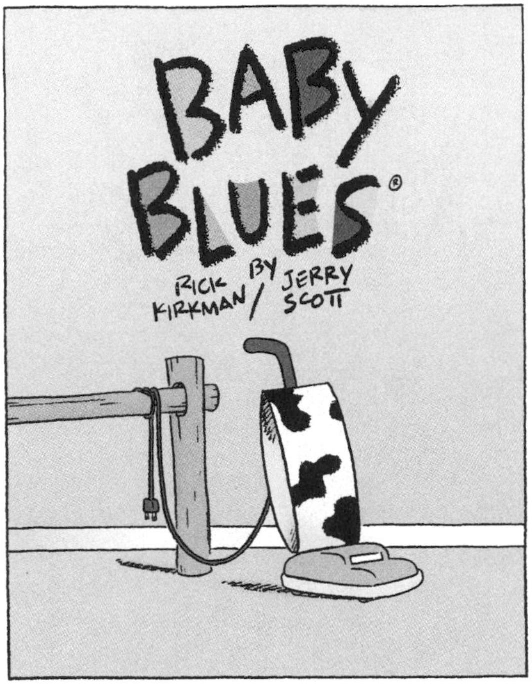
BABY BLUES®
BY RICK KIRKMAN / JERRY SCOTT

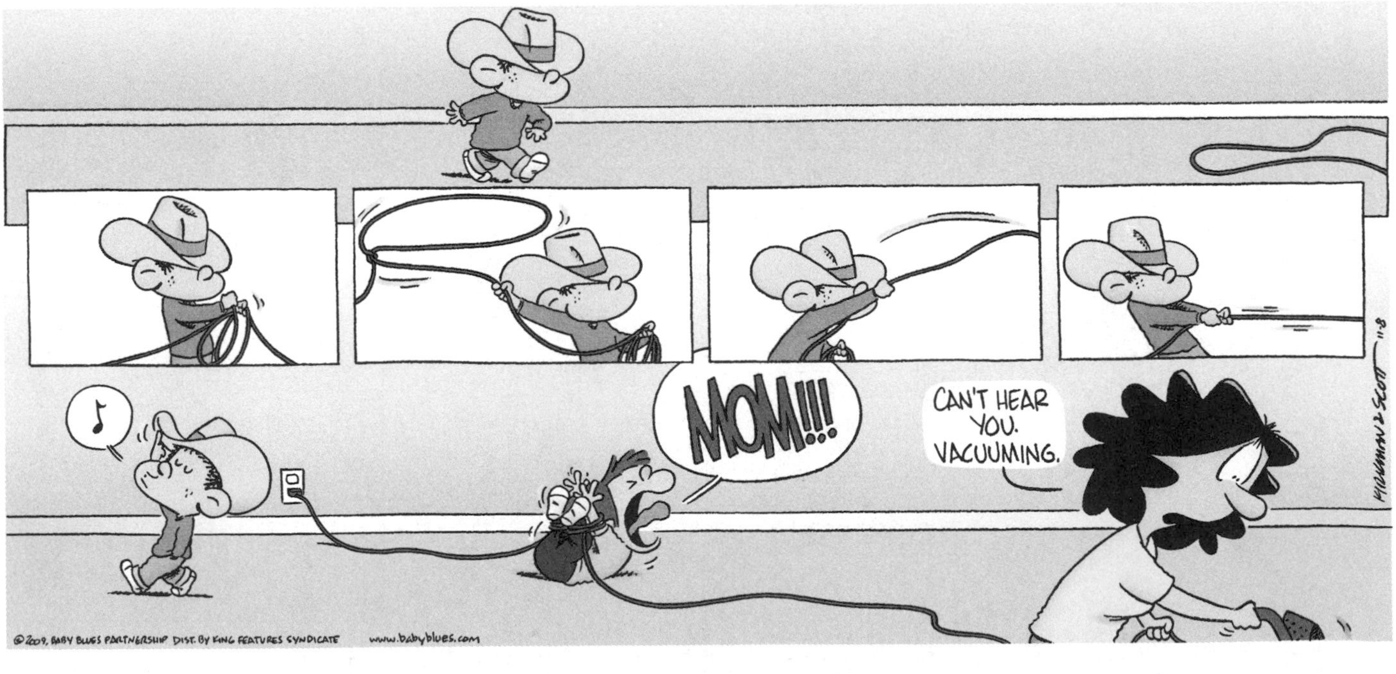
MOM!!!
CAN'T HEAR YOU. VACUUMING.
©2009, BABY BLUES PARTNERSHIP DIST. BY KING FEATURES SYNDICATE www.babyblues.com

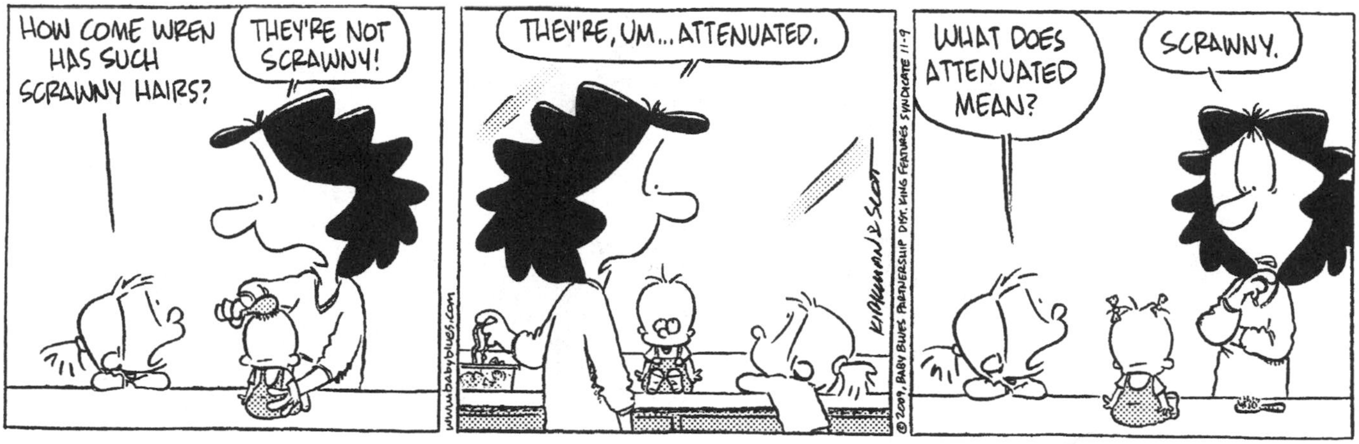
HOW COME WREN HAS SUCH SCRAWNY HAIRS?
THEY'RE NOT SCRAWNY!
www.babyblues.com
THEY'RE, UM... ATTENUATED.
KIRKMAN & SCOTT
© 2009, BABY BLUES PARTNERSHIP DIST. BY KING FEATURES SYNDICATE 11-9
WHAT DOES ATTENUATED MEAN?
SCRAWNY.

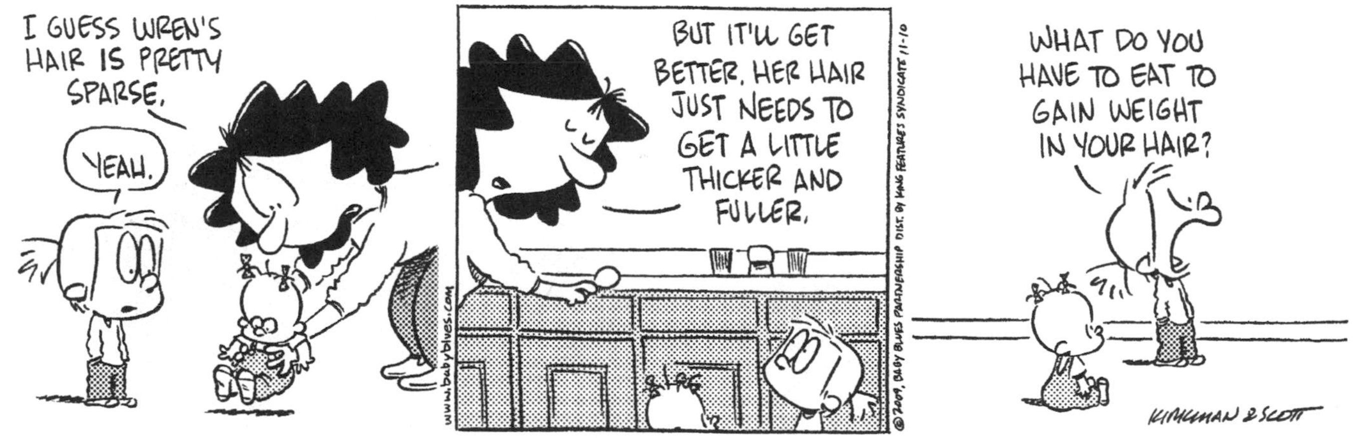
I GUESS WREN'S HAIR IS PRETTY SPARSE.
YEAH.
www.babyblues.com
BUT IT'LL GET BETTER. HER HAIR JUST NEEDS TO GET A LITTLE THICKER AND FULLER.
© 2009, BABY BLUES PARTNERSHIP DIST. BY KING FEATURES SYNDICATE 11-10
WHAT DO YOU HAVE TO EAT TO GAIN WEIGHT IN YOUR HAIR?
KIRKMAN & SCOTT

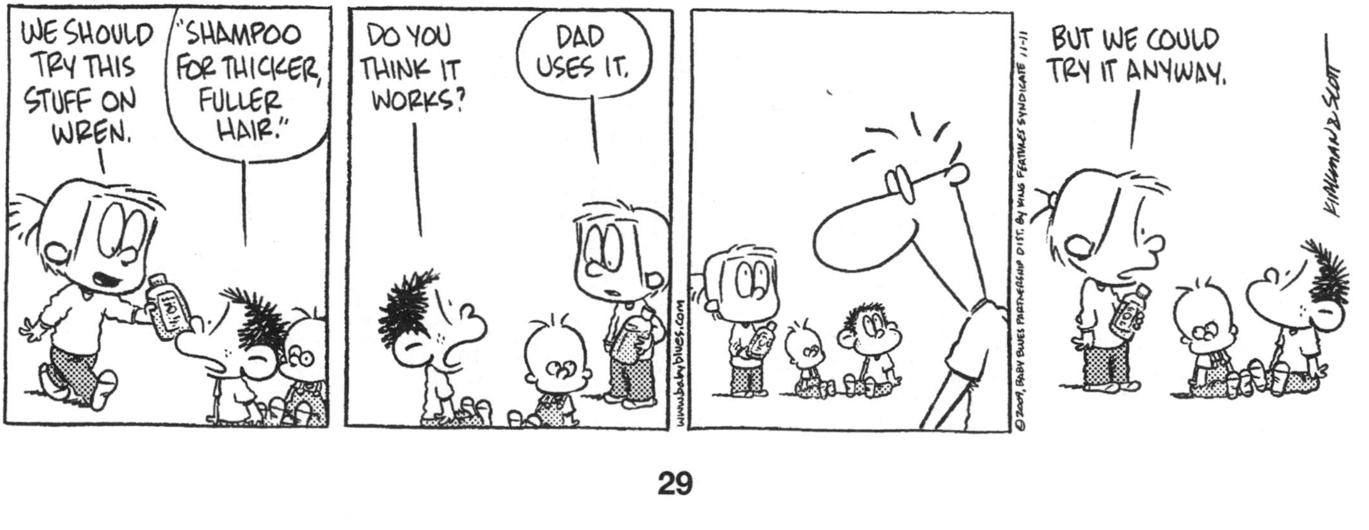
WE SHOULD TRY THIS STUFF ON WREN.
"SHAMPOO FOR THICKER, FULLER HAIR."
DO YOU THINK IT WORKS?
DAD USES IT.
www.babyblues.com
© 2009, BABY BLUES PARTNERSHIP DIST. BY KING FEATURES SYNDICATE 11-11
BUT WE COULD TRY IT ANYWAY.
KIRKMAN & SCOTT

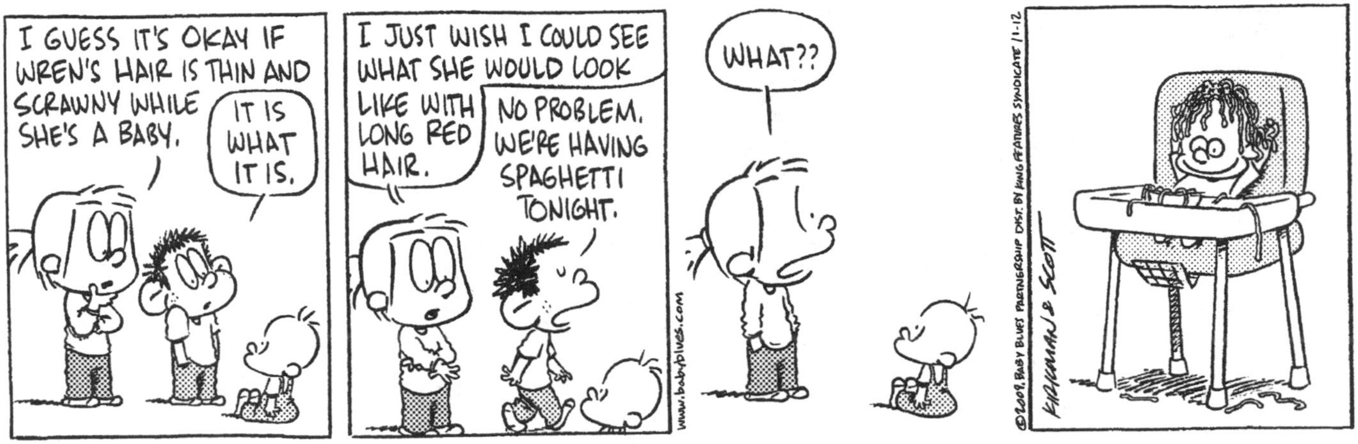
I GUESS IT'S OKAY IF WREN'S HAIR IS THIN AND SCRAWNY WHILE SHE'S A BABY.
IT IS WHAT IT IS.
I JUST WISH I COULD SEE WHAT SHE WOULD LOOK LIKE WITH LONG RED HAIR.
NO PROBLEM. WE'RE HAVING SPAGHETTI TONIGHT.
www.babyblues.com
WHAT??
©2009, BABY BLUES PARTNERSHIP DIST. BY KING FEATURES SYNDICATE 11-12
KIRKMAN & SCOTT

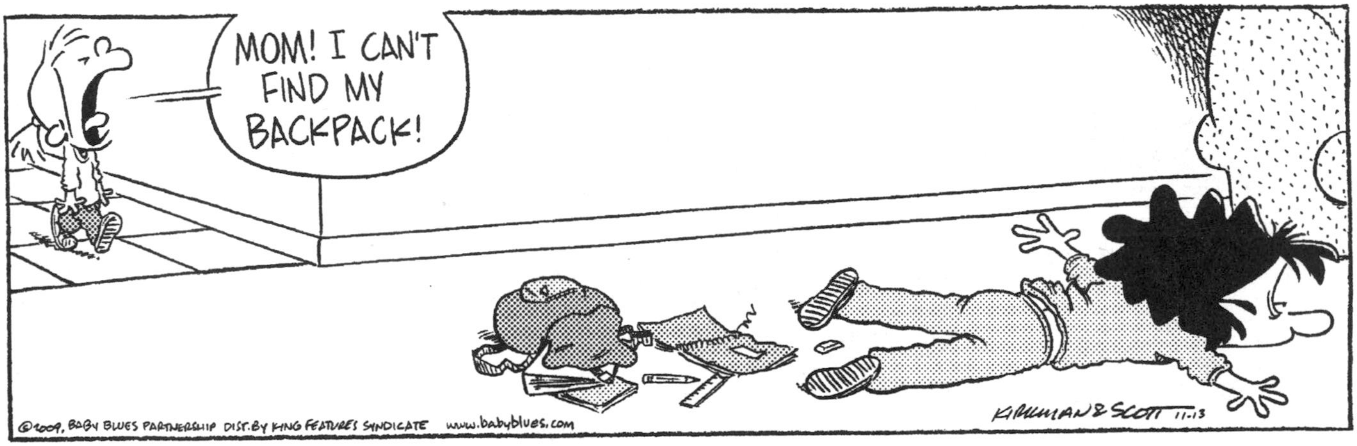
MOM! I CAN'T FIND MY BACKPACK!
©2009, BABY BLUES PARTNERSHIP DIST. BY KING FEATURES SYNDICATE www.babyblues.com
KIRKMAN & SCOTT 11-13

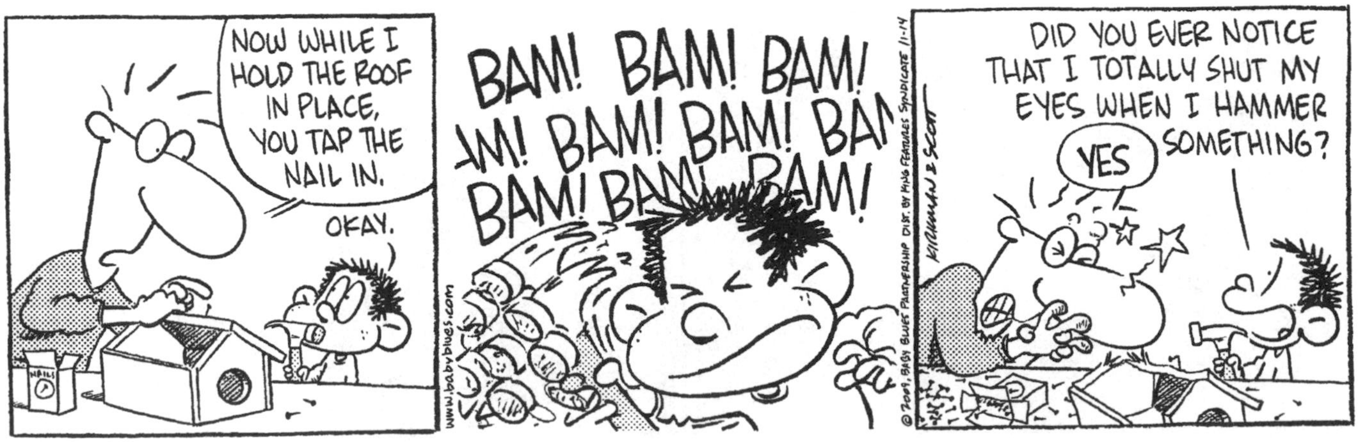
NOW WHILE I HOLD THE ROOF IN PLACE, YOU TAP THE NAIL IN.
OKAY.
www.babyblues.com
BAM! BAM! BAM!
AM! BAM! BAM! BAM
BAM! BAM! BAM!
©2009, BABY BLUES PARTNERSHIP DIST. BY KING FEATURES SYNDICATE 11-14
KIRKMAN & SCOTT
DID YOU EVER NOTICE THAT I TOTALLY SHUT MY EYES WHEN I HAMMER SOMETHING?
YES

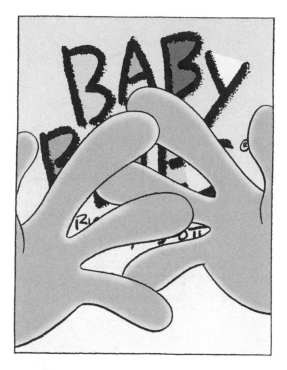

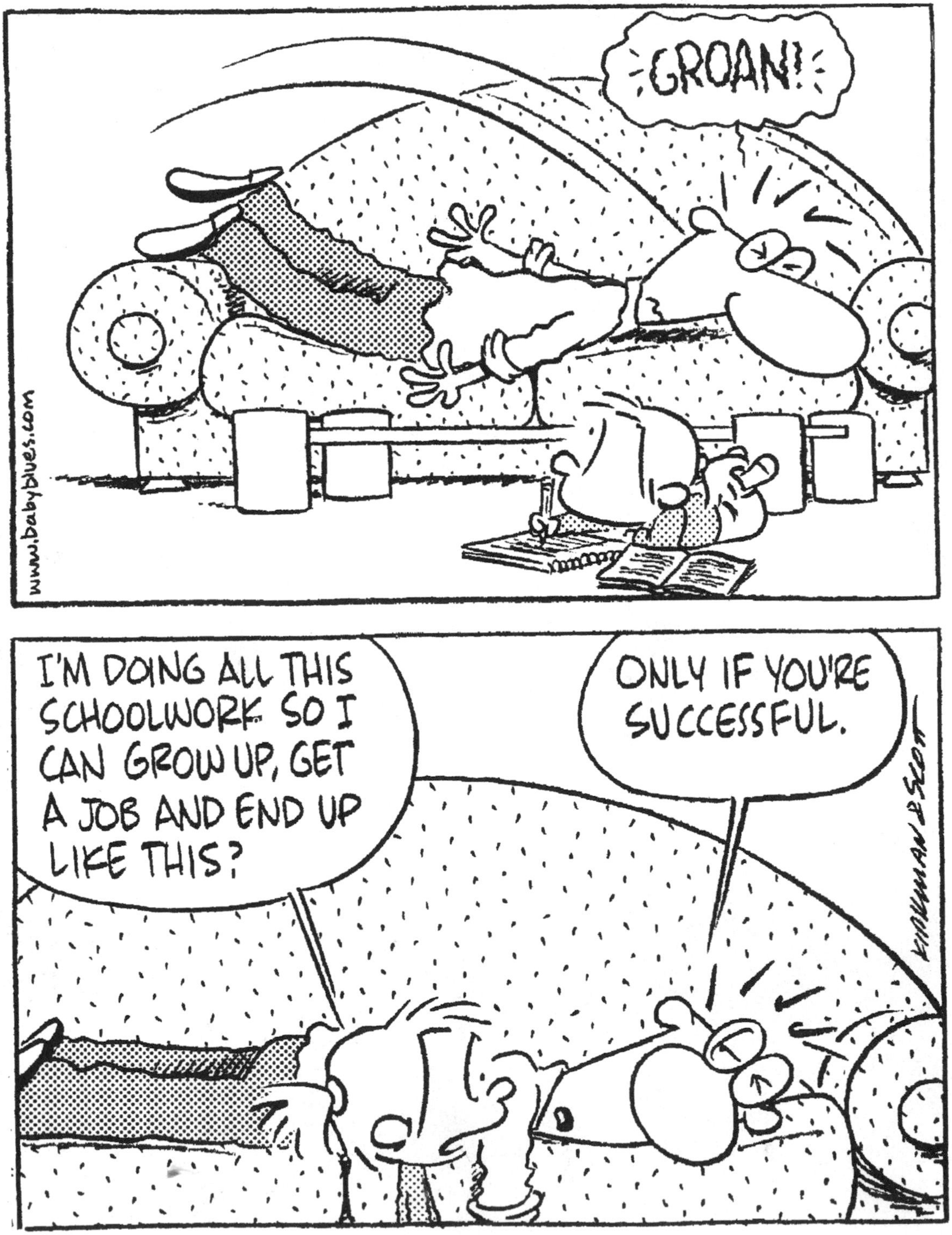
GROAN!
www.babyblues.com
I'M DOING ALL THIS SCHOOLWORK SO I CAN GROW UP, GET A JOB AND END UP LIKE THIS?
ONLY IF YOU'RE SUCCESSFUL.
KIRKMAN & SCOTT

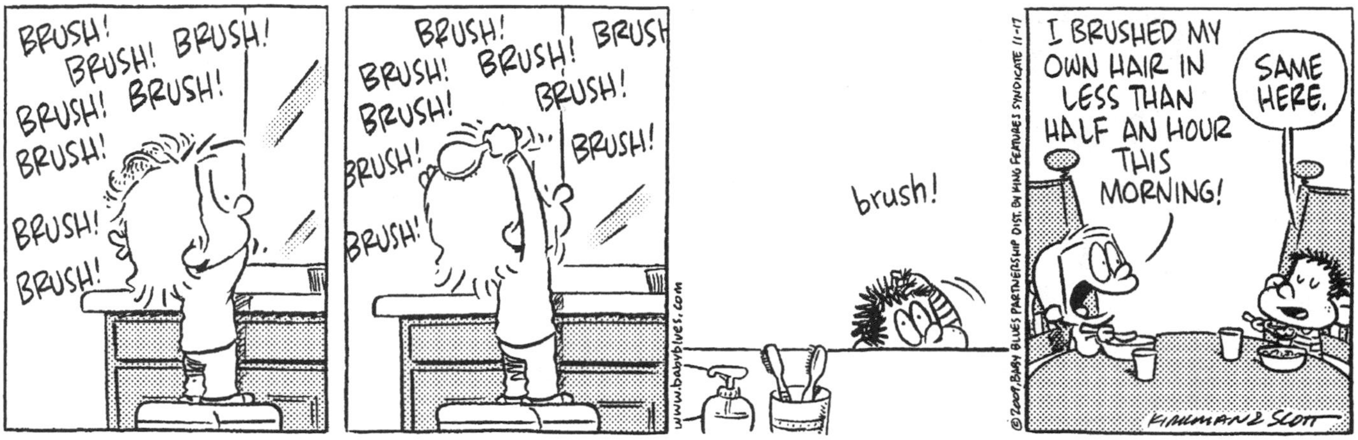
BRUSH! BRUSH! BRUSH! BRUSH! BRUSH! BRUSH! BRUSH! BRUSH!
BRUSH! BRUSH! BRUSH! BRUSH! BRUSH! BRUSH! BRUSH! BRUSH!
brush!
I BRUSHED MY OWN HAIR IN LESS THAN HALF AN HOUR THIS MORNING!
SAME HERE.
www.babyblues.com
© 2009, BABY BLUES PARTNERSHIP DIST. BY KING FEATURES SYNDICATE 11-17
KIRKMAN & SCOTT

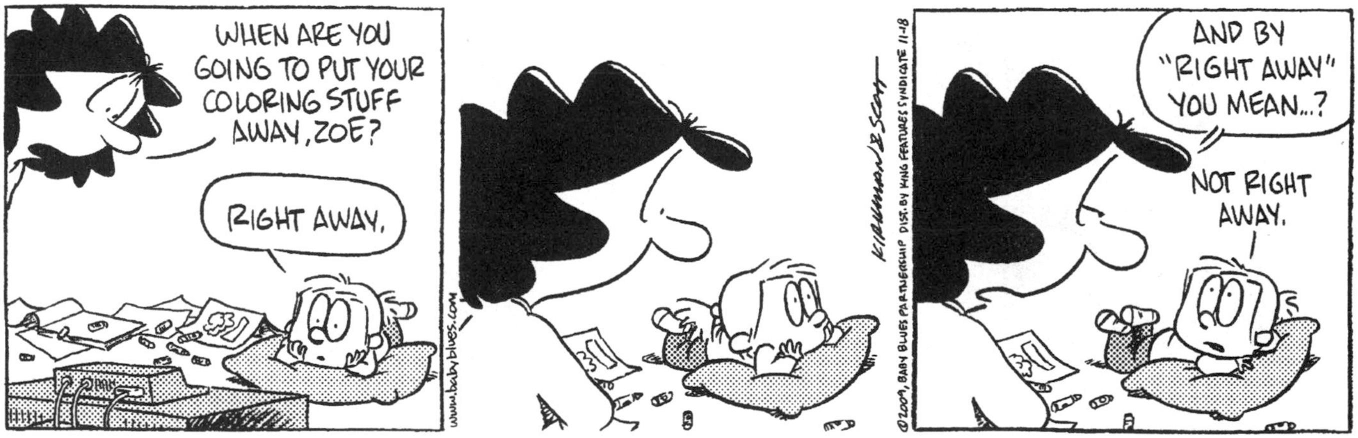
WHEN ARE YOU GOING TO PUT YOUR COLORING STUFF AWAY, ZOE?
RIGHT AWAY.
www.babyblues.com
KIRKMAN & SCOTT
© 2009, BABY BLUES PARTNERSHIP DIST. BY KING FEATURES SYNDICATE 11-18
AND BY "RIGHT AWAY" YOU MEAN...?
NOT RIGHT AWAY.

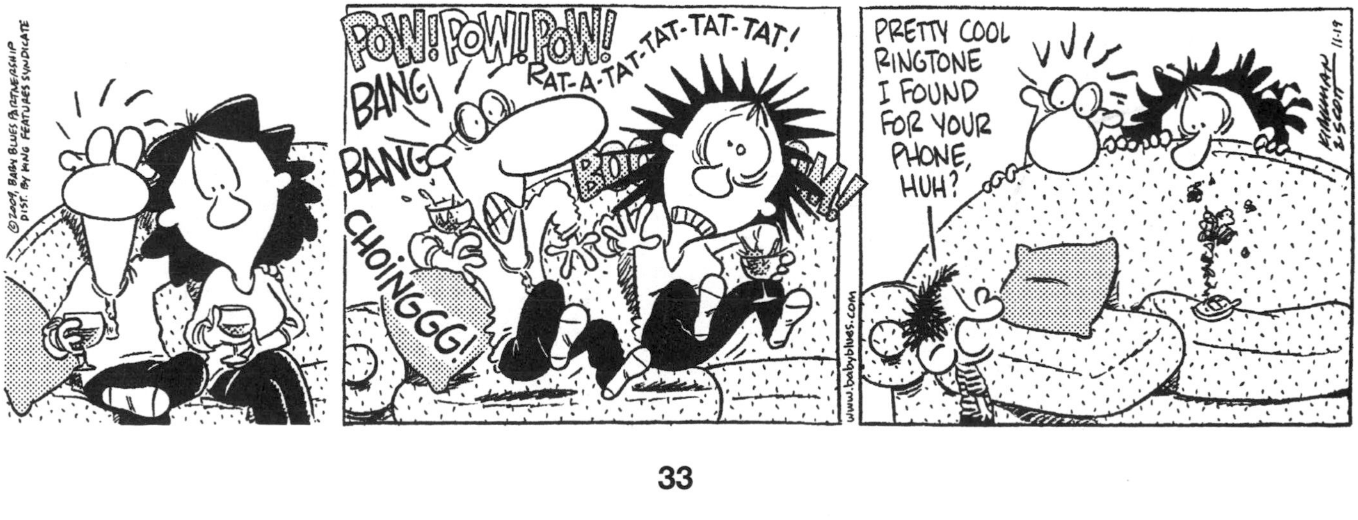
© 2009, BABY BLUES PARTNERSHIP DIST. BY KING FEATURES SYNDICATE
POW! POW! POW!
BANG!
RAT-A-TAT-TAT-TAT-TAT!
BANG
CHOINGGG!
www.babyblues.com
PRETTY COOL RINGTONE I FOUND FOR YOUR PHONE, HUH?
11-19
KIRKMAN & SCOTT

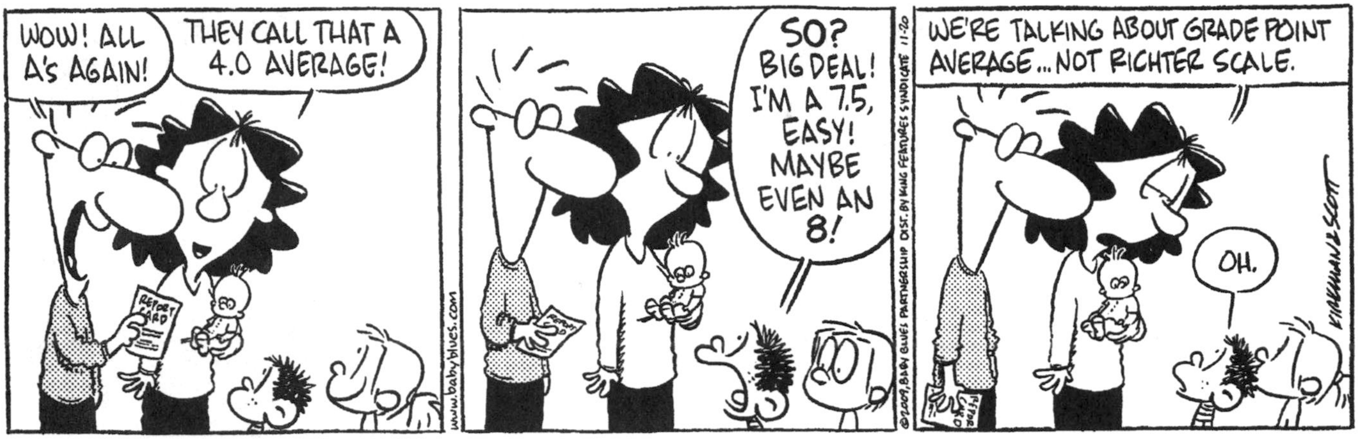
WOW! ALL A's AGAIN!
THEY CALL THAT A 4.0 AVERAGE!
REPORT CARD
www.babyblues.com
SO? BIG DEAL! I'M A 7.5, EASY! MAYBE EVEN AN 8!
©2009, BABY BLUES PARTNERSHIP DIST. BY KING FEATURES SYNDICATE 11-20
WE'RE TALKING ABOUT GRADE POINT AVERAGE... NOT RICHTER SCALE.
OH.
KIRKMAN & SCOTT

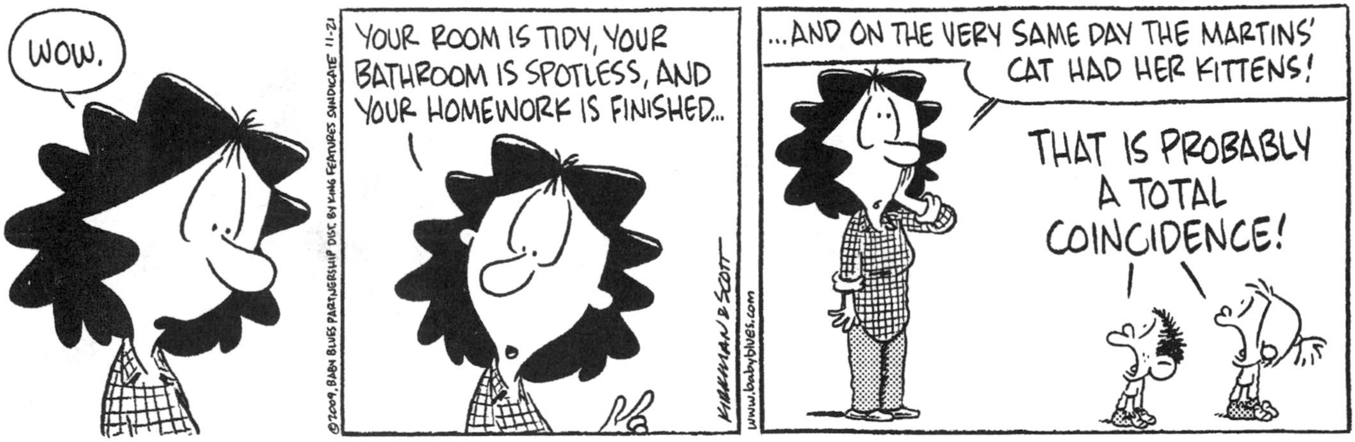
WOW.
©2009, BABY BLUES PARTNERSHIP DIST. BY KING FEATURES SYNDICATE 11-21
YOUR ROOM IS TIDY, YOUR BATHROOM IS SPOTLESS, AND YOUR HOMEWORK IS FINISHED...
KIRKMAN & SCOTT
www.babyblues.com
...AND ON THE VERY SAME DAY THE MARTINS' CAT HAD HER KITTENS!
THAT IS PROBABLY A TOTAL COINCIDENCE!

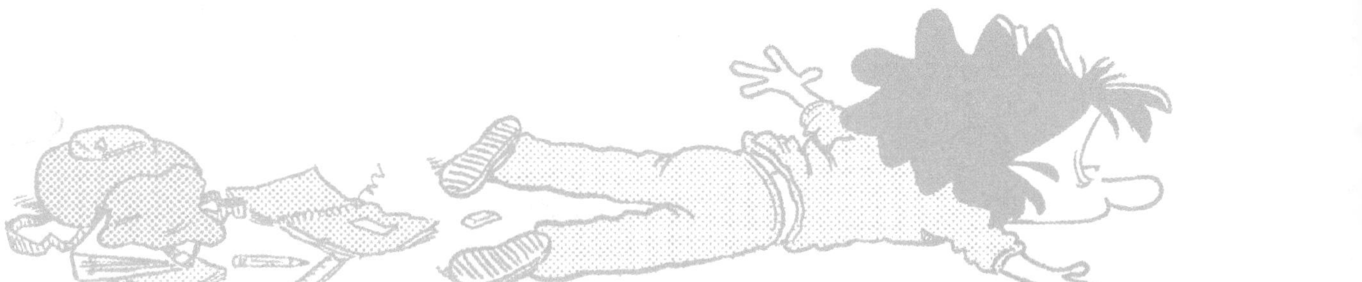

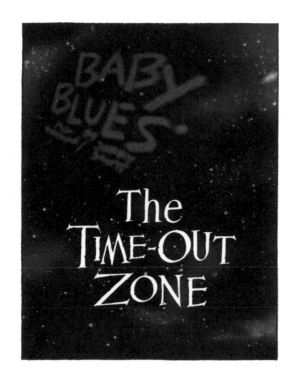

BABY BLUES
The TIME-OUT ZONE

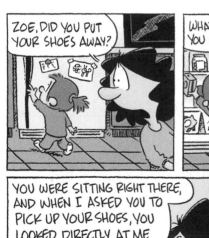

ZOE, DID YOU PUT YOUR SHOES AWAY?
WHAT DO YOU MEAN?
I MEAN, DID YOU PUT YOUR SHOES AWAY?
WAS I SUPPOSED TO PUT MY SHOES AWAY?
YES! I ASKED YOU TO DO IT FIVE MINUTES AGO!
ARE YOU SURE?
YES I'M SURE!
YOU WERE SITTING RIGHT THERE, AND WHEN I ASKED YOU TO PICK UP YOUR SHOES, YOU LOOKED DIRECTLY AT ME AND SAID, "OKAY, MOM."
OH.
AND THAT MADE YOU THINK I WAS LISTENING TO YOU?
www.babyblues.com
OF ALL THE TIME-OUTS I'VE SEEN, THIS IS THE TIME-OUTIEST!
MFGLB!
KIRKMAN & SCOTT 11-22

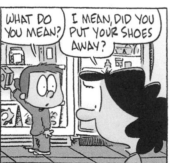

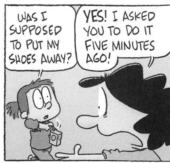

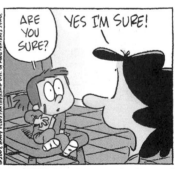

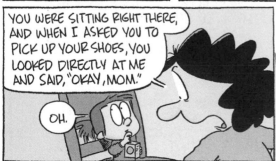

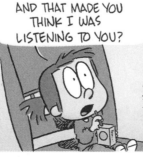

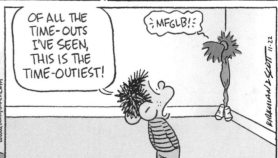

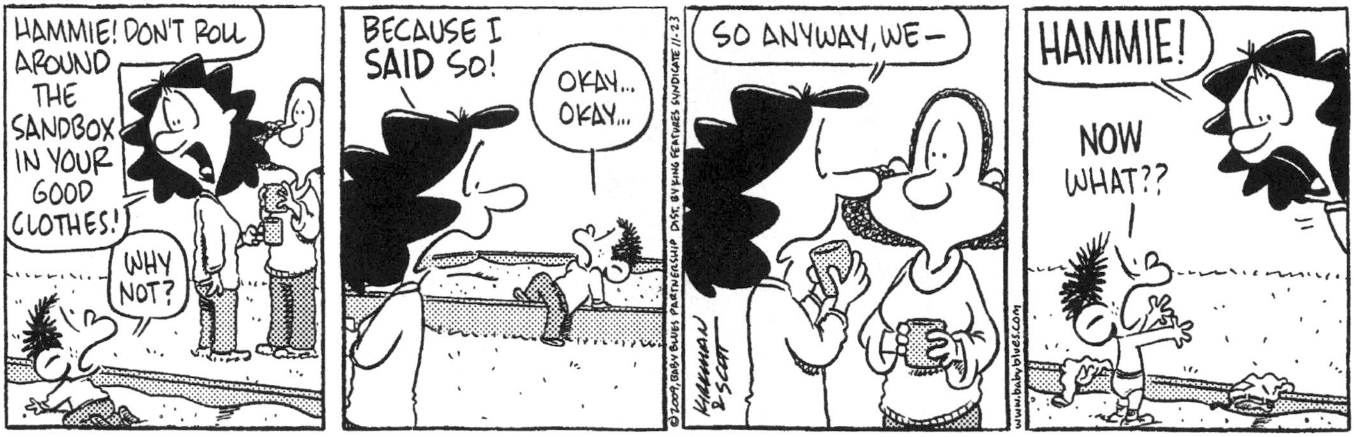
HAMMIE! DON'T ROLL AROUND THE SANDBOX IN YOUR GOOD CLOTHES!
WHY NOT?
BECAUSE I SAID SO!
OKAY... OKAY...
©2009, BABY BLUES PARTNERSHIP DIST. BY KING FEATURES SYNDICATE 11-23
KIRKMAN & SCOTT
SO ANYWAY, WE–
www.babyblues.com
HAMMIE!
NOW WHAT??

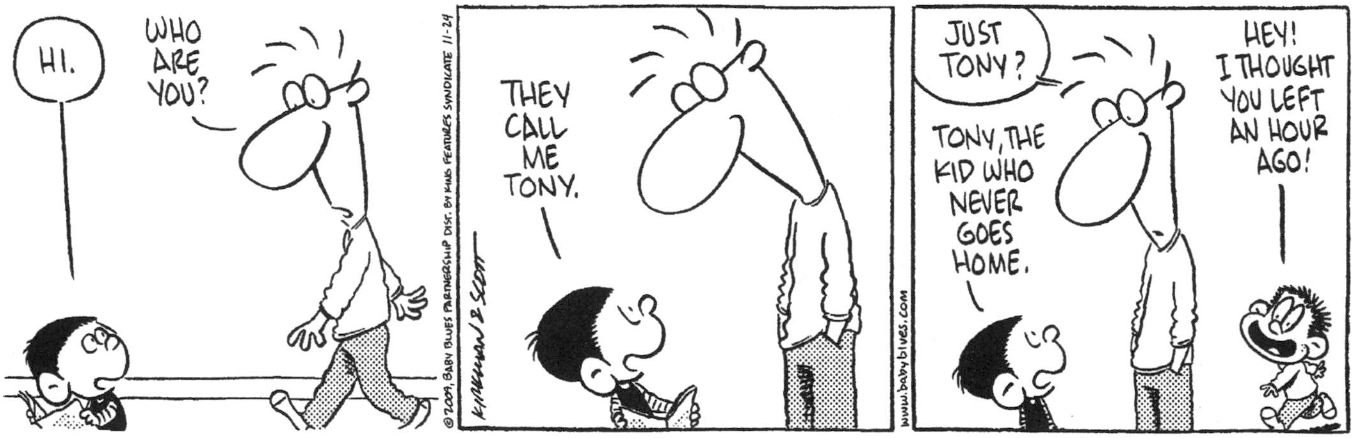
HI.
WHO ARE YOU?
©2009, BABY BLUES PARTNERSHIP DIST. BY KING FEATURES SYNDICATE 11-24
KIRKMAN & SCOTT
THEY CALL ME TONY.
www.babyblues.com
JUST TONY?
TONY, THE KID WHO NEVER GOES HOME.
HEY! I THOUGHT YOU LEFT AN HOUR AGO!

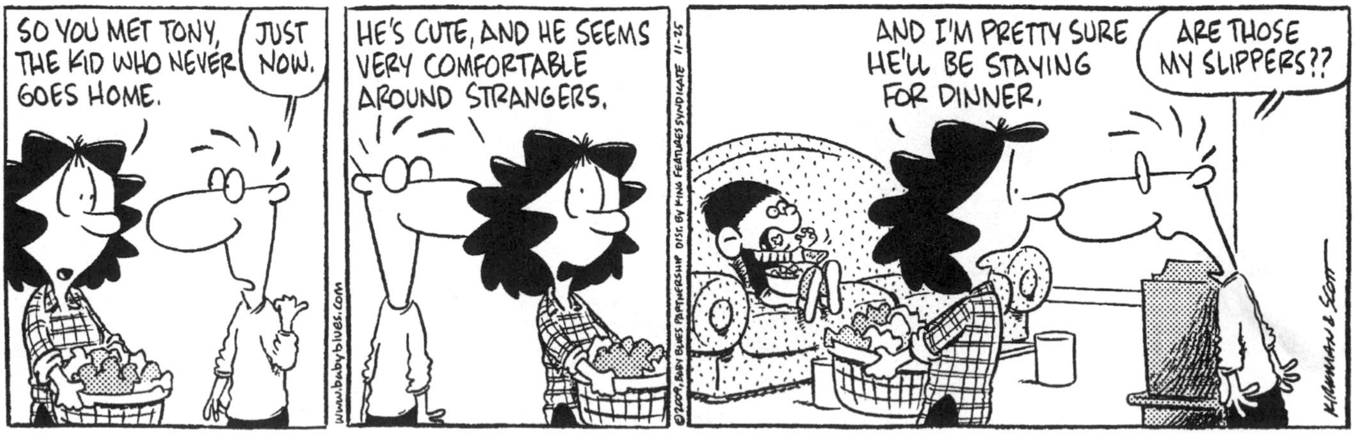
SO YOU MET TONY, THE KID WHO NEVER GOES HOME.
JUST NOW.
www.babyblues.com
HE'S CUTE, AND HE SEEMS VERY COMFORTABLE AROUND STRANGERS.
©2009, BABY BLUES PARTNERSHIP DIST. BY KING FEATURES SYNDICATE 11-25
AND I'M PRETTY SURE HE'LL BE STAYING FOR DINNER.
ARE THOSE MY SLIPPERS??
KIRKMAN & SCOTT

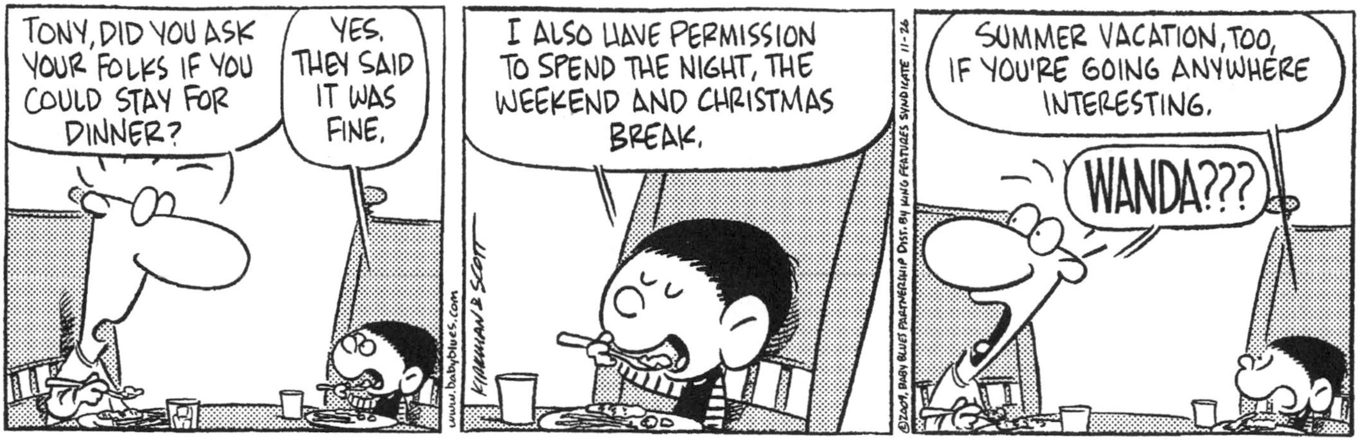
TONY, DID YOU ASK YOUR FOLKS IF YOU COULD STAY FOR DINNER?
YES. THEY SAID IT WAS FINE.
I ALSO HAVE PERMISSION TO SPEND THE NIGHT, THE WEEKEND AND CHRISTMAS BREAK.
SUMMER VACATION, TOO, IF YOU'RE GOING ANYWHERE INTERESTING.
WANDA???
www.babyblues.com
KIRKMAN & SCOTT
©2009, BABY BLUES PARTNERSHIP DIST. BY KING FEATURES SYNDICATE 11-26

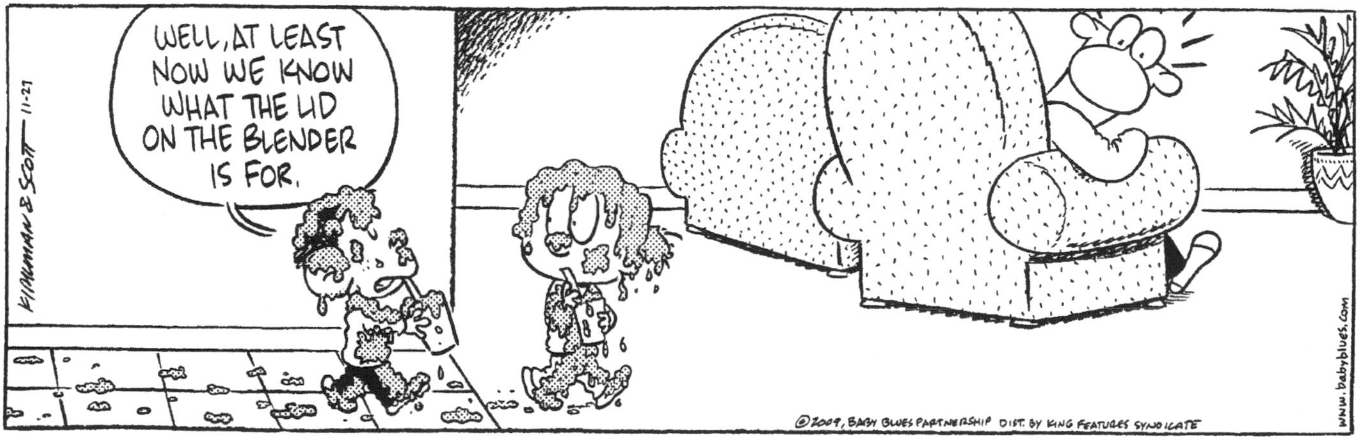
WELL, AT LEAST NOW WE KNOW WHAT THE LID ON THE BLENDER IS FOR.
KIRKMAN & SCOTT 11-27
©2009, BABY BLUES PARTNERSHIP DIST. BY KING FEATURES SYNDICATE
www.babyblues.com

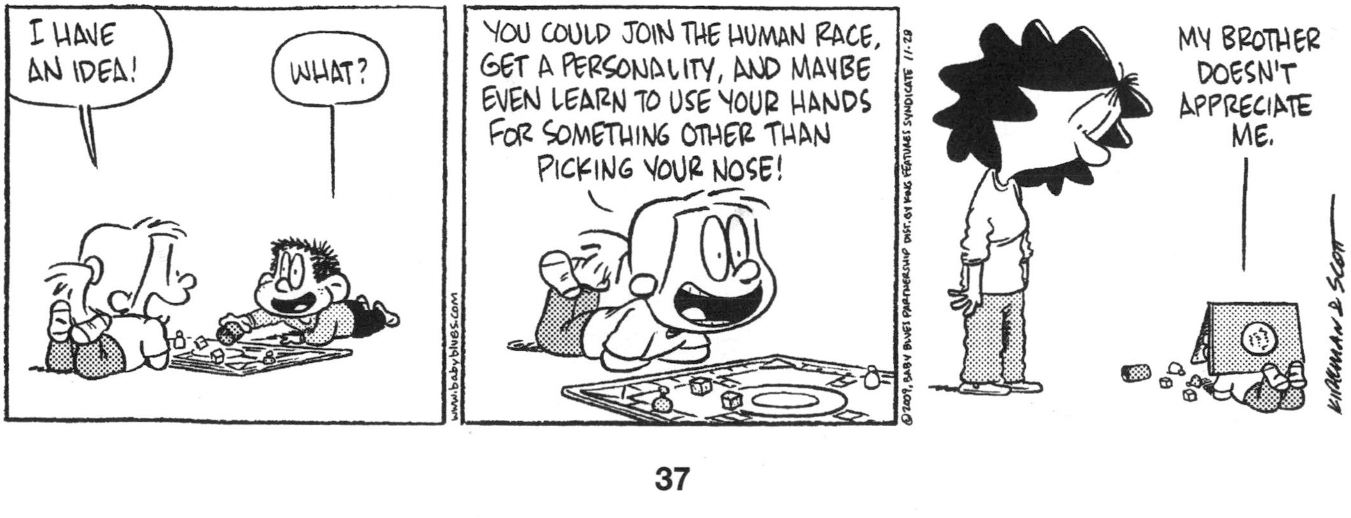
I HAVE AN IDEA!
WHAT?
YOU COULD JOIN THE HUMAN RACE, GET A PERSONALITY, AND MAYBE EVEN LEARN TO USE YOUR HANDS FOR SOMETHING OTHER THAN PICKING YOUR NOSE!
MY BROTHER DOESN'T APPRECIATE ME.
www.babyblues.com
©2009, BABY BLUES PARTNERSHIP DIST. BY KING FEATURES SYNDICATE 11-28
KIRKMAN & SCOTT

BABY BLUES®
BY RICK KIRKMAN / JERRY SCOTT

OKAY...DOES EVERYONE UNDERSTAND THIS CHAPTER?
YES!
HAVE YOU ALL FINISHED THE SAMPLE PROBLEMS?
YES!
ARE THERE ANY QUESTIONS ABOUT THE HOMEWORK?
NO!
TODAY
Art
2:00
WHAT'S THIS CHAPTER ABOUT?
HOW AM I SUPPOSED TO KNOW??
©2009, BABY BLUES PARTNERSHIP DIST. BY KING FEATURES SYNDICATE
KIRKMAN & SCOTT 11-29
www.babyblues.com

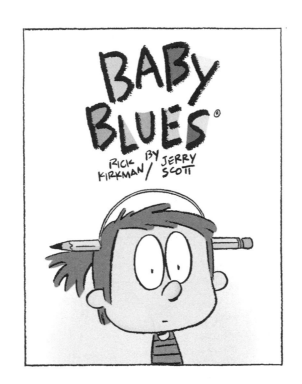

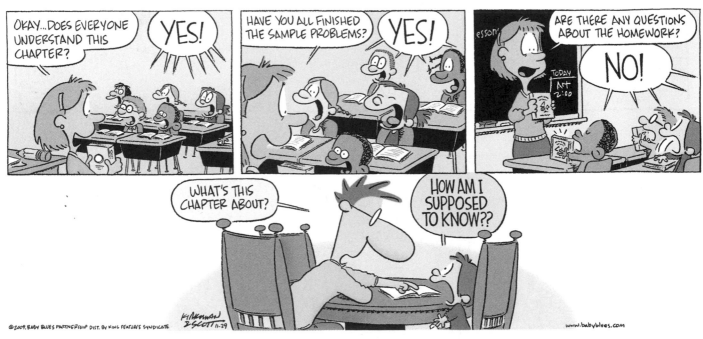

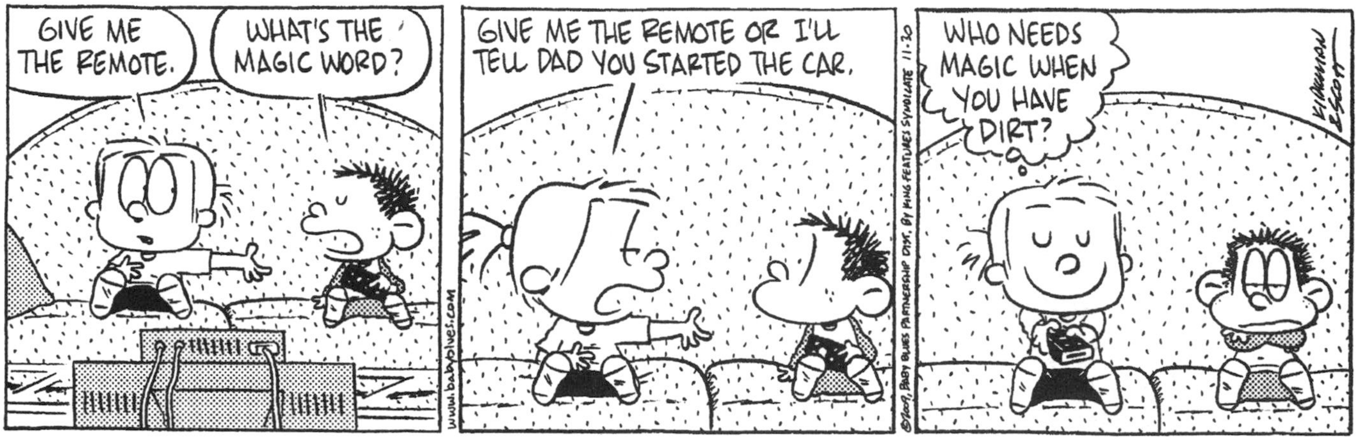
GIVE ME THE REMOTE.
WHAT'S THE MAGIC WORD?
GIVE ME THE REMOTE OR I'LL TELL DAD YOU STARTED THE CAR.
WHO NEEDS MAGIC WHEN YOU HAVE DIRT?
KIRKMAN & SCOTT
www.babyblues.com

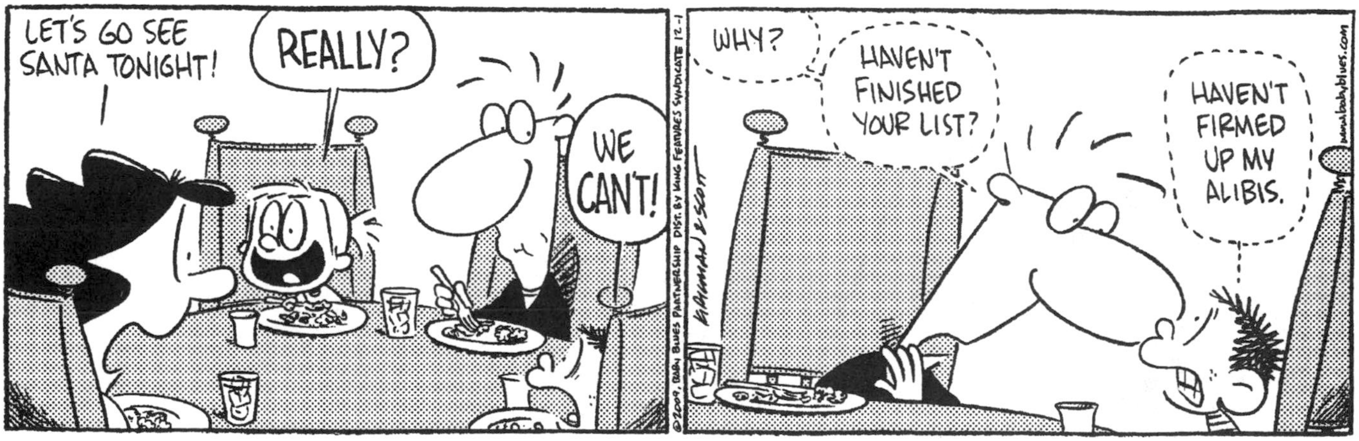
LET'S GO SEE SANTA TONIGHT!
REALLY?
WE CAN'T!
WHY?
HAVEN'T FINISHED YOUR LIST?
HAVEN'T FIRMED UP MY ALIBIS.
KIRKMAN & SCOTT
www.babyblues.com

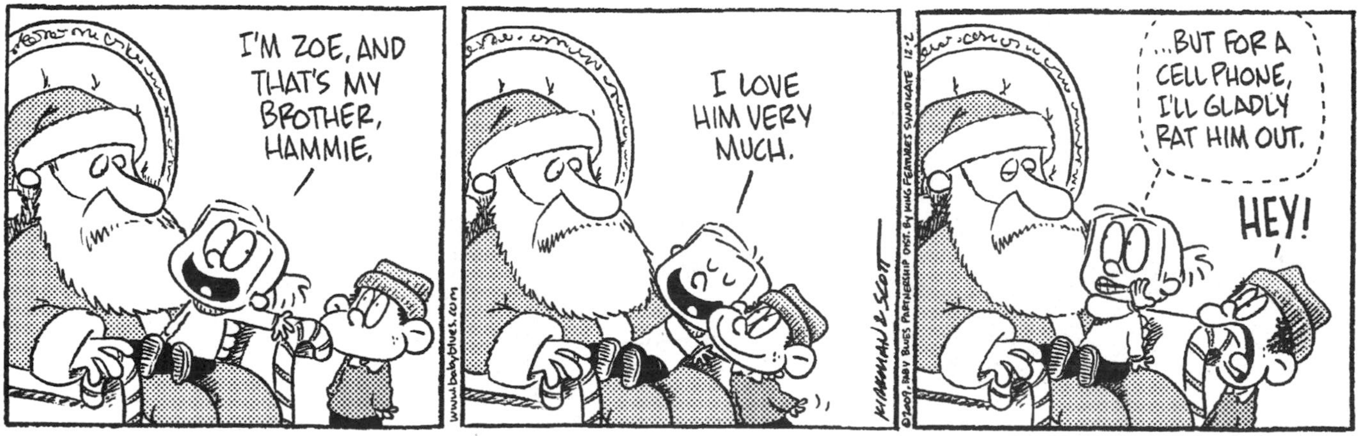
I'M ZOE, AND THAT'S MY BROTHER, HAMMIE.
I LOVE HIM VERY MUCH.
...BUT FOR A CELL PHONE, I'LL GLADLY RAT HIM OUT.
HEY!
KIRKMAN & SCOTT
www.babyblues.com

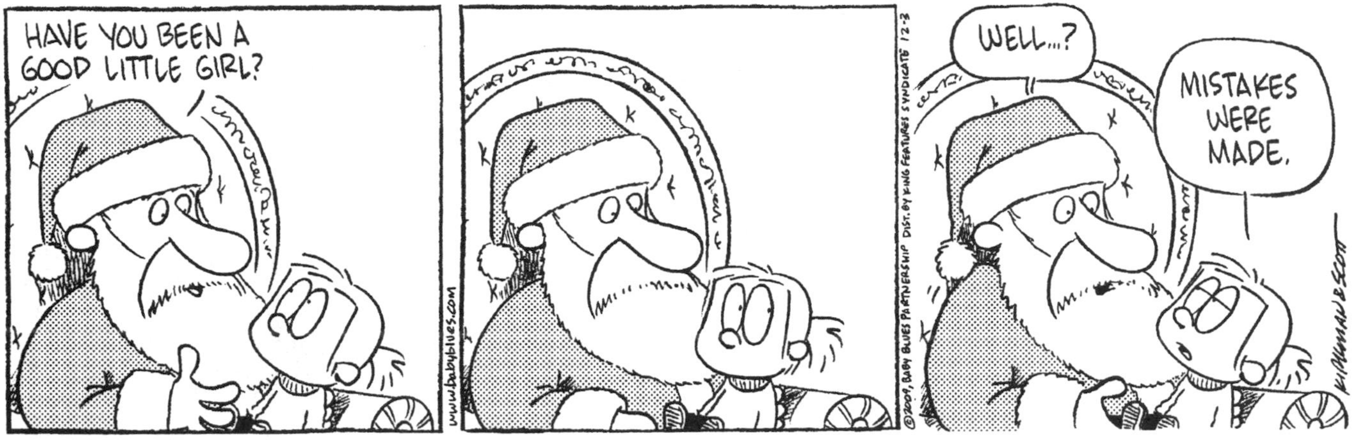
HAVE YOU BEEN A GOOD LITTLE GIRL?
WELL...?
MISTAKES WERE MADE.

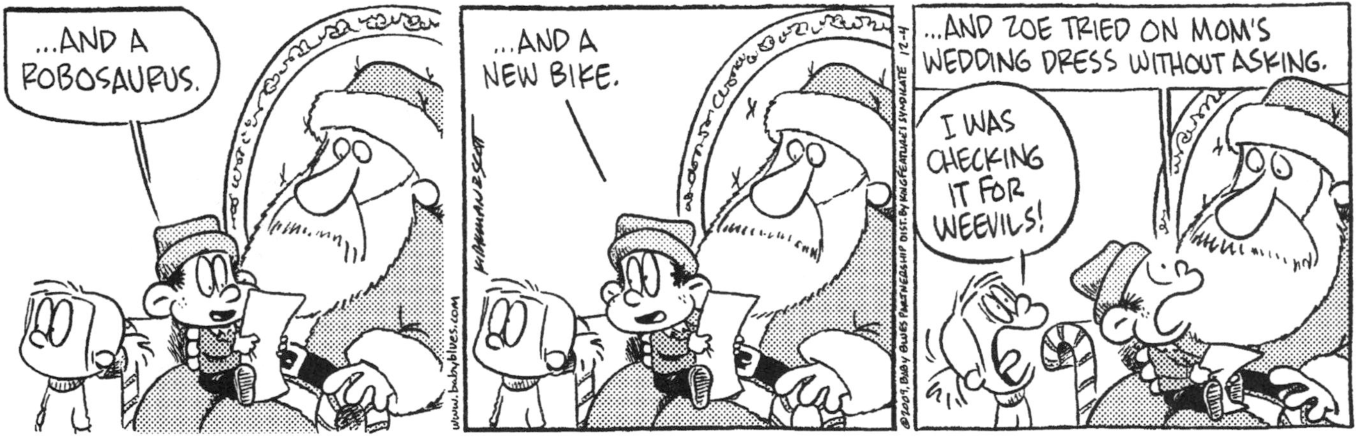
...AND A ROBOSAURUS.
...AND A NEW BIKE.
...AND ZOE TRIED ON MOM'S WEDDING DRESS WITHOUT ASKING.
I WAS CHECKING IT FOR WEEVILS!

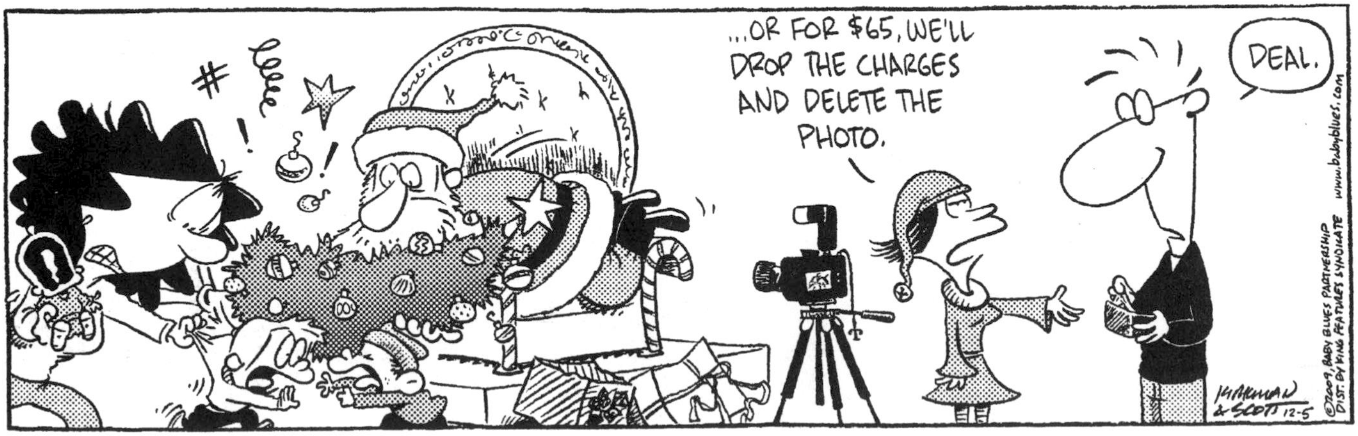
...OR FOR $65, WE'LL DROP THE CHARGES AND DELETE THE PHOTO.
DEAL.

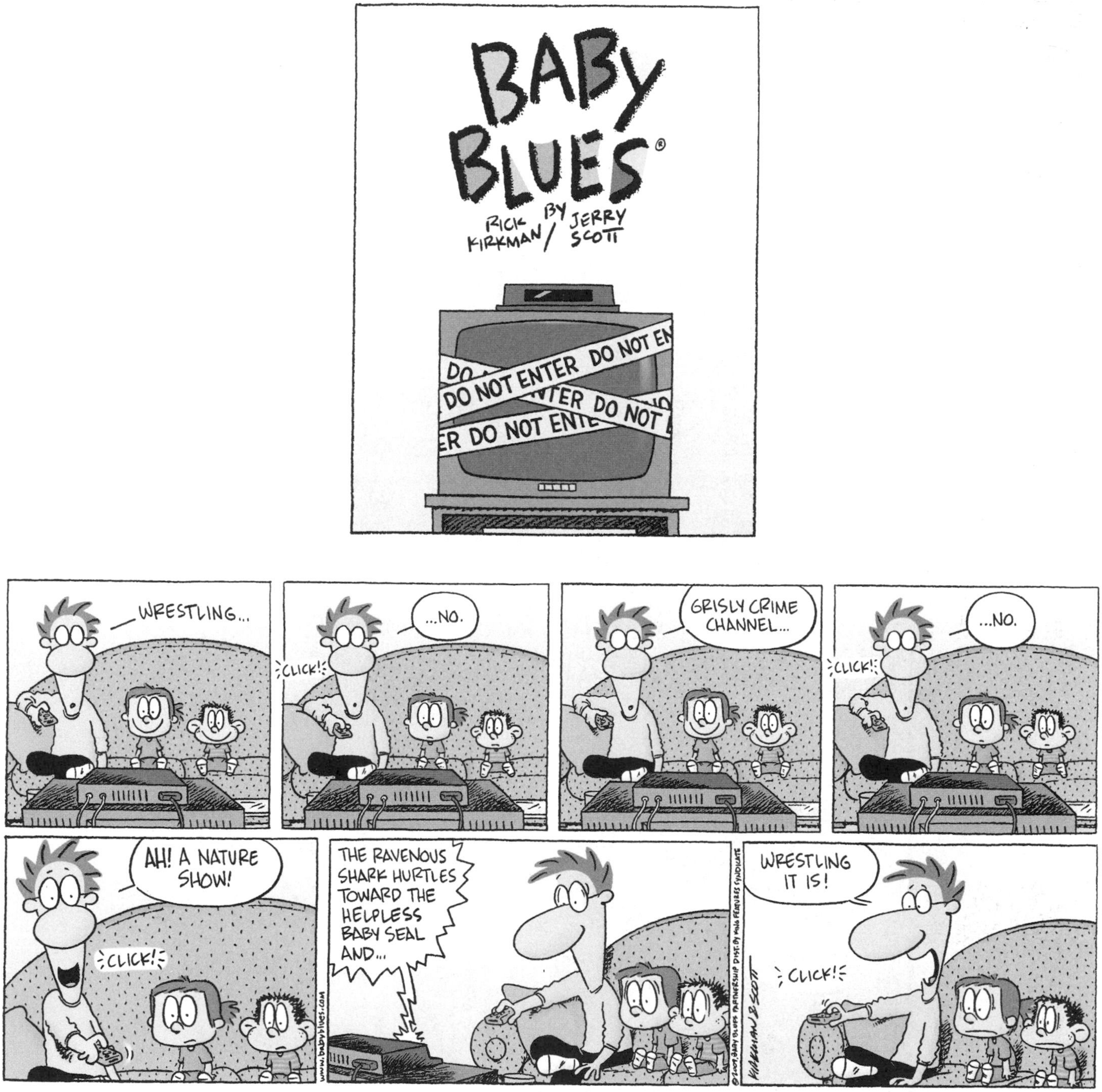
BABY BLUES®
BY RICK KIRKMAN / JERRY SCOTT
DO NOT ENTER DO NOT EN
DO NOT ENTER
DO NOT ENTE
ER DO NOT
WRESTLING...
CLICK!
...NO.
GRISLY CRIME CHANNEL...
CLICK!
...NO.
AH! A NATURE SHOW!
CLICK!
www.babyblues.com
THE RAVENOUS SHARK HURTLES TOWARD THE HELPLESS BABY SEAL AND...
©2009, BABY BLUES PARTNERSHIP DIST. BY KING FEATURES SYNDICATE
KIRKMAN & SCOTT
WRESTLING IT IS!
CLICK!

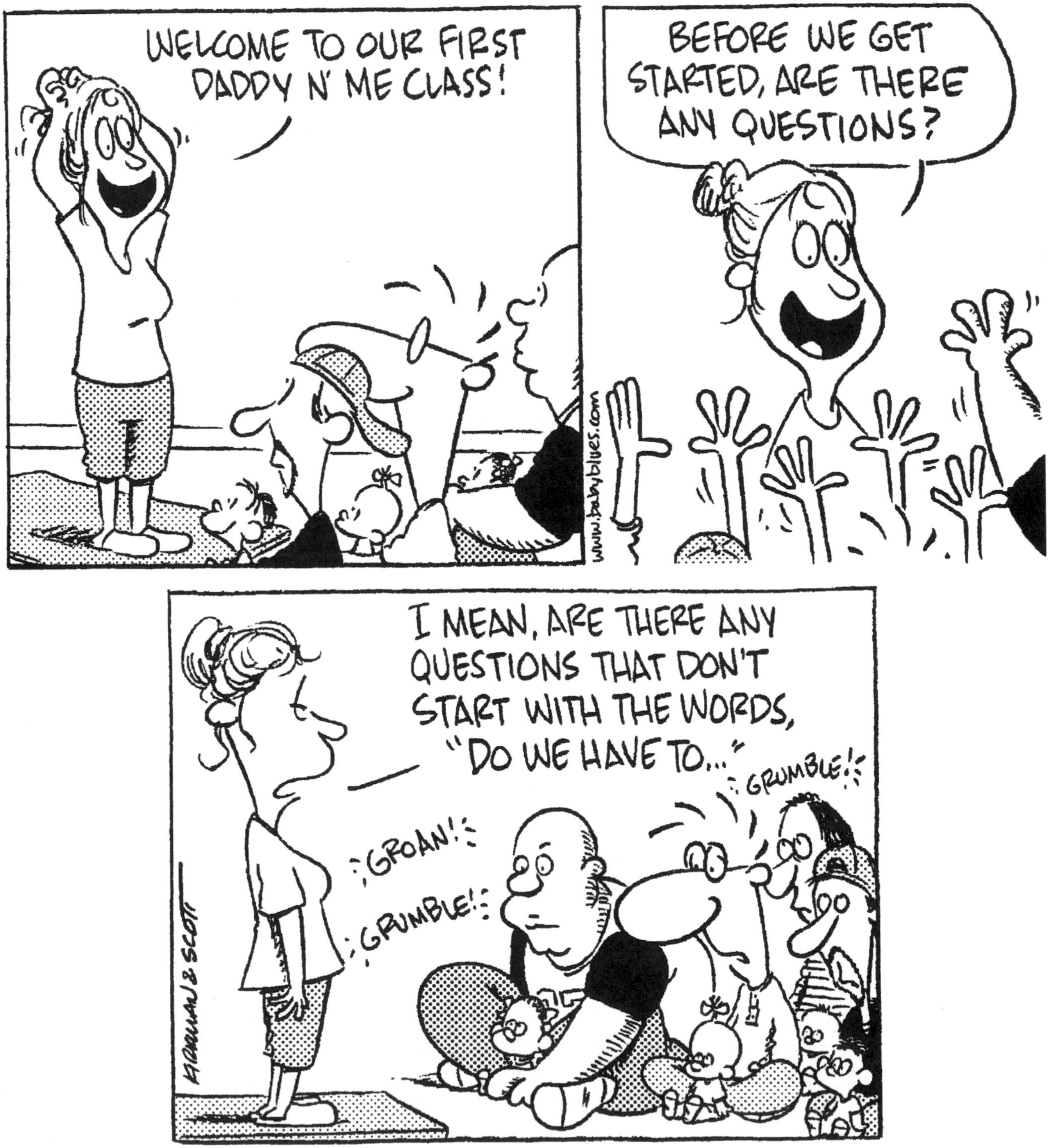
WELCOME TO OUR FIRST DADDY N' ME CLASS!
www.babyblues.com
BEFORE WE GET STARTED, ARE THERE ANY QUESTIONS?
I MEAN, ARE THERE ANY QUESTIONS THAT DON'T START WITH THE WORDS, "DO WE HAVE TO..."
GROAN!
GRUMBLE!
GRUMBLE!
KIRKMAN & SCOTT

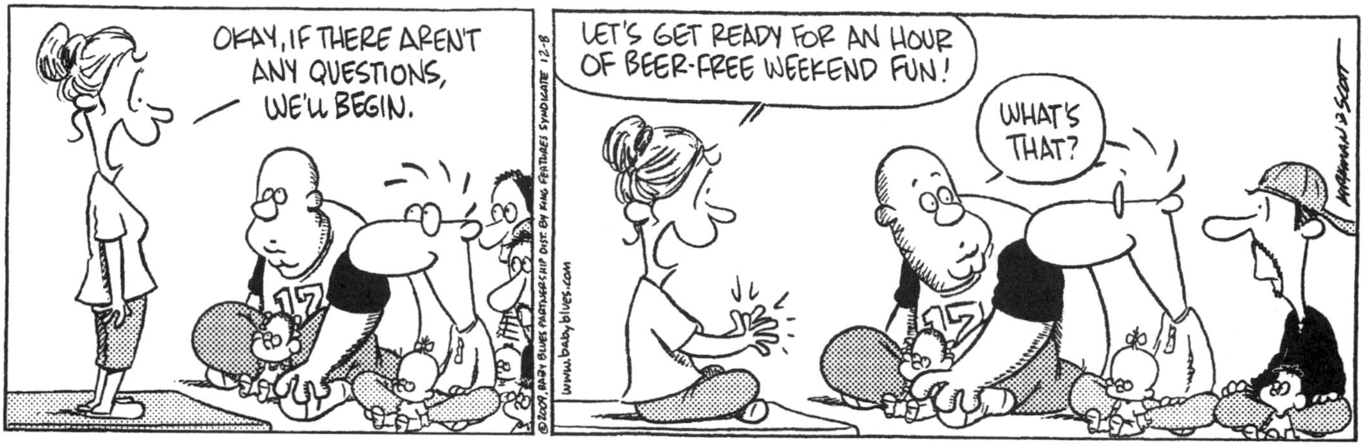
OKAY, IF THERE AREN'T ANY QUESTIONS, WE'LL BEGIN.
LET'S GET READY FOR AN HOUR OF BEER-FREE WEEKEND FUN!
WHAT'S THAT?
©2009, BABY BLUES PARTNERSHIP DIST. BY KING FEATURES SYNDICATE 12-8
www.babyblues.com
KIRKMAN & SCOTT

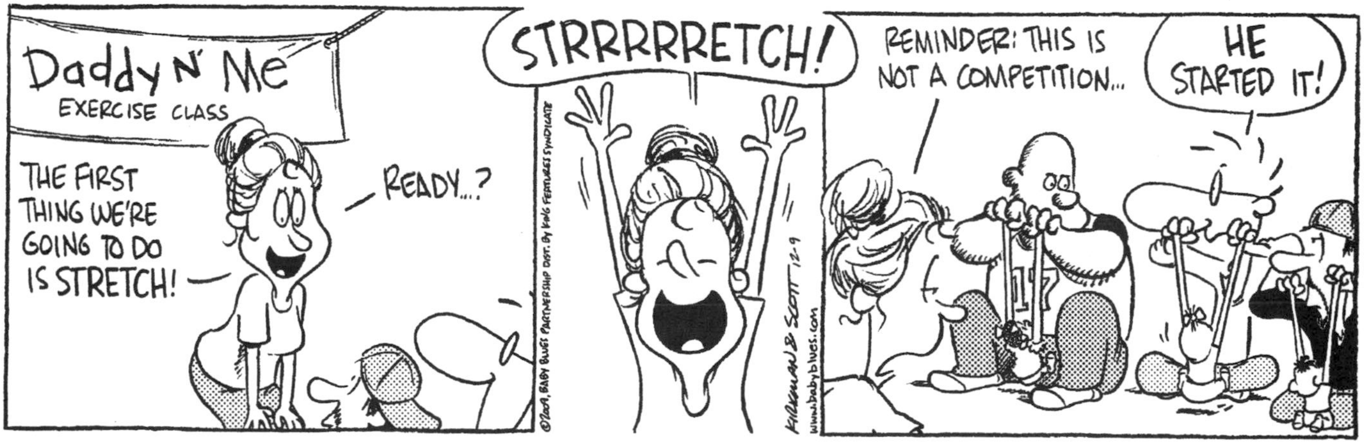
Daddy N' Me
EXERCISE CLASS
THE FIRST THING WE'RE GOING TO DO IS STRETCH!
READY...?
STRRRRRETCH!
REMINDER: THIS IS NOT A COMPETITION...
HE STARTED IT!
©2009, BABY BLUES PARTNERSHIP DIST. BY KING FEATURES SYNDICATE
KIRKMAN & SCOTT 12-9
www.babyblues.com

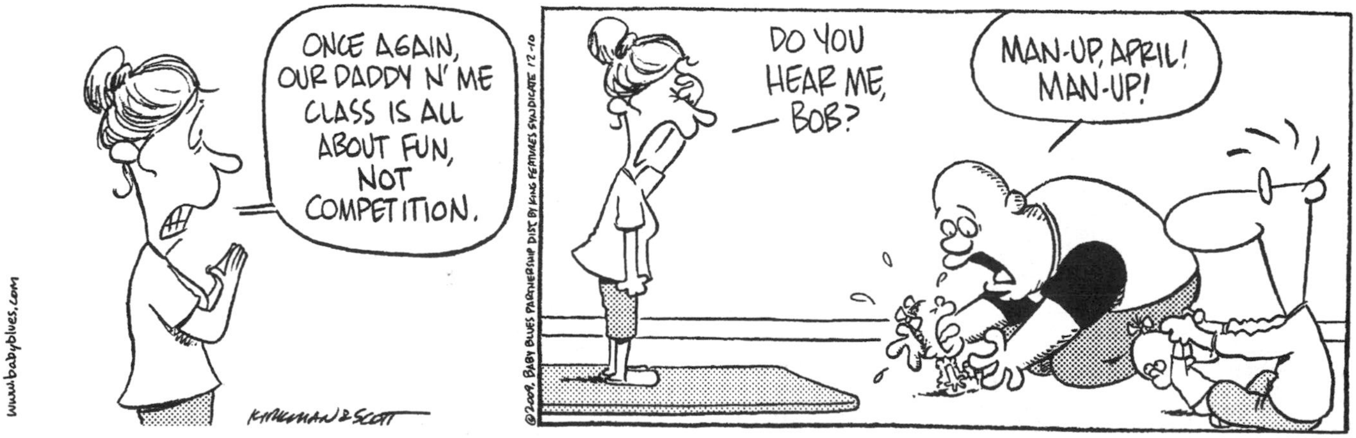
ONCE AGAIN, OUR DADDY N' ME CLASS IS ALL ABOUT FUN, NOT COMPETITION.
DO YOU HEAR ME, BOB?
MAN-UP, APRIL! MAN-UP!
www.babyblues.com
KIRKMAN & SCOTT
©2009, BABY BLUES PARTNERSHIP DIST. BY KING FEATURES SYNDICATE 12-10

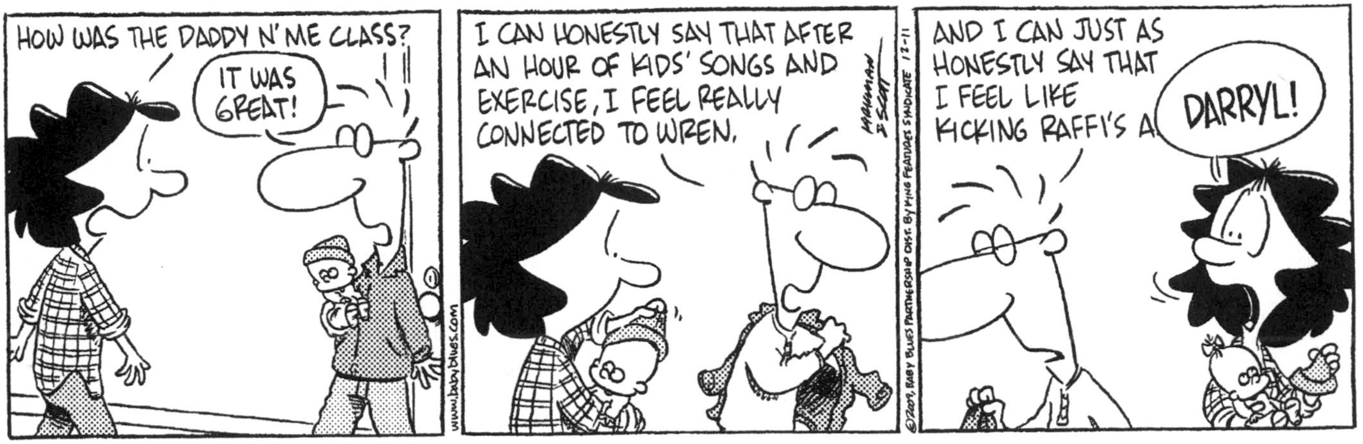
HOW WAS THE DADDY N' ME CLASS?
IT WAS GREAT!
www.babyblues.com
I CAN HONESTLY SAY THAT AFTER AN HOUR OF KIDS' SONGS AND EXERCISE, I FEEL REALLY CONNECTED TO WREN.
KIRKMAN & SCOTT
©2009, BABY BLUES PARTNERSHIP DIST. BY KING FEATURES SYNDICATE 12-11
AND I CAN JUST AS HONESTLY SAY THAT I FEEL LIKE KICKING RAFFI'S A
DARRYL!

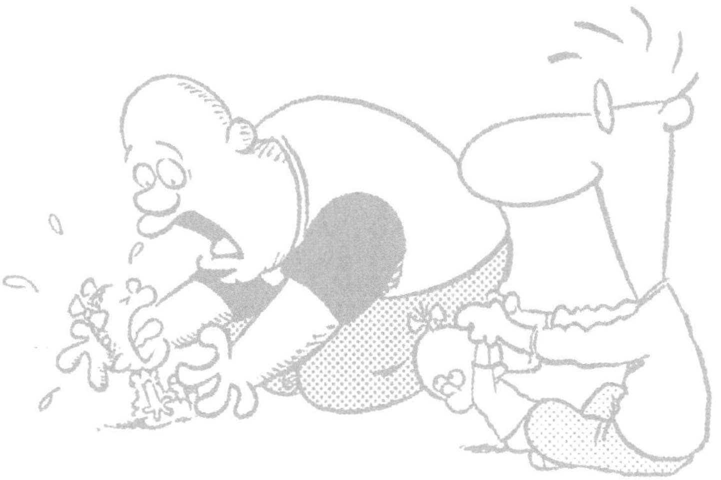

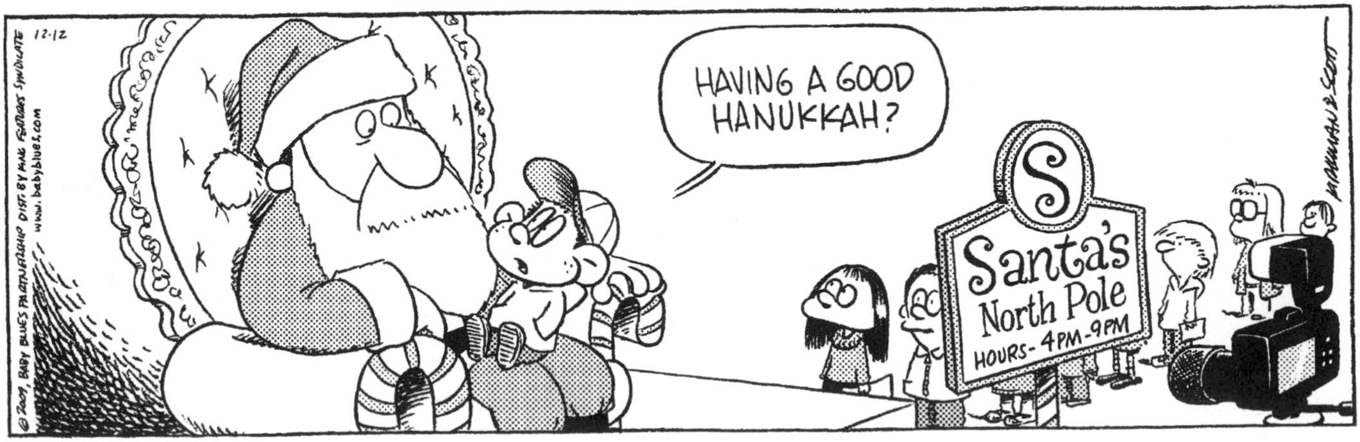
12-12
©2009, BABY BLUES PARTNERSHIP DIST. BY KING FEATURES SYNDICATE
www.babyblues.com
HAVING A GOOD HANUKKAH?
S
Santa's North Pole
HOURS- 4PM-9PM
KIRKMAN & SCOTT

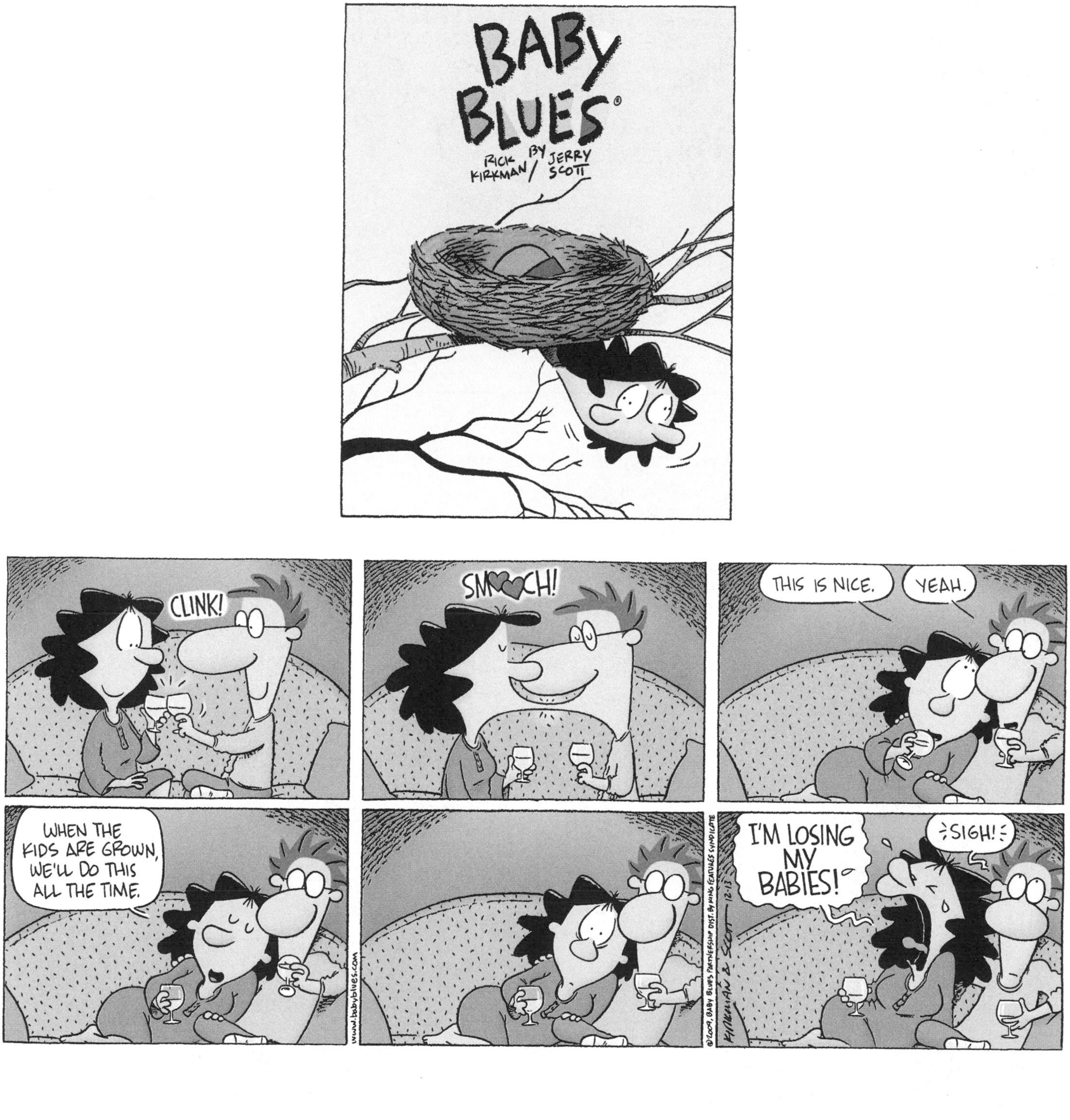
BABY BLUES®
RICK KIRKMAN / BY / JERRY SCOTT
CLINK!
SMOOCH!
THIS IS NICE.
YEAH.
WHEN THE KIDS ARE GROWN, WE'LL DO THIS ALL THE TIME.
www.babyblues.com
©2009, BABY BLUES PARTNERSHIP DIST. BY KING FEATURES SYNDICATE
KIRKMAN & SCOTT 12-13
I'M LOSING MY BABIES!
SIGH!

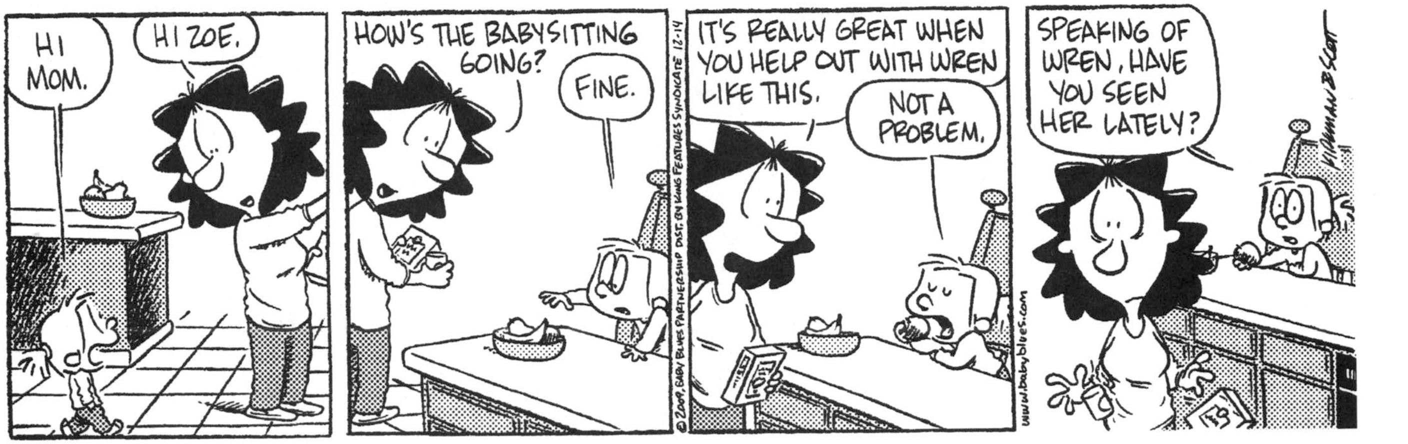
HI MOM.
HI ZOE.
HOW'S THE BABYSITTING GOING?
FINE.
IT'S REALLY GREAT WHEN YOU HELP OUT WITH WREN LIKE THIS.
NOT A PROBLEM.
SPEAKING OF WREN, HAVE YOU SEEN HER LATELY?
© 2009, BABY BLUES PARTNERSHIP DIST. BY KING FEATURES SYNDICATE 12-14
www.babyblues.com
KIRKMAN & SCOTT

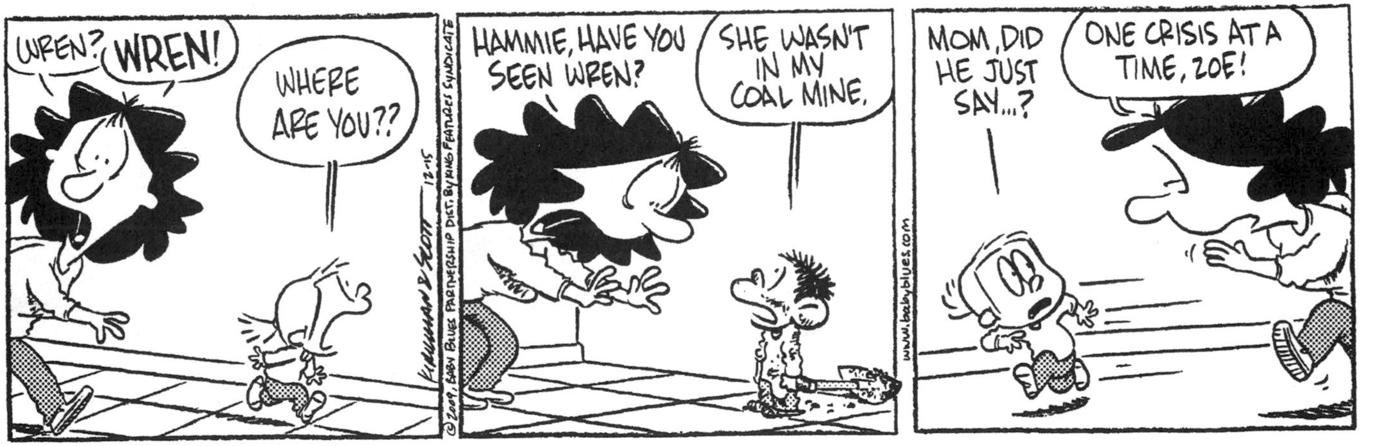
WREN?
WREN!
WHERE ARE YOU??
HAMMIE, HAVE YOU SEEN WREN?
SHE WASN'T IN MY COAL MINE.
MOM, DID HE JUST SAY...?
ONE CRISIS AT A TIME, ZOE!
© 2009, BABY BLUES PARTNERSHIP DIST. BY KING FEATURES SYNDICATE 12-15
KIRKMAN & SCOTT
www.babyblues.com

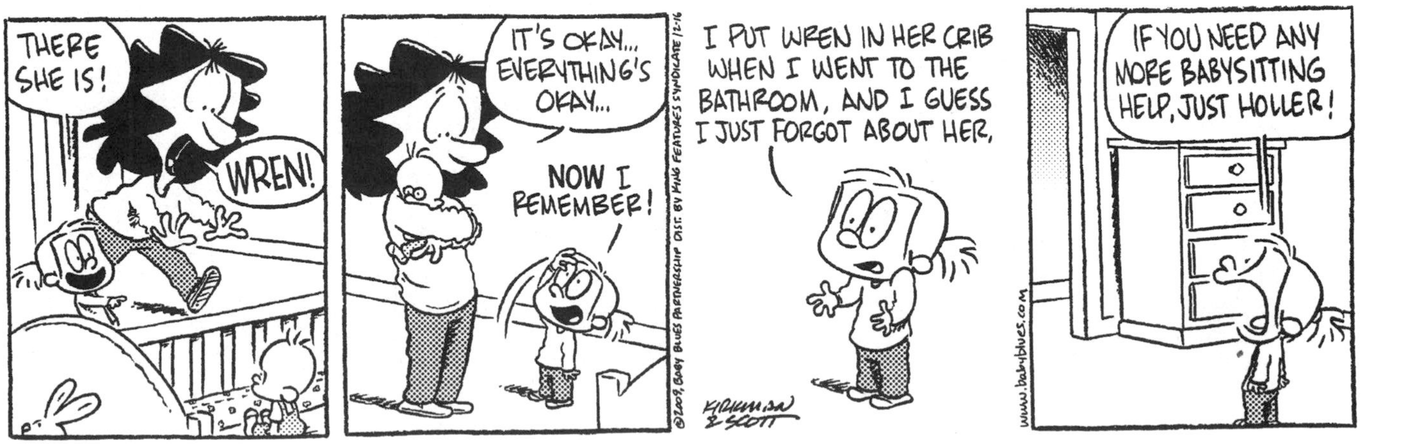
THERE SHE IS!
WREN!
IT'S OKAY... EVERYTHING'S OKAY...
NOW I REMEMBER!
I PUT WREN IN HER CRIB WHEN I WENT TO THE BATHROOM, AND I GUESS I JUST FORGOT ABOUT HER.
IF YOU NEED ANY MORE BABYSITTING HELP, JUST HOLLER!
© 2009, BABY BLUES PARTNERSHIP DIST. BY KING FEATURES SYNDICATE 12-16
KIRKMAN & SCOTT
www.babyblues.com

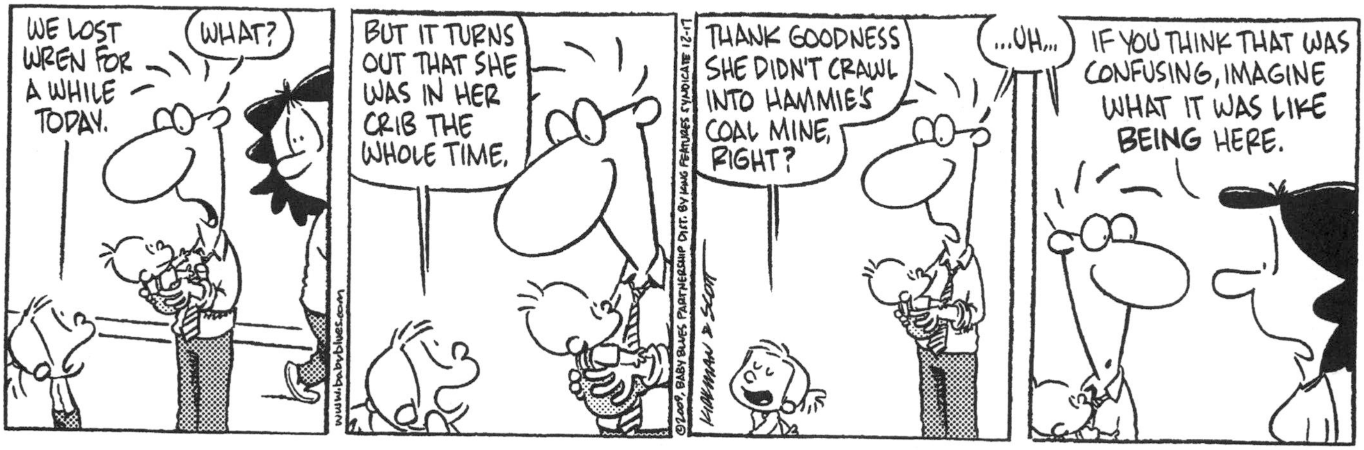
WE LOST WREN FOR A WHILE TODAY.
WHAT?
BUT IT TURNS OUT THAT SHE WAS IN HER CRIB THE WHOLE TIME.
THANK GOODNESS SHE DIDN'T CRAWL INTO HAMMIE'S COAL MINE, RIGHT?
...UH...
IF YOU THINK THAT WAS CONFUSING, IMAGINE WHAT IT WAS LIKE BEING HERE.
www.babyblues.com
©2009, BABY BLUES PARTNERSHIP DIST. BY KING FEATURES SYNDICATE 12-17
KIRKMAN & SCOTT

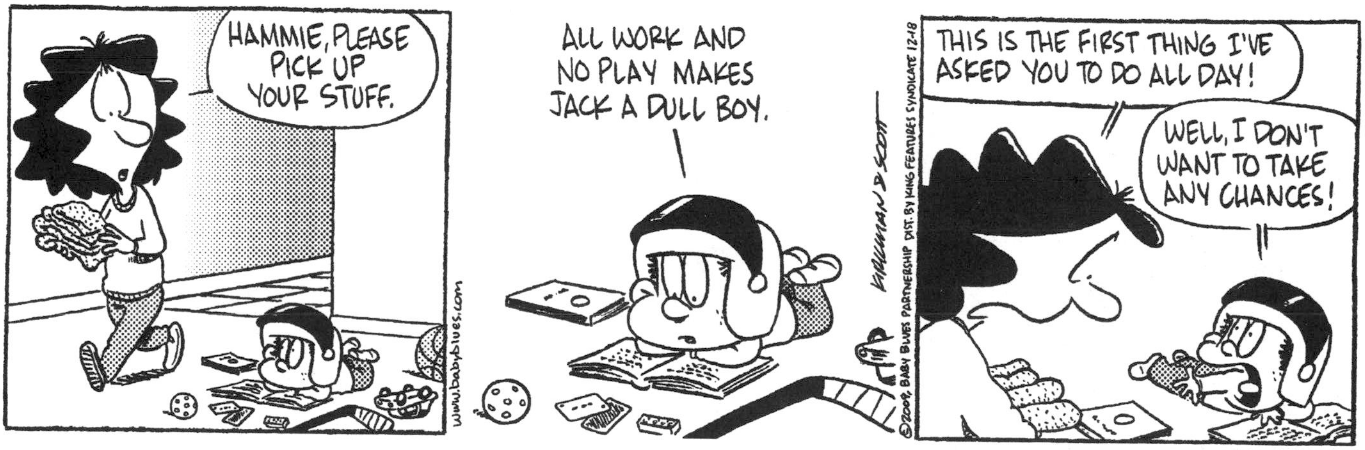
HAMMIE, PLEASE PICK UP YOUR STUFF.
ALL WORK AND NO PLAY MAKES JACK A DULL BOY.
THIS IS THE FIRST THING I'VE ASKED YOU TO DO ALL DAY!
WELL, I DON'T WANT TO TAKE ANY CHANCES!
www.babyblues.com
©2009, BABY BLUES PARTNERSHIP DIST. BY KING FEATURES SYNDICATE 12-18
KIRKMAN & SCOTT

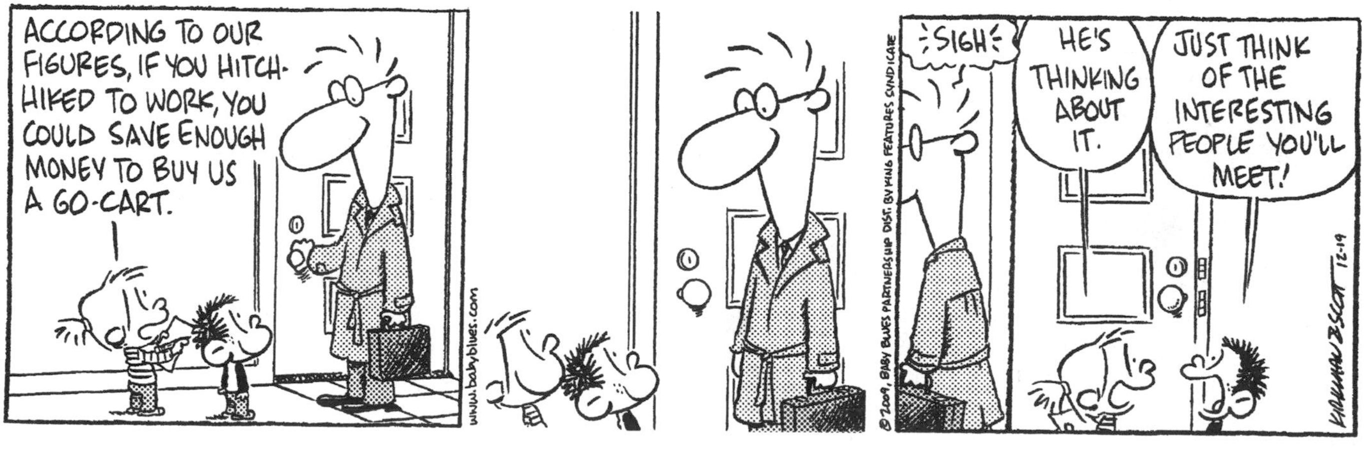
ACCORDING TO OUR FIGURES, IF YOU HITCH-HIKED TO WORK, YOU COULD SAVE ENOUGH MONEY TO BUY US A GO-CART.
SIGH
HE'S THINKING ABOUT IT.
JUST THINK OF THE INTERESTING PEOPLE YOU'LL MEET!
www.babyblues.com
©2009, BABY BLUES PARTNERSHIP DIST. BY KING FEATURES SYNDICATE
KIRKMAN & SCOTT 12-19

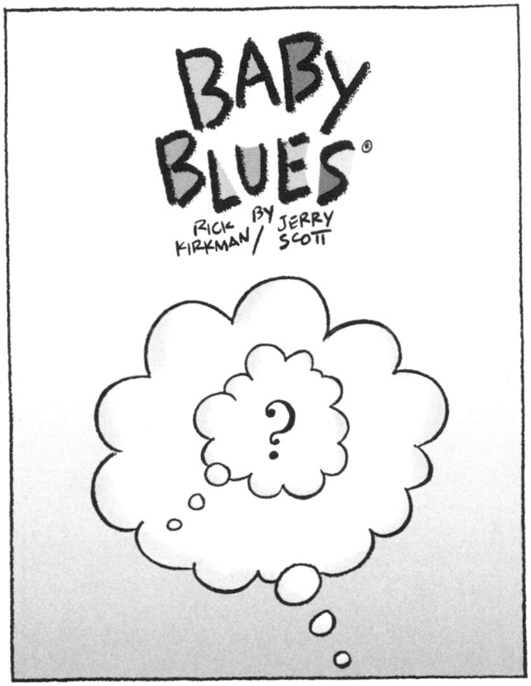
BABY BLUES®
BY RICK KIRKMAN / JERRY SCOTT
?

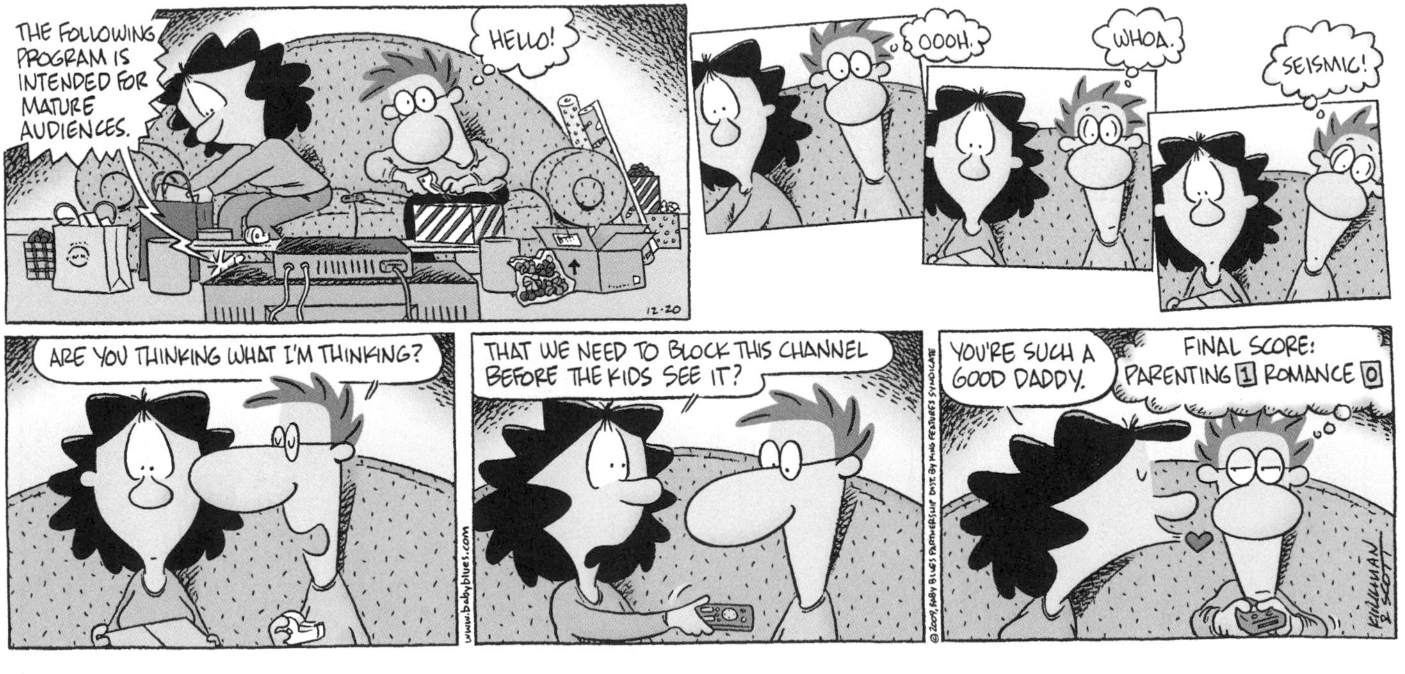
THE FOLLOWING PROGRAM IS INTENDED FOR MATURE AUDIENCES.
HELLO!
12-20
OOOH.
WHOA.
SEISMIC!
ARE YOU THINKING WHAT I'M THINKING?
www.babyblues.com
THAT WE NEED TO BLOCK THIS CHANNEL BEFORE THE KIDS SEE IT?
©2009, BABY BLUES PARTNERSHIP DIST. BY KING FEATURES SYNDICATE
YOU'RE SUCH A GOOD DADDY.
FINAL SCORE: PARENTING 1 ROMANCE 0
KIRKMAN & SCOTT

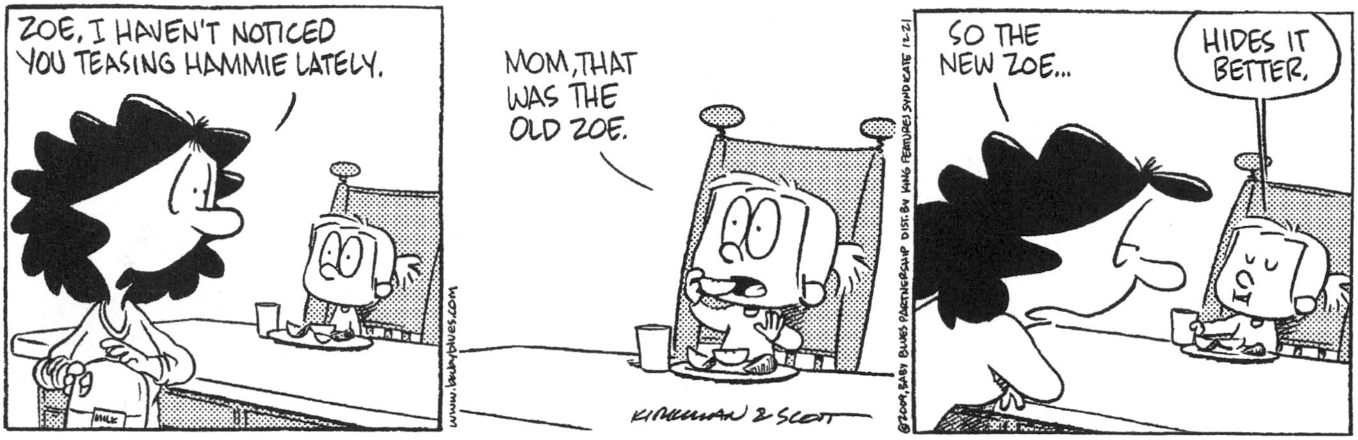
ZOE, I HAVEN'T NOTICED YOU TEASING HAMMIE LATELY.
MOM, THAT WAS THE OLD ZOE.
SO THE NEW ZOE...
HIDES IT BETTER.
KIRKMAN & SCOTT
www.babyblues.com
©2009, BABY BLUES PARTNERSHIP DIST. BY KING FEATURES SYNDICATE 12-21

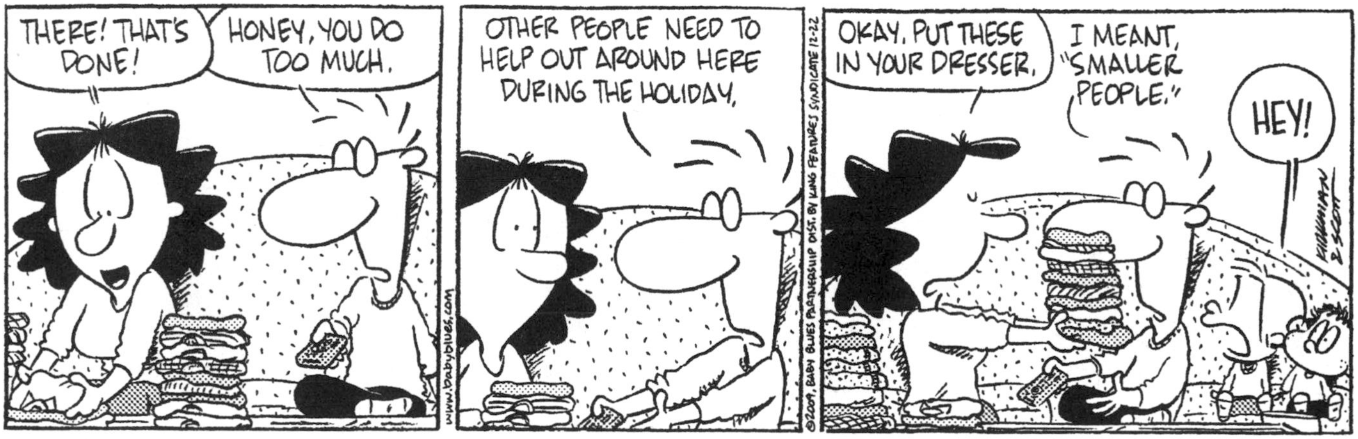
THERE! THAT'S DONE!
HONEY, YOU DO TOO MUCH.
OTHER PEOPLE NEED TO HELP OUT AROUND HERE DURING THE HOLIDAY.
OKAY, PUT THESE IN YOUR DRESSER.
I MEANT, "SMALLER PEOPLE."
HEY!
KIRKMAN & SCOTT
www.babyblues.com
©2009, BABY BLUES PARTNERSHIP DIST. BY KING FEATURES SYNDICATE 12-22

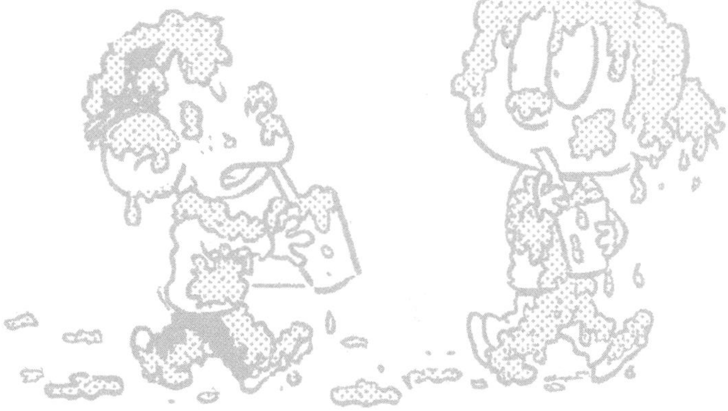

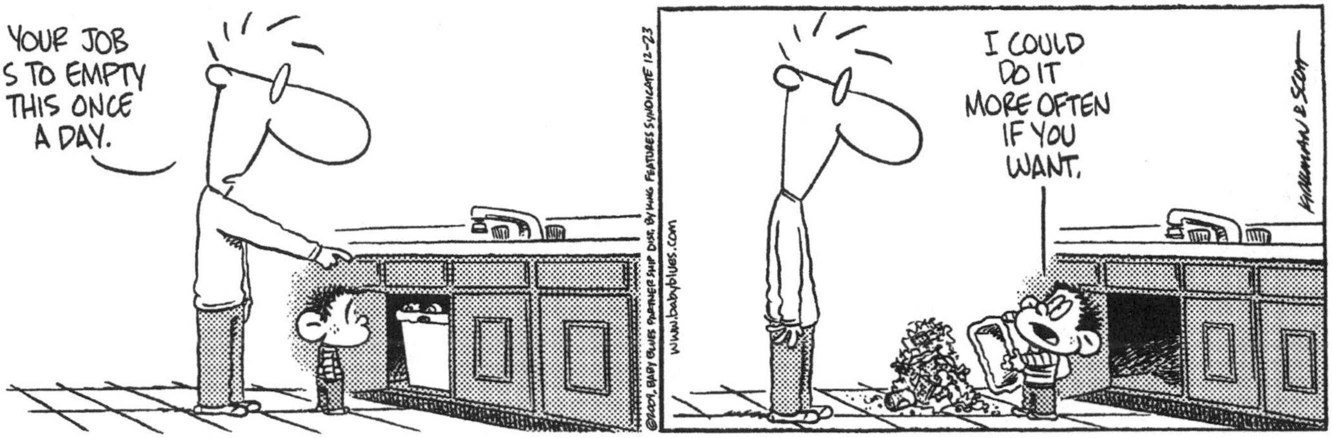
YOUR JOB IS TO EMPTY THIS ONCE A DAY.
I COULD DO IT MORE OFTEN IF YOU WANT.
©2009, BABY BLUES PARTNERSHIP DIST. BY KING FEATURES SYNDICATE 12-23
www.babyblues.com
KIRKMAN & SCOTT

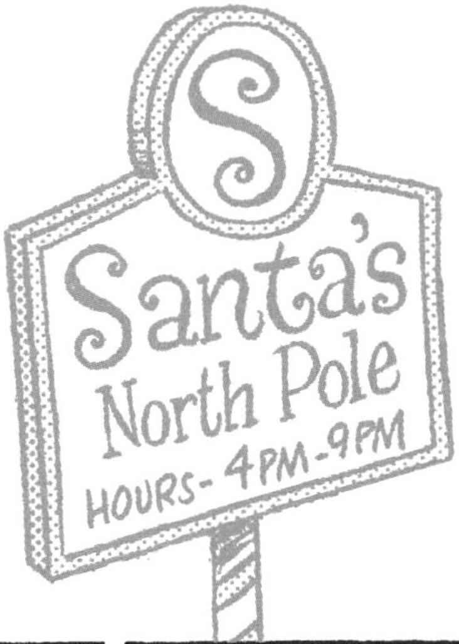
S
Santa's
North Pole
HOURS- 4PM-9PM

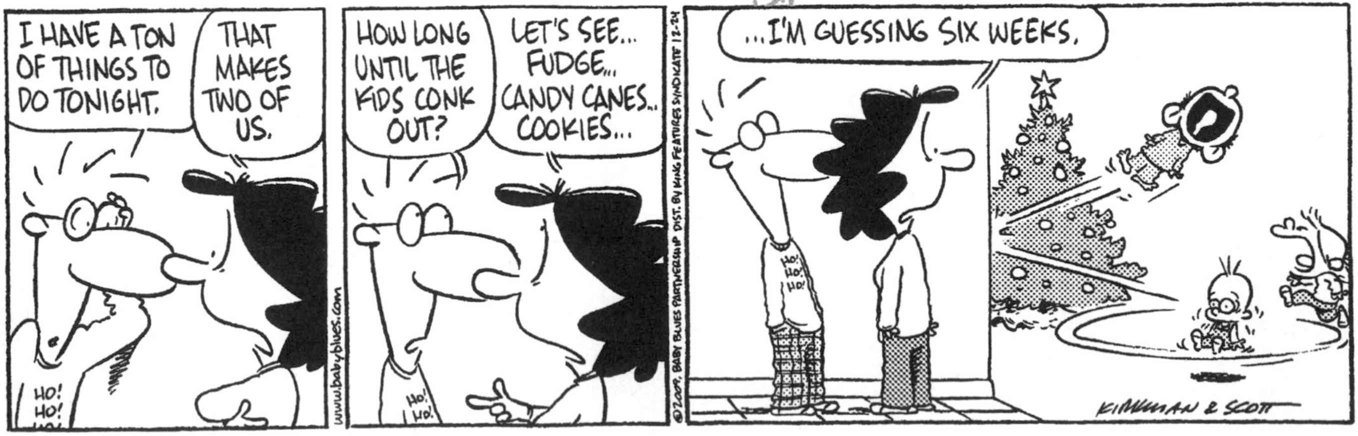
I HAVE A TON OF THINGS TO DO TONIGHT.
THAT MAKES TWO OF US.
HO! HO!
www.babyblues.com
HOW LONG UNTIL THE KIDS CONK OUT?
LET'S SEE... FUDGE... CANDY CANES... COOKIES...
HO! HO!
©2009, BABY BLUES PARTNERSHIP DIST. BY KING FEATURES SYNDICATE 12-24
...I'M GUESSING SIX WEEKS.
HO! HO! HO!
KIRKMAN & SCOTT

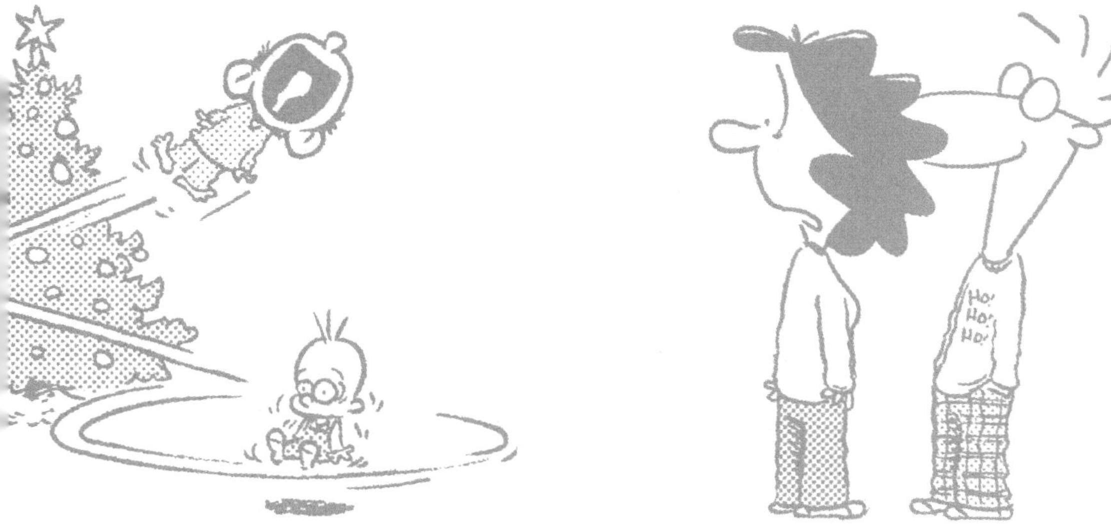
HO! HO! HO!

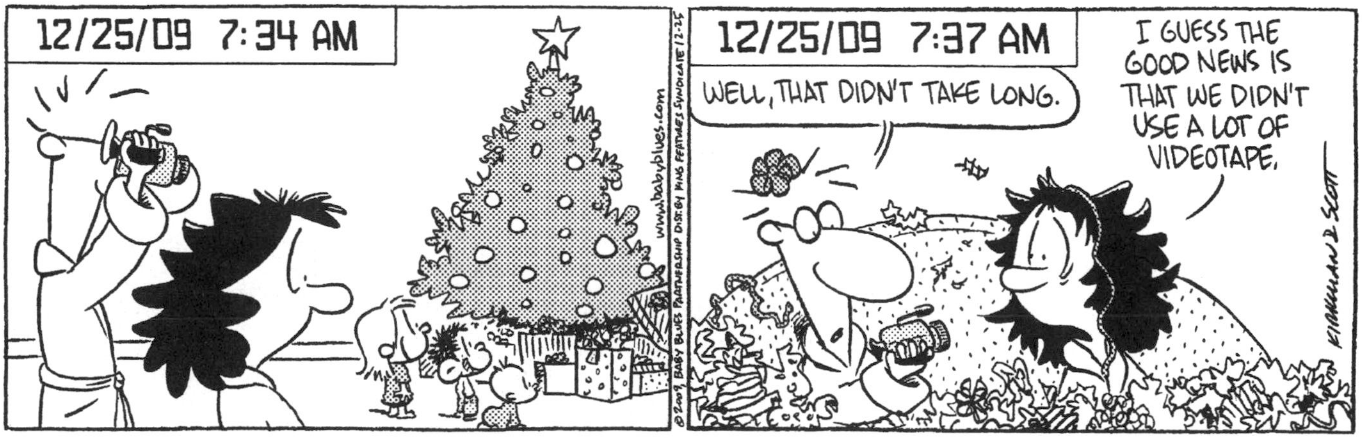
12/25/09 7:34 AM
www.babyblues.com
© 2009, Baby Blues Partnership Dist. by King Features Syndicate 12-25
12/25/09 7:37 AM
WELL, THAT DIDN'T TAKE LONG.
I GUESS THE GOOD NEWS IS THAT WE DIDN'T USE A LOT OF VIDEOTAPE.
KIRKMAN & SCOTT

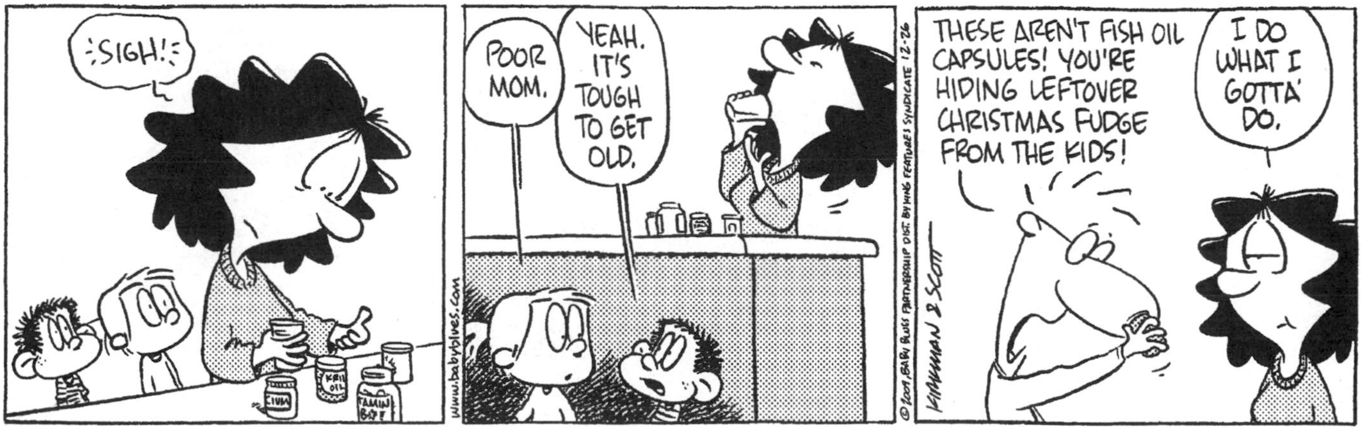
SIGH!
www.babyblues.com
POOR MOM.
YEAH. IT'S TOUGH TO GET OLD.
© 2009, Baby Blues Partnership Dist. by King Features Syndicate 12-26
KIRKMAN & SCOTT
THESE AREN'T FISH OIL CAPSULES! YOU'RE HIDING LEFTOVER CHRISTMAS FUDGE FROM THE KIDS!
I DO WHAT I GOTTA' DO.

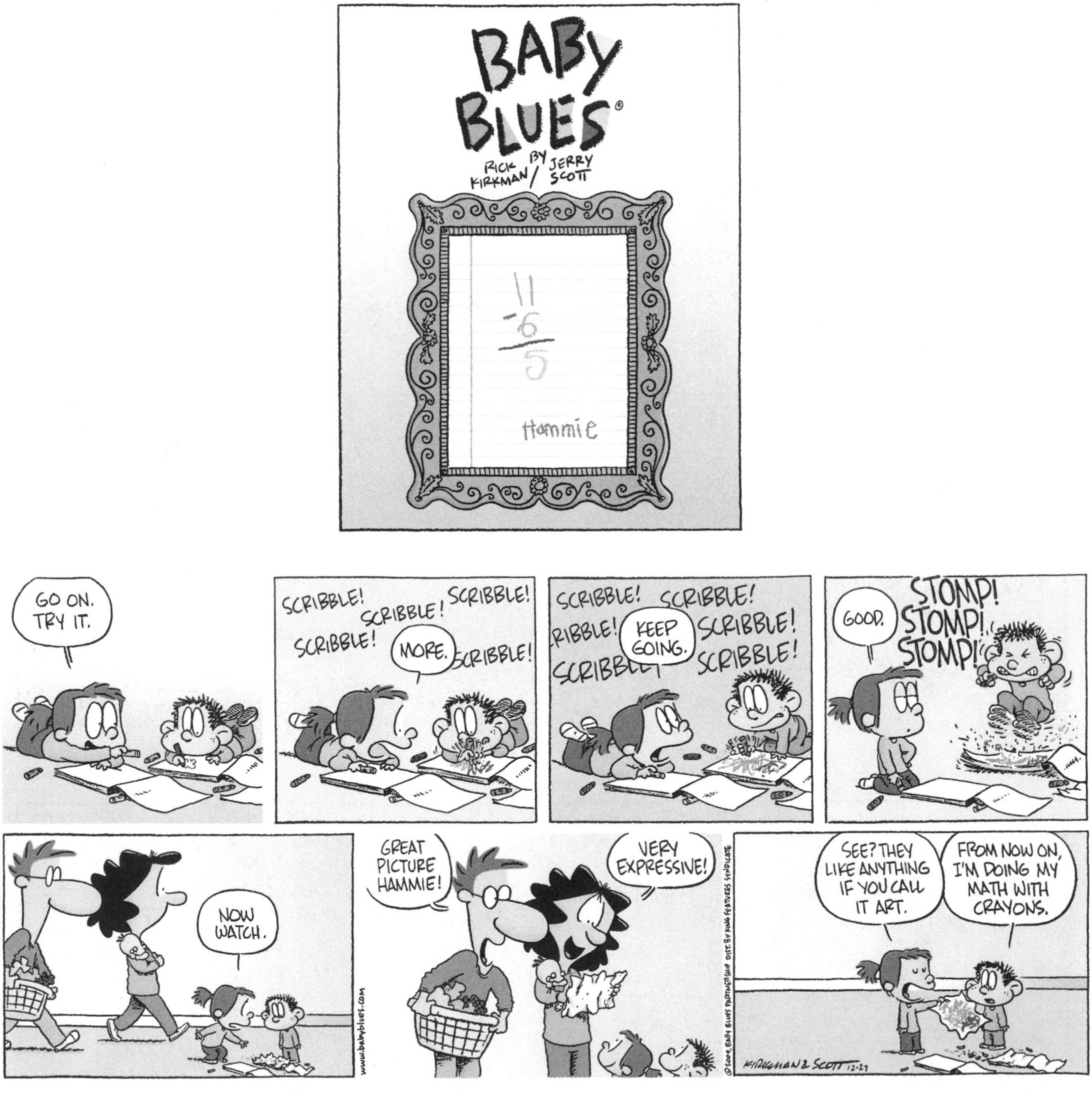
BABY BLUES®
BY RICK KIRKMAN / JERRY SCOTT
11
-6
5
Hammie
GO ON. TRY IT.
SCRIBBLE! SCRIBBLE! SCRIBBLE! SCRIBBLE! SCRIBBLE!
MORE.
SCRIBBLE! SCRIBBLE! SCRIBBLE! SCRIBBLE! SCRIBBLE!
KEEP GOING.
GOOD.
STOMP! STOMP! STOMP!
NOW WATCH.
www.babyblues.com
GREAT PICTURE HAMMIE!
VERY EXPRESSIVE!
SEE? THEY LIKE ANYTHING IF YOU CALL IT ART.
FROM NOW ON, I'M DOING MY MATH WITH CRAYONS.
KIRKMAN & SCOTT 12-27

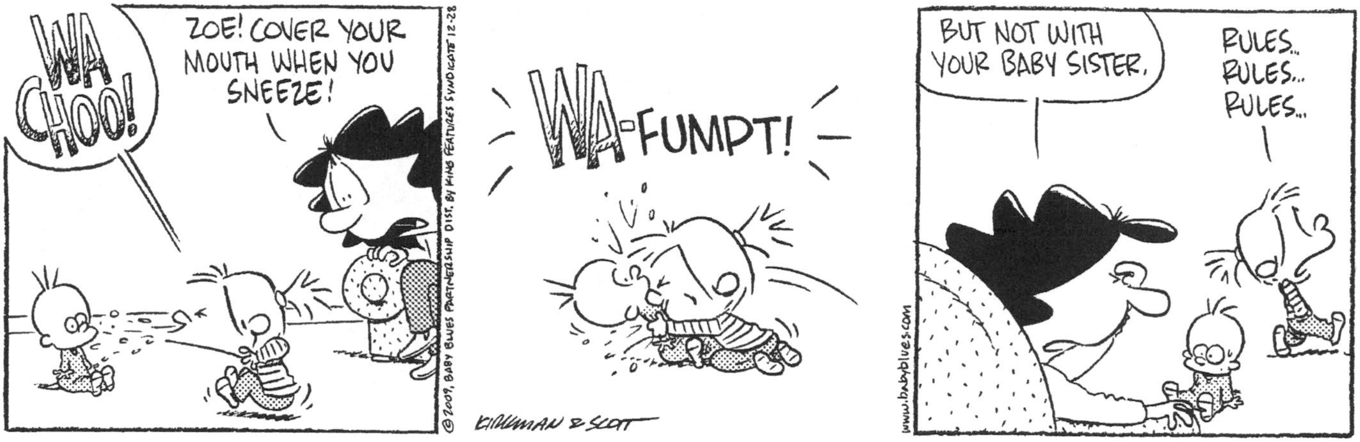
WA CHOO!
ZOE! COVER YOUR MOUTH WHEN YOU SNEEZE!
© 2009, BABY BLUES PARTNERSHIP DIST. BY KING FEATURES SYNDICATE 12-28
WA-FUMPT!
KIRKMAN & SCOTT
BUT NOT WITH YOUR BABY SISTER.
RULES.. RULES.. RULES..
www.babyblues.com

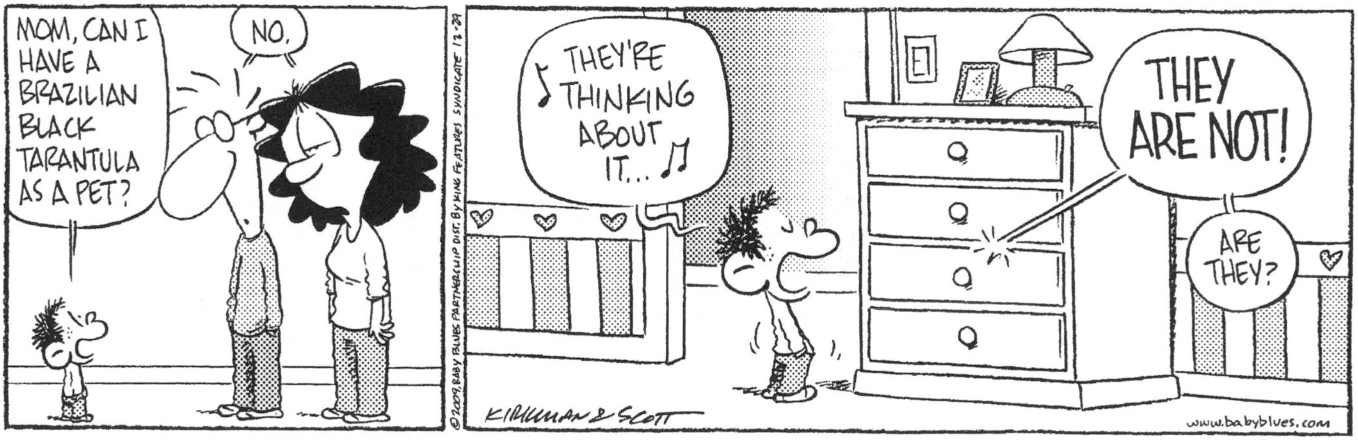
MOM, CAN I HAVE A BRAZILIAN BLACK TARANTULA AS A PET?
NO.
© 2009, BABY BLUES PARTNERSHIP DIST. BY KING FEATURES SYNDICATE 12-29
THEY'RE THINKING ABOUT IT...
THEY ARE NOT!
ARE THEY?
KIRKMAN & SCOTT
www.babyblues.com

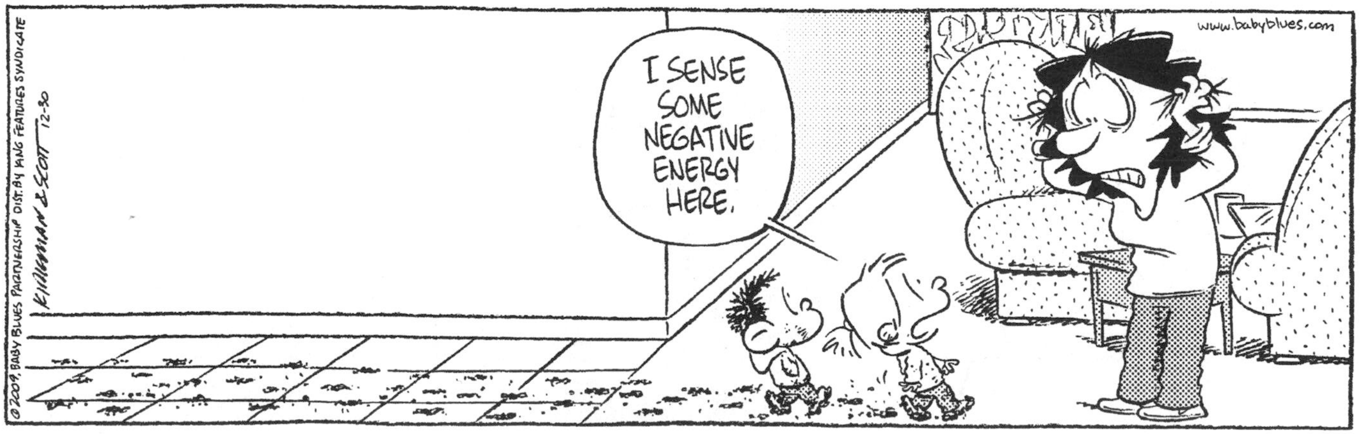
© 2009, BABY BLUES PARTNERSHIP DIST. BY KING FEATURES SYNDICATE
KIRKMAN & SCOTT 12-30
I SENSE SOME NEGATIVE ENERGY HERE.
www.babyblues.com

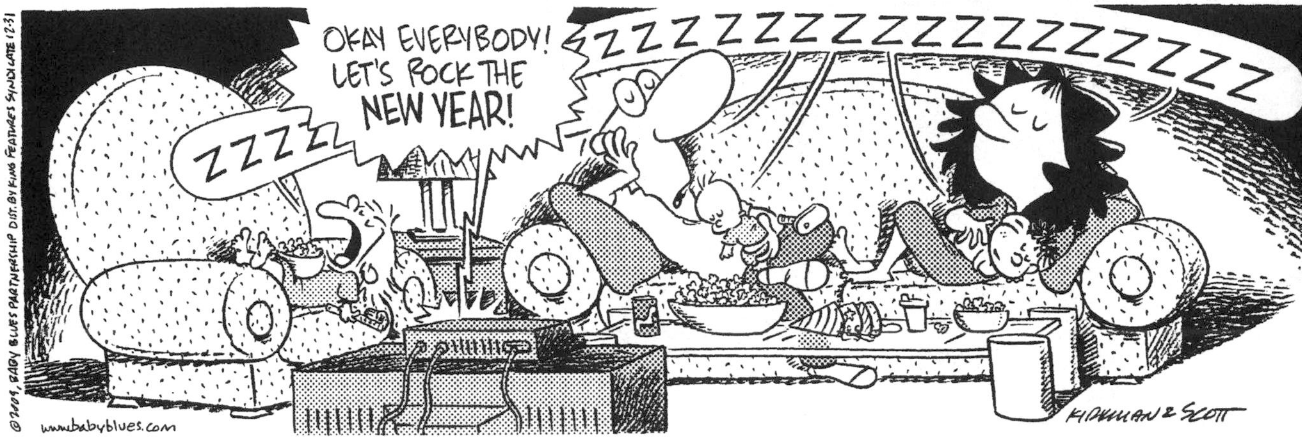

ZZZZ
OKAY EVERYBODY! LET'S ROCK THE NEW YEAR!
ZZZZZZZZZZZZZZZZZZZZ
© 2009, BABY BLUES PARTNERSHIP DIST. BY KING FEATURES SYNDICATE 12-31
www.babyblues.com
KIRKMAN & SCOTT

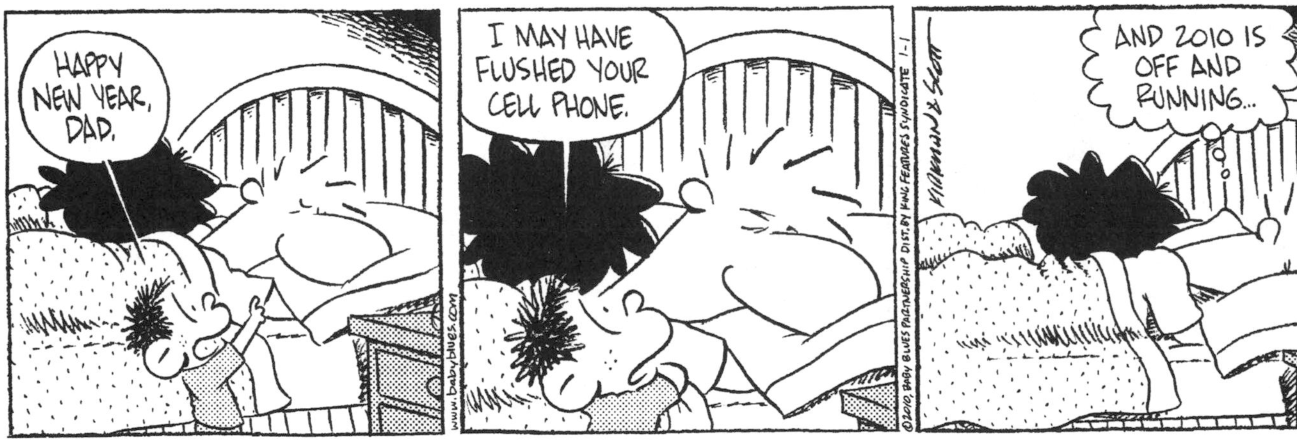

HAPPY NEW YEAR, DAD.
www.babyblues.com
I MAY HAVE FLUSHED YOUR CELL PHONE.
© 2010, BABY BLUES PARTNERSHIP DIST. BY KING FEATURES SYNDICATE 1-1
KIRKMAN & SCOTT
AND 2010 IS OFF AND RUNNING...

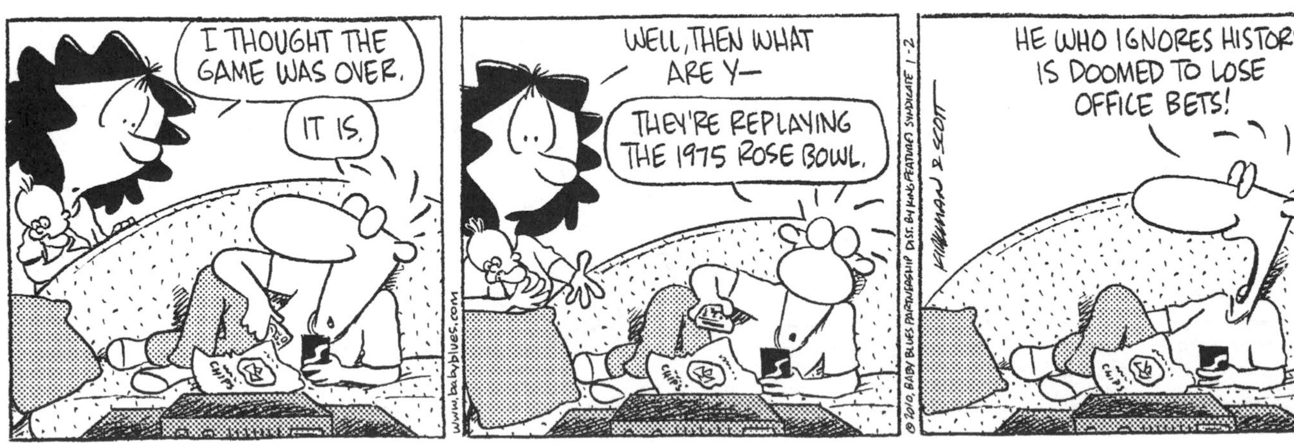

I THOUGHT THE GAME WAS OVER.
IT IS.
www.babyblues.com
WELL, THEN WHAT ARE Y—
THEY'RE REPLAYING THE 1975 ROSE BOWL.
© 2010, BABY BLUES PARTNERSHIP DIST. BY KING FEATURES SYNDICATE 1-2
KIRKMAN & SCOTT
HE WHO IGNORES HISTORY IS DOOMED TO LOSE OFFICE BETS!

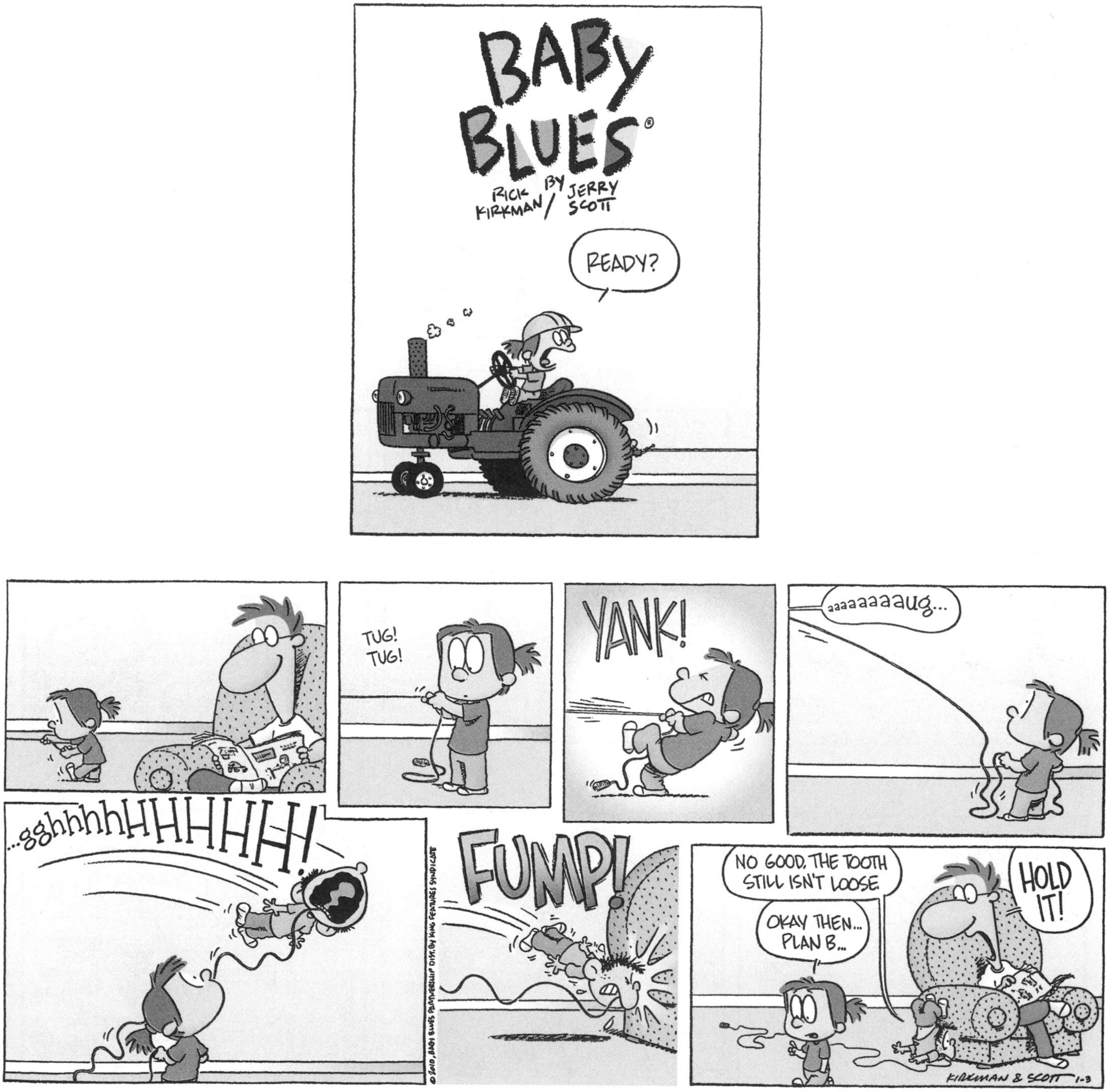
BABY BLUES®
BY RICK KIRKMAN / JERRY SCOTT
READY?
TUG! TUG!
YANK!
aaaaaaaaug...
...gghhhhHHHHH!
© 2010, BABY BLUES PARTNERSHIP DIST. BY KING FEATURES SYNDICATE
FUMP!
NO GOOD. THE TOOTH STILL ISN'T LOOSE.
OKAY THEN... PLAN B...
HOLD IT!
KIRKMAN & SCOTT 1-3

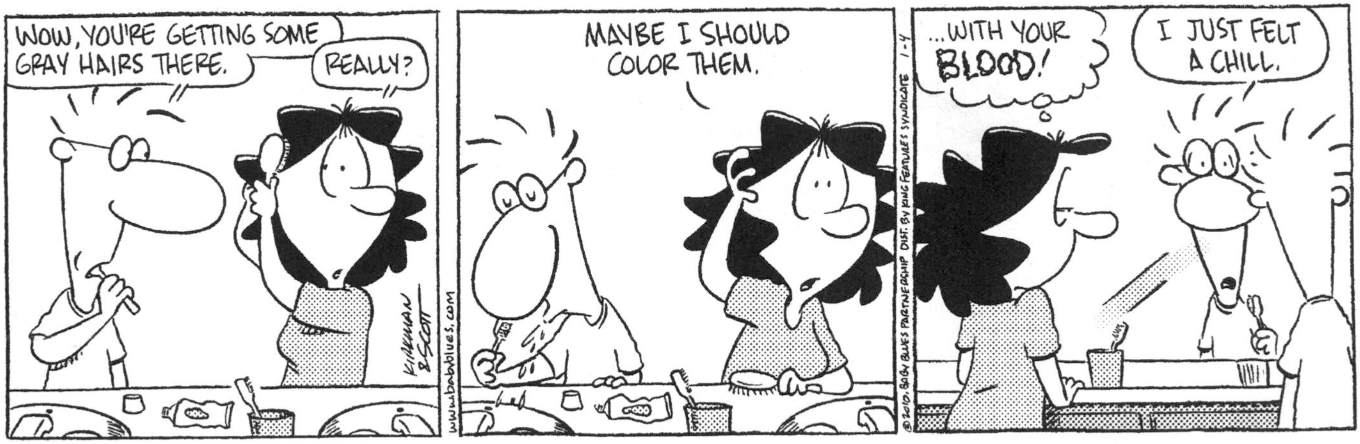

WOW, YOU'RE GETTING SOME GRAY HAIRS THERE.
REALLY?
KIRKMAN & SCOTT
www.babyblues.com
MAYBE I SHOULD COLOR THEM.
1-4
©2010, BABY BLUES PARTNERSHIP DIST. BY KING FEATURES SYNDICATE
...WITH YOUR BLOOD!
I JUST FELT A CHILL.

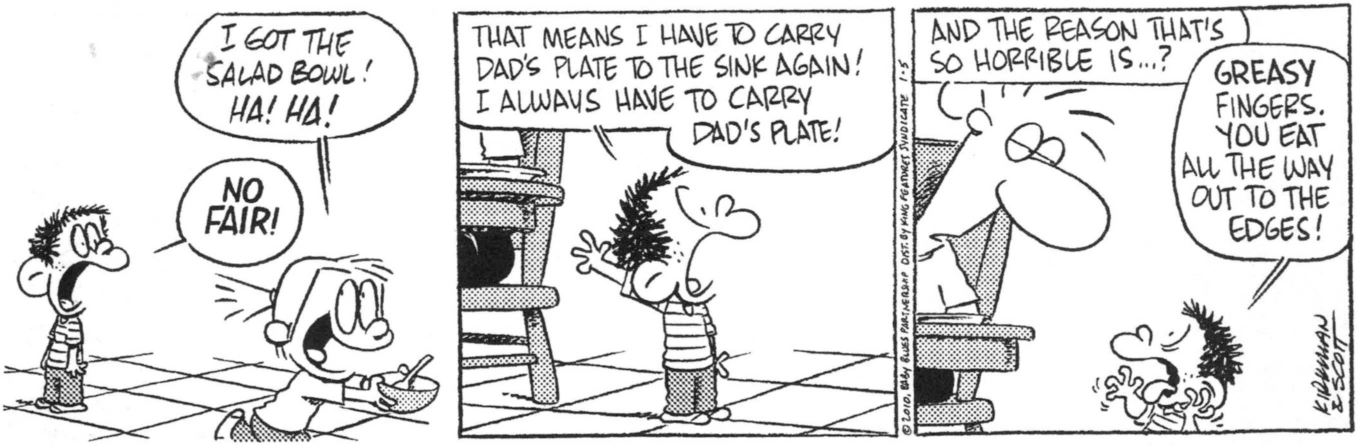

I GOT THE SALAD BOWL! HA! HA!
NO FAIR!
THAT MEANS I HAVE TO CARRY DAD'S PLATE TO THE SINK AGAIN! I ALWAYS HAVE TO CARRY DAD'S PLATE!
1-5
©2010, BABY BLUES PARTNERSHIP DIST. BY KING FEATURES SYNDICATE
AND THE REASON THAT'S SO HORRIBLE IS...?
GREASY FINGERS. YOU EAT ALL THE WAY OUT TO THE EDGES!
KIRKMAN & SCOTT

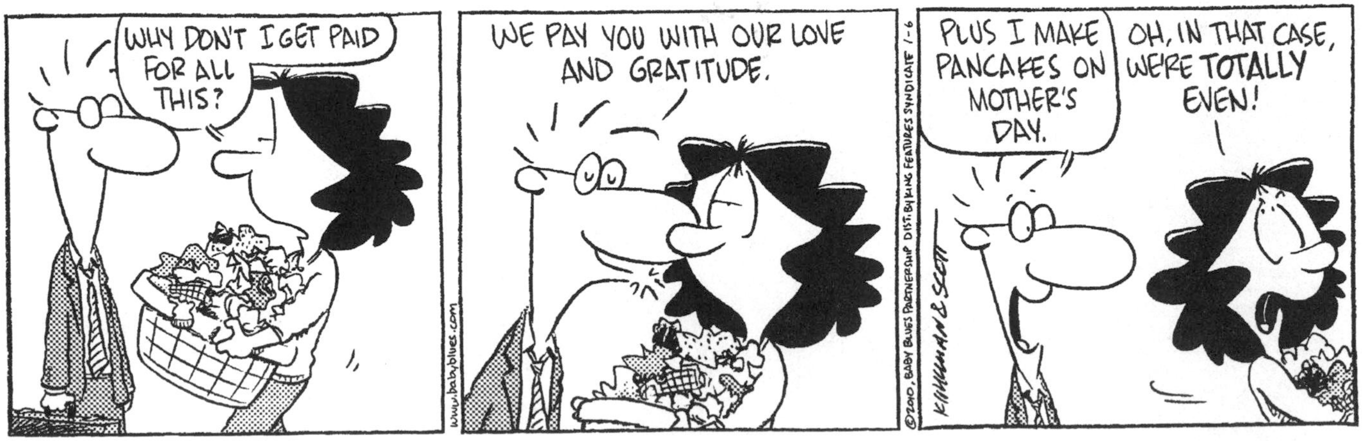

WHY DON'T I GET PAID FOR ALL THIS?
www.babyblues.com
WE PAY YOU WITH OUR LOVE AND GRATITUDE.
1-6
©2010, BABY BLUES PARTNERSHIP DIST. BY KING FEATURES SYNDICATE
KIRKMAN & SCOTT
PLUS I MAKE PANCAKES ON MOTHER'S DAY.
OH, IN THAT CASE, WE'RE TOTALLY EVEN!

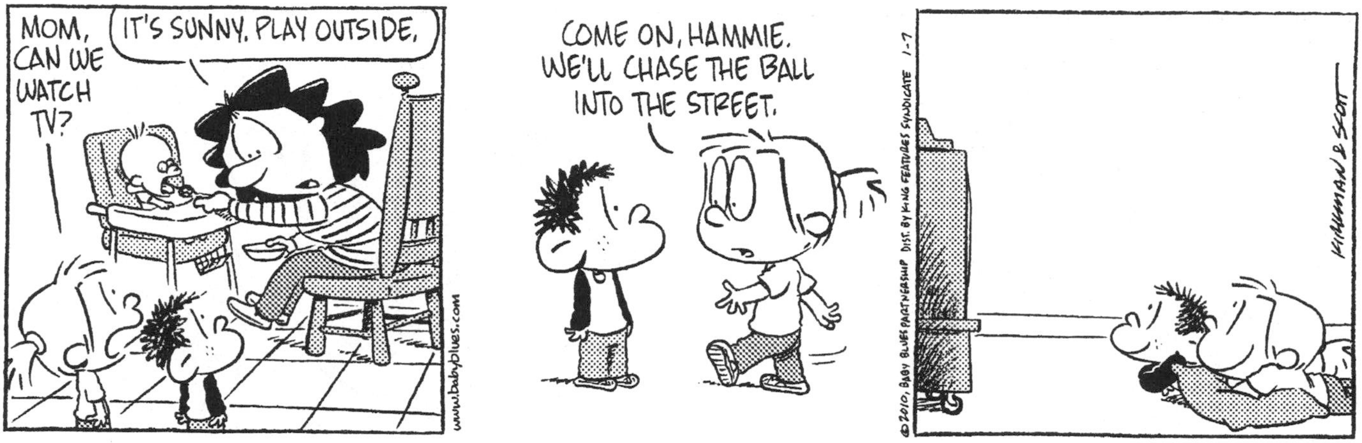
MOM, CAN WE WATCH TV?
IT'S SUNNY. PLAY OUTSIDE.
www.babyblues.com
COME ON, HAMMIE. WE'LL CHASE THE BALL INTO THE STREET.
© 2010, BABY BLUES PARTNERSHIP DIST. BY KING FEATURES SYNDICATE 1-7
KIRKMAN & SCOTT

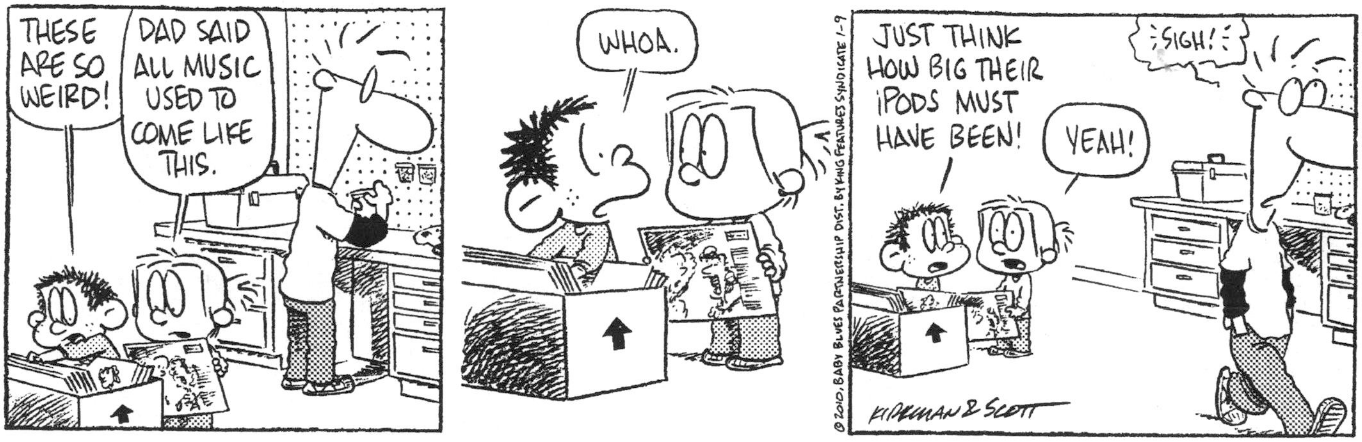
THESE ARE SO WEIRD!
DAD SAID ALL MUSIC USED TO COME LIKE THIS.
WHOA.
© 2010, BABY BLUES PARTNERSHIP DIST. BY KING FEATURES SYNDICATE 1-9
JUST THINK HOW BIG THEIR iPODS MUST HAVE BEEN!
YEAH!
SIGH!
KIRKMAN & SCOTT

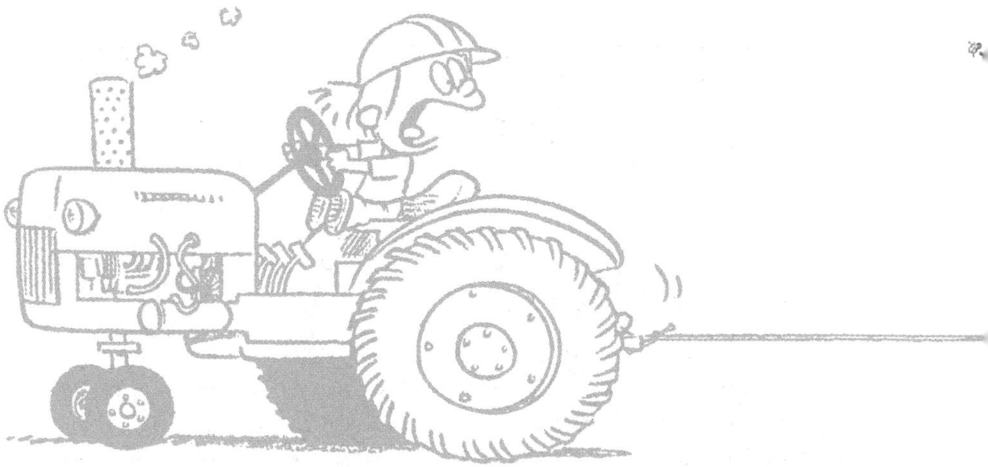

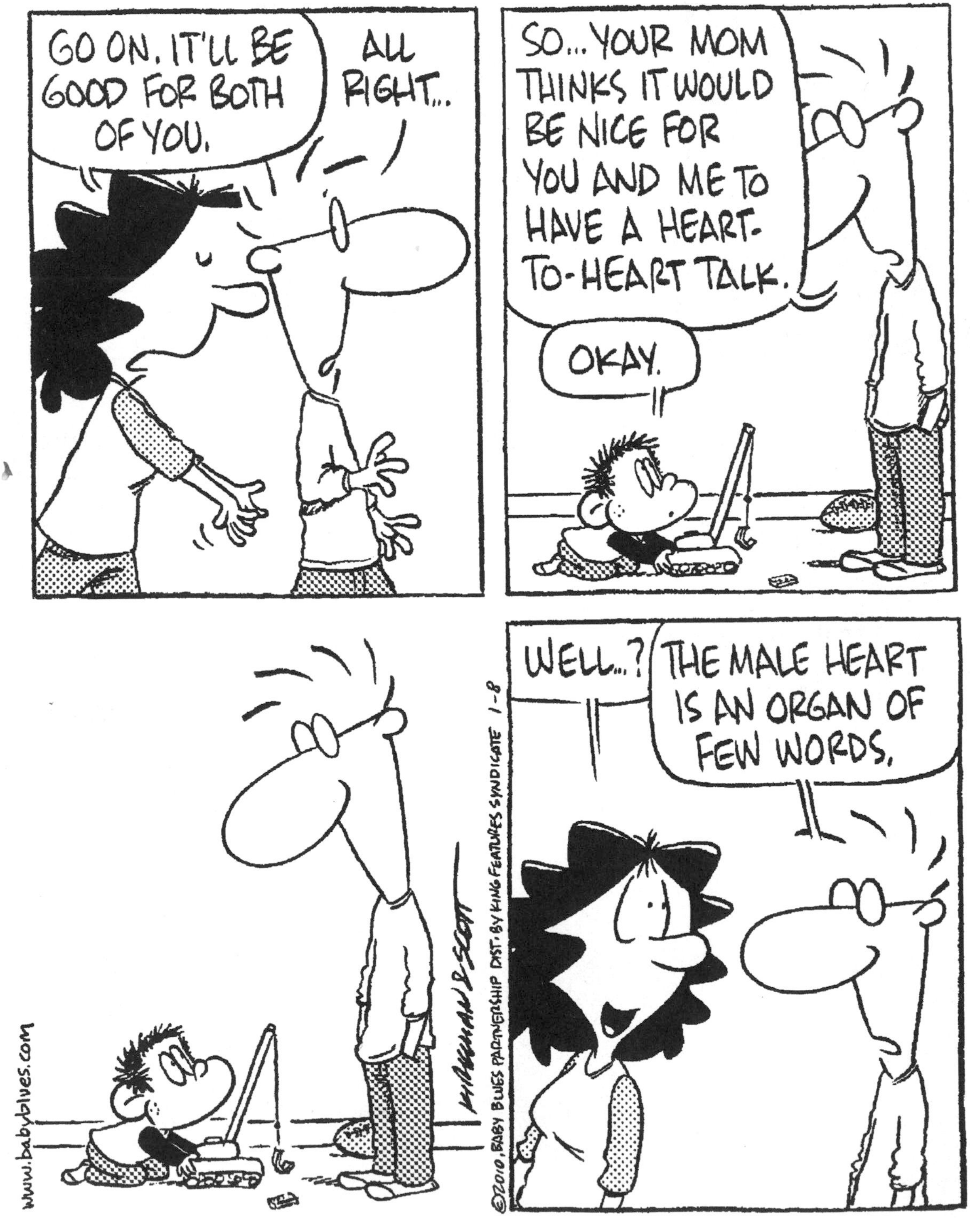
GO ON. IT'LL BE GOOD FOR BOTH OF YOU.
ALL RIGHT...
SO... YOUR MOM THINKS IT WOULD BE NICE FOR YOU AND ME TO HAVE A HEART-TO-HEART TALK.
OKAY.
WELL...?
THE MALE HEART IS AN ORGAN OF FEW WORDS.
www.babyblues.com
©2010, BABY BLUES PARTNERSHIP DIST. BY KING FEATURES SYNDICATE 1-8

BABY BLUES®
BY RICK KIRKMAN / JERRY SCOTT
GUIDE STAR
START HOME
END ?????????

HEY MOM, THERE'S A KID AT SCHOOL I WANT TO PLAY WITH.
CAN YOU DRIVE ME OVER TO HIS HOUSE?
www.babyblues.com
MAYBE. WHAT'S HIS NAME?
I DUNNO.
WELL, WHERE DOES HE LIVE?
NOT SURE.
IS HE IN YOUR CLASS?
NOPE.
DO YOU EVER PLAY TOGETHER ON THE PLAYGROUND?
NEVER.
©2010, BABY BLUES PARTNERSHIP DIST. BY KING FEATURES SYNDICATE 1-10
SO WHY—
HE HAS A SNAKE.
SAY NO! SAY NO! SAY NO!
KIRKMAN & SCOTT

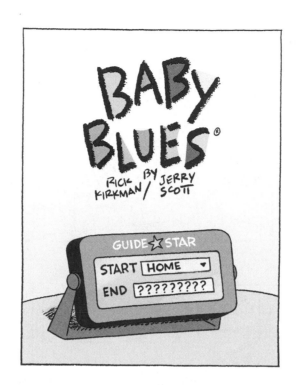

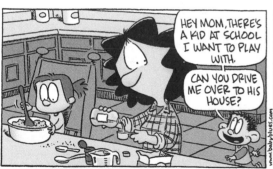

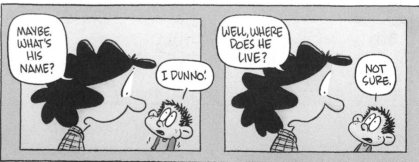

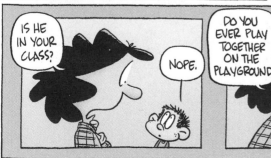

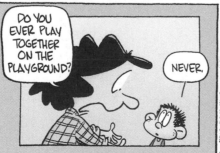

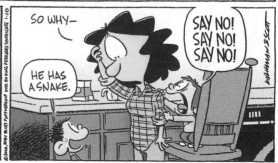

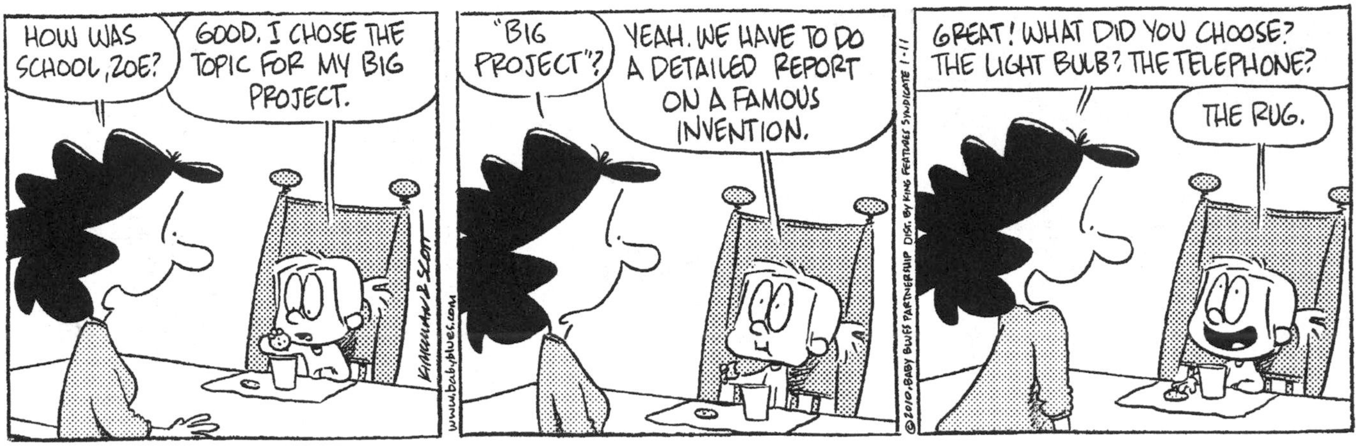
HOW WAS SCHOOL, ZOE?
GOOD. I CHOSE THE TOPIC FOR MY BIG PROJECT.
KIRKMAN & SCOTT
www.babyblues.com
"BIG PROJECT"?
YEAH. WE HAVE TO DO A DETAILED REPORT ON A FAMOUS INVENTION.
©2010, BABY BLUES PARTNERSHIP DIST. BY KING FEATURES SYNDICATE 1-11
GREAT! WHAT DID YOU CHOOSE? THE LIGHT BULB? THE TELEPHONE?
THE RUG.

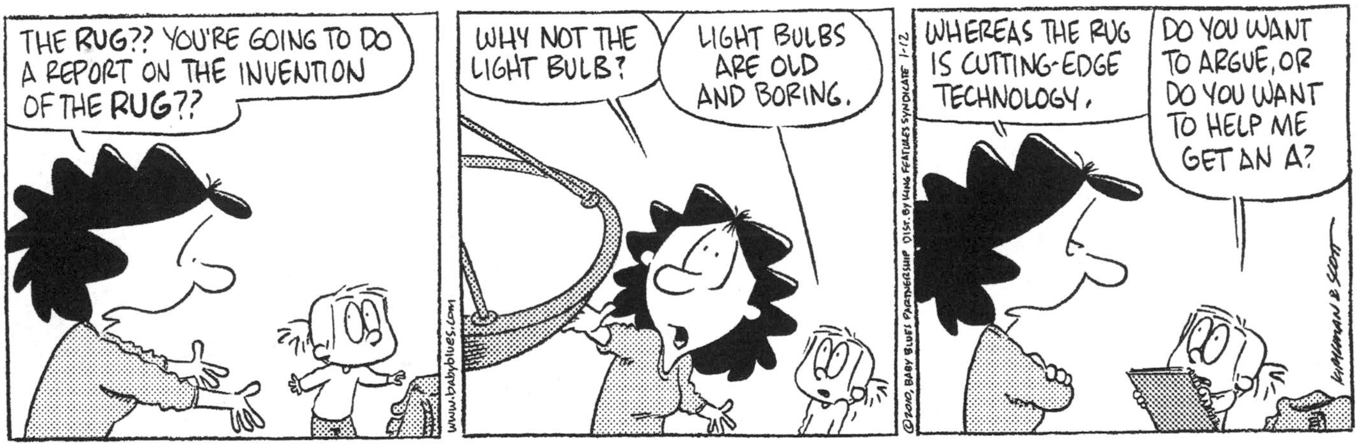
THE RUG?? YOU'RE GOING TO DO A REPORT ON THE INVENTION OF THE RUG??
www.babyblues.com
WHY NOT THE LIGHT BULB?
LIGHT BULBS ARE OLD AND BORING.
©2010, BABY BLUES PARTNERSHIP DIST. BY KING FEATURES SYNDICATE 1-12
WHEREAS THE RUG IS CUTTING-EDGE TECHNOLOGY.
DO YOU WANT TO ARGUE, OR DO YOU WANT TO HELP ME GET AN A?
KIRKMAN & SCOTT

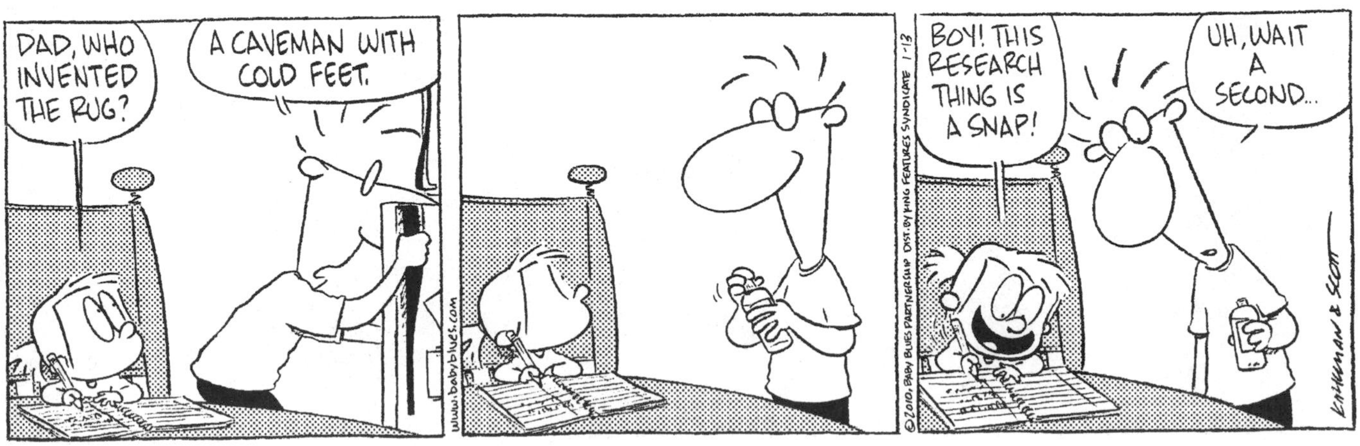
DAD, WHO INVENTED THE RUG?
A CAVEMAN WITH COLD FEET.
www.babyblues.com
©2010, BABY BLUES PARTNERSHIP DIST. BY KING FEATURES SYNDICATE 1-13
BOY! THIS RESEARCH THING IS A SNAP!
UH, WAIT A SECOND...
KIRKMAN & SCOTT

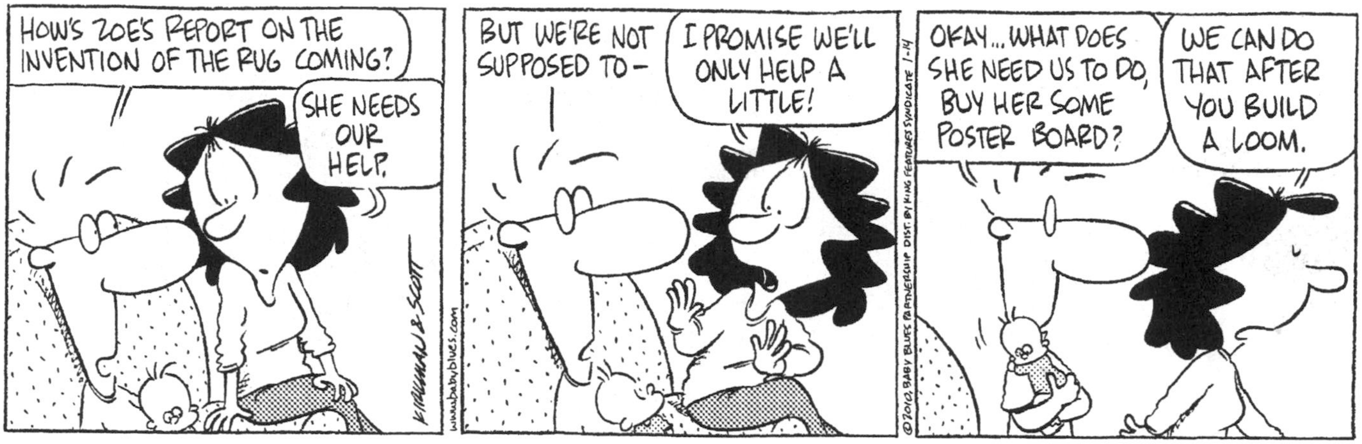
HOW'S ZOE'S REPORT ON THE INVENTION OF THE RUG COMING?
SHE NEEDS OUR HELP.
KIRKMAN & SCOTT
www.babyblues.com
BUT WE'RE NOT SUPPOSED TO–
I PROMISE WE'LL ONLY HELP A LITTLE!
©2010, BABY BLUES PARTNERSHIP DIST. BY KING FEATURES SYNDICATE 1-14
OKAY... WHAT DOES SHE NEED US TO DO, BUY HER SOME POSTER BOARD?
WE CAN DO THAT AFTER YOU BUILD A LOOM.

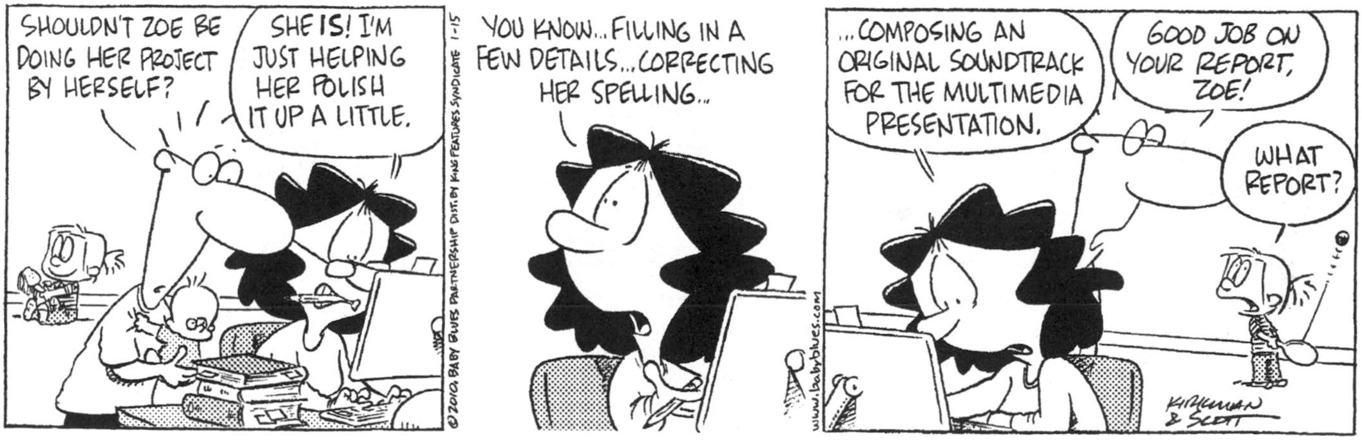
SHOULDN'T ZOE BE DOING HER PROJECT BY HERSELF?
SHE IS! I'M JUST HELPING HER POLISH IT UP A LITTLE.
©2010, BABY BLUES PARTNERSHIP DIST. BY KING FEATURES SYNDICATE 1-15
YOU KNOW... FILLING IN A FEW DETAILS... CORRECTING HER SPELLING...
www.babyblues.com
...COMPOSING AN ORIGINAL SOUNDTRACK FOR THE MULTIMEDIA PRESENTATION.
GOOD JOB ON YOUR REPORT, ZOE!
WHAT REPORT?
KIRKMAN & SCOTT

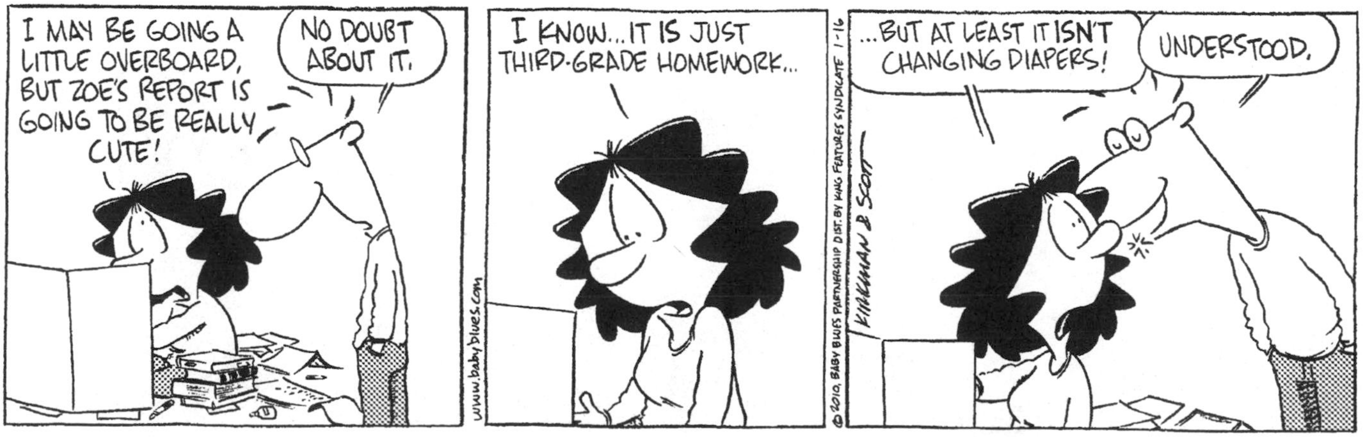
I MAY BE GOING A LITTLE OVERBOARD, BUT ZOE'S REPORT IS GOING TO BE REALLY CUTE!
NO DOUBT ABOUT IT.
www.babyblues.com
I KNOW... IT IS JUST THIRD-GRADE HOMEWORK...
KIRKMAN & SCOTT
©2010, BABY BLUES PARTNERSHIP DIST. BY KING FEATURES SYNDICATE 1-16
...BUT AT LEAST IT ISN'T CHANGING DIAPERS!
UNDERSTOOD.

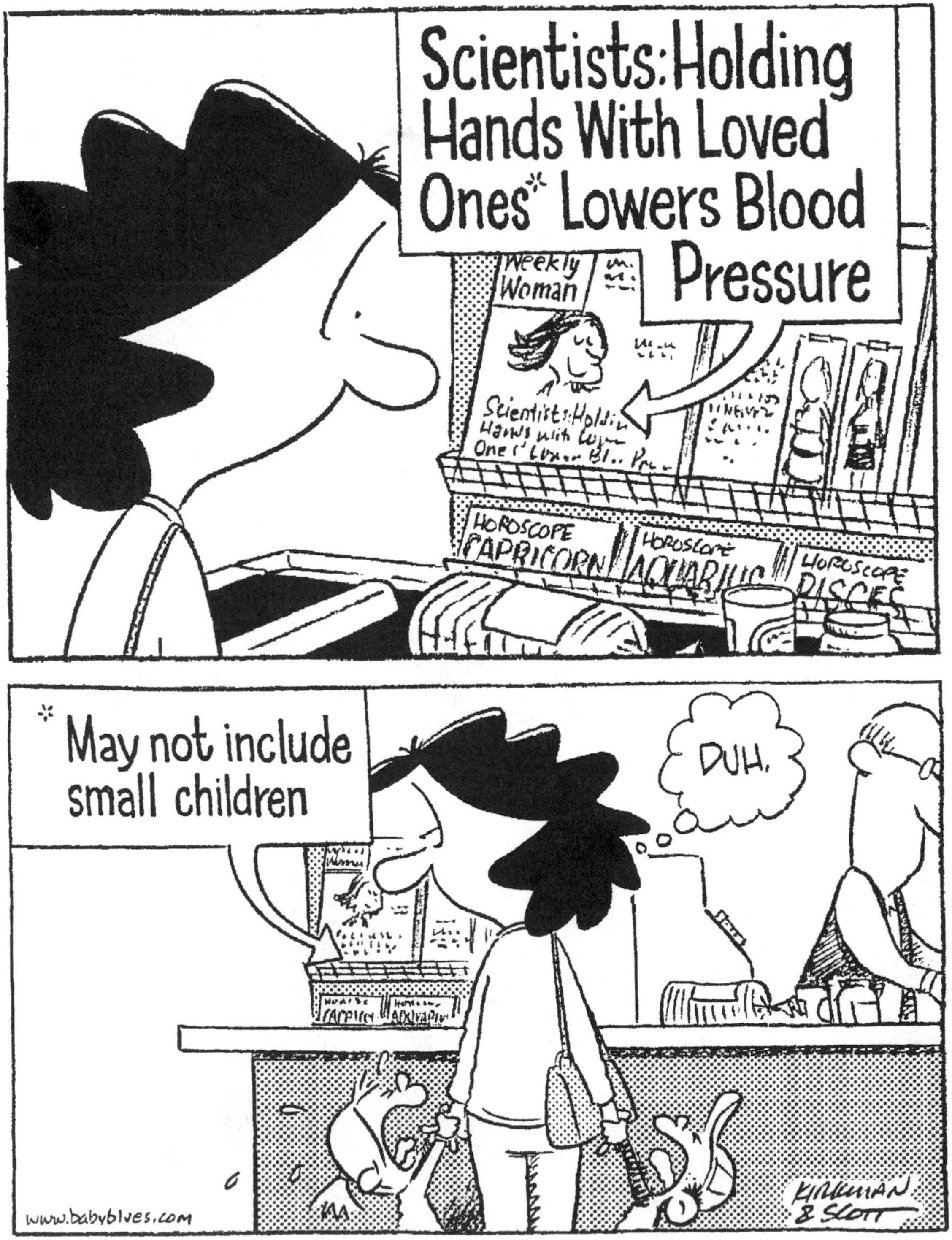
Scientists: Holding Hands With Loved Ones* Lowers Blood Pressure
Weekly Woman
HOROSCOPE
HOROSCOPE
HOROSCOPE
* May not include small children
DUH.
www.babyblues.com
KIRKMAN & SCOTT

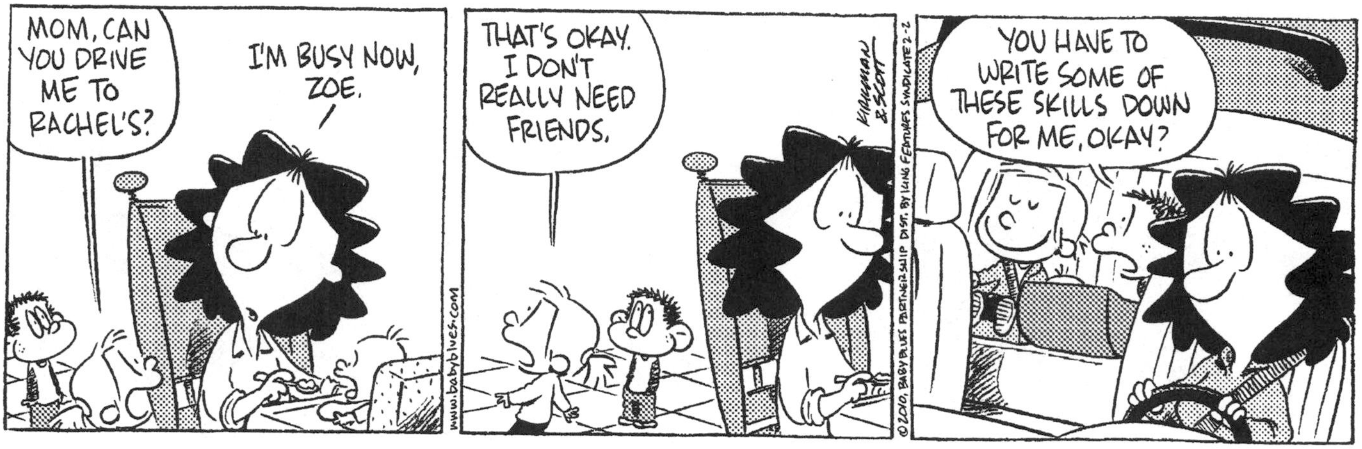
MOM, CAN YOU DRIVE ME TO RACHEL'S?
I'M BUSY NOW, ZOE.
www.babyblues.com
THAT'S OKAY. I DON'T REALLY NEED FRIENDS.
KIRKMAN & SCOTT
© 2010, BABY BLUES PARTNERSHIP DIST. BY KING FEATURES SYNDICATE 2-2
YOU HAVE TO WRITE SOME OF THESE SKILLS DOWN FOR ME, OKAY?

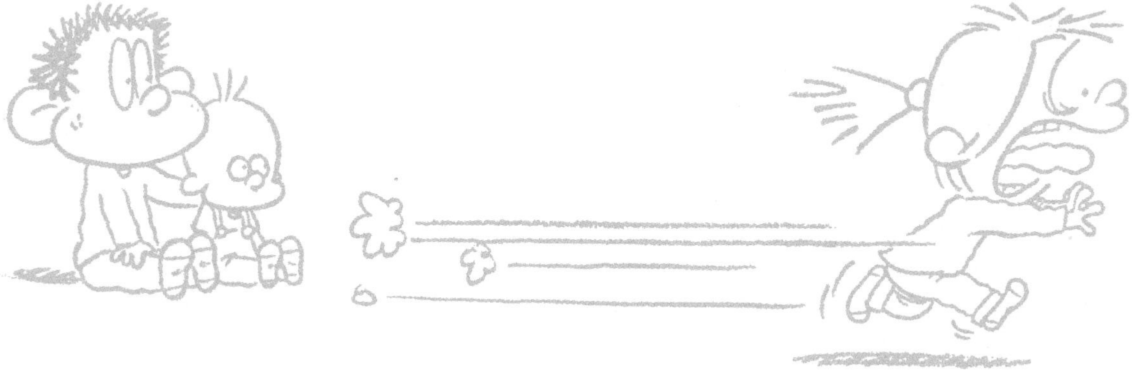

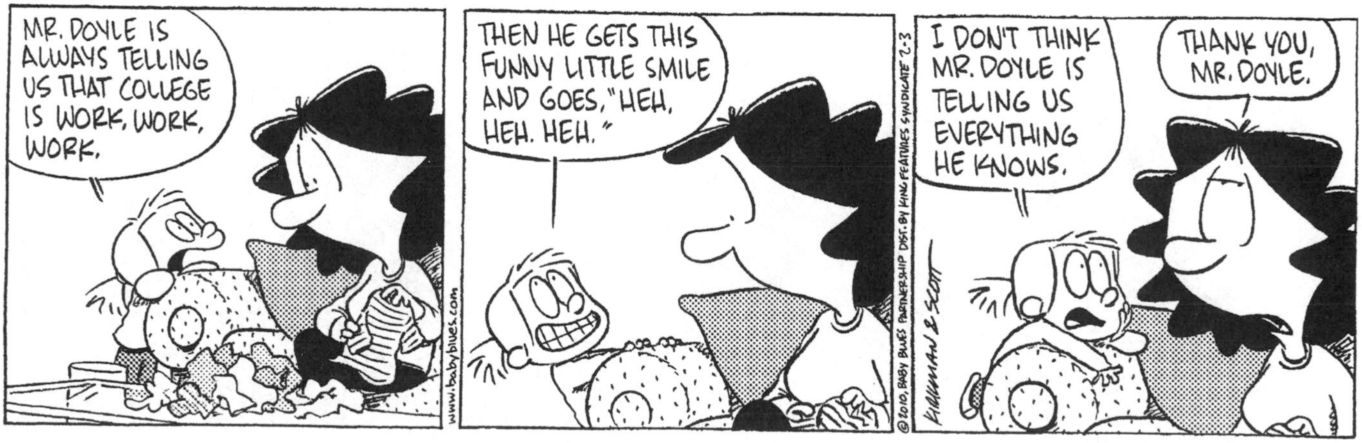
MR. DOYLE IS ALWAYS TELLING US THAT COLLEGE IS WORK, WORK, WORK.
www.babyblues.com
THEN HE GETS THIS FUNNY LITTLE SMILE AND GOES, "HEH, HEH. HEH."
© 2010, BABY BLUES PARTNERSHIP DIST. BY KING FEATURES SYNDICATE 2-3
KIRKMAN & SCOTT
I DON'T THINK MR. DOYLE IS TELLING US EVERYTHING HE KNOWS.
THANK YOU, MR. DOYLE.

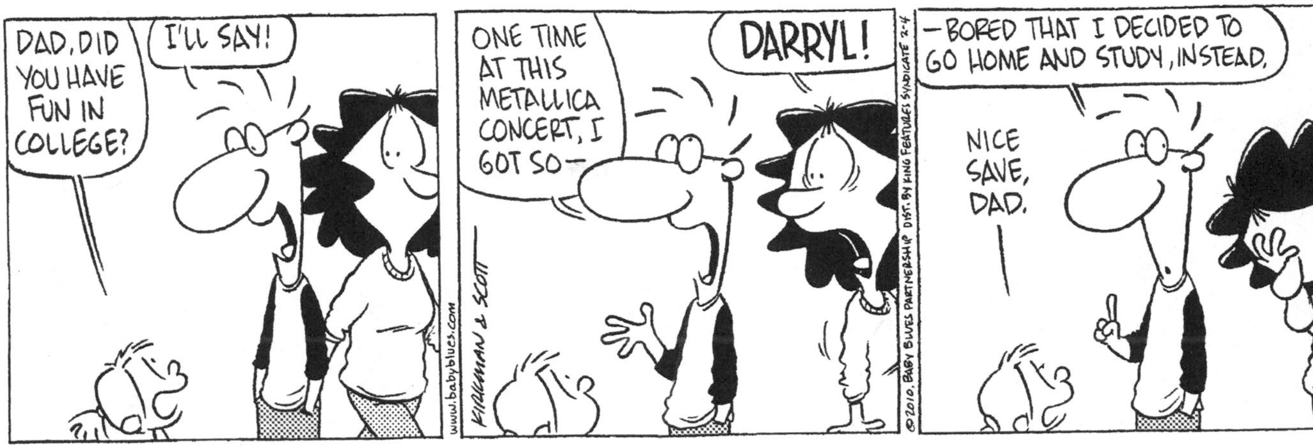
DAD, DID YOU HAVE FUN IN COLLEGE?
I'LL SAY!
www.babyblues.com
KIRKMAN & SCOTT
ONE TIME AT THIS METALLICA CONCERT, I GOT SO—
DARRYL!
©2010, BABY BLUES PARTNERSHIP DIST. BY KING FEATURES SYNDICATE 2-4
—BORED THAT I DECIDED TO GO HOME AND STUDY, INSTEAD.
NICE SAVE, DAD.

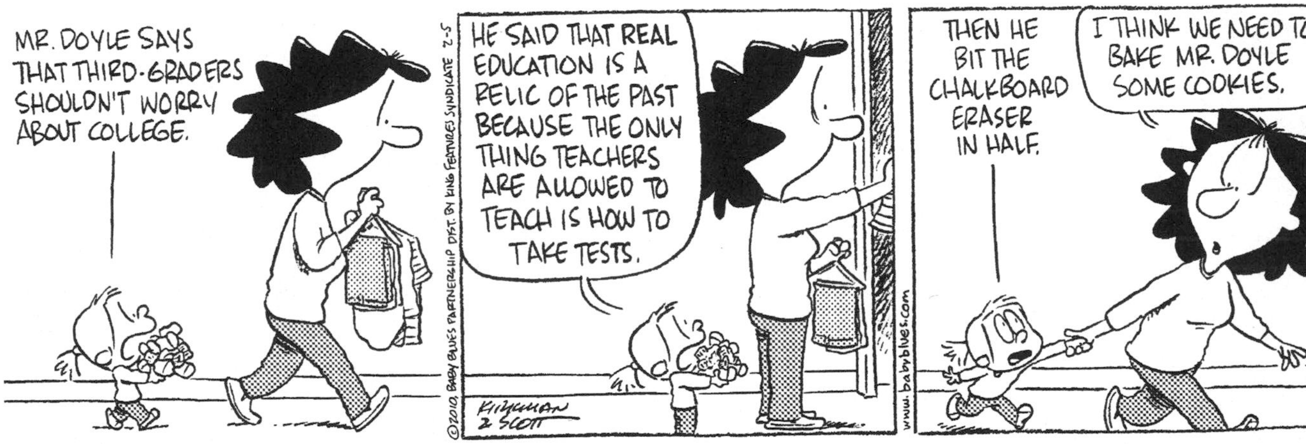
MR. DOYLE SAYS THAT THIRD-GRADERS SHOULDN'T WORRY ABOUT COLLEGE.
©2010, BABY BLUES PARTNERSHIP DIST. BY KING FEATURES SYNDICATE 2-5
KIRKMAN & SCOTT
HE SAID THAT REAL EDUCATION IS A RELIC OF THE PAST BECAUSE THE ONLY THING TEACHERS ARE ALLOWED TO TEACH IS HOW TO TAKE TESTS.
www.babyblues.com
THEN HE BIT THE CHALKBOARD ERASER IN HALF.
I THINK WE NEED TO BAKE MR. DOYLE SOME COOKIES.

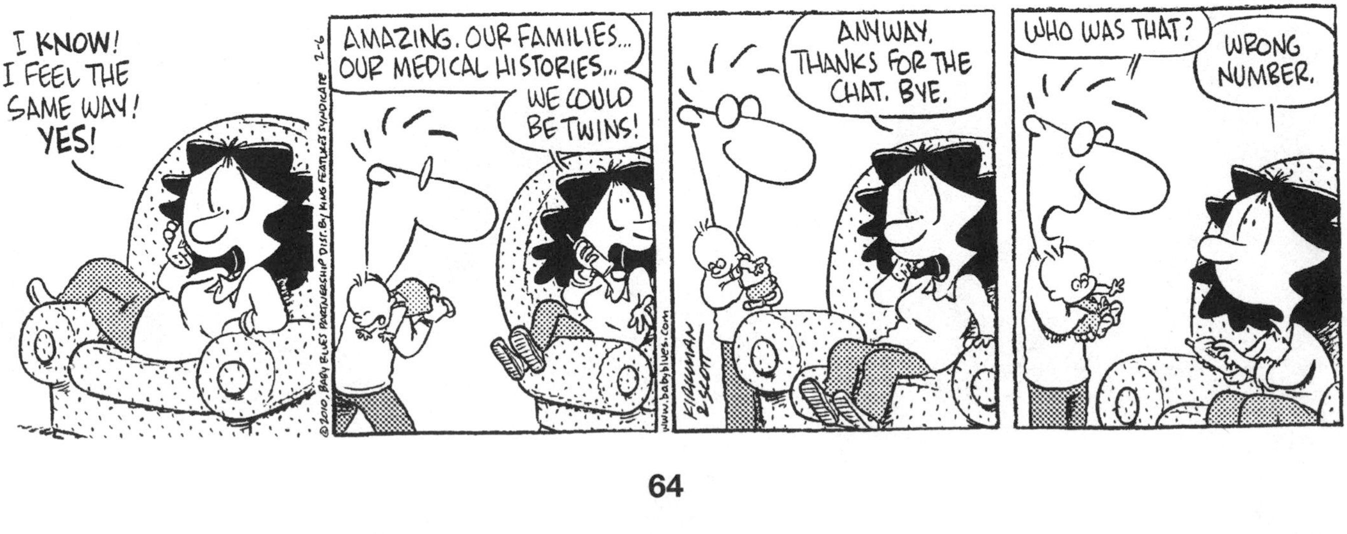
I KNOW! I FEEL THE SAME WAY! YES!
©2010, BABY BLUES PARTNERSHIP DIST. BY KING FEATURES SYNDICATE 2-6
AMAZING. OUR FAMILIES... OUR MEDICAL HISTORIES...
WE COULD BE TWINS!
www.babyblues.com
KIRKMAN & SCOTT
ANYWAY. THANKS FOR THE CHAT. BYE.
WHO WAS THAT?
WRONG NUMBER.

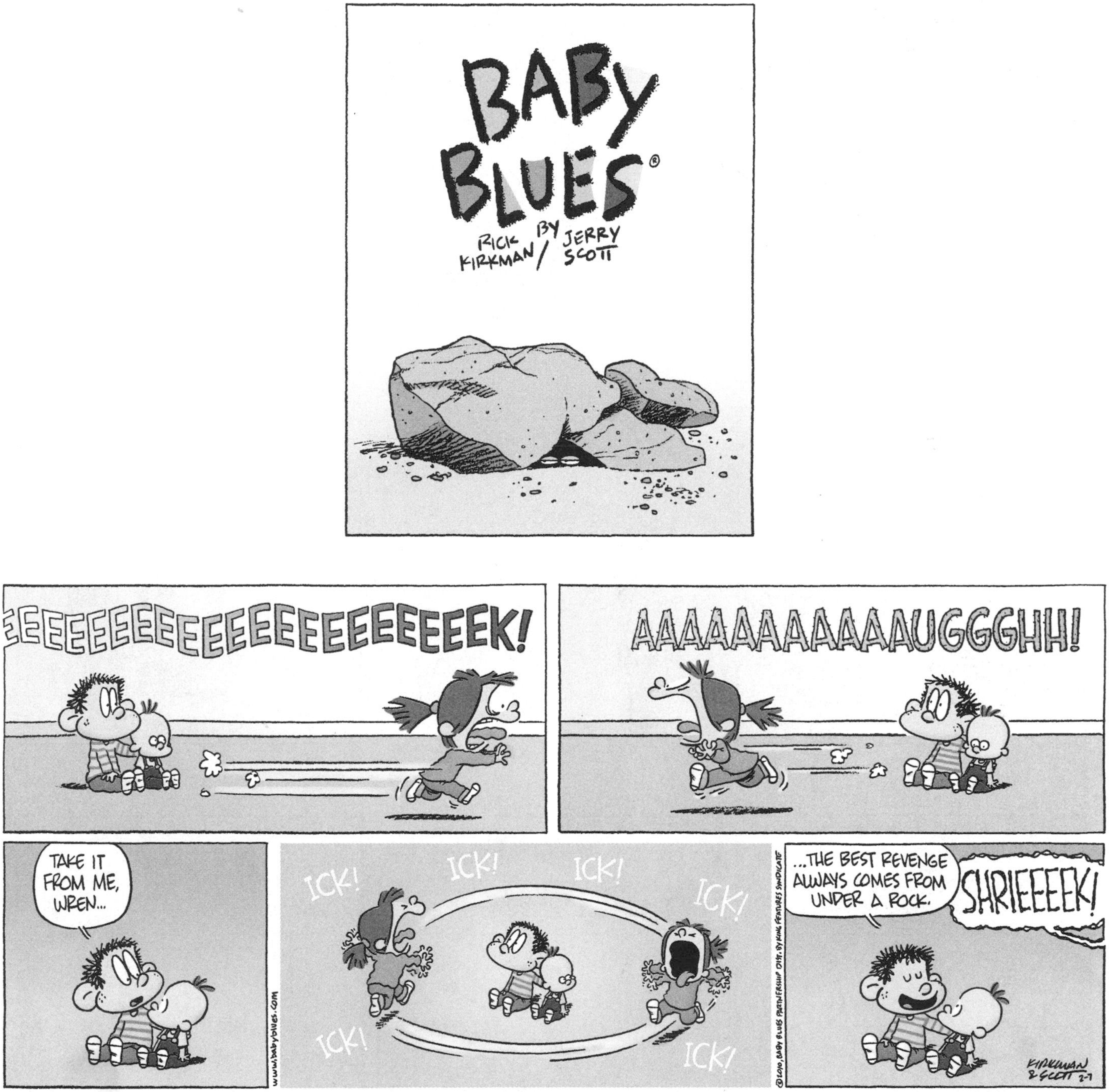

BABY BLUES®
BY RICK KIRKMAN / JERRY SCOTT
EEEEEEEEEEEEEEEEEEEEEEEK!
AAAAAAAAAAAAUGGGHH!
TAKE IT FROM ME, WREN...
ICK! ICK! ICK! ICK! ICK! ICK!
...THE BEST REVENGE ALWAYS COMES FROM UNDER A ROCK.
SHRIEEEEK!
www.babyblues.com
©2010, BABY BLUES PARTNERSHIP DIST. BY KING FEATURES SYNDICATE
KIRKMAN & SCOTT

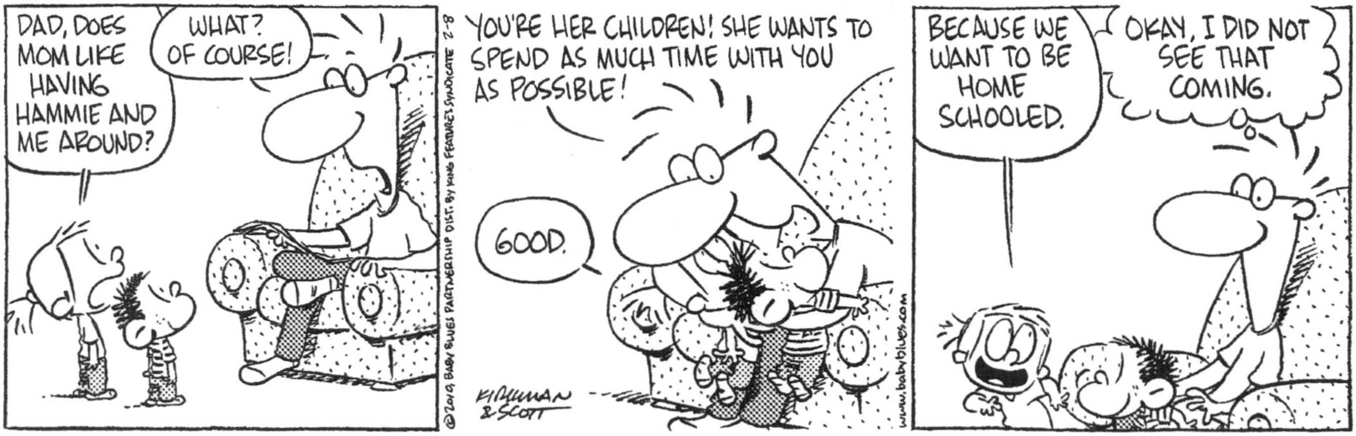
DAD, DOES MOM LIKE HAVING HAMMIE AND ME AROUND?
WHAT? OF COURSE!
YOU'RE HER CHILDREN! SHE WANTS TO SPEND AS MUCH TIME WITH YOU AS POSSIBLE!
GOOD.
BECAUSE WE WANT TO BE HOME SCHOOLED.
OKAY, I DID NOT SEE THAT COMING.
©2010, BABY BLUES PARTNERSHIP DIST. BY KING FEATURES SYNDICATE 2-8
KIRKMAN & SCOTT
www.babyblues.com

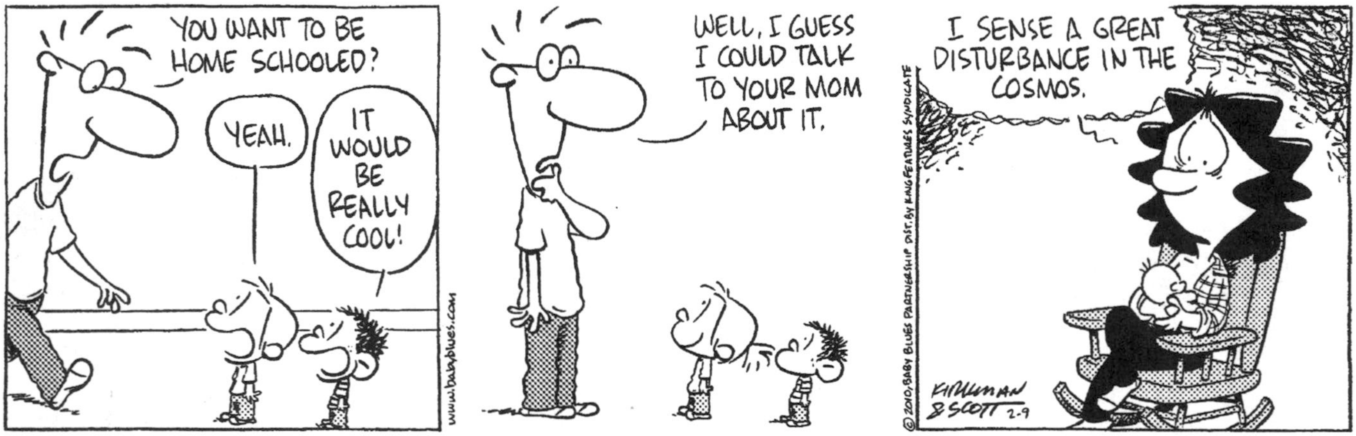
YOU WANT TO BE HOME SCHOOLED?
YEAH.
IT WOULD BE REALLY COOL!
WELL, I GUESS I COULD TALK TO YOUR MOM ABOUT IT.
I SENSE A GREAT DISTURBANCE IN THE COSMOS.
www.babyblues.com
©2010, BABY BLUES PARTNERSHIP DIST. BY KING FEATURES SYNDICATE
KIRKMAN & SCOTT 2-9

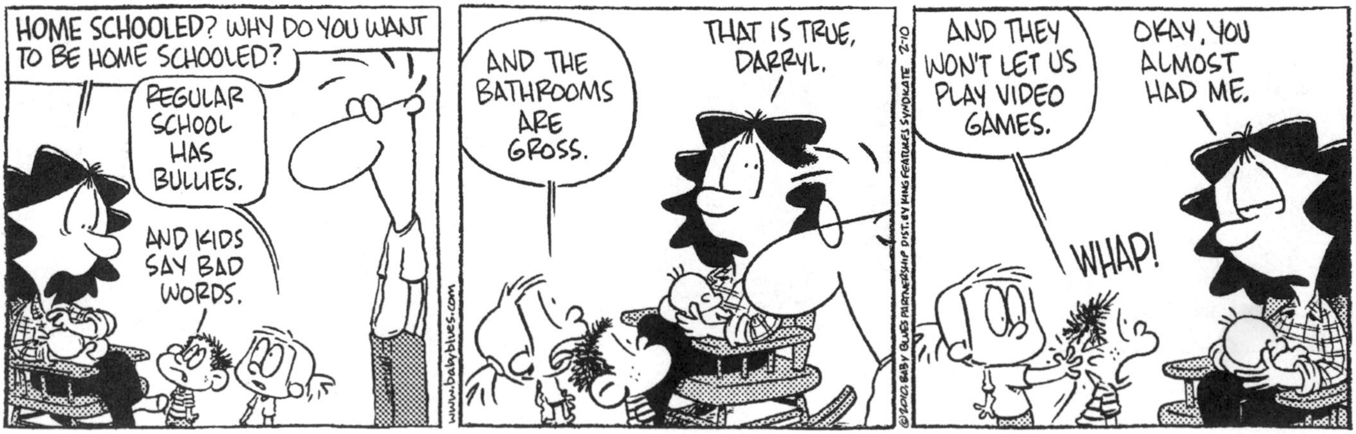
HOME SCHOOLED? WHY DO YOU WANT TO BE HOME SCHOOLED?
REGULAR SCHOOL HAS BULLIES.
AND KIDS SAY BAD WORDS.
AND THE BATHROOMS ARE GROSS.
THAT IS TRUE, DARRYL.
AND THEY WON'T LET US PLAY VIDEO GAMES.
WHAP!
OKAY, YOU ALMOST HAD ME.
www.babyblues.com
©2010, BABY BLUES PARTNERSHIP DIST. BY KING FEATURES SYNDICATE 2-10

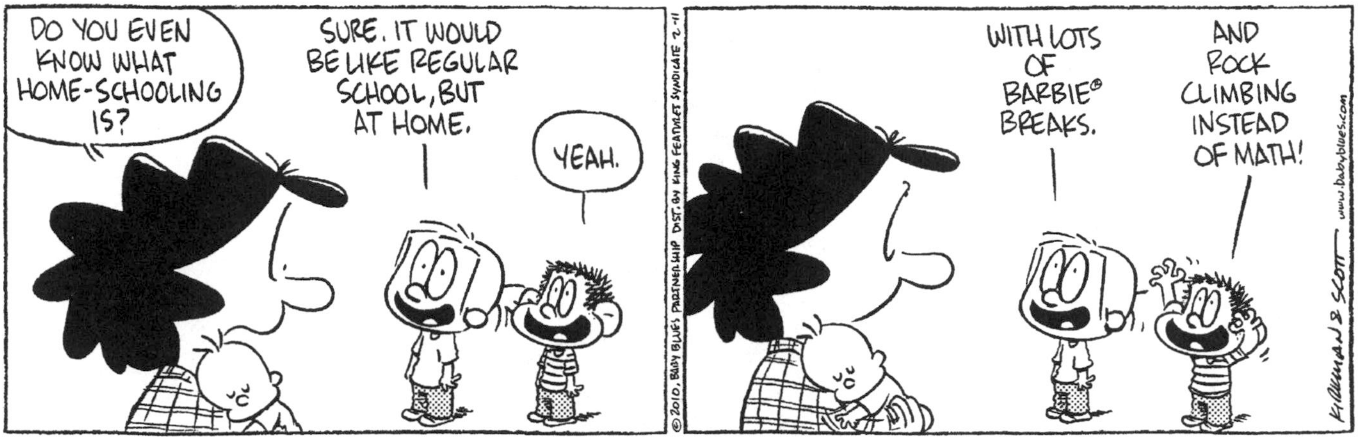
DO YOU EVEN KNOW WHAT HOME-SCHOOLING IS?
SURE. IT WOULD BE LIKE REGULAR SCHOOL, BUT AT HOME.
YEAH.
WITH LOTS OF BARBIE® BREAKS.
AND ROCK CLIMBING INSTEAD OF MATH!

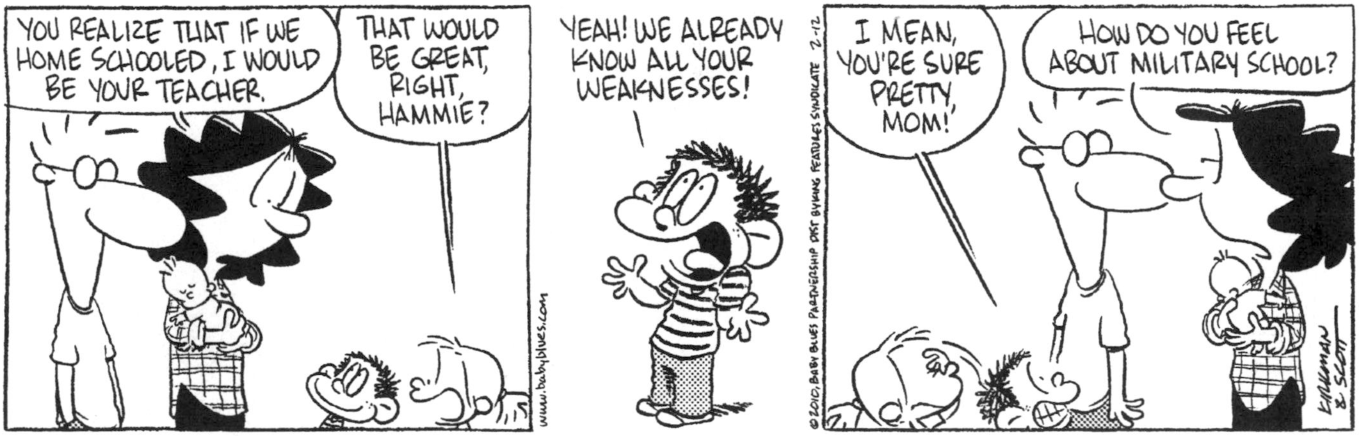
YOU REALIZE THAT IF WE HOME SCHOOLED, I WOULD BE YOUR TEACHER.
THAT WOULD BE GREAT, RIGHT, HAMMIE?
YEAH! WE ALREADY KNOW ALL YOUR WEAKNESSES!
I MEAN, YOU'RE SURE PRETTY, MOM!
HOW DO YOU FEEL ABOUT MILITARY SCHOOL?

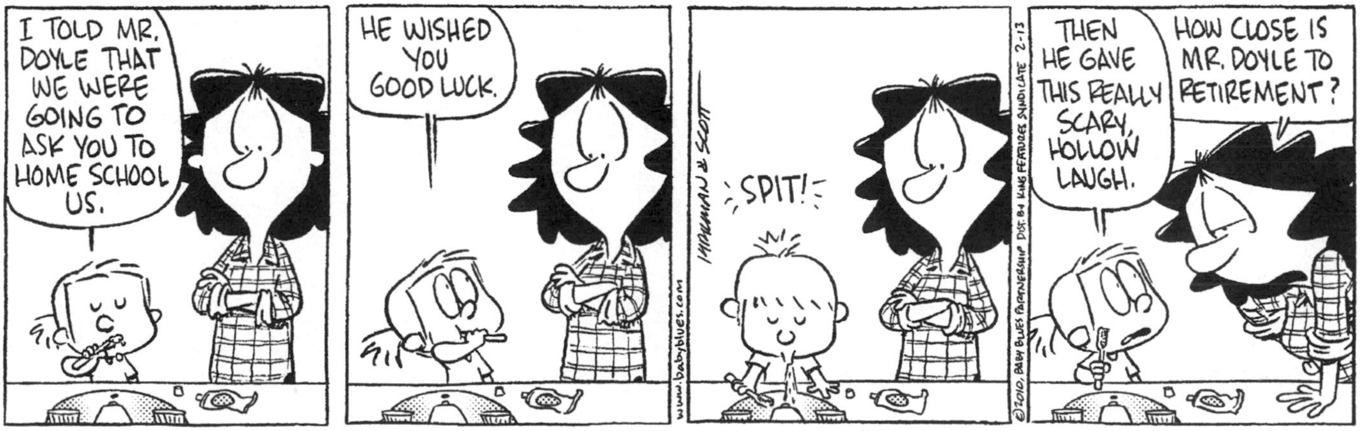
I TOLD MR. DOYLE THAT WE WERE GOING TO ASK YOU TO HOME SCHOOL US.
HE WISHED YOU GOOD LUCK.
SPIT!
THEN HE GAVE THIS REALLY SCARY, HOLLOW LAUGH.
HOW CLOSE IS MR. DOYLE TO RETIREMENT?

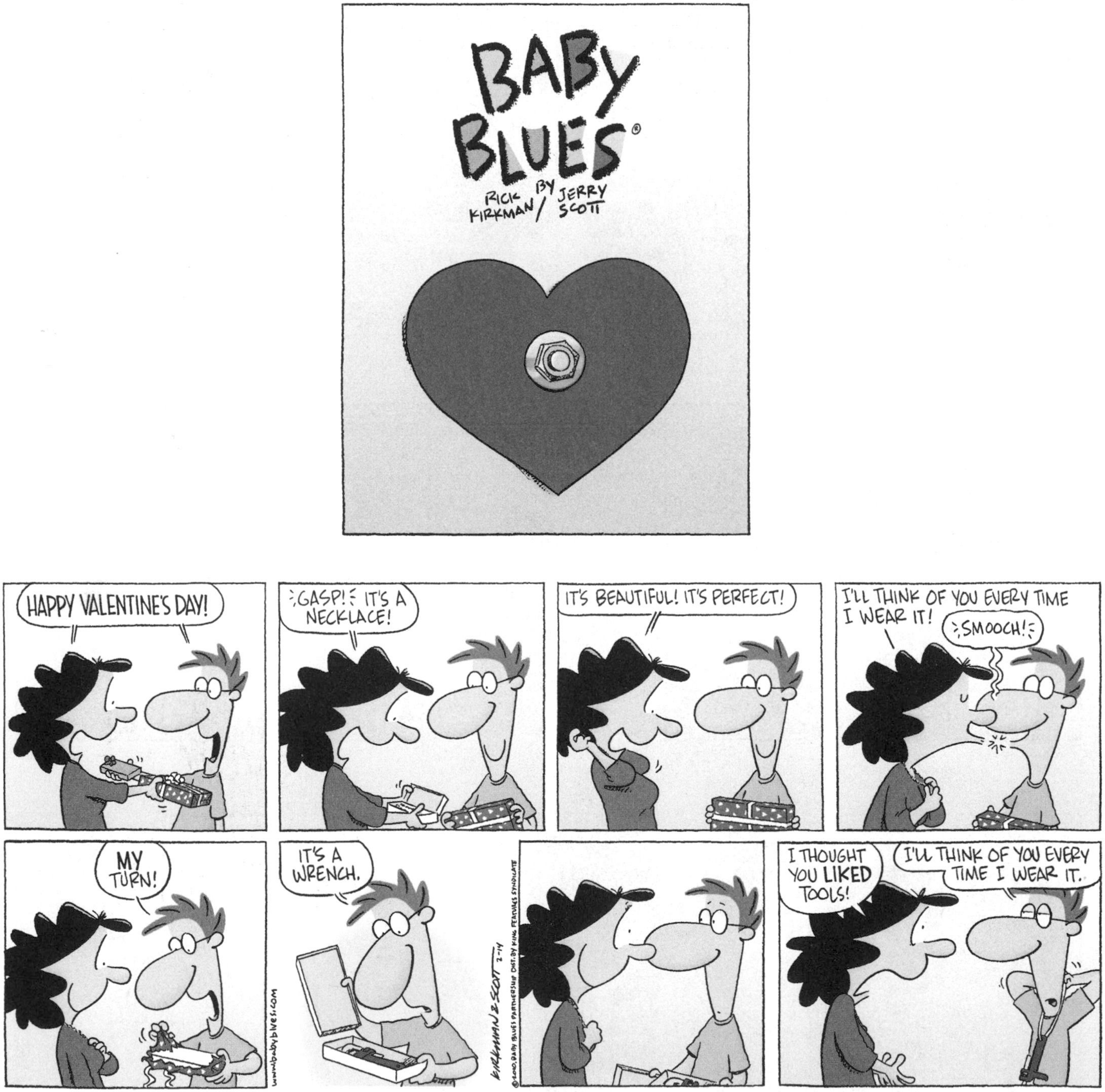
BABY BLUES®
BY RICK KIRKMAN / JERRY SCOTT
HAPPY VALENTINE'S DAY!
GASP! IT'S A NECKLACE!
IT'S BEAUTIFUL! IT'S PERFECT!
I'LL THINK OF YOU EVERY TIME I WEAR IT!
SMOOCH!
MY TURN!
www.babyblues.com
IT'S A WRENCH.
KIRKMAN & SCOTT
I THOUGHT YOU LIKED TOOLS!
I'LL THINK OF YOU EVERY TIME I WEAR IT.

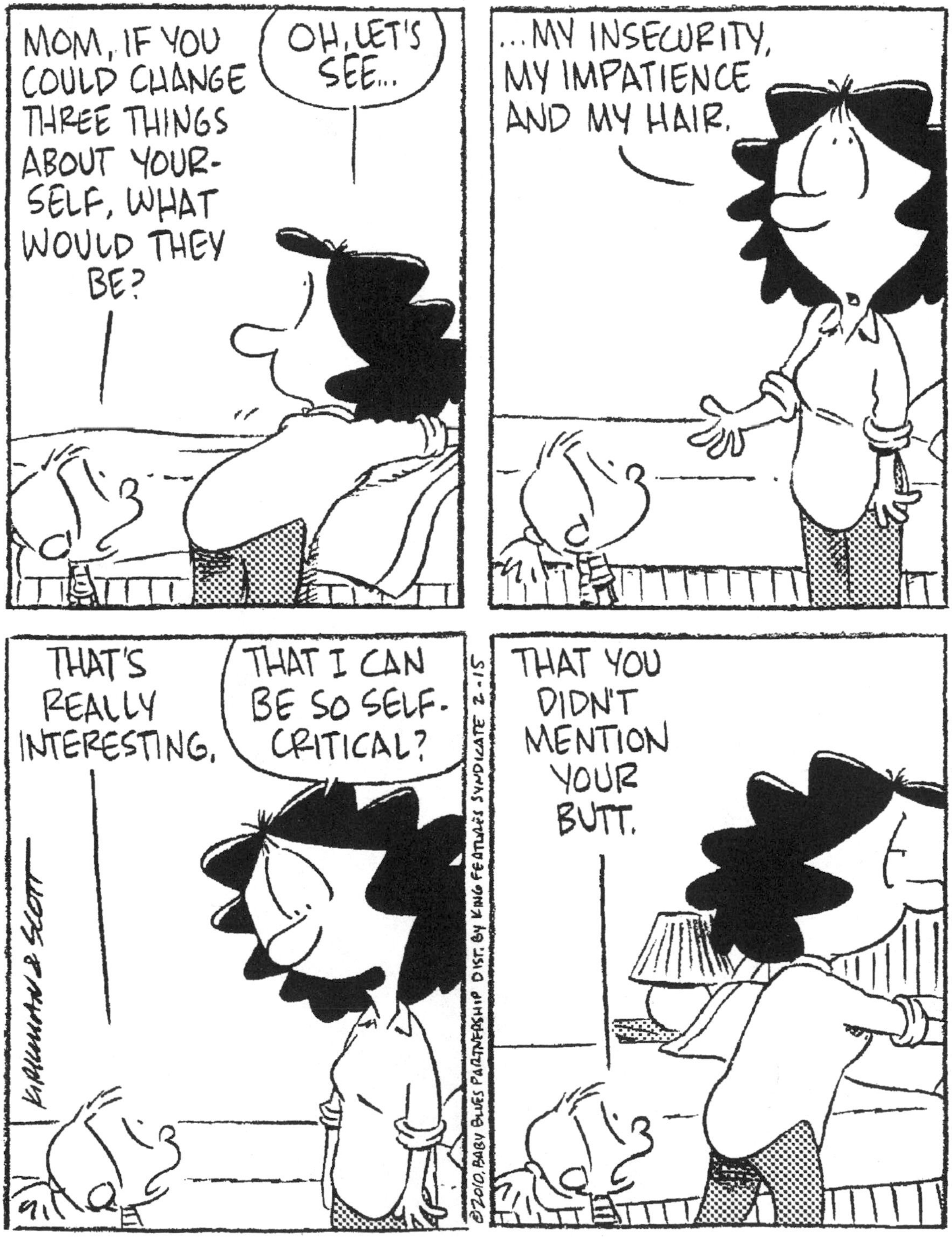

MOM, IF YOU COULD CHANGE THREE THINGS ABOUT YOURSELF, WHAT WOULD THEY BE?
OH, LET'S SEE...
...MY INSECURITY, MY IMPATIENCE AND MY HAIR.
THAT'S REALLY INTERESTING.
THAT I CAN BE SO SELF-CRITICAL?
THAT YOU DIDN'T MENTION YOUR BUTT.
KIRKMAN & SCOTT
©2010, BABY BLUES PARTNERSHIP DIST. BY KING FEATURES SYNDICATE 2-15

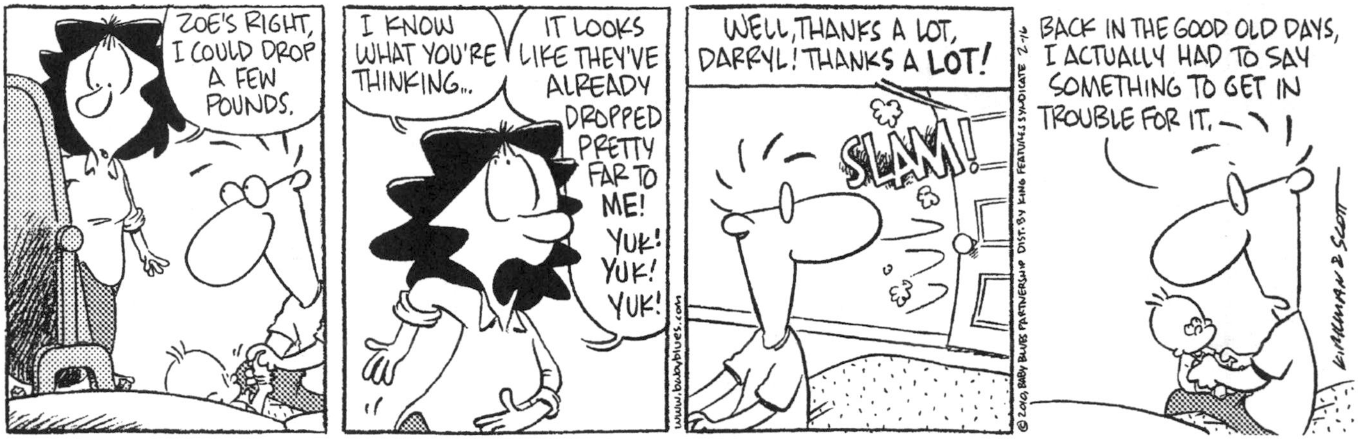
ZOE'S RIGHT, I COULD DROP A FEW POUNDS.
I KNOW WHAT YOU'RE THINKING...
IT LOOKS LIKE THEY'VE ALREADY DROPPED PRETTY FAR TO ME!
YUK! YUK! YUK!
www.babyblues.com
WELL, THANKS A LOT, DARRYL! THANKS A LOT!
SLAM!
© 2010, BABY BLUES PARTNERSHIP DIST. BY KING FEATURES SYNDICATE 2-16
BACK IN THE GOOD OLD DAYS, I ACTUALLY HAD TO SAY SOMETHING TO GET IN TROUBLE FOR IT.
KIRKMAN & SCOTT

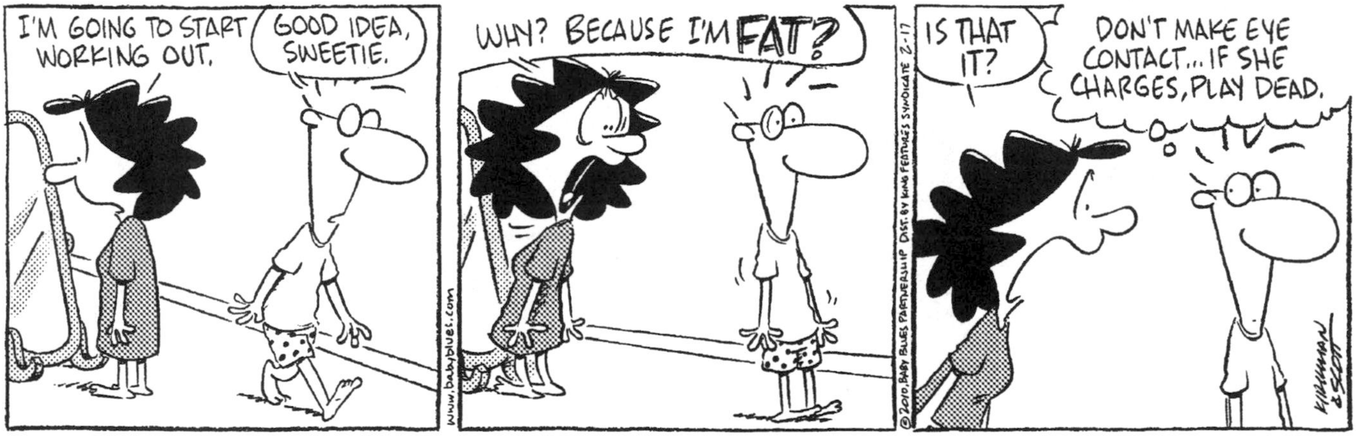
I'M GOING TO START WORKING OUT.
GOOD IDEA, SWEETIE.
www.babyblues.com
WHY? BECAUSE I'M FAT?
© 2010, BABY BLUES PARTNERSHIP DIST. BY KING FEATURES SYNDICATE 2-17
IS THAT IT?
DON'T MAKE EYE CONTACT... IF SHE CHARGES, PLAY DEAD.
KIRKMAN & SCOTT

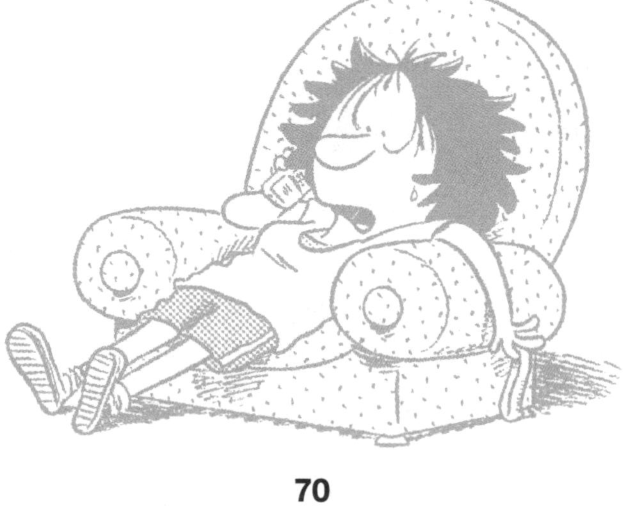

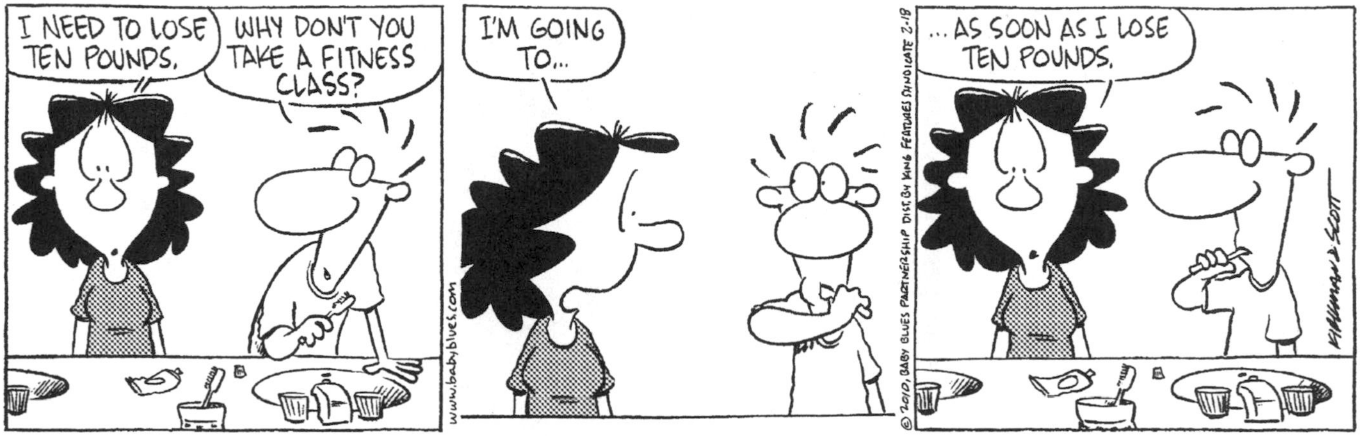
I NEED TO LOSE TEN POUNDS.
WHY DON'T YOU TAKE A FITNESS CLASS?
I'M GOING TO...
... AS SOON AS I LOSE TEN POUNDS.

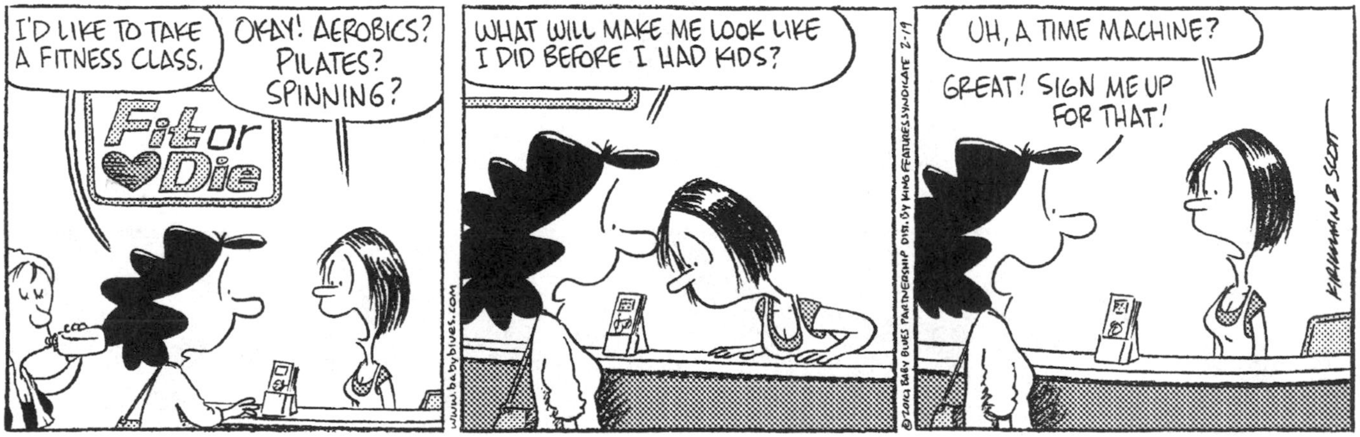
I'D LIKE TO TAKE A FITNESS CLASS.
OKAY! AEROBICS? PILATES? SPINNING?
Fit or Die
WHAT WILL MAKE ME LOOK LIKE I DID BEFORE I HAD KIDS?
UH, A TIME MACHINE?
GREAT! SIGN ME UP FOR THAT!

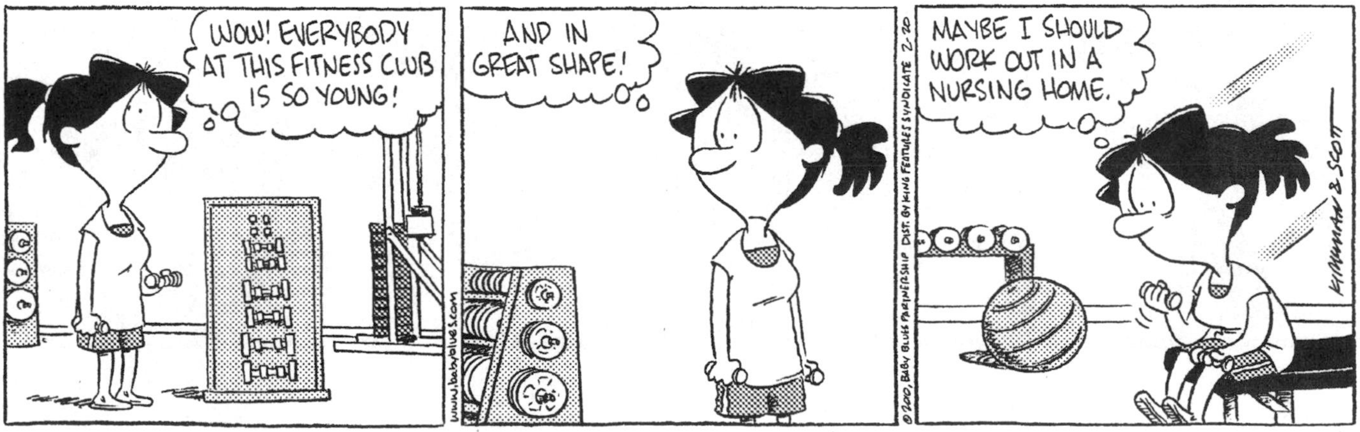
WOW! EVERYBODY AT THIS FITNESS CLUB IS SO YOUNG!
AND IN GREAT SHAPE!
MAYBE I SHOULD WORK OUT IN A NURSING HOME.

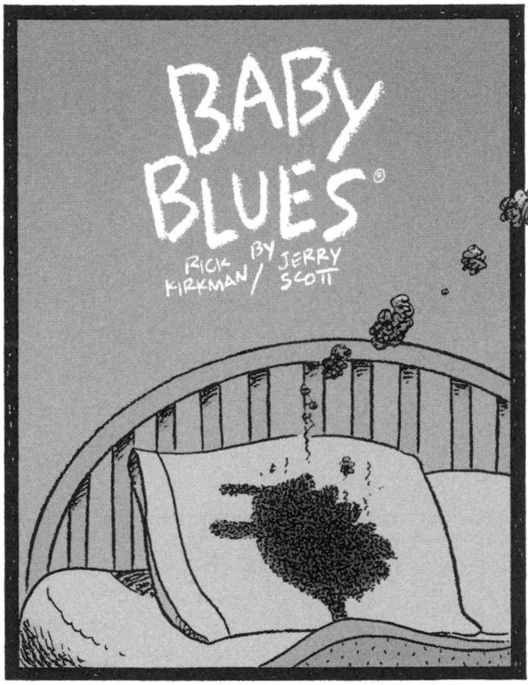
BABY BLUES®
RICK KIRKMAN / BY JERRY SCOTT

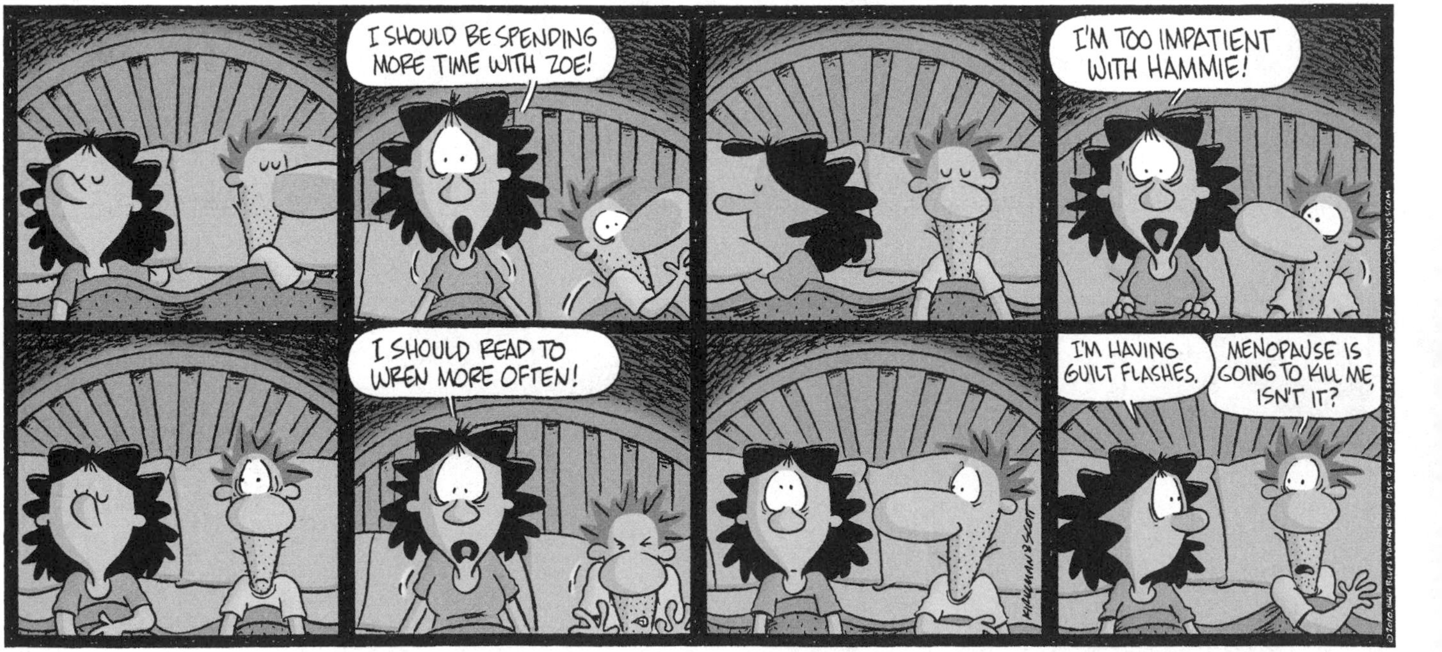
I SHOULD BE SPENDING MORE TIME WITH ZOE!
I'M TOO IMPATIENT WITH HAMMIE!
I SHOULD READ TO WREN MORE OFTEN!
I'M HAVING GUILT FLASHES.
MENOPAUSE IS GOING TO KILL ME, ISN'T IT?

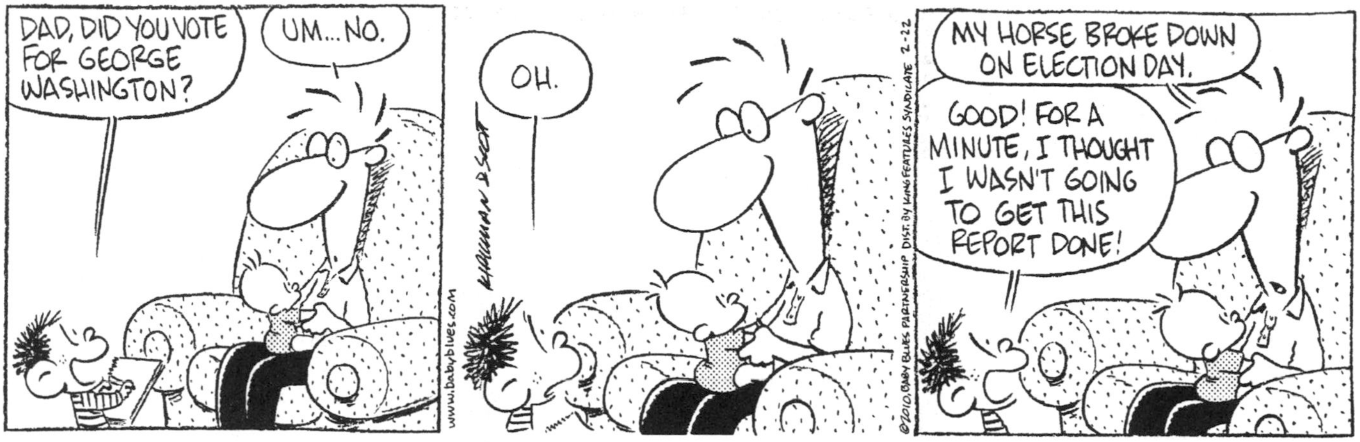
DAD, DID YOU VOTE FOR GEORGE WASHINGTON?
UM...NO.
www.babyblues.com
KIRKMAN & SCOTT
OH.
©2010, BABY BLUES PARTNERSHIP DIST. BY KING FEATURES SYNDICATE 2-22
MY HORSE BROKE DOWN ON ELECTION DAY.
GOOD! FOR A MINUTE, I THOUGHT I WASN'T GOING TO GET THIS REPORT DONE!

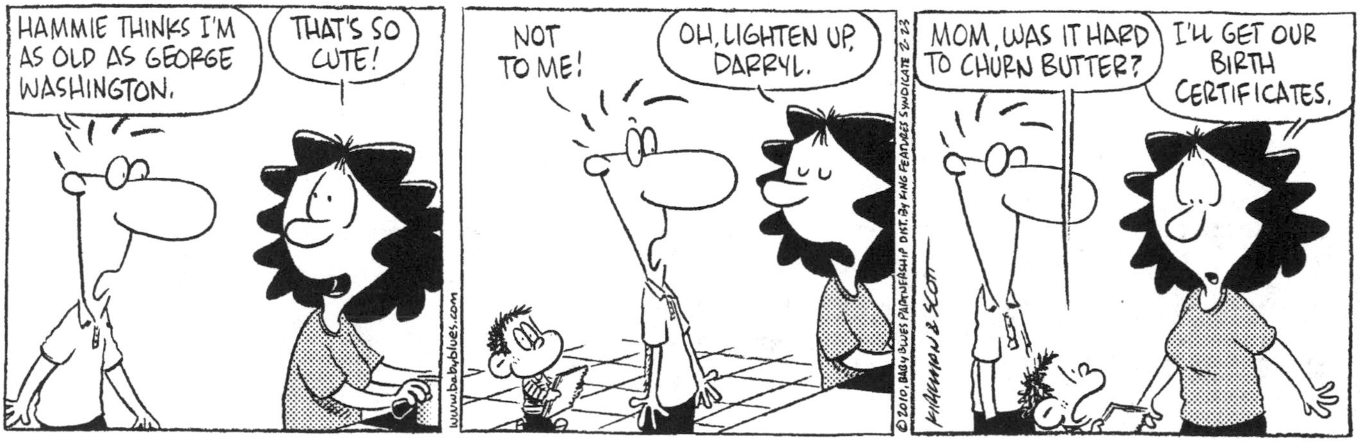
HAMMIE THINKS I'M AS OLD AS GEORGE WASHINGTON.
THAT'S SO CUTE!
www.babyblues.com
NOT TO ME!
OH, LIGHTEN UP, DARRYL.
©2010, BABY BLUES PARTNERSHIP DIST. BY KING FEATURES SYNDICATE 2-23
KIRKMAN & SCOTT
MOM, WAS IT HARD TO CHURN BUTTER?
I'LL GET OUR BIRTH CERTIFICATES.

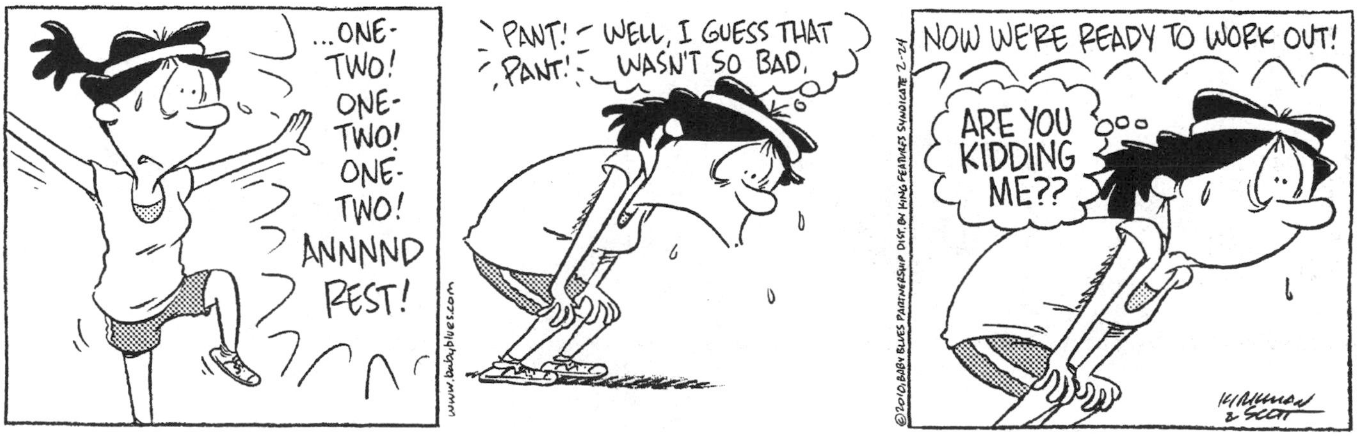
...ONE-TWO! ONE-TWO! ONE-TWO! ANNNND REST!
www.babyblues.com
PANT! PANT!
WELL, I GUESS THAT WASN'T SO BAD.
©2010, BABY BLUES PARTNERSHIP DIST. BY KING FEATURES SYNDICATE 2-24
NOW WE'RE READY TO WORK OUT!
ARE YOU KIDDING ME??
KIRKMAN & SCOTT

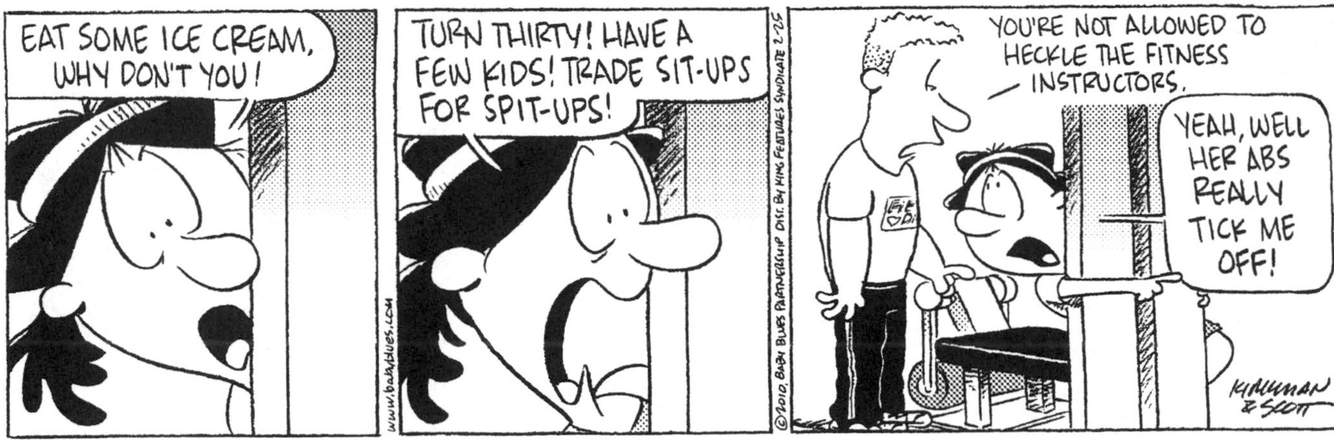
EAT SOME ICE CREAM, WHY DON'T YOU!
TURN THIRTY! HAVE A FEW KIDS! TRADE SIT-UPS FOR SPIT-UPS!
YOU'RE NOT ALLOWED TO HECKLE THE FITNESS INSTRUCTORS.
YEAH, WELL HER ABS REALLY TICK ME OFF!
www.babyblues.com
©2010, BABY BLUES PARTNERSHIP DIST. BY KING FEATURES SYNDICATE 2-25
KIRKMAN & SCOTT

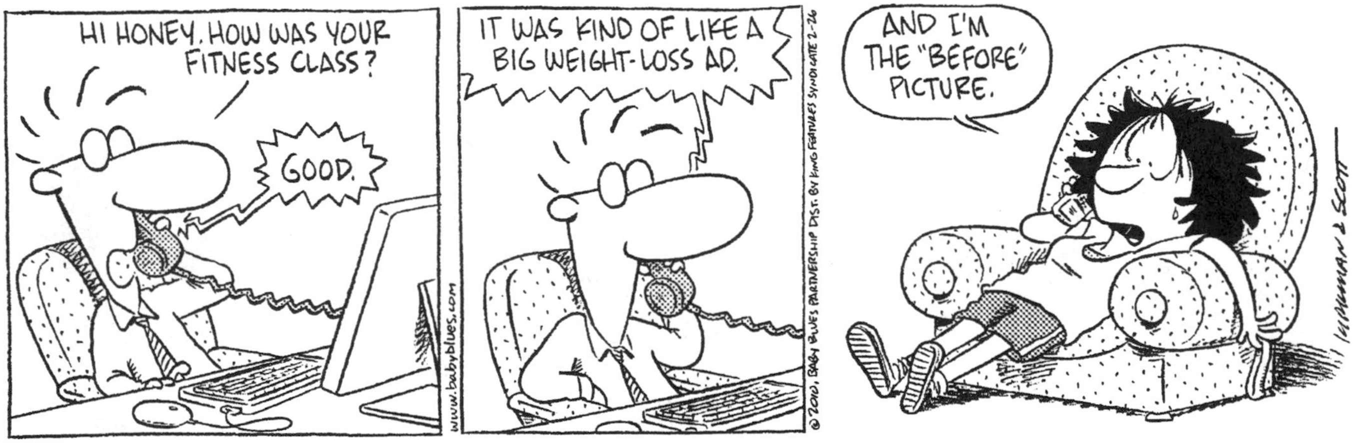
HI HONEY. HOW WAS YOUR FITNESS CLASS?
GOOD.
IT WAS KIND OF LIKE A BIG WEIGHT-LOSS AD.
AND I'M THE "BEFORE" PICTURE.
www.babyblues.com
©2010, BABY BLUES PARTNERSHIP DIST. BY KING FEATURES SYNDICATE 2-26
KIRKMAN & SCOTT

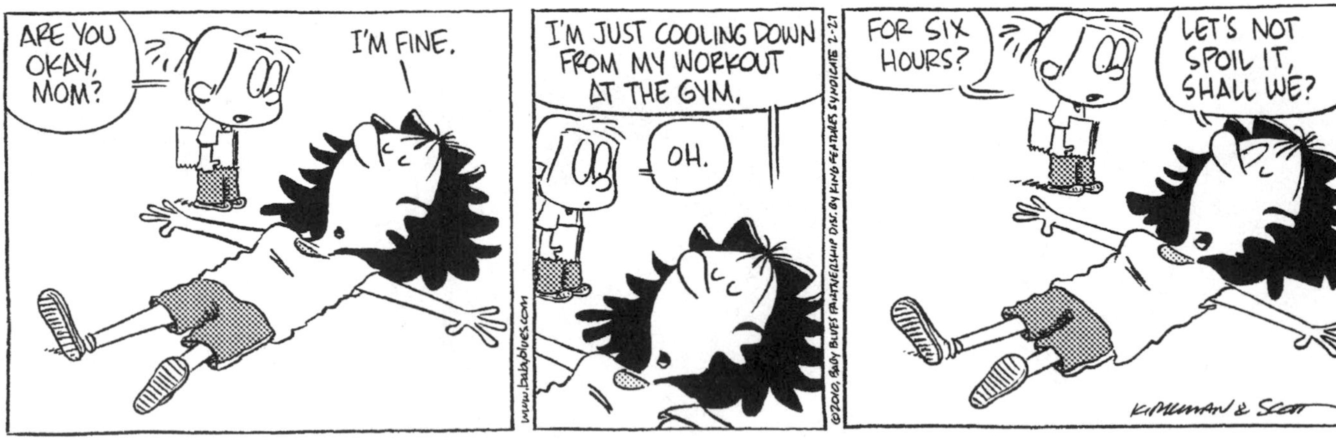
ARE YOU OKAY, MOM?
I'M FINE.
I'M JUST COOLING DOWN FROM MY WORKOUT AT THE GYM.
OH.
FOR SIX HOURS?
LET'S NOT SPOIL IT, SHALL WE?
www.babyblues.com
©2010, BABY BLUES PARTNERSHIP DIST. BY KING FEATURES SYNDICATE 2-27
KIRKMAN & SCOTT

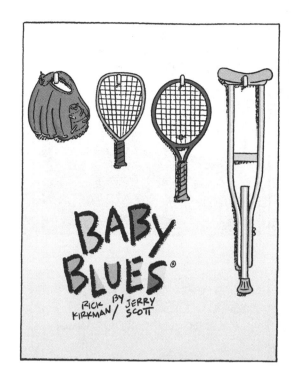

BABY BLUES®
BY RICK KIRKMAN / JERRY SCOTT

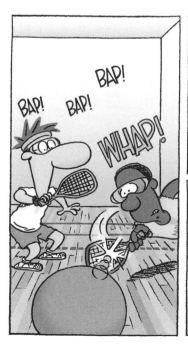

BAP! BAP! BAP!
WHAP!
OW!
SHOULDER?
YEAH, I TWEAKED IT PITCHING BATTING PRACTICE TO HAMMIE.
SAME HERE, BUT MINE'S FROM PUSHING KEESHA ON THE SWINGS.
I THOUGHT IT WAS FROM THE TIME YOU TOOK HER SLEDDING.
NOPE. YOU'RE THINKING ABOUT THE BRUISED RIBS.
OH, THAT'S RIGHT. I REMEMBER NOW BECAUSE IT WAS RIGHT AFTER I MESSED UP MY KNEE PLAYING SOCCER WITH ZOE.
www.babyblues.com
KIRKMAN & SCOTT 2-28
©2010 BABY BLUES PARTNERSHIP DIST. BY KING FEATURES SYNDICATE
REMEMBER WHEN OUR INJURIES WERE CAUSED BY STUPIDITY AND NOT KIDS.

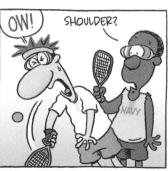

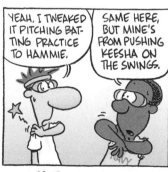

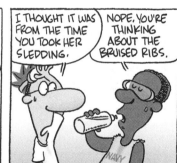

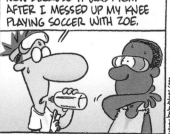

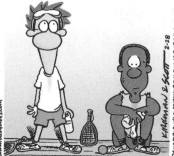

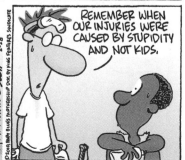

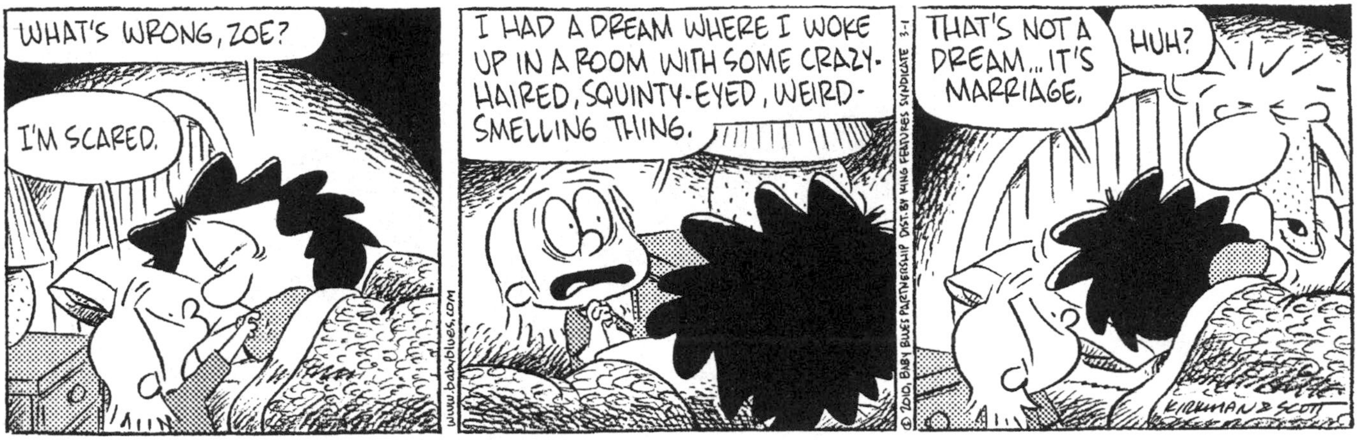
WHAT'S WRONG, ZOE?
I'M SCARED.
I HAD A DREAM WHERE I WOKE UP IN A ROOM WITH SOME CRAZY-HAIRED, SQUINTY-EYED, WEIRD-SMELLING THING.
THAT'S NOT A DREAM... IT'S MARRIAGE.
HUH?
www.babyblues.com
© 2010, BABY BLUES PARTNERSHIP DIST. BY KING FEATURES SYNDICATE 3-1
KIRKMAN & SCOTT

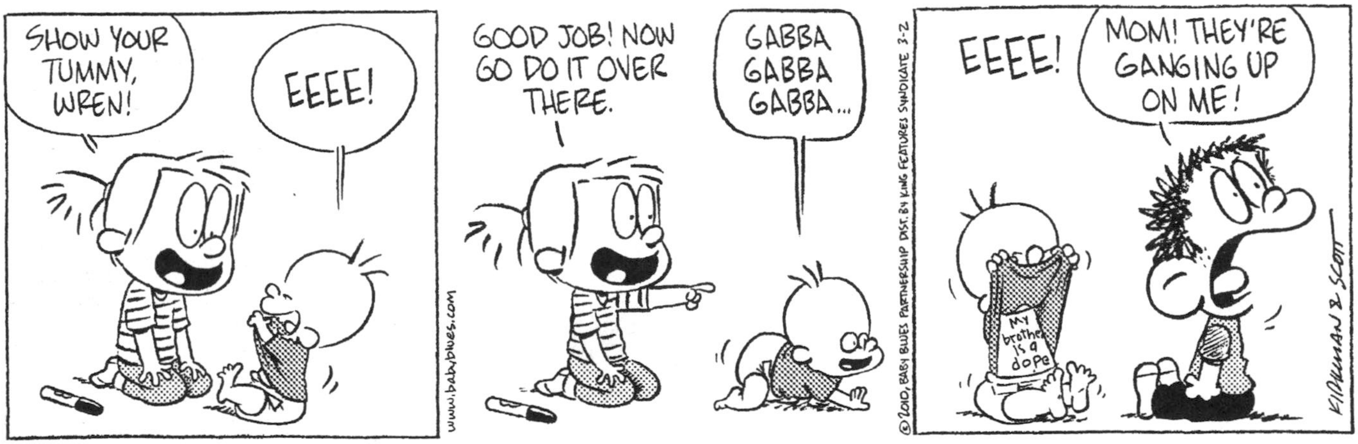
SHOW YOUR TUMMY, WREN!
EEEE!
GOOD JOB! NOW GO DO IT OVER THERE.
GABBA GABBA GABBA...
EEEE!
MOM! THEY'RE GANGING UP ON ME!
My brother is a dope
www.babyblues.com
© 2010, BABY BLUES PARTNERSHIP DIST. BY KING FEATURES SYNDICATE 3-2
KIRKMAN & SCOTT

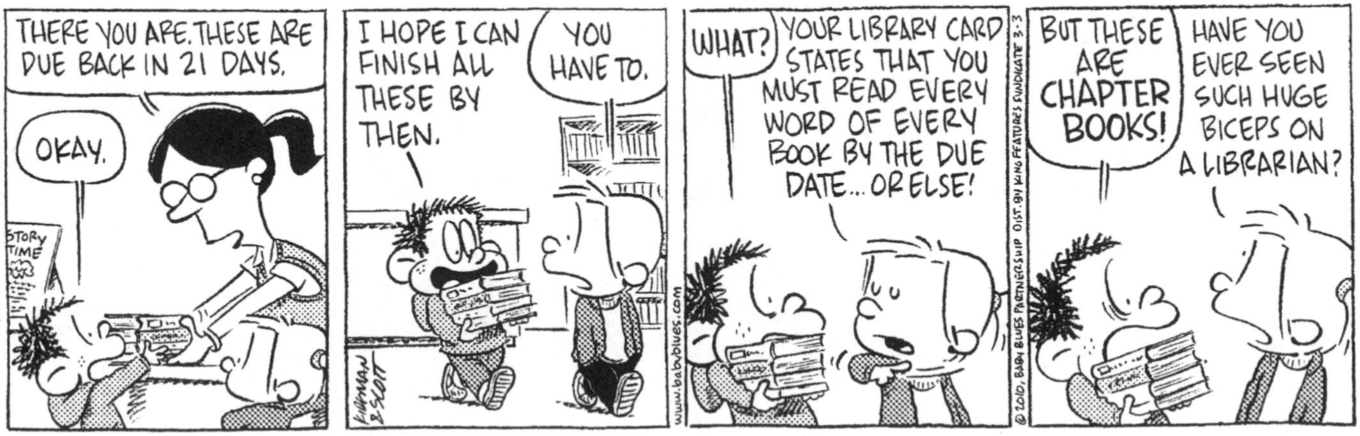
THERE YOU ARE. THESE ARE DUE BACK IN 21 DAYS.
OKAY.
STORY TIME
I HOPE I CAN FINISH ALL THESE BY THEN.
YOU HAVE TO.
WHAT?
YOUR LIBRARY CARD STATES THAT YOU MUST READ EVERY WORD OF EVERY BOOK BY THE DUE DATE... OR ELSE!
BUT THESE ARE CHAPTER BOOKS!
HAVE YOU EVER SEEN SUCH HUGE BICEPS ON A LIBRARIAN?
KIRKMAN & SCOTT
www.babyblues.com
© 2010, BABY BLUES PARTNERSHIP DIST. BY KING FEATURES SYNDICATE 3-3

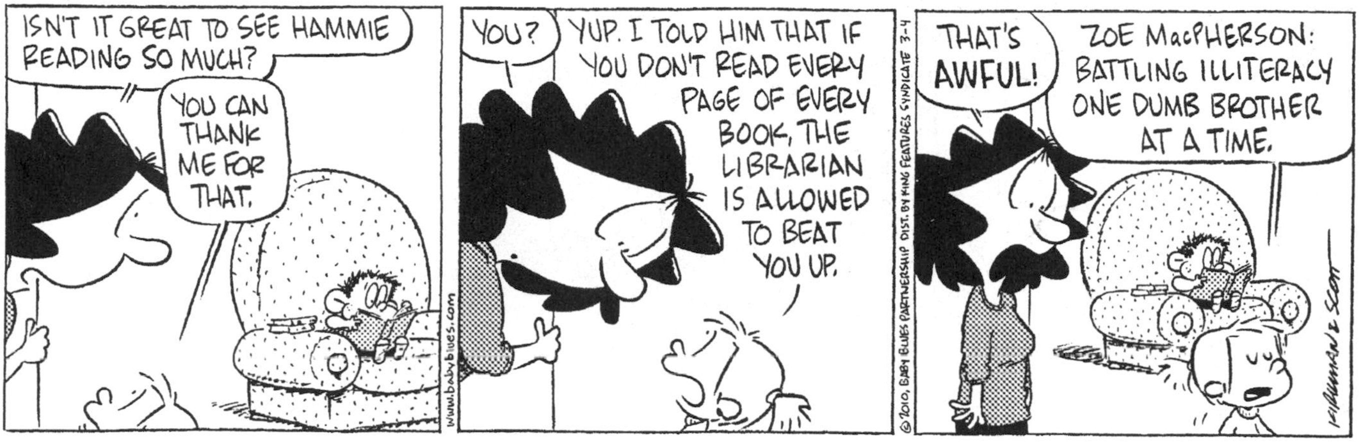
ISN'T IT GREAT TO SEE HAMMIE READING SO MUCH?
YOU CAN THANK ME FOR THAT.
YOU?
YUP. I TOLD HIM THAT IF YOU DON'T READ EVERY PAGE OF EVERY BOOK, THE LIBRARIAN IS ALLOWED TO BEAT YOU UP.
THAT'S AWFUL!
ZOE MacPHERSON: BATTLING ILLITERACY ONE DUMB BROTHER AT A TIME.
www.babyblues.com
© 2010, BABY BLUES PARTNERSHIP DIST. BY KING FEATURES SYNDICATE 3-4
KIRKMAN & SCOTT

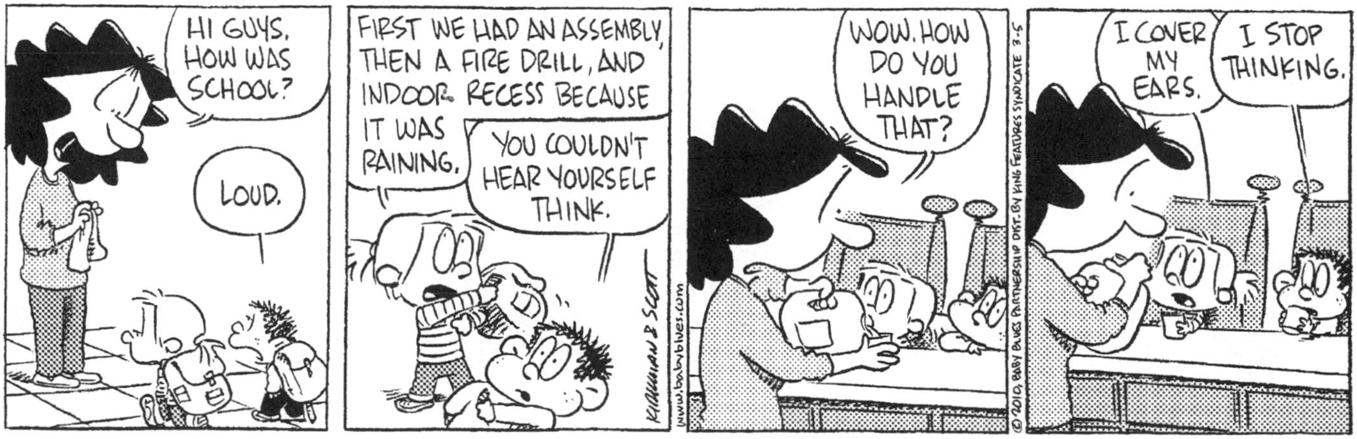
HI GUYS. HOW WAS SCHOOL?
LOUD.
FIRST WE HAD AN ASSEMBLY, THEN A FIRE DRILL, AND INDOOR RECESS BECAUSE IT WAS RAINING.
YOU COULDN'T HEAR YOURSELF THINK.
KIRKMAN & SCOTT
www.babyblues.com
WOW. HOW DO YOU HANDLE THAT?
© 2010, BABY BLUES PARTNERSHIP DIST. BY KING FEATURES SYNDICATE 3-5
I COVER MY EARS.
I STOP THINKING.

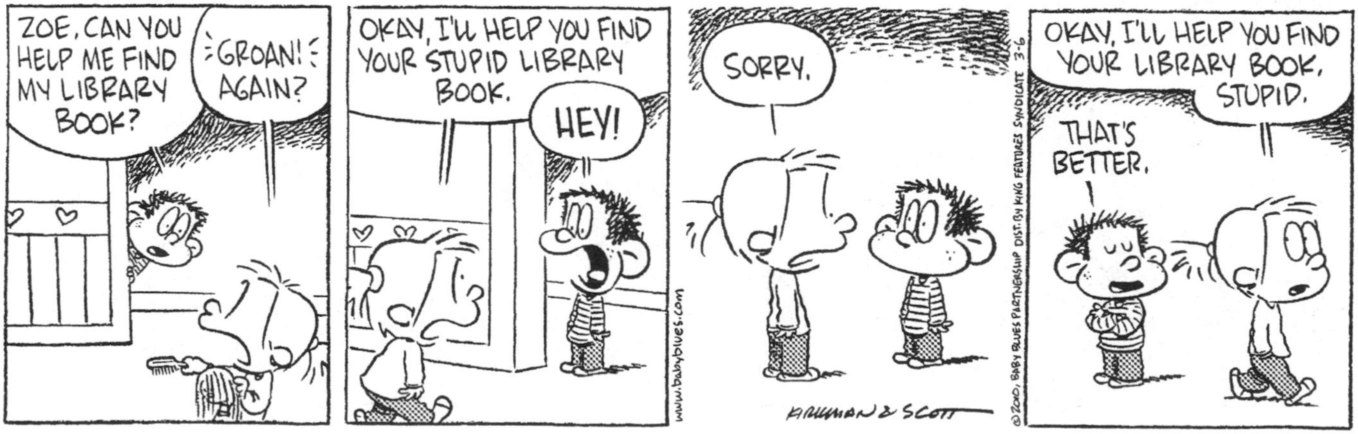
ZOE, CAN YOU HELP ME FIND MY LIBRARY BOOK?
GROAN! AGAIN?
OKAY, I'LL HELP YOU FIND YOUR STUPID LIBRARY BOOK.
HEY!
www.babyblues.com
SORRY.
KIRKMAN & SCOTT
© 2010, BABY BLUES PARTNERSHIP DIST. BY KING FEATURES SYNDICATE 3-6
OKAY, I'LL HELP YOU FIND YOUR LIBRARY BOOK, STUPID.
THAT'S BETTER.

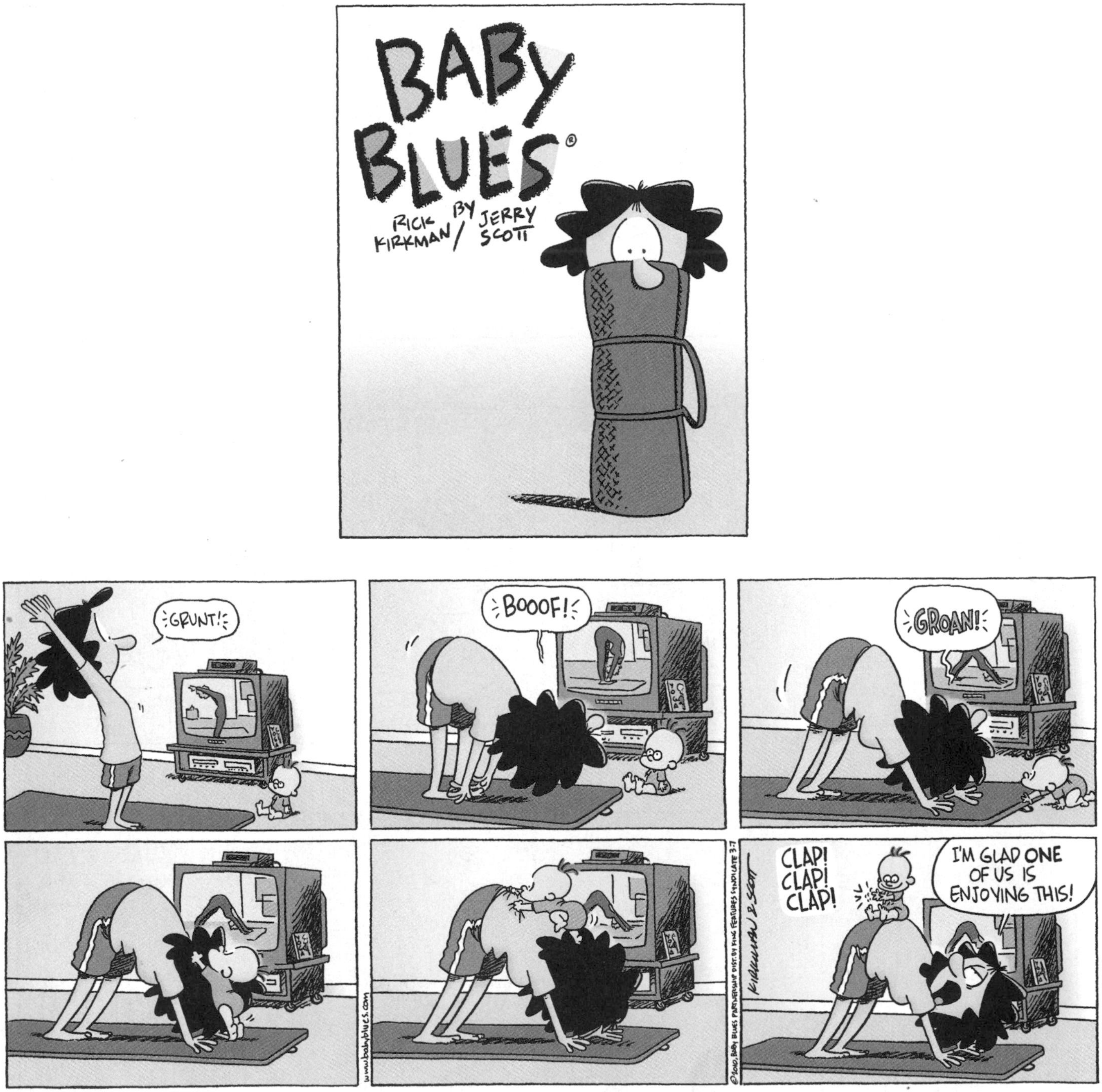

BABY BLUES®
BY RICK KIRKMAN / JERRY SCOTT
GRUNT!
BOOOF!
GROAN!
www.babyblues.com
CLAP! CLAP! CLAP!
I'M GLAD ONE OF US IS ENJOYING THIS!

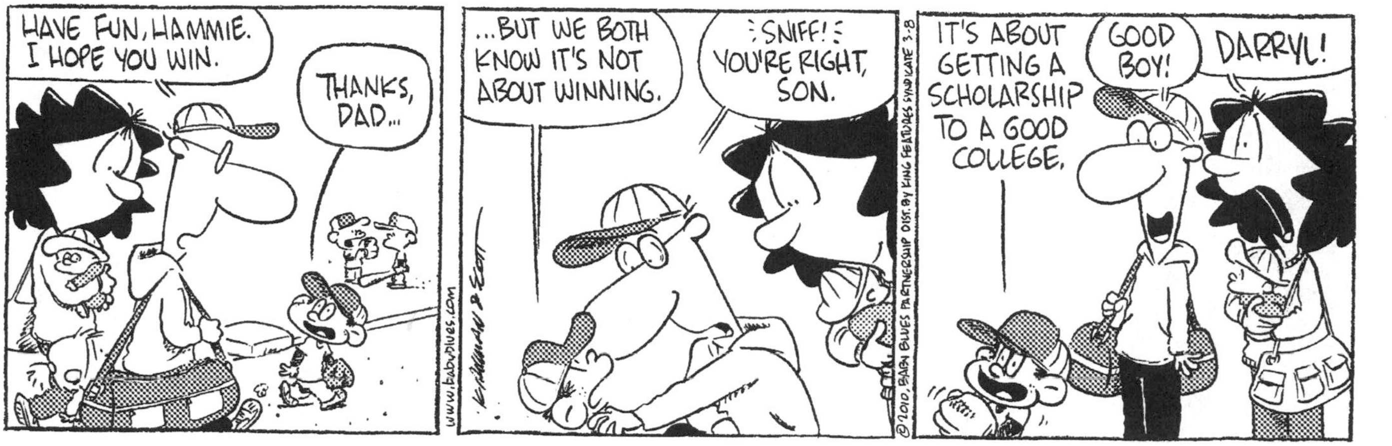
HAVE FUN, HAMMIE. I HOPE YOU WIN.
THANKS, DAD...
...BUT WE BOTH KNOW IT'S NOT ABOUT WINNING.
SNIFF! YOU'RE RIGHT, SON.
IT'S ABOUT GETTING A SCHOLARSHIP TO A GOOD COLLEGE.
GOOD BOY!
DARRYL!
www.babyblues.com
KIRKMAN & SCOTT
© 2010, BABY BLUES PARTNERSHIP DIST. BY KING FEATURES SYNDICATE 3-8

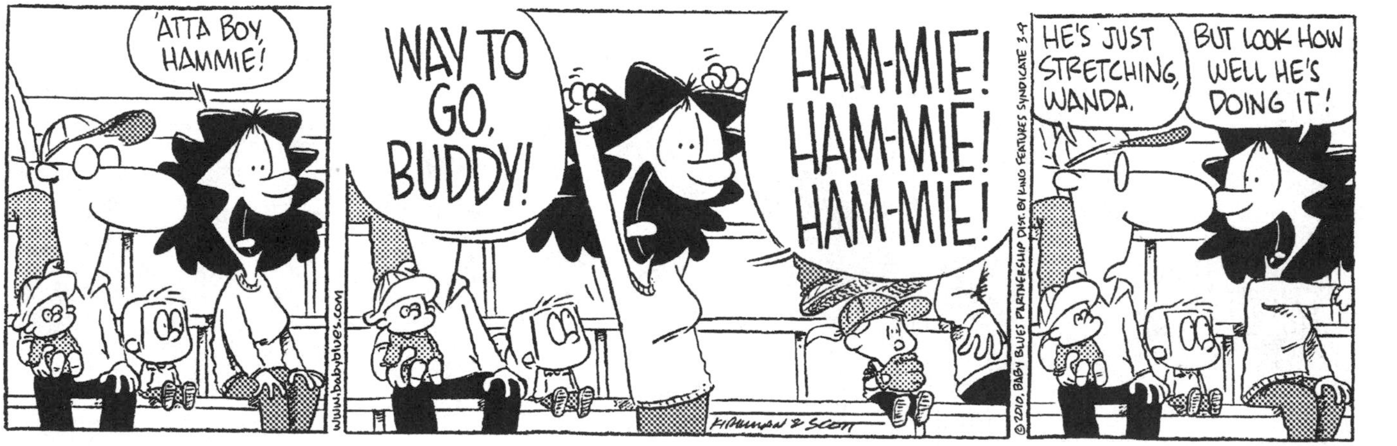
'ATTA BOY, HAMMIE!
WAY TO GO, BUDDY!
HAM-MIE! HAM-MIE! HAM-MIE!
HE'S JUST STRETCHING, WANDA.
BUT LOOK HOW WELL HE'S DOING IT!
www.babyblues.com
KIRKMAN & SCOTT
© 2010, BABY BLUES PARTNERSHIP DIST. BY KING FEATURES SYNDICATE 3-9

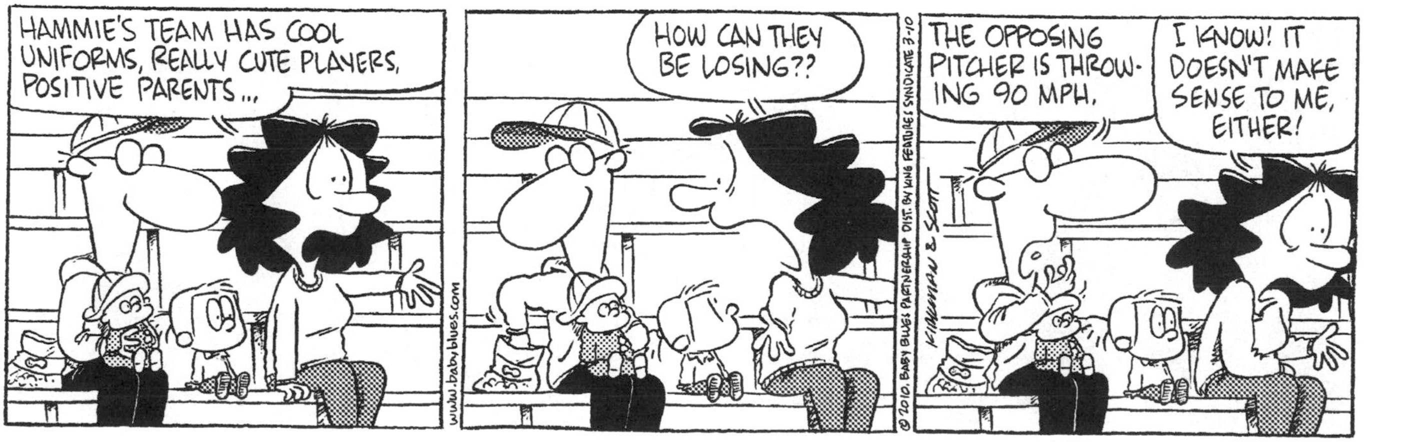
HAMMIE'S TEAM HAS COOL UNIFORMS, REALLY CUTE PLAYERS, POSITIVE PARENTS...
HOW CAN THEY BE LOSING??
THE OPPOSING PITCHER IS THROWING 90 MPH.
I KNOW! IT DOESN'T MAKE SENSE TO ME, EITHER!
www.babyblues.com
KIRKMAN & SCOTT
© 2010, BABY BLUES PARTNERSHIP DIST. BY KING FEATURES SYNDICATE 3-10

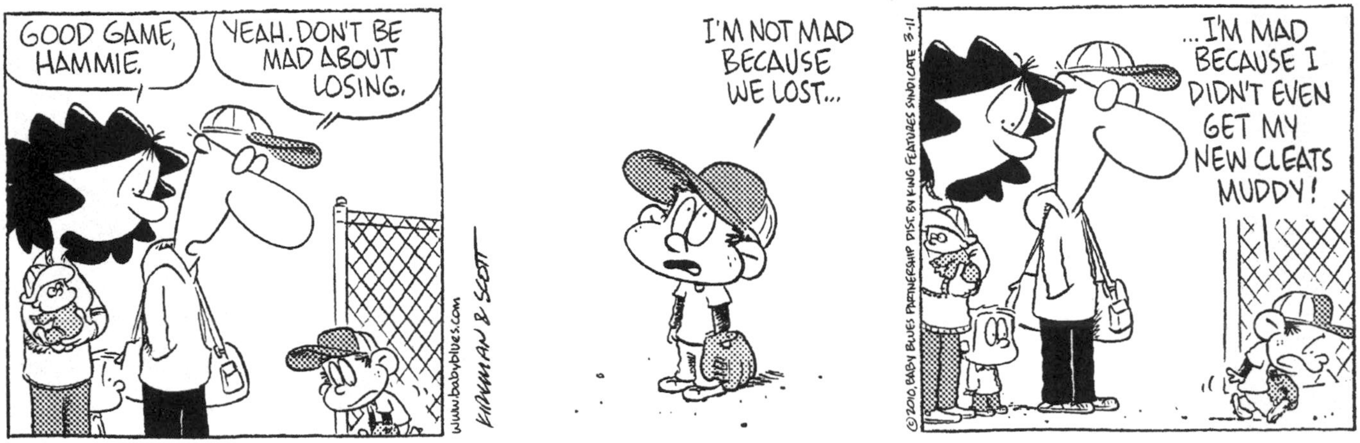
GOOD GAME, HAMMIE.
YEAH. DON'T BE MAD ABOUT LOSING.
www.babyblues.com
KIRKMAN & SCOTT
I'M NOT MAD BECAUSE WE LOST...
© 2010, BABY BLUES PARTNERSHIP DIST. BY KING FEATURES SYNDICATE 3-11
...I'M MAD BECAUSE I DIDN'T EVEN GET MY NEW CLEATS MUDDY!

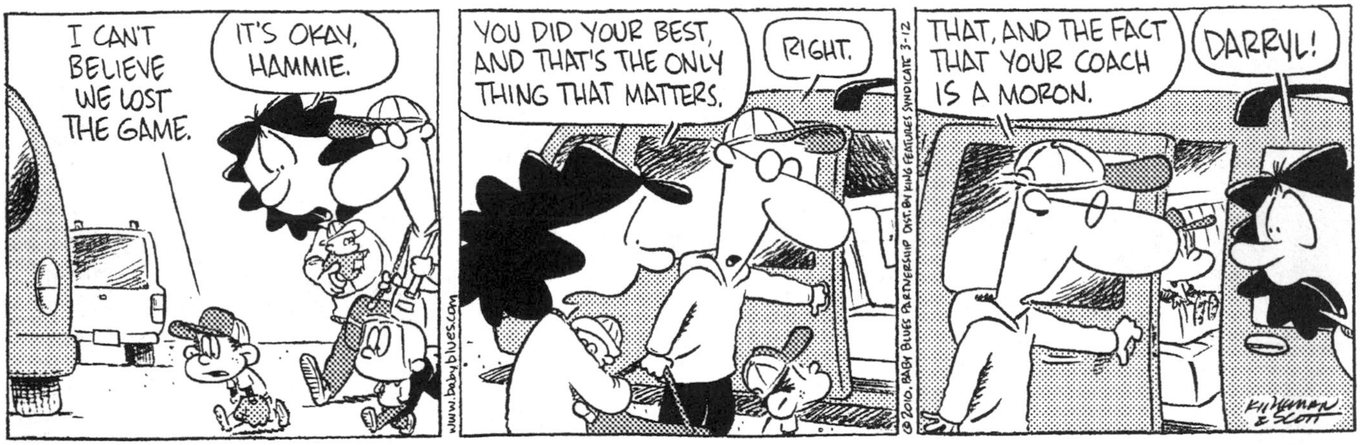
I CAN'T BELIEVE WE LOST THE GAME.
IT'S OKAY, HAMMIE.
www.babyblues.com
YOU DID YOUR BEST, AND THAT'S THE ONLY THING THAT MATTERS.
RIGHT.
© 2010, BABY BLUES PARTNERSHIP DIST. BY KING FEATURES SYNDICATE 3-12
THAT, AND THE FACT THAT YOUR COACH IS A MORON.
DARRYL!
KIRKMAN & SCOTT

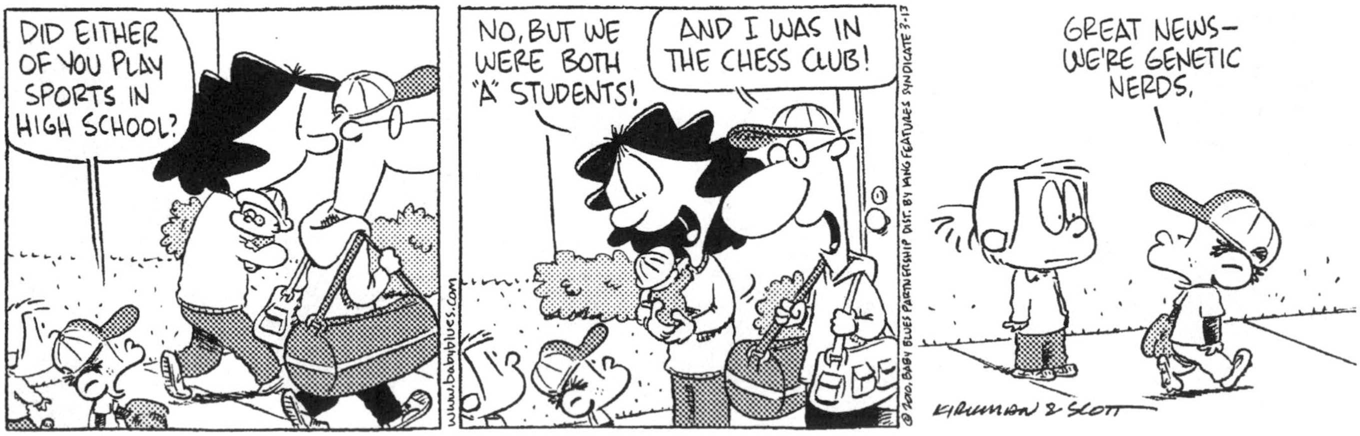
DID EITHER OF YOU PLAY SPORTS IN HIGH SCHOOL?
www.babyblues.com
NO, BUT WE WERE BOTH "A" STUDENTS!
AND I WAS IN THE CHESS CLUB!
© 2010, BABY BLUES PARTNERSHIP DIST. BY KING FEATURES SYNDICATE 3-13
GREAT NEWS— WE'RE GENETIC NERDS.
KIRKMAN & SCOTT

Rick Kirkman & Jerry Scott's
BABY BLUES®

ARE YOU OKAY, DARRYL?
YEAH. JUST THINKING.
HOW WOULD YOU FEEL ABOUT TAKING A YEAR OFF AND TRAVELING AROUND THE WORLD WITH THE KIDS?
WHAT?
THINK OF THE ADVENTURE! THINK OF THE FAMILY BONDING!
BRAAP! BRAAP! BRAAP!
I CAN'T HEAR YOU! I CAN'T HEAR YOU! I CAN'T HEAR YOU!
www.babyblues.com
BLORT!
©2010, BABY BLUES PARTNERSHIP DIST. BY KING FEATURES SYNDICATE
ON SECOND THOUGHT, JUST THINK OF THE ADVENTURE.
YEAH, I'LL DO IT WHILE I'M EXPLORING THE WONDERS OF SPOT-TREATING BARF STAINS.
KIRKMAN & SCOTT
3-14

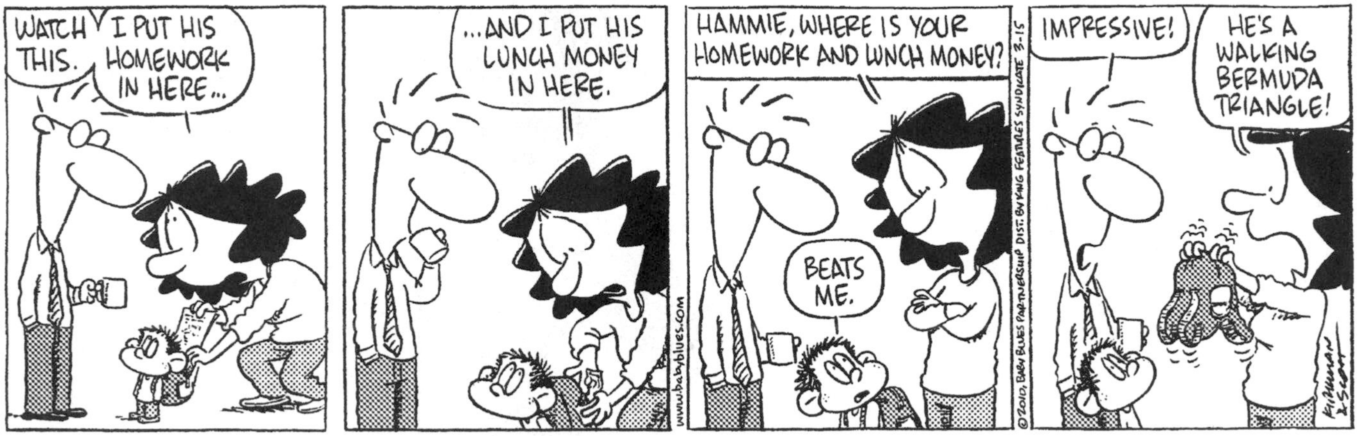
WATCH THIS.
I PUT HIS HOMEWORK IN HERE...
...AND I PUT HIS LUNCH MONEY IN HERE.
www.babyblues.com
HAMMIE, WHERE IS YOUR HOMEWORK AND LUNCH MONEY?
BEATS ME.
©2010, BABY BLUES PARTNERSHIP DIST. BY KING FEATURES SYNDICATE 3-15
IMPRESSIVE!
HE'S A WALKING BERMUDA TRIANGLE!
KIRKMAN & SCOTT

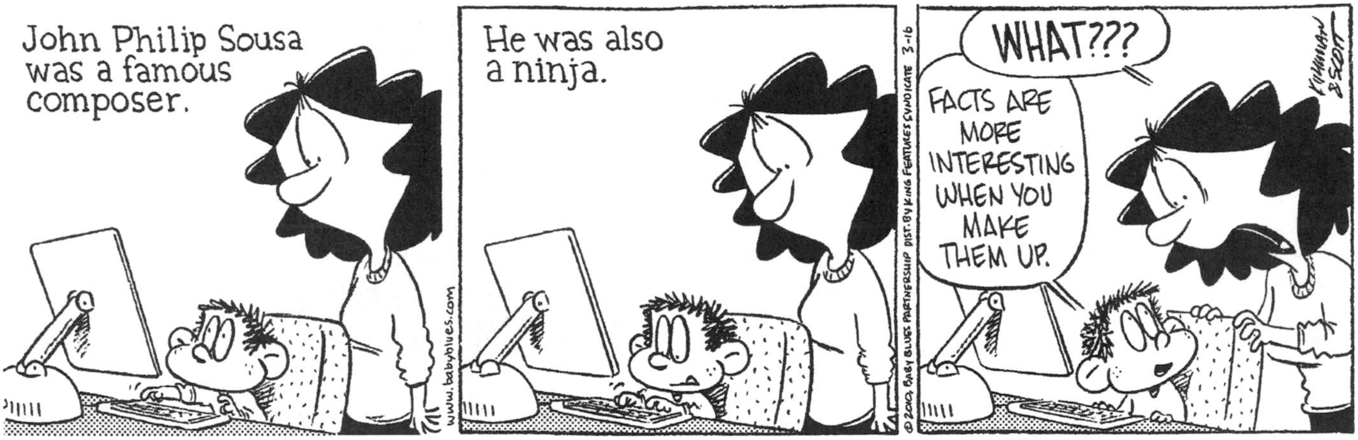
John Philip Sousa was a famous composer.
www.babyblues.com
He was also a ninja.
©2010, BABY BLUES PARTNERSHIP DIST. BY KING FEATURES SYNDICATE 3-16
WHAT???
FACTS ARE MORE INTERESTING WHEN YOU MAKE THEM UP.
KIRKMAN & SCOTT

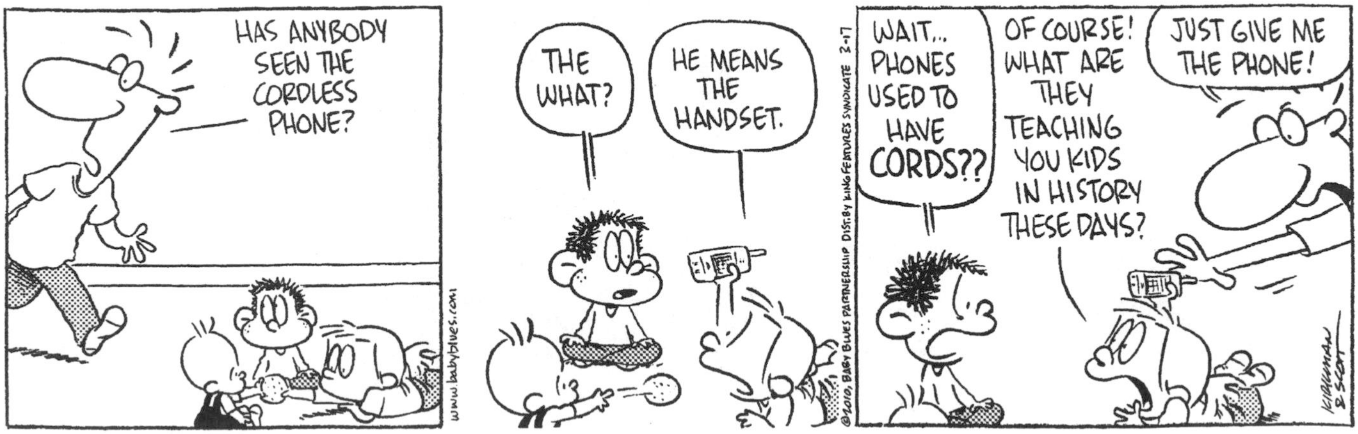
HAS ANYBODY SEEN THE CORDLESS PHONE?
www.babyblues.com
THE WHAT?
HE MEANS THE HANDSET.
©2010, BABY BLUES PARTNERSHIP DIST. BY KING FEATURES SYNDICATE 3-17
WAIT... PHONES USED TO HAVE CORDS??
OF COURSE! WHAT ARE THEY TEACHING YOU KIDS IN HISTORY THESE DAYS?
JUST GIVE ME THE PHONE!
KIRKMAN & SCOTT

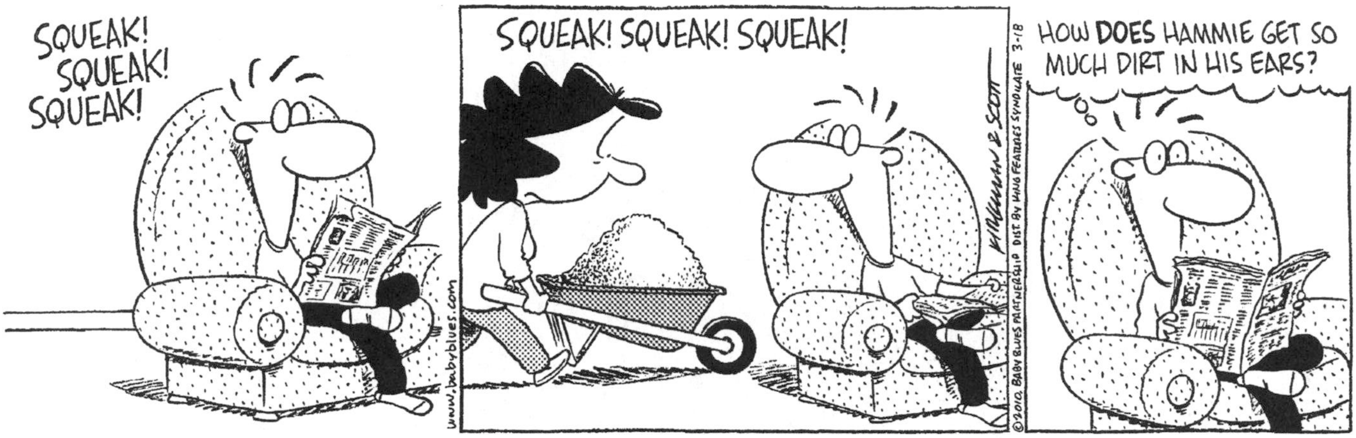
SQUEAK! SQUEAK! SQUEAK!
www.babyblues.com
SQUEAK! SQUEAK! SQUEAK!
KIRKMAN & SCOTT
©2010, BABY BLUES PARTNERSHIP DIST. BY KING FEATURES SYNDICATE 3-18
HOW **DOES** HAMMIE GET SO MUCH DIRT IN HIS EARS?

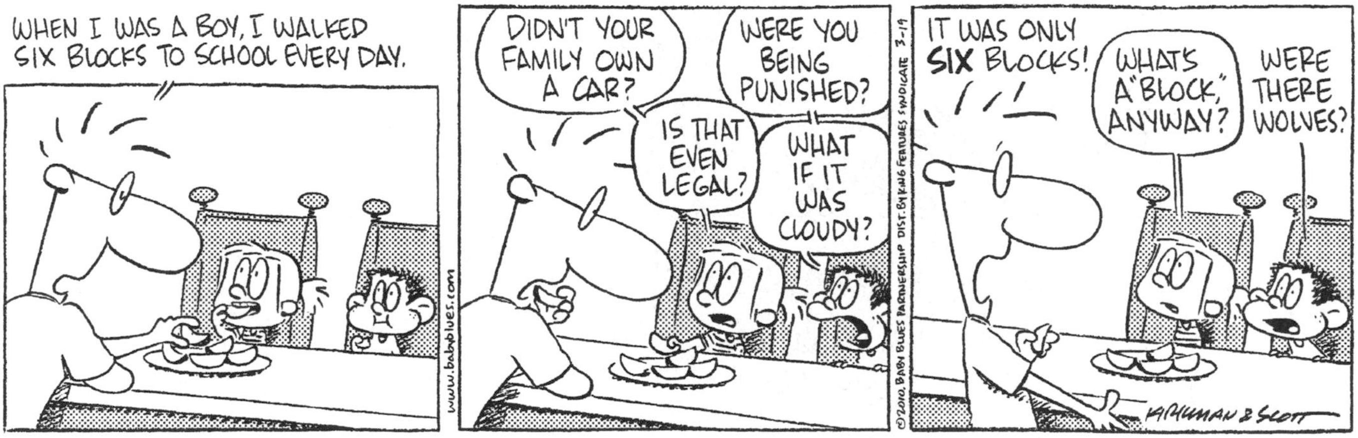
WHEN I WAS A BOY, I WALKED SIX BLOCKS TO SCHOOL EVERY DAY.
www.babyblues.com
DIDN'T YOUR FAMILY OWN A CAR?
WERE YOU BEING PUNISHED?
IS THAT EVEN LEGAL?
WHAT IF IT WAS CLOUDY?
©2010, BABY BLUES PARTNERSHIP DIST. BY KING FEATURES SYNDICATE 3-19
IT WAS ONLY **SIX** BLOCKS!
WHAT'S A "BLOCK," ANYWAY?
WERE THERE WOLVES?
KIRKMAN & SCOTT

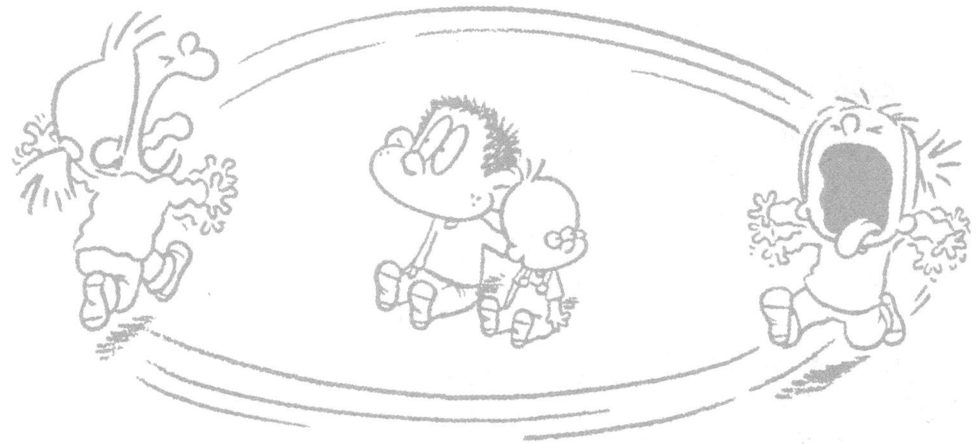

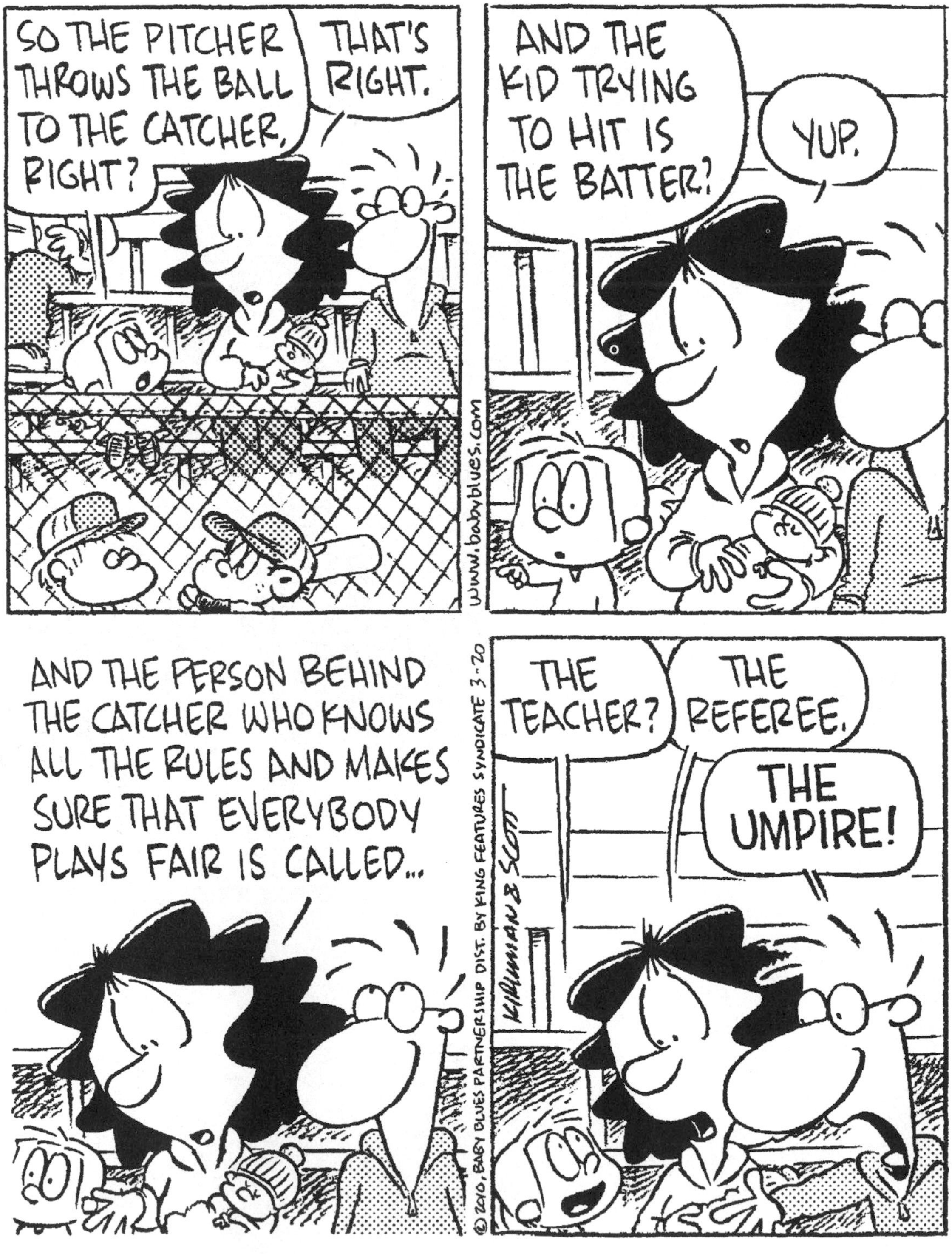
SO THE PITCHER THROWS THE BALL TO THE CATCHER, RIGHT?
THAT'S RIGHT.
AND THE KID TRYING TO HIT IS THE BATTER?
YUP.
AND THE PERSON BEHIND THE CATCHER WHO KNOWS ALL THE RULES AND MAKES SURE THAT EVERYBODY PLAYS FAIR IS CALLED...
THE TEACHER?
THE REFEREE.
THE UMPIRE!
www.babyblues.com
© 2010, BABY BLUES PARTNERSHIP DIST. BY KING FEATURES SYNDICATE 3-20
KIRKMAN & SCOTT

BABY BLUES®
BY RICK KIRKMAN / JERRY SCOTT

HEY HONEY, IF YOU'RE GOING TO THE KITCHEN, CAN YOU BRING ME A GLASS OF WATER?
SURE.
THERE.
PLUNK!
ARE YOU MAD?
KINDA.
ABOUT WHAT?
YOU'VE GOT TO BE KIDDING ME.
ABOUT WHAT?
GAAA! SOMETIMES YOU CAN BE SO CLUELESS!
KIRKMAN & SCOTT 3-21
www.babyblues.com
©2010 BABY BLUES PARTNERSHIP DIST. BY KING FEATURES SYNDICATE
ABOUT WHAT?

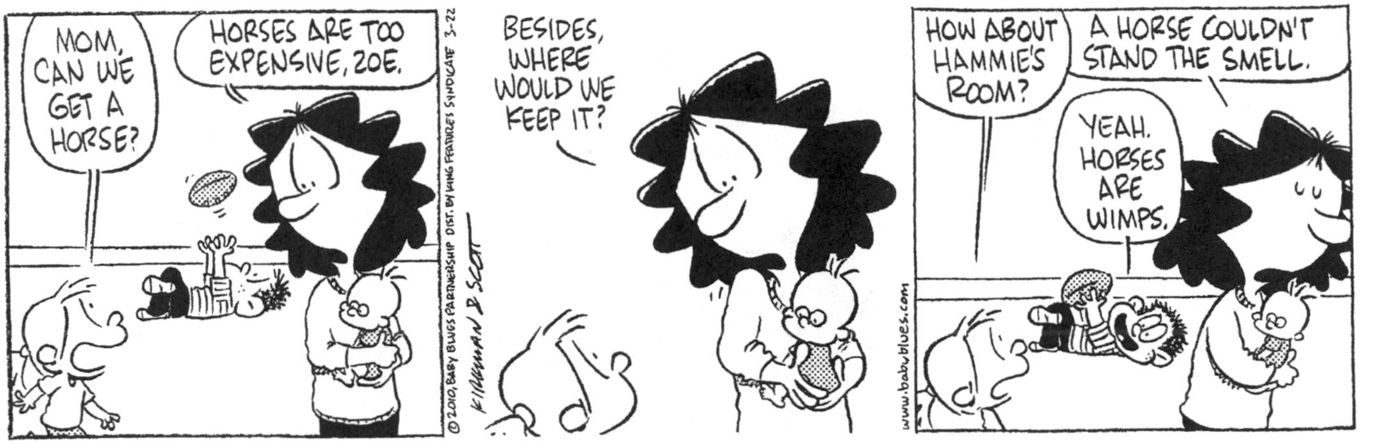
MOM, CAN WE GET A HORSE?
HORSES ARE TOO EXPENSIVE, ZOE.
© 2010, BABY BLUES PARTNERSHIP DIST. BY KING FEATURES SYNDICATE 3-22
KIRKMAN & SCOTT
BESIDES, WHERE WOULD WE KEEP IT?
HOW ABOUT HAMMIE'S ROOM?
A HORSE COULDN'T STAND THE SMELL.
YEAH. HORSES ARE WIMPS.
www.babyblues.com

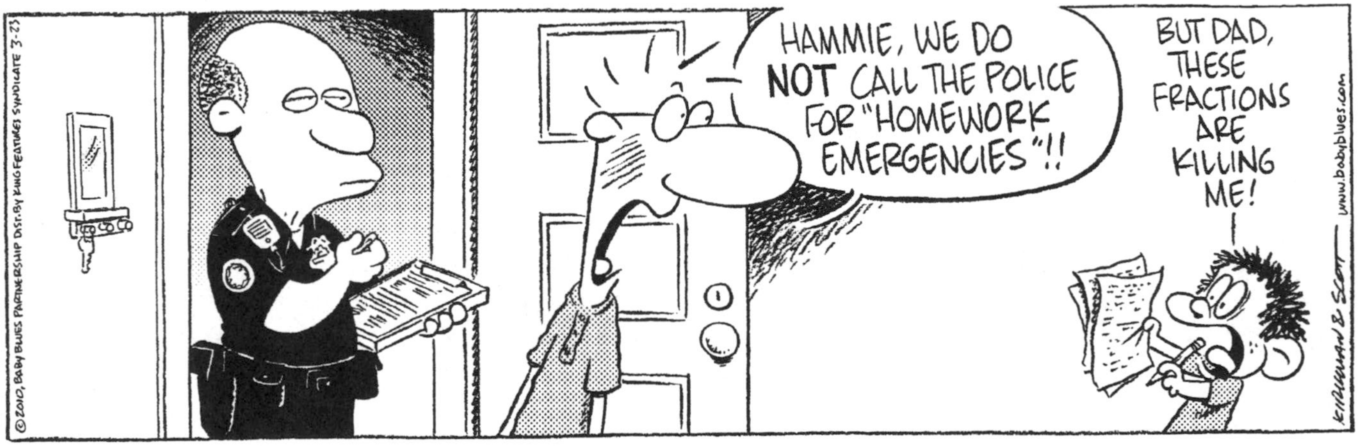
© 2010, BABY BLUES PARTNERSHIP DIST. BY KING FEATURES SYNDICATE 3-23
HAMMIE, WE DO **NOT** CALL THE POLICE FOR "HOMEWORK EMERGENCIES"!!
BUT DAD, THESE FRACTIONS ARE KILLING ME!
KIRKMAN & SCOTT
www.babyblues.com

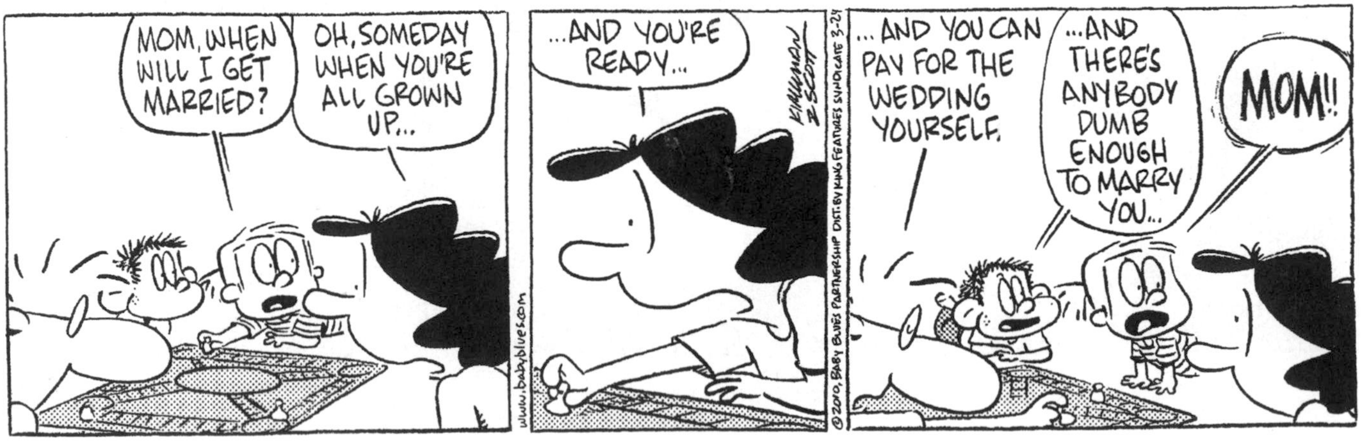
MOM, WHEN WILL I GET MARRIED?
OH, SOMEDAY WHEN YOU'RE ALL GROWN UP...
www.babyblues.com
...AND YOU'RE READY...
KIRKMAN & SCOTT
© 2010, BABY BLUES PARTNERSHIP DIST. BY KING FEATURES SYNDICATE 3-24
...AND YOU CAN PAY FOR THE WEDDING YOURSELF.
...AND THERE'S ANYBODY DUMB ENOUGH TO MARRY YOU...
MOM!!

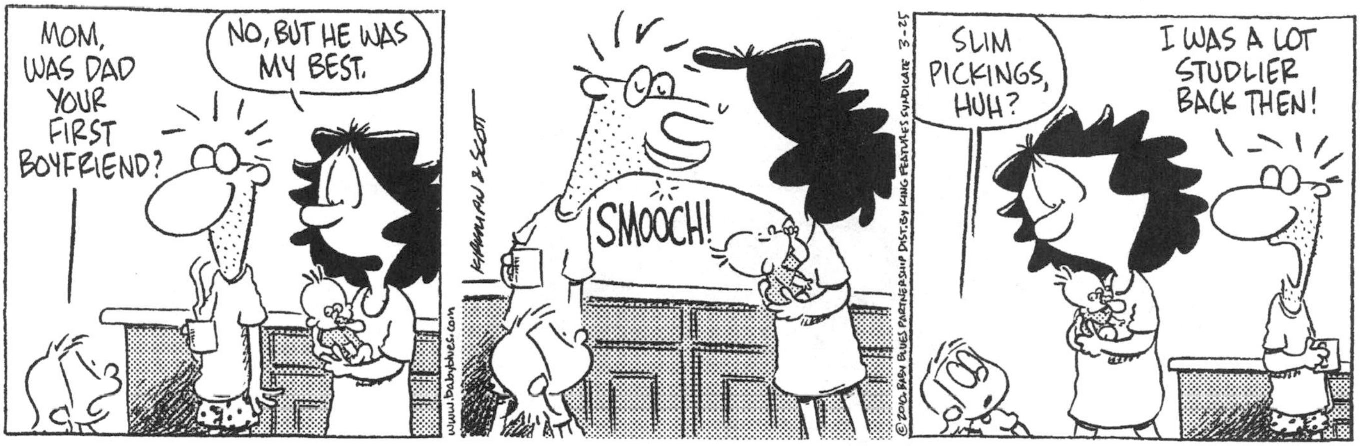
MOM, WAS DAD YOUR FIRST BOYFRIEND?
NO, BUT HE WAS MY BEST.
www.babyblues.com
KIRKMAN & SCOTT
SMOOCH!
©2010, BABY BLUES PARTNERSHIP DIST. BY KING FEATURES SYNDICATE 3-25
SLIM PICKINGS, HUH?
I WAS A LOT STUDLIER BACK THEN!

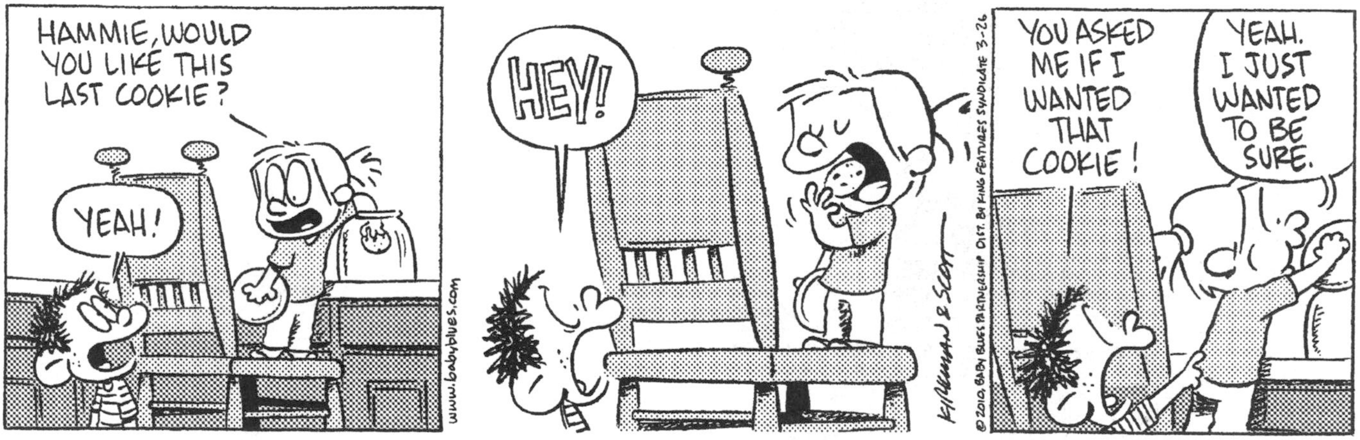
HAMMIE, WOULD YOU LIKE THIS LAST COOKIE?
YEAH!
www.babyblues.com
HEY!
KIRKMAN & SCOTT
©2010, BABY BLUES PARTNERSHIP DIST. BY KING FEATURES SYNDICATE 3-26
YOU ASKED ME IF I WANTED THAT COOKIE!
YEAH. I JUST WANTED TO BE SURE.

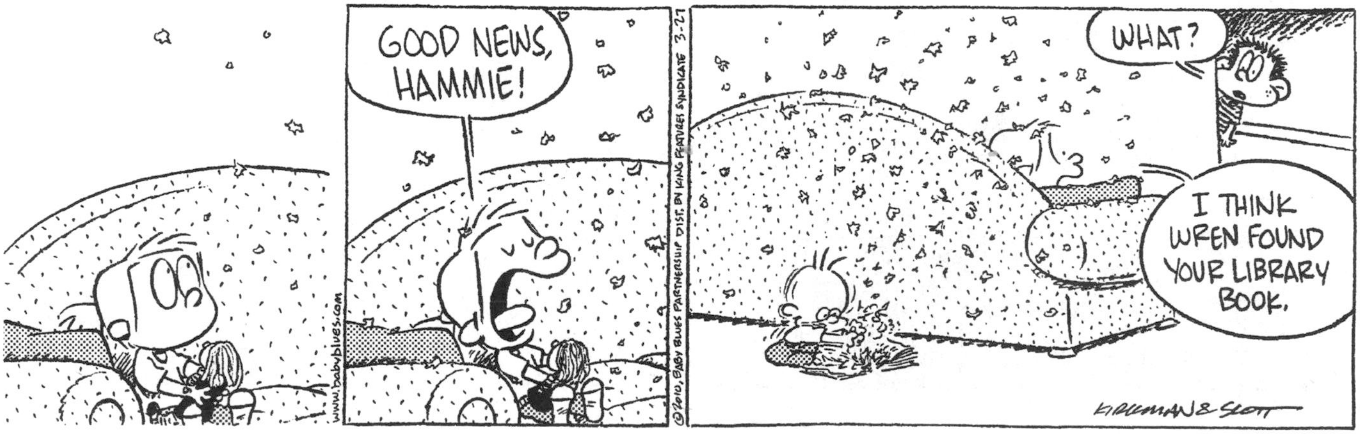
www.babyblues.com
GOOD NEWS, HAMMIE!
©2010, BABY BLUES PARTNERSHIP DIST. BY KING FEATURES SYNDICATE 3-27
WHAT?
I THINK WREN FOUND YOUR LIBRARY BOOK.
KIRKMAN & SCOTT

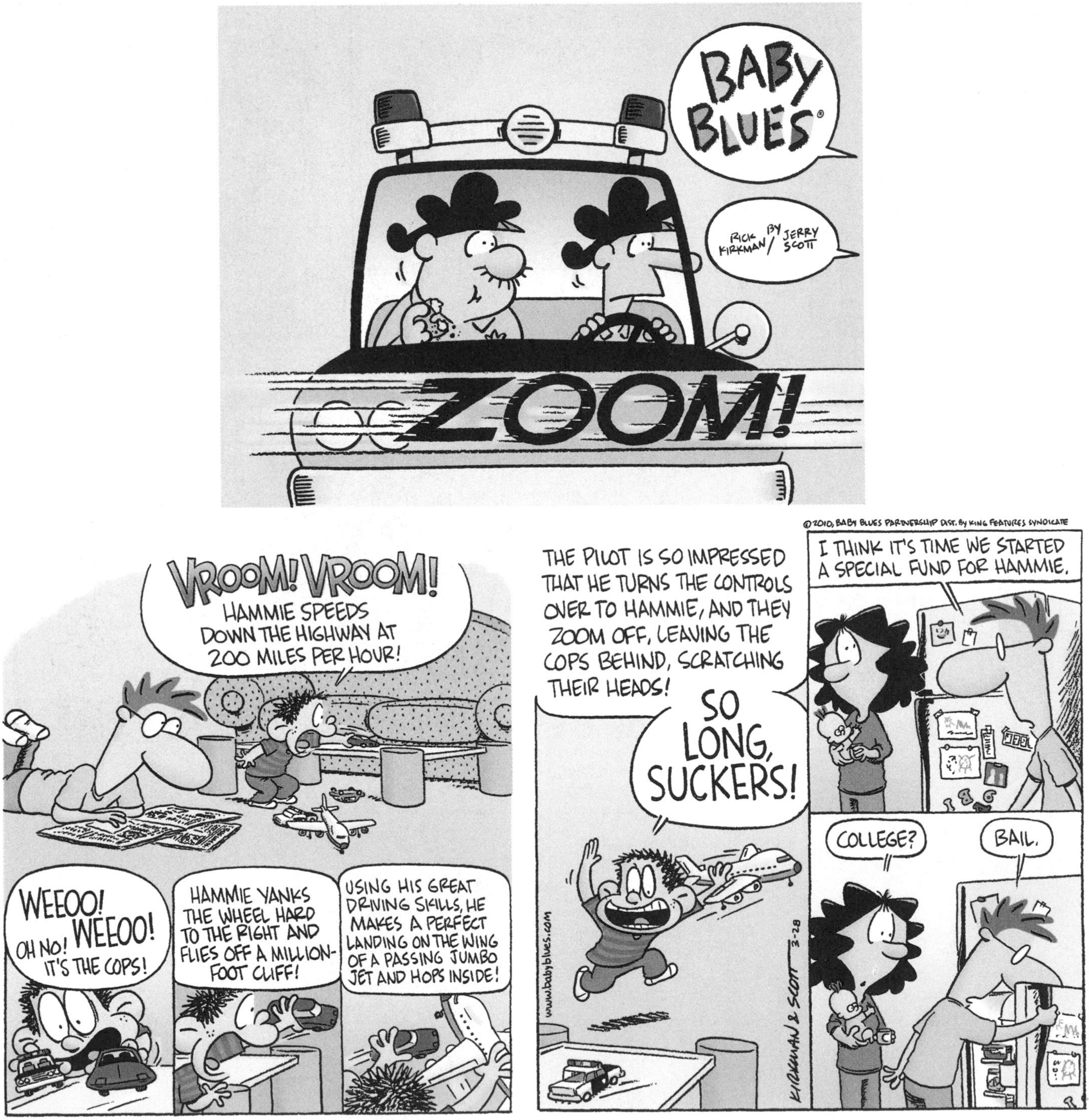
BABY BLUES®
BY RICK KIRKMAN / JERRY SCOTT
ZOOM!
VROOM! VROOM! HAMMIE SPEEDS DOWN THE HIGHWAY AT 200 MILES PER HOUR!
WEEOO! WEEOO! OH NO! IT'S THE COPS!
HAMMIE YANKS THE WHEEL HARD TO THE RIGHT AND FLIES OFF A MILLION-FOOT CLIFF!
USING HIS GREAT DRIVING SKILLS, HE MAKES A PERFECT LANDING ON THE WING OF A PASSING JUMBO JET AND HOPS INSIDE!
THE PILOT IS SO IMPRESSED THAT HE TURNS THE CONTROLS OVER TO HAMMIE, AND THEY ZOOM OFF, LEAVING THE COPS BEHIND, SCRATCHING THEIR HEADS!
SO LONG, SUCKERS!
www.babyblues.com
KIRKMAN & SCOTT 3-28
©2010, BABY BLUES PARTNERSHIP DIST. BY KING FEATURES SYNDICATE
I THINK IT'S TIME WE STARTED A SPECIAL FUND FOR HAMMIE.
COLLEGE?
BAIL.

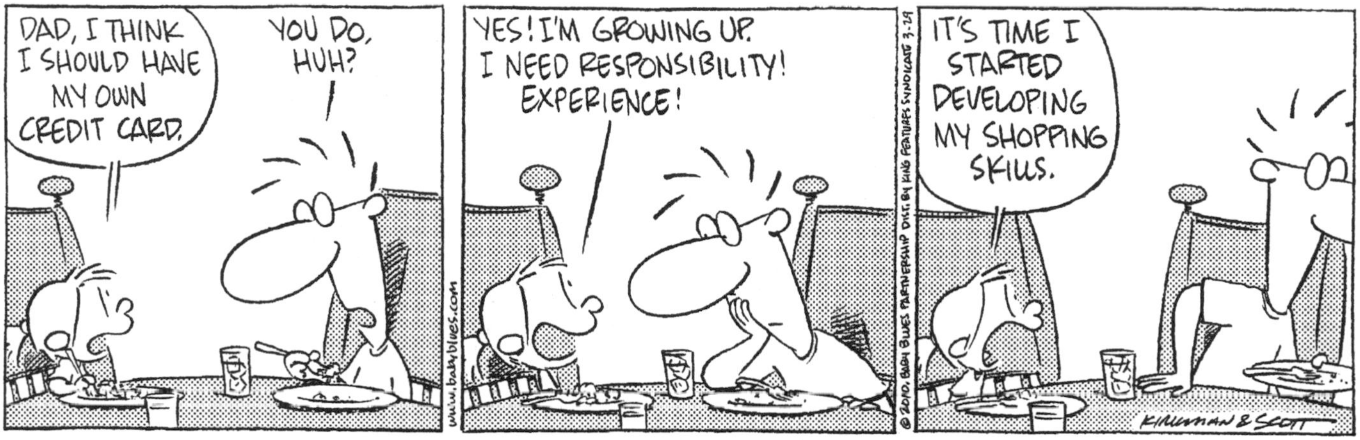
DAD, I THINK I SHOULD HAVE MY OWN CREDIT CARD.
YOU DO, HUH?
YES! I'M GROWING UP. I NEED RESPONSIBILITY! EXPERIENCE!
IT'S TIME I STARTED DEVELOPING MY SHOPPING SKILLS.
www.babyblues.com
© 2010, BABY BLUES PARTNERSHIP DIST. BY KING FEATURES SYNDICATE 3-29
KIRKMAN & SCOTT

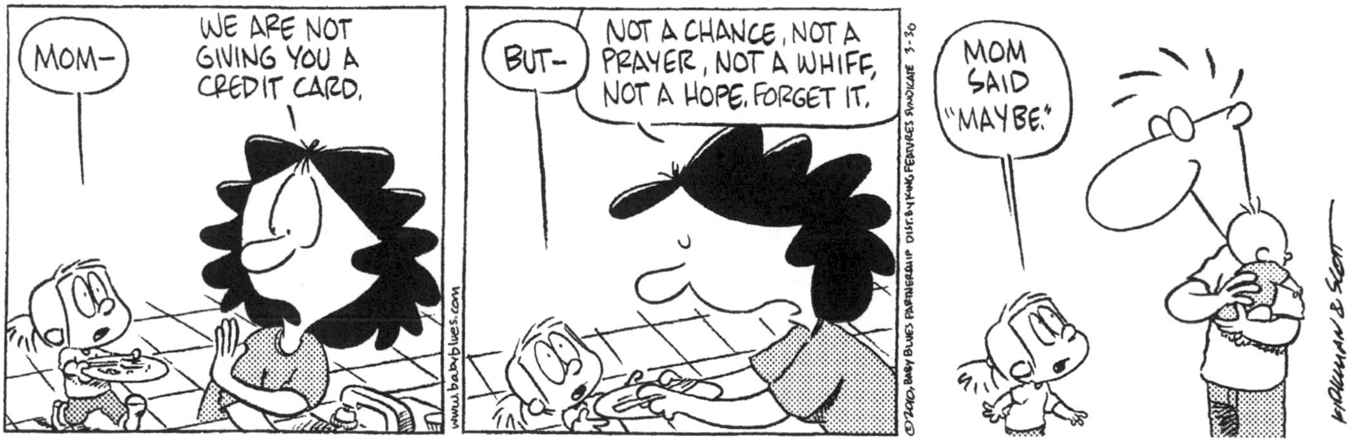
MOM-
WE ARE NOT GIVING YOU A CREDIT CARD.
BUT-
NOT A CHANCE, NOT A PRAYER, NOT A WHIFF, NOT A HOPE. FORGET IT.
MOM SAID "MAYBE."
www.babyblues.com
© 2010, BABY BLUES PARTNERSHIP DIST. BY KING FEATURES SYNDICATE 3-30
KIRKMAN & SCOTT

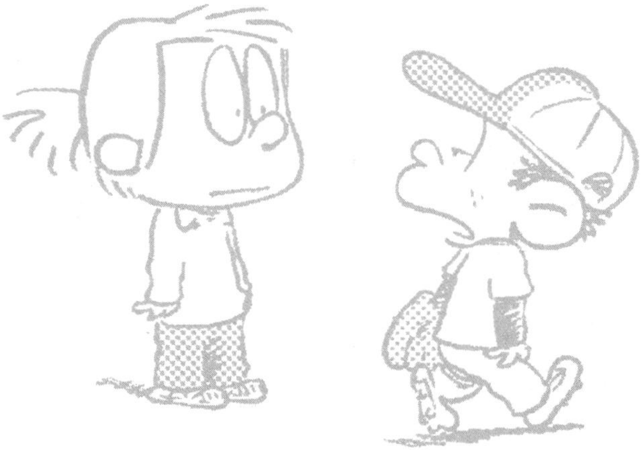

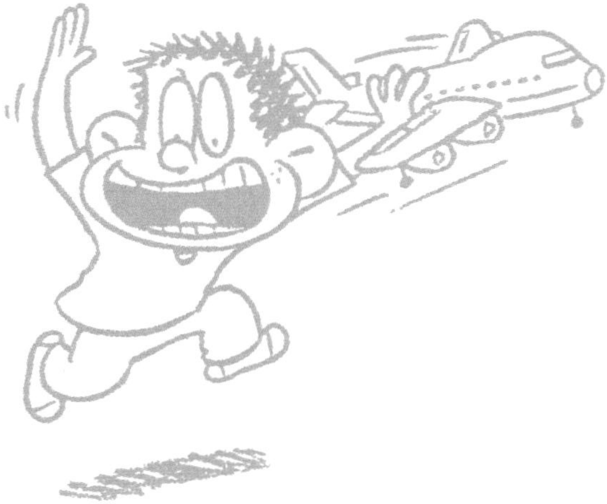

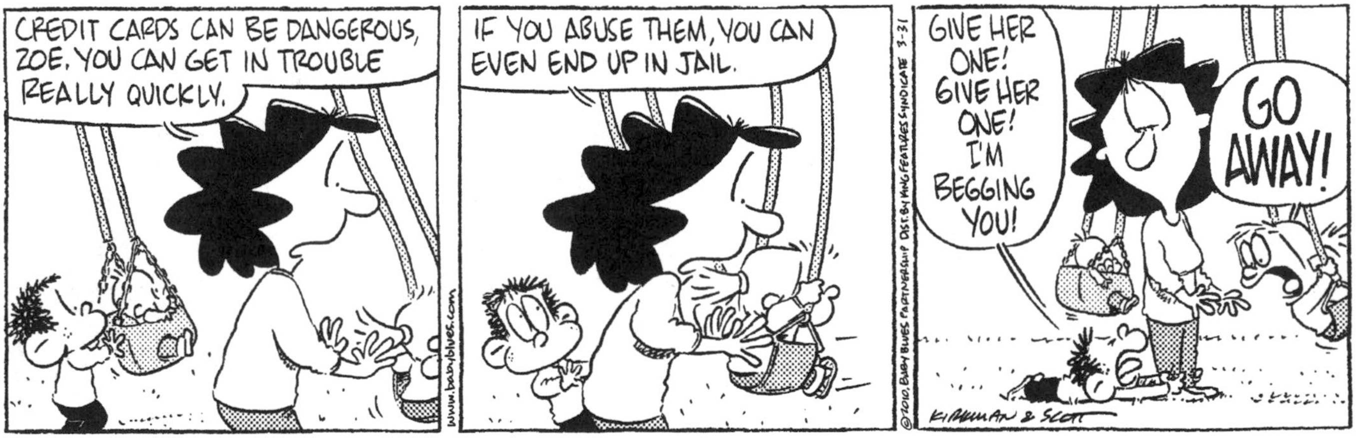

CREDIT CARDS CAN BE DANGEROUS, ZOE. YOU CAN GET IN TROUBLE REALLY QUICKLY.
www.babyblues.com
IF YOU ABUSE THEM, YOU CAN EVEN END UP IN JAIL.
©2010, BABY BLUES PARTNERSHIP DIST. BY KING FEATURES SYNDICATE 3-31
GIVE HER ONE! GIVE HER ONE! I'M BEGGING YOU!
GO AWAY!
KIRKMAN & SCOTT

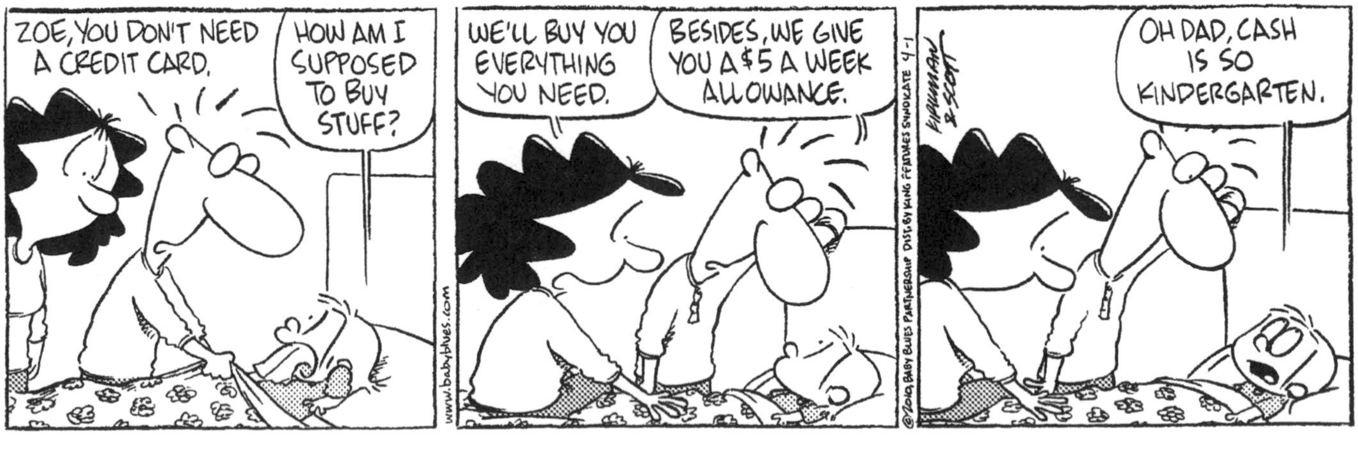

ZOE, YOU DON'T NEED A CREDIT CARD.
HOW AM I SUPPOSED TO BUY STUFF?
www.babyblues.com
WE'LL BUY YOU EVERYTHING YOU NEED.
BESIDES, WE GIVE YOU A $5 A WEEK ALLOWANCE.
©2010, BABY BLUES PARTNERSHIP DIST. BY KING FEATURES SYNDICATE 4-1
KIRKMAN & SCOTT
OH DAD, CASH IS SO KINDERGARTEN.

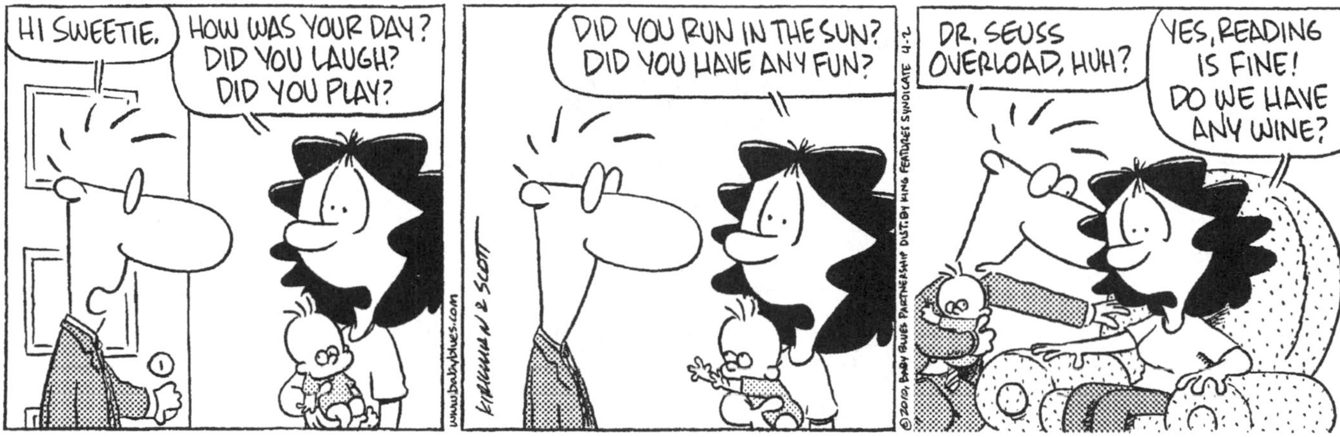
HI SWEETIE.
HOW WAS YOUR DAY? DID YOU LAUGH? DID YOU PLAY?
www.babyblues.com
KIRKMAN & SCOTT
DID YOU RUN IN THE SUN? DID YOU HAVE ANY FUN?
©2010, BABY BLUES PARTNERSHIP DIST. BY KING FEATURES SYNDICATE 4-2
DR. SEUSS OVERLOAD, HUH?
YES, READING IS FINE! DO WE HAVE ANY WINE?

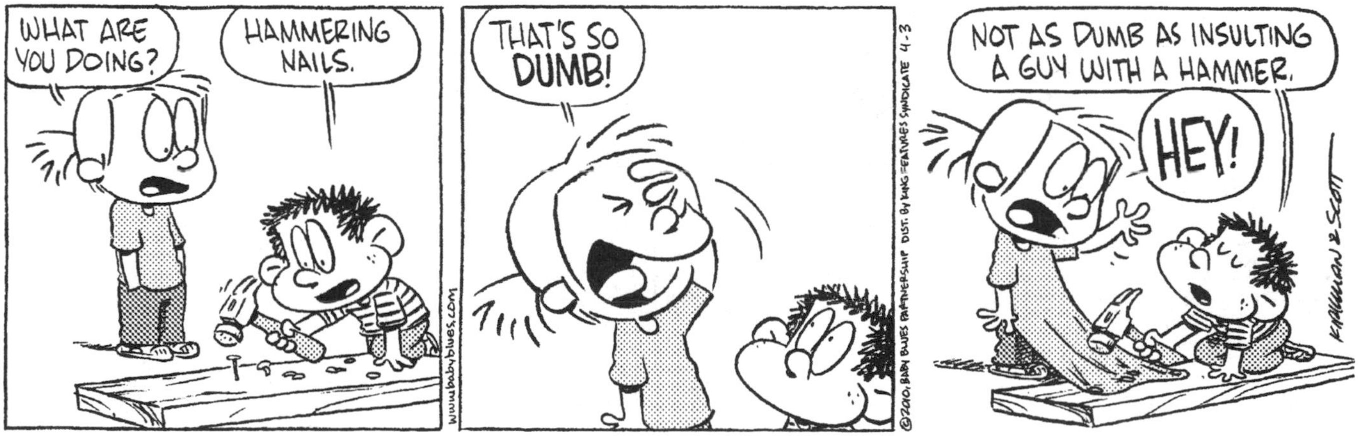
WHAT ARE YOU DOING?
HAMMERING NAILS.
www.babyblues.com
THAT'S SO DUMB!
©2010, BABY BLUES PARTNERSHIP DIST. BY KING FEATURES SYNDICATE 4-3
NOT AS DUMB AS INSULTING A GUY WITH A HAMMER.
HEY!
KIRKMAN & SCOTT

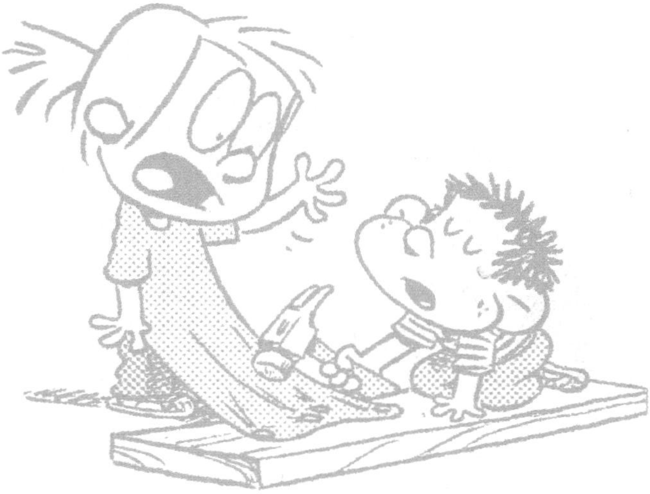

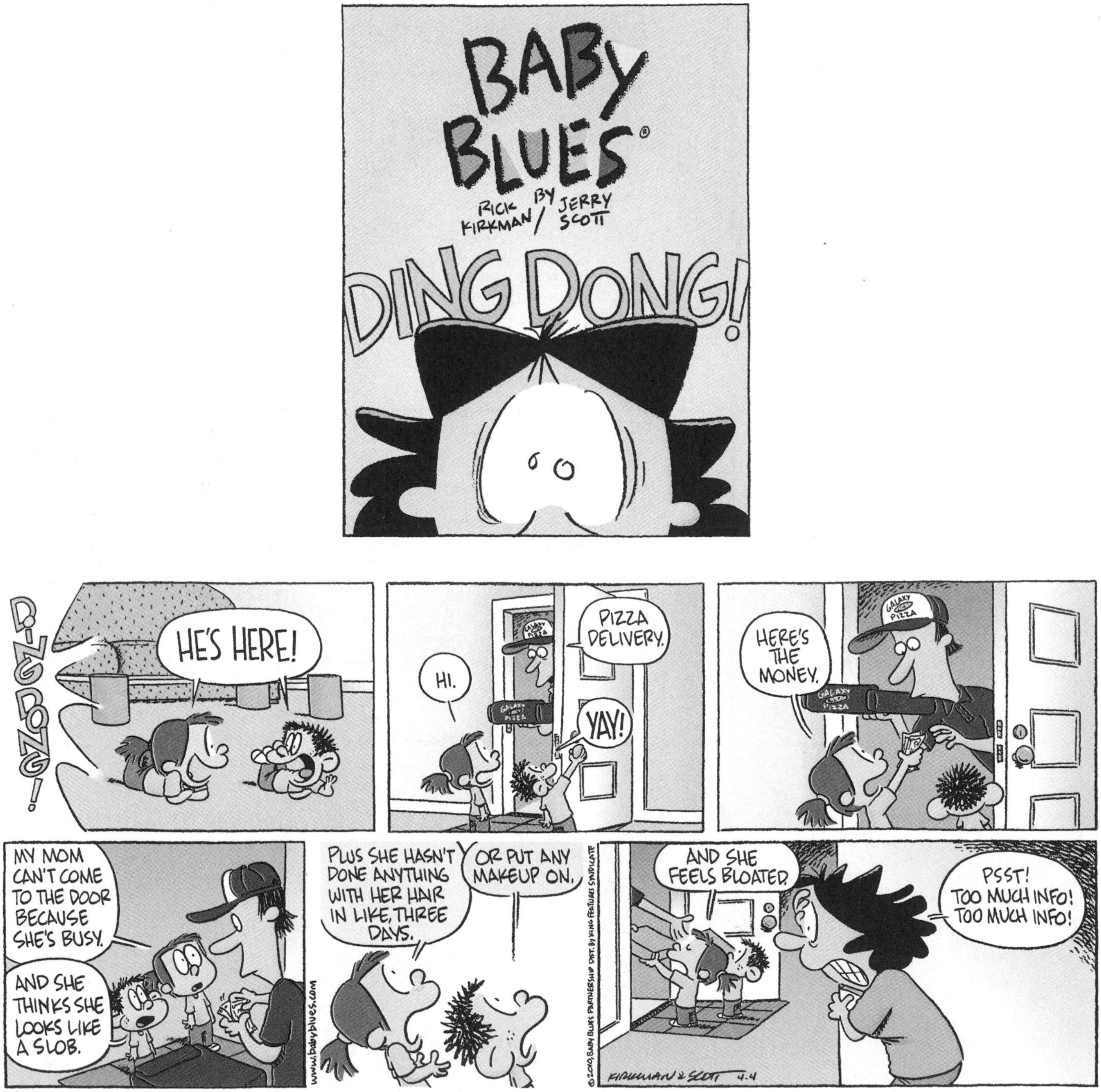
BABY BLUES®
BY RICK KIRKMAN / JERRY SCOTT
DING DONG!
DING DONG!
HE'S HERE!
HI.
PIZZA DELIVERY.
YAY!
HERE'S THE MONEY.
MY MOM CAN'T COME TO THE DOOR BECAUSE SHE'S BUSY.
AND SHE THINKS SHE LOOKS LIKE A SLOB.
www.babyblues.com
PLUS SHE HASN'T DONE ANYTHING WITH HER HAIR IN LIKE, THREE DAYS.
OR PUT ANY MAKEUP ON.
©2010, BABY BLUES PARTNERSHIP DIST. BY KING FEATURES SYNDICATE
AND SHE FEELS BLOATED.
PSST! TOO MUCH INFO! TOO MUCH INFO!
KIRKMAN & SCOTT 4-4

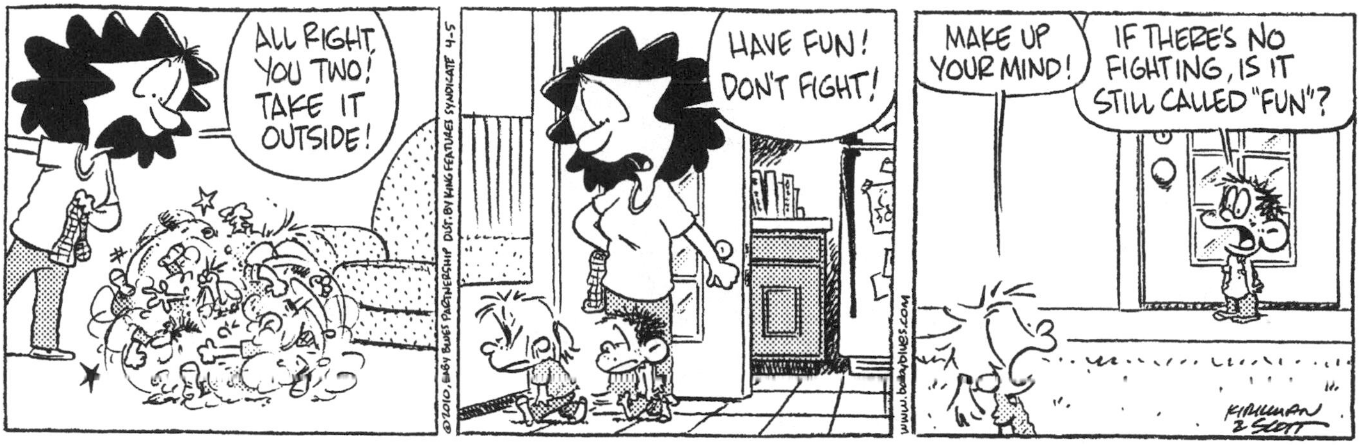
ALL RIGHT, YOU TWO! TAKE IT OUTSIDE!
©2010, BABY BLUES PARTNERSHIP DIST. BY KING FEATURES SYNDICATE 4-5
HAVE FUN! DON'T FIGHT!
www.babyblues.com
MAKE UP YOUR MIND!
IF THERE'S NO FIGHTING, IS IT STILL CALLED "FUN"?
KIRKMAN & SCOTT

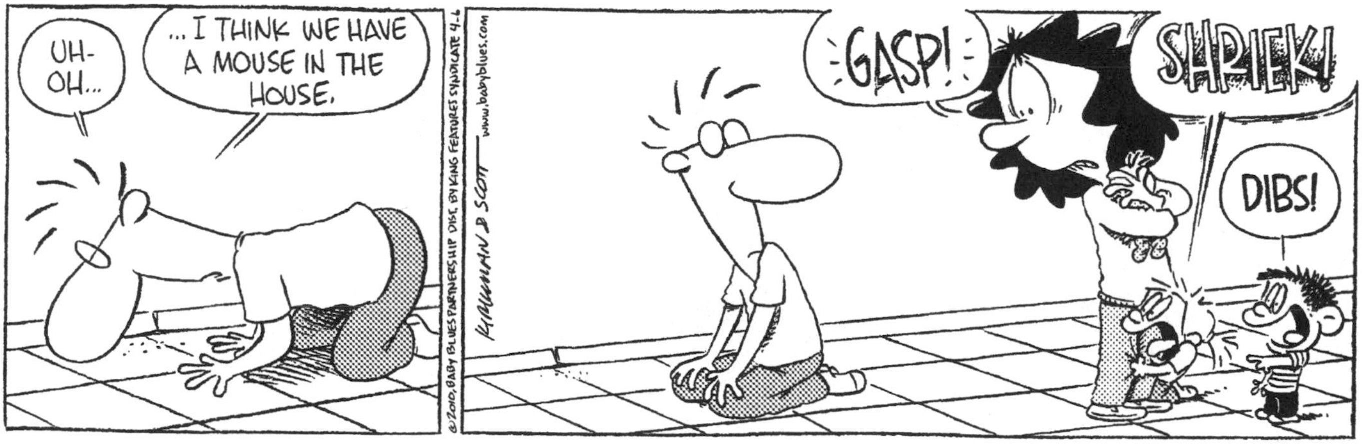
UH-OH...
...I THINK WE HAVE A MOUSE IN THE HOUSE.
©2010, BABY BLUES PARTNERSHIP DIST. BY KING FEATURES SYNDICATE 4-6
KIRKMAN & SCOTT
www.babyblues.com
GASP!
SHRIEK!
DIBS!

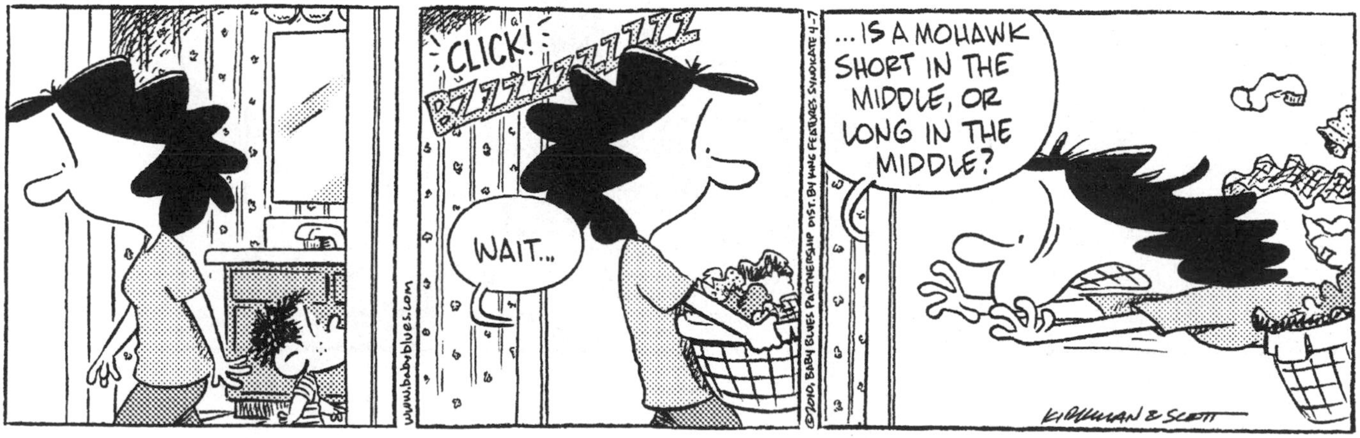
www.babyblues.com
CLICK!
BZZZZZZZZZZZ
WAIT...
©2010, BABY BLUES PARTNERSHIP DIST. BY KING FEATURES SYNDICATE 4-7
...IS A MOHAWK SHORT IN THE MIDDLE, OR LONG IN THE MIDDLE?
KIRKMAN & SCOTT

JUST REMEMBER, WREN, MOST THINGS ARE HARD BEFORE THEY'RE EASY.

KIRKMAN & SCOTT — 4-8

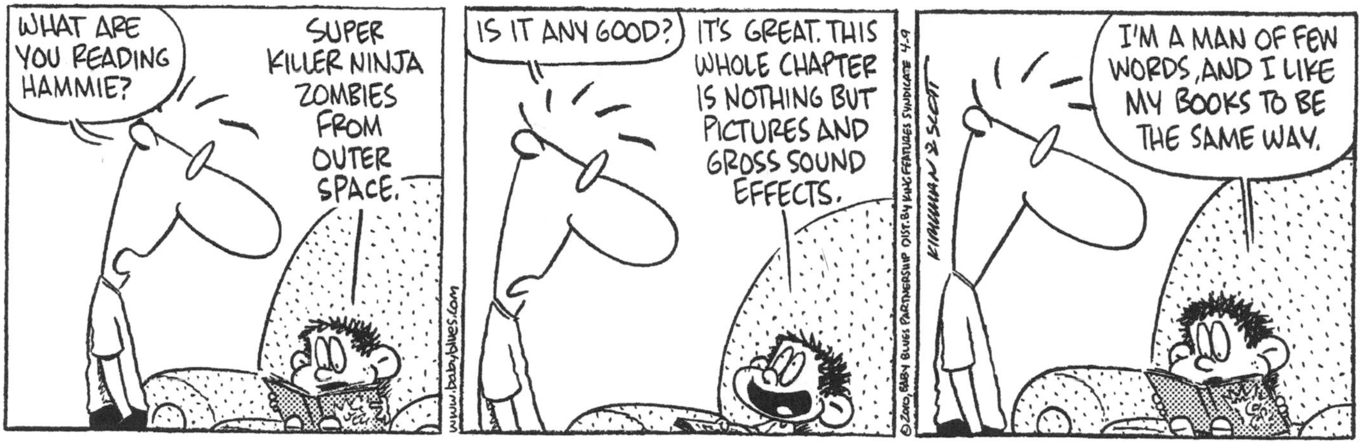
WHAT ARE YOU READING HAMMIE?
SUPER KILLER NINJA ZOMBIES FROM OUTER SPACE.
www.babyblues.com
IS IT ANY GOOD?
IT'S GREAT. THIS WHOLE CHAPTER IS NOTHING BUT PICTURES AND GROSS SOUND EFFECTS.
©2010, BABY BLUES PARTNERSHIP DIST. BY KING FEATURES SYNDICATE 4-9
KIRKMAN & SCOTT
I'M A MAN OF FEW WORDS, AND I LIKE MY BOOKS TO BE THE SAME WAY.

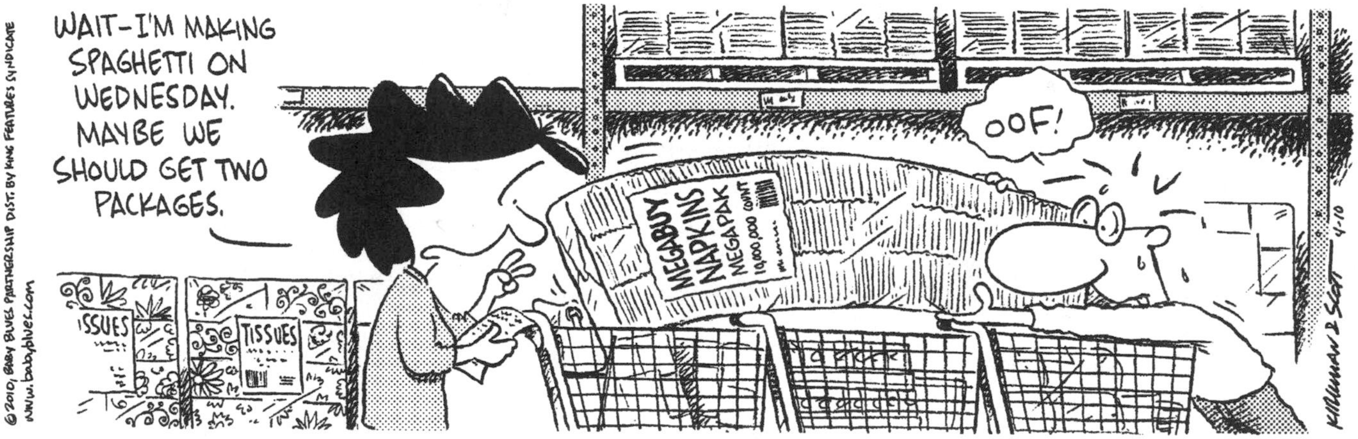
©2010, BABY BLUES PARTNERSHIP DIST. BY KING FEATURES SYNDICATE
www.babyblues.com
WAIT- I'M MAKING SPAGHETTI ON WEDNESDAY. MAYBE WE SHOULD GET TWO PACKAGES.
OOF!
MEGABUY NAPKINS MEGAPAK 10,000,000 COUNT
TISSUES
4-10
KIRKMAN & SCOTT

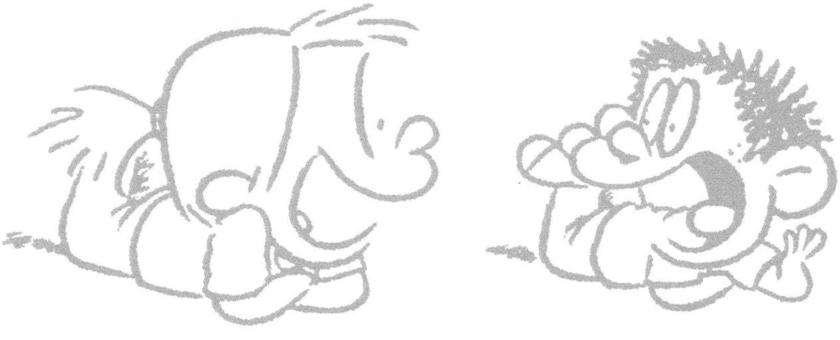

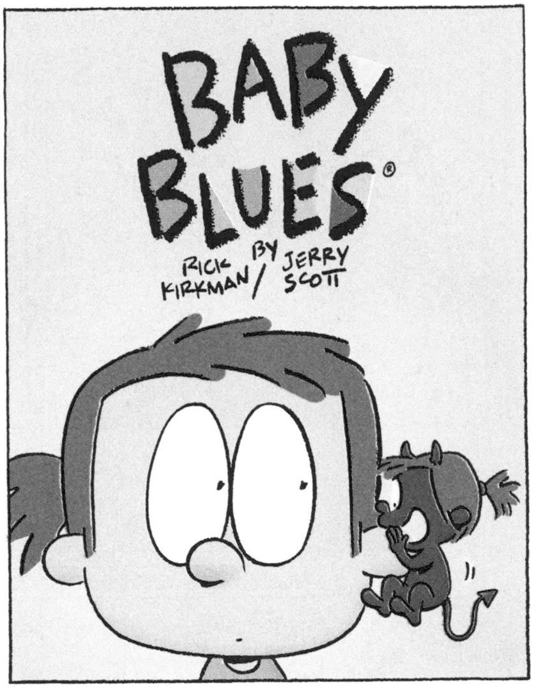
BABY BLUES®
BY RICK KIRKMAN / JERRY SCOTT

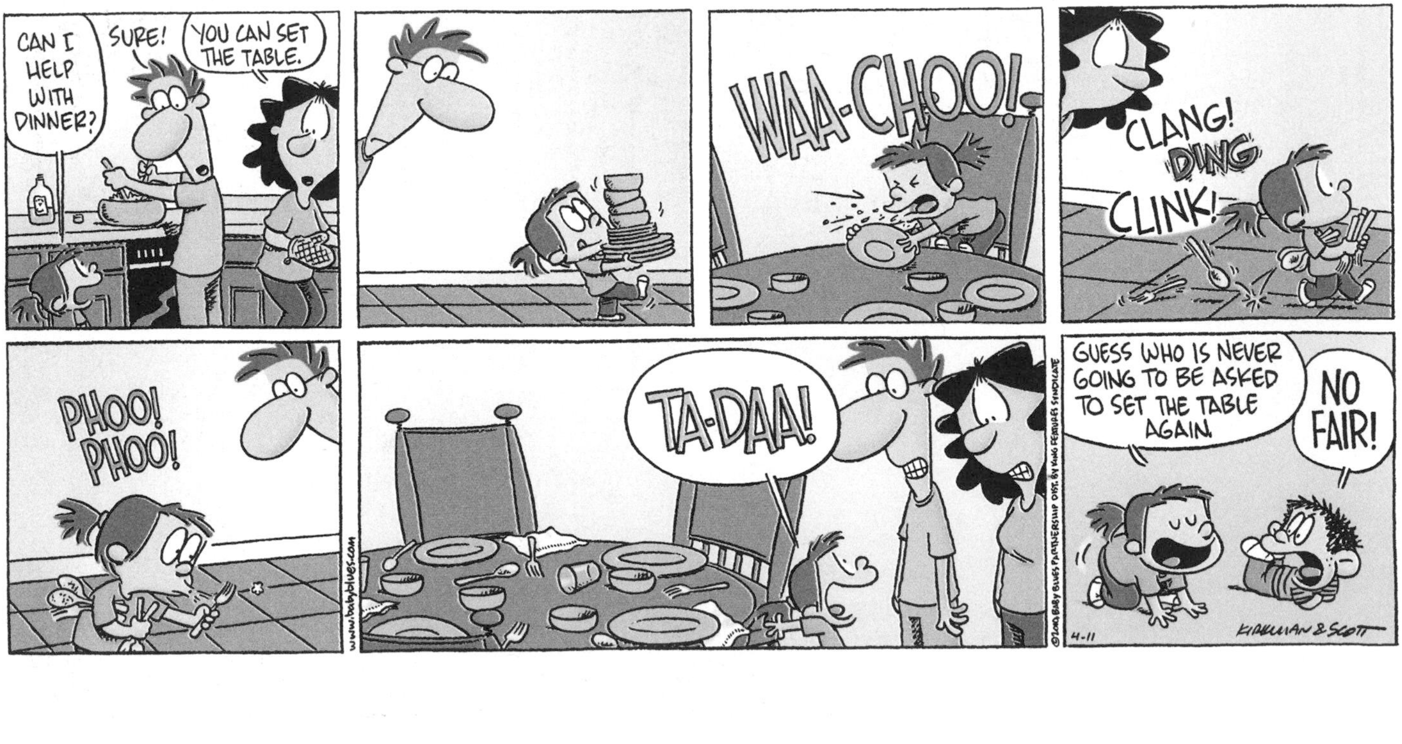
CAN I HELP WITH DINNER?
SURE!
YOU CAN SET THE TABLE.
WAA-CHOO!
CLANG!
DING
CLINK!
PHOO! PHOO!
www.babyblues.com
TA-DAA!
©2003 BABY BLUES PARTNERSHIP DIST. BY KING FEATURES SYNDICATE
GUESS WHO IS NEVER GOING TO BE ASKED TO SET THE TABLE AGAIN.
NO FAIR!
4-11
KIRKMAN & SCOTT

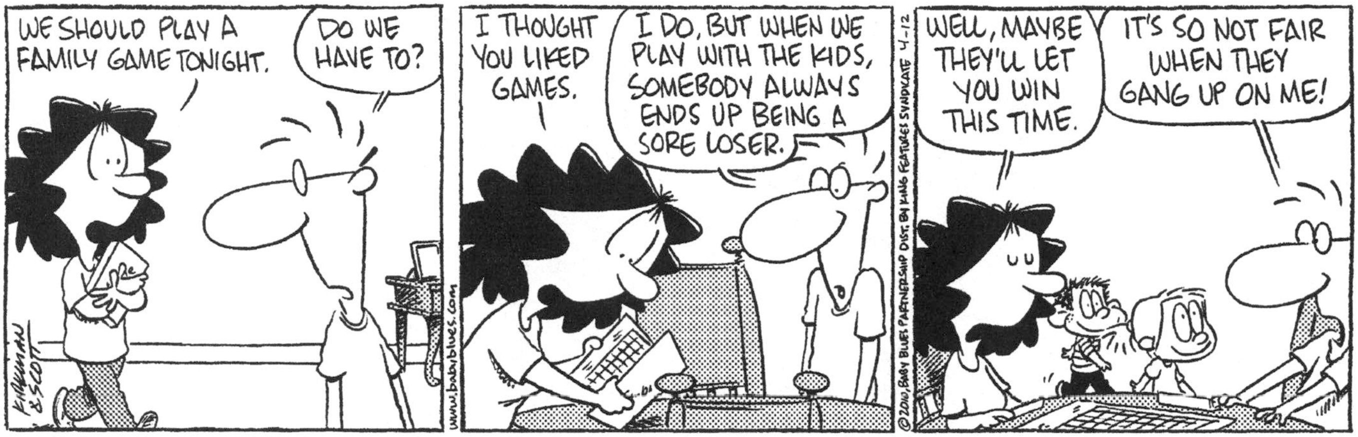
WE SHOULD PLAY A FAMILY GAME TONIGHT.
DO WE HAVE TO?
KIRKMAN & SCOTT
www.babyblues.com
I THOUGHT YOU LIKED GAMES.
I DO, BUT WHEN WE PLAY WITH THE KIDS, SOMEBODY ALWAYS ENDS UP BEING A SORE LOSER.
©2010, BABY BLUES PARTNERSHIP DIST. BY KING FEATURES SYNDICATE 4-12
WELL, MAYBE THEY'LL LET YOU WIN THIS TIME.
IT'S SO NOT FAIR WHEN THEY GANG UP ON ME!

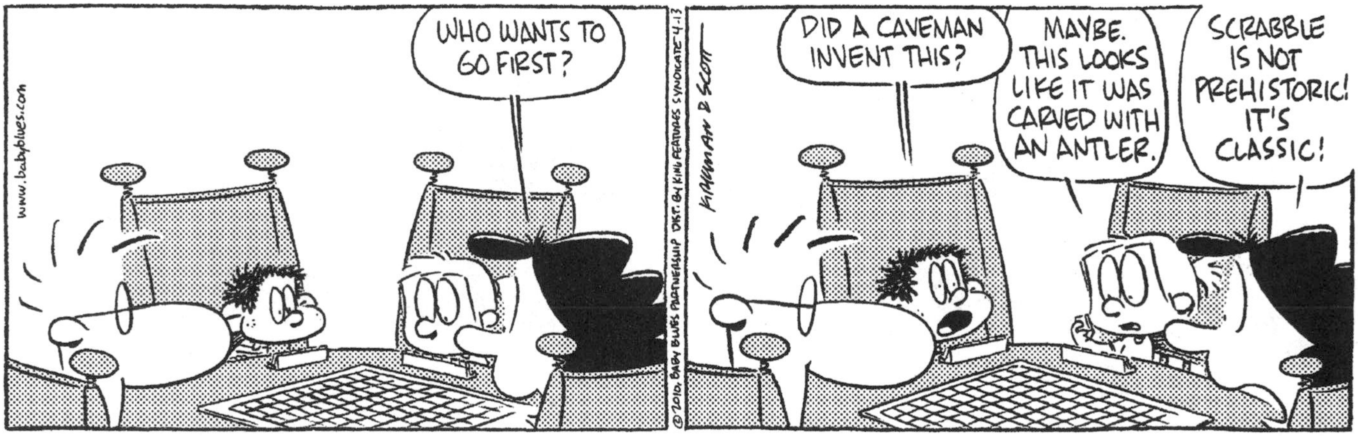
www.babyblues.com
WHO WANTS TO GO FIRST?
©2010, BABY BLUES PARTNERSHIP DIST. BY KING FEATURES SYNDICATE 4-13
KIRKMAN & SCOTT
DID A CAVEMAN INVENT THIS?
MAYBE. THIS LOOKS LIKE IT WAS CARVED WITH AN ANTLER.
SCRABBLE IS NOT PREHISTORIC! IT'S CLASSIC!

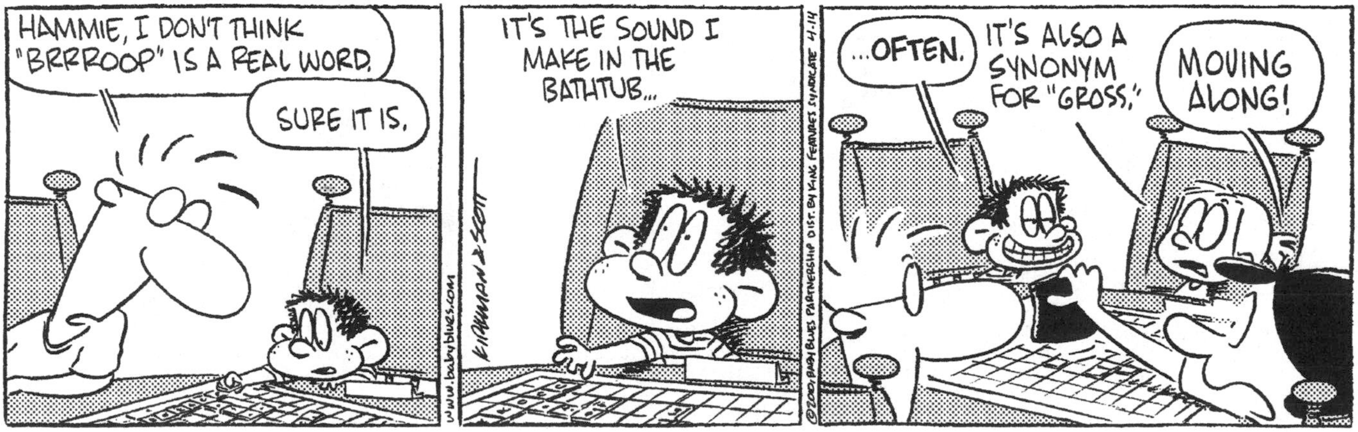
HAMMIE, I DON'T THINK "BRRROOP" IS A REAL WORD.
SURE IT IS.
www.babyblues.com
IT'S THE SOUND I MAKE IN THE BATHTUB...
KIRKMAN & SCOTT
©2010, BABY BLUES PARTNERSHIP DIST. BY KING FEATURES SYNDICATE 4-14
...OFTEN.
IT'S ALSO A SYNONYM FOR "GROSS."
MOVING ALONG!

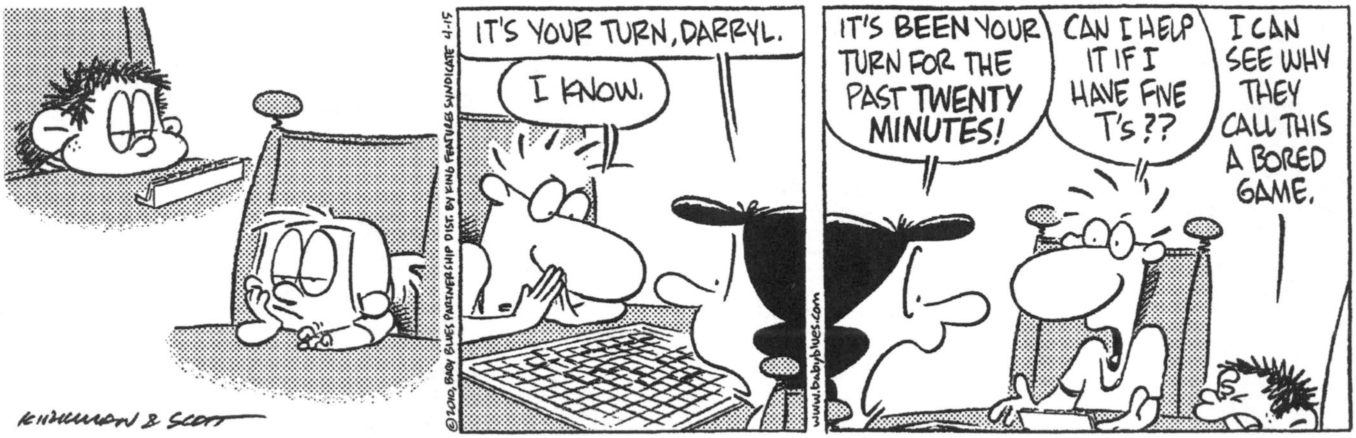
IT'S YOUR TURN, DARRYL.
I KNOW.
IT'S BEEN YOUR TURN FOR THE PAST TWENTY MINUTES!
CAN I HELP IT IF I HAVE FIVE T's??
I CAN SEE WHY THEY CALL THIS A BORED GAME.

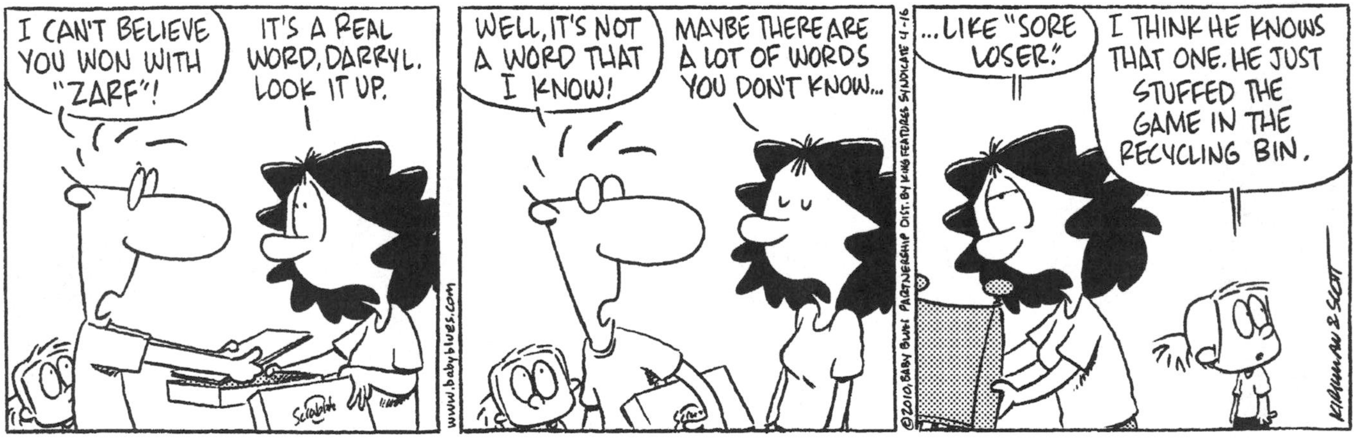
I CAN'T BELIEVE YOU WON WITH "ZARF"!
IT'S A REAL WORD, DARRYL. LOOK IT UP.
WELL, IT'S NOT A WORD THAT I KNOW!
MAYBE THERE ARE A LOT OF WORDS YOU DON'T KNOW...
...LIKE "SORE LOSER."
I THINK HE KNOWS THAT ONE. HE JUST STUFFED THE GAME IN THE RECYCLING BIN.

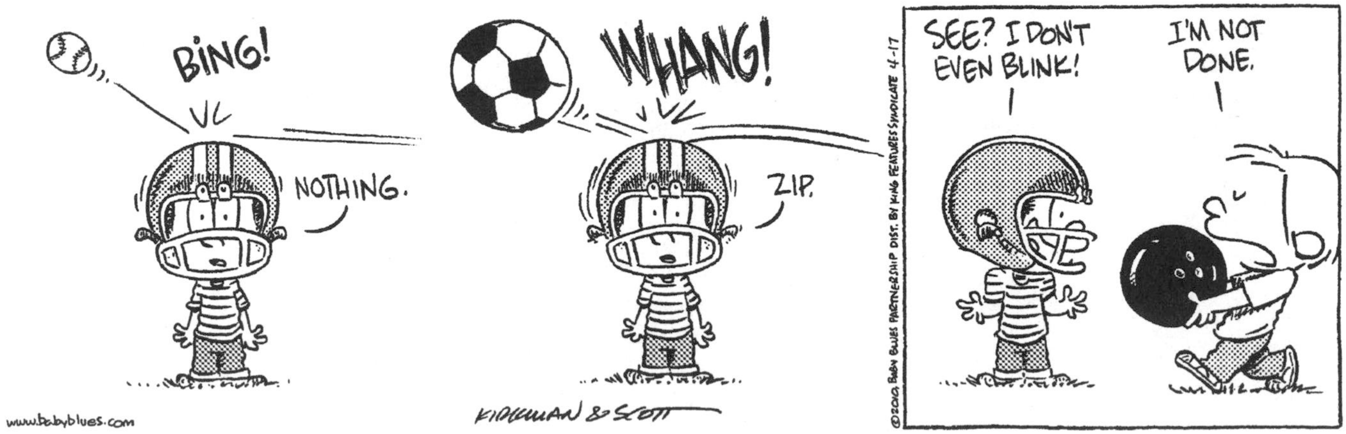
BING!
NOTHING.
WHANG!
ZIP.
SEE? I DON'T EVEN BLINK!
I'M NOT DONE.

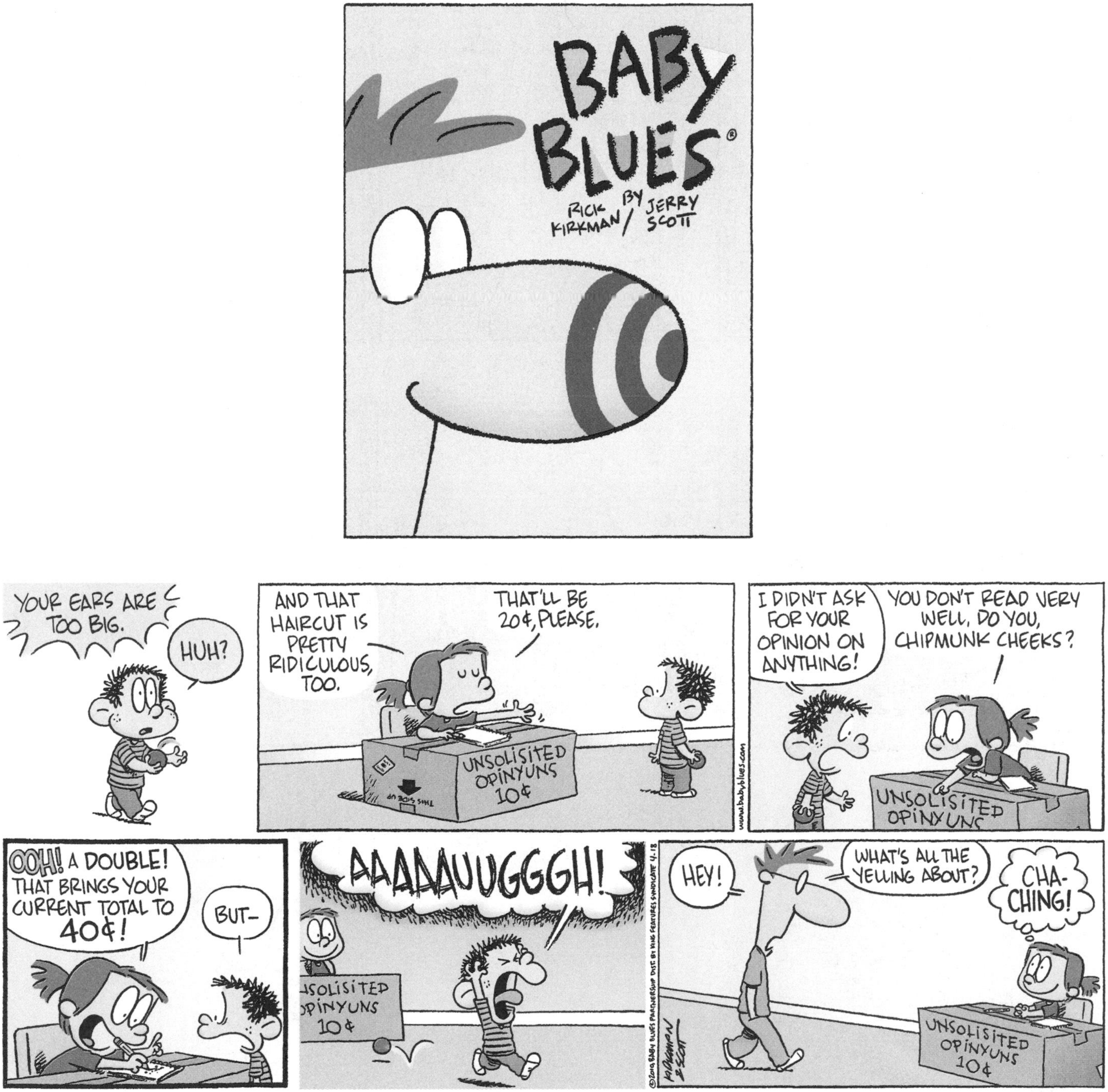
BABY BLUES®
BY RICK KIRKMAN / JERRY SCOTT
YOUR EARS ARE TOO BIG.
HUH?
AND THAT HAIRCUT IS PRETTY RIDICULOUS, TOO.
THAT'LL BE 20¢, PLEASE.
UNSOLISITED OPINYUNS 10¢
THIS SIDE UP
www.babyblues.com
I DIDN'T ASK FOR YOUR OPINION ON ANYTHING!
YOU DON'T READ VERY WELL, DO YOU, CHIPMUNK CHEEKS?
UNSOLISITED OPINYUNS
OOH! A DOUBLE! THAT BRINGS YOUR CURRENT TOTAL TO 40¢!
BUT–
AAAAAUUGGGH!
UNSOLISITED OPINYUNS 10¢
©2010 BABY BLUES PARTNERSHIP DIST. BY KING FEATURES SYNDICATE 4-18
KIRKMAN & SCOTT
HEY!
WHAT'S ALL THE YELLING ABOUT?
CHA-CHING!
UNSOLISITED OPINYUNS 10¢

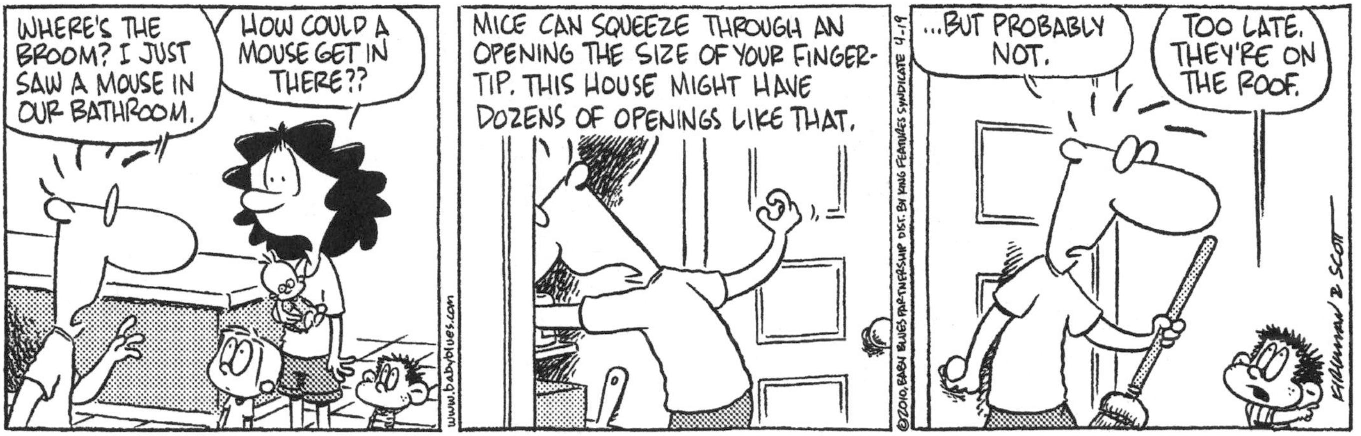
WHERE'S THE BROOM? I JUST SAW A MOUSE IN OUR BATHROOM.
HOW COULD A MOUSE GET IN THERE??
www.babyblues.com
MICE CAN SQUEEZE THROUGH AN OPENING THE SIZE OF YOUR FINGER-TIP. THIS HOUSE MIGHT HAVE DOZENS OF OPENINGS LIKE THAT.
©2010 BABY BLUES PARTNERSHIP DIST. BY KING FEATURES SYNDICATE 4-19
...BUT PROBABLY NOT.
TOO LATE. THEY'RE ON THE ROOF.
KIRKMAN & SCOTT

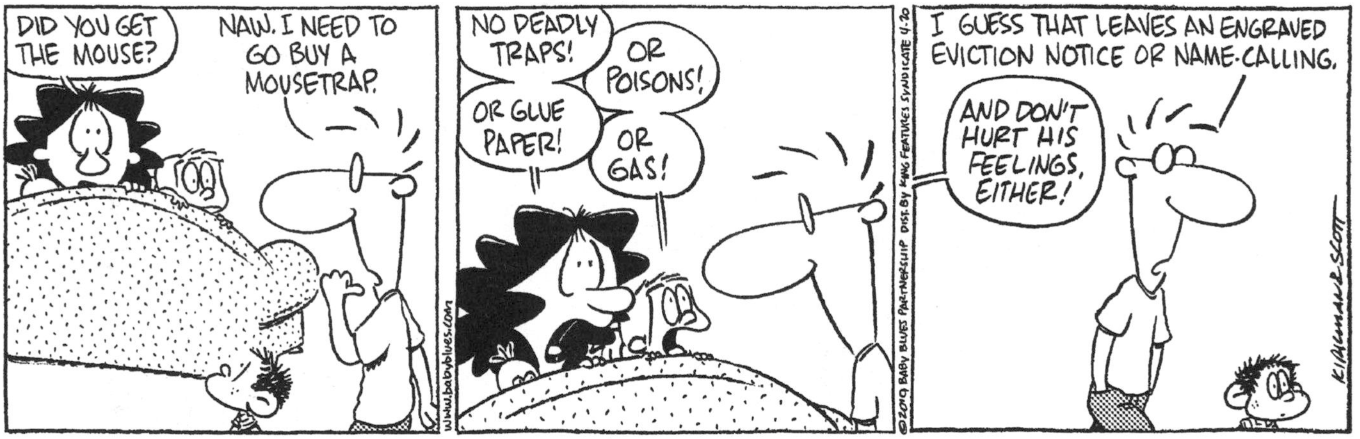
DID YOU GET THE MOUSE?
NAW. I NEED TO GO BUY A MOUSETRAP.
www.babyblues.com
NO DEADLY TRAPS!
OR POISONS!
OR GLUE PAPER!
OR GAS!
©2010 BABY BLUES PARTNERSHIP DIST. BY KING FEATURES SYNDICATE 4-20
I GUESS THAT LEAVES AN ENGRAVED EVICTION NOTICE OR NAME-CALLING.
AND DON'T HURT HIS FEELINGS, EITHER!
KIRKMAN & SCOTT

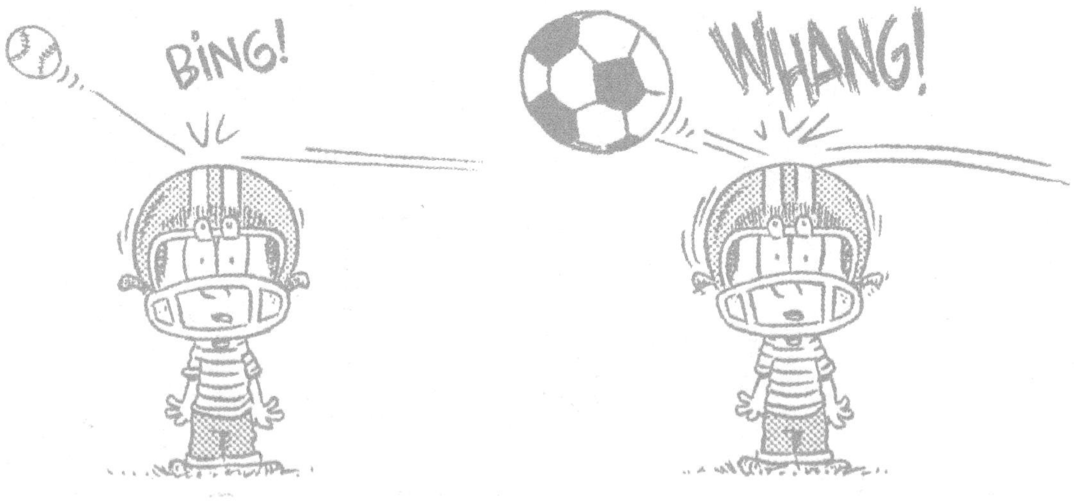
BING!
WHANG!

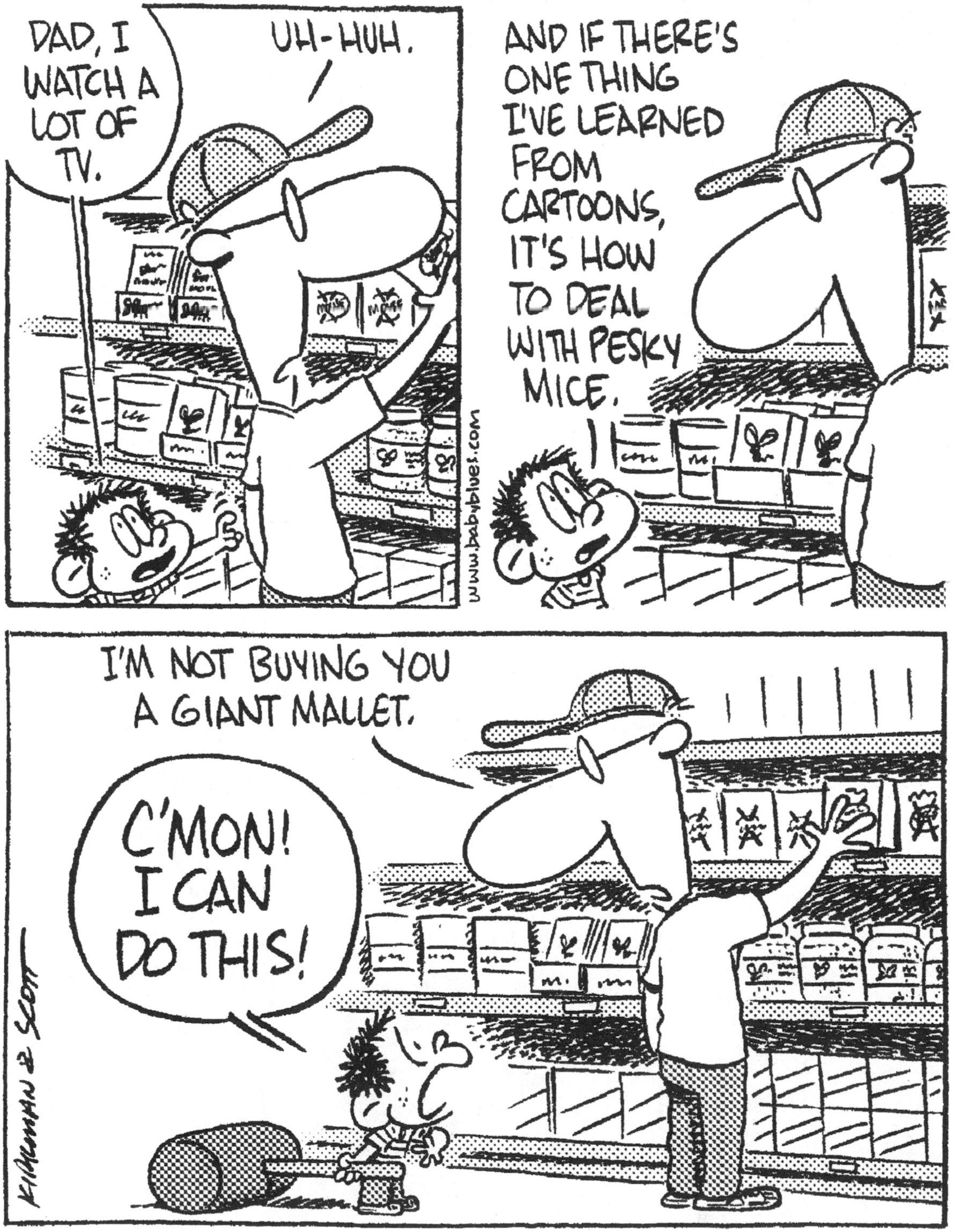
DAD, I WATCH A LOT OF TV.
UH-HUH.
www.babyblues.com
AND IF THERE'S ONE THING I'VE LEARNED FROM CARTOONS, IT'S HOW TO DEAL WITH PESKY MICE.
I'M NOT BUYING YOU A GIANT MALLET.
C'MON! I CAN DO THIS!
KIRKMAN & SCOTT

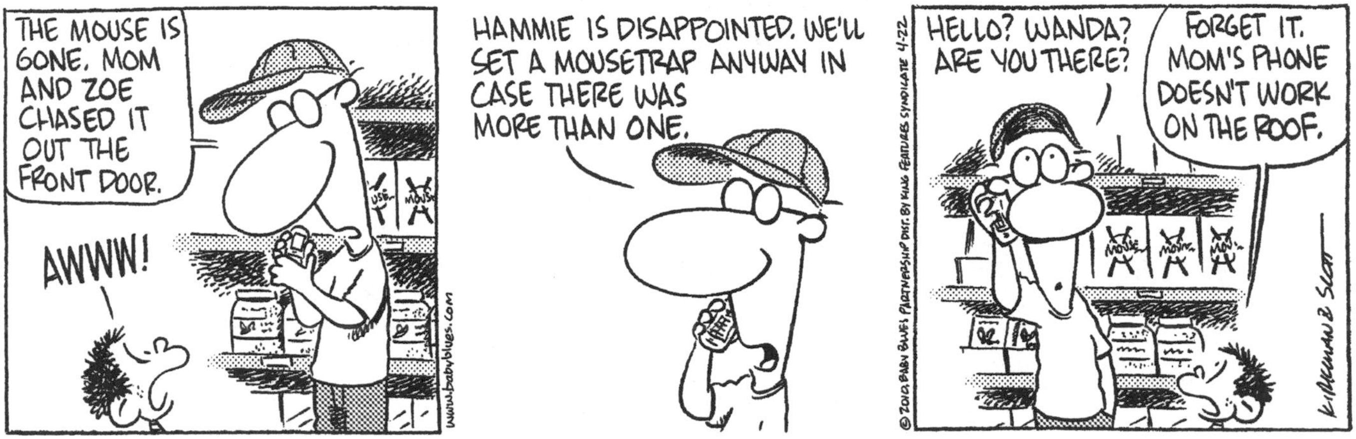
THE MOUSE IS GONE. MOM AND ZOE CHASED IT OUT THE FRONT DOOR.
AWWW!
www.babyblues.com
HAMMIE IS DISAPPOINTED. WE'LL SET A MOUSETRAP ANYWAY IN CASE THERE WAS MORE THAN ONE.
© 2010 BABY BLUES PARTNERSHIP DIST. BY KING FEATURES SYNDICATE 4-22
HELLO? WANDA? ARE YOU THERE?
FORGET IT. MOM'S PHONE DOESN'T WORK ON THE ROOF.
KIRKMAN & SCOTT

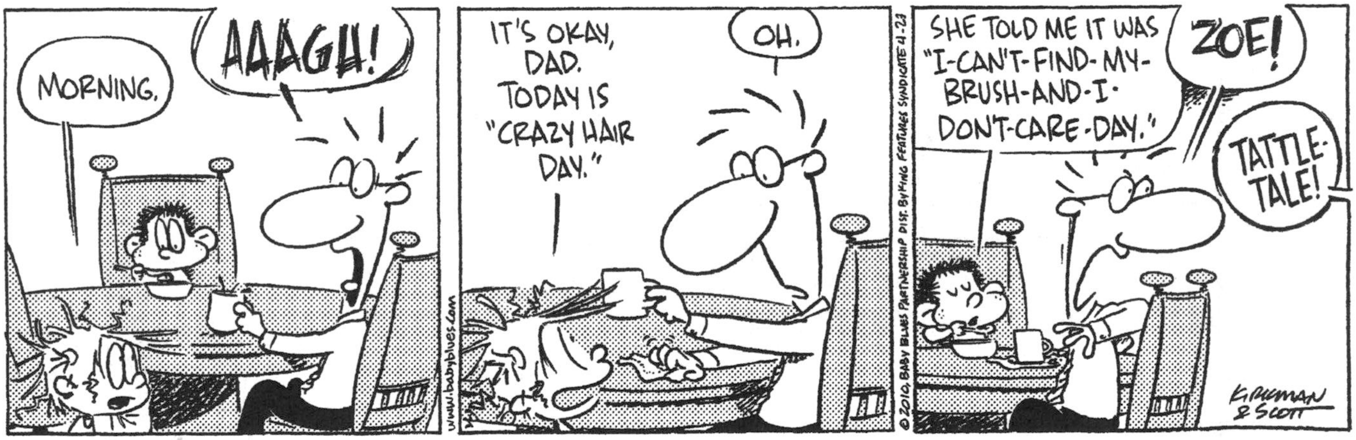
MORNING.
AAAGH!
www.babyblues.com
IT'S OKAY, DAD. TODAY IS "CRAZY HAIR DAY."
OH.
© 2010 BABY BLUES PARTNERSHIP DIST. BY KING FEATURES SYNDICATE 4-23
SHE TOLD ME IT WAS "I-CAN'T-FIND-MY-BRUSH-AND-I-DON'T-CARE-DAY."
ZOE!
TATTLE-TALE!
KIRKMAN & SCOTT

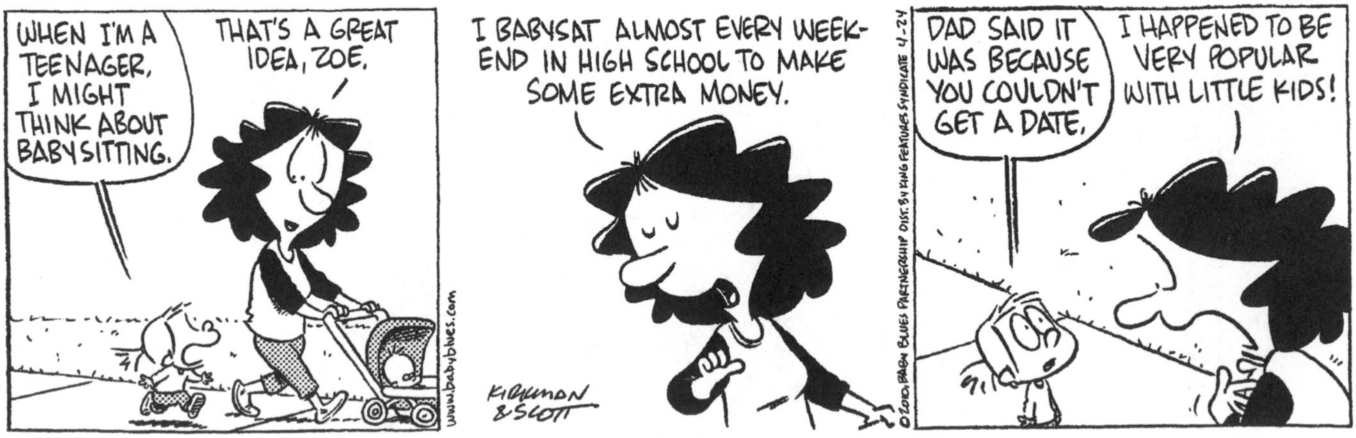
WHEN I'M A TEENAGER, I MIGHT THINK ABOUT BABYSITTING.
THAT'S A GREAT IDEA, ZOE.
www.babyblues.com
KIRKMAN & SCOTT
I BABYSAT ALMOST EVERY WEEKEND IN HIGH SCHOOL TO MAKE SOME EXTRA MONEY.
© 2010 BABY BLUES PARTNERSHIP DIST. BY KING FEATURES SYNDICATE 4-24
DAD SAID IT WAS BECAUSE YOU COULDN'T GET A DATE.
I HAPPENED TO BE VERY POPULAR WITH LITTLE KIDS!

BABY BLUES®
BY
RICK KIRKMAN / JERRY SCOTT

AAAAAUGGHHH!
ZOE, YOU LEFT YOUR GUM IN YOUR JEANS POCKET!
I DID?
YES! AND NOW IT'S STUCK ALL OVER THE INSIDE OF THE DRYER AND MOST OF THE OTHER CLOTHES!
I'M SORRY! I'M SORRY!
IT'LL NEVER HAPPEN AGAIN! I PROMISE! I PROMISE! I PROMISE!
CALM DOWN, ZOE. IT'S NOT THE END OF THE WORLD.
KIRKMAN & SCOTT 4-25
©2010 BABY BLUES PARTNERSHIP DIST. BY KING FEATURES SYNDICATE
I FORGIVE YOU.
YOU DO?
www.babyblues.com
CAN I HAVE ANOTHER PIECE OF GUM NOW?

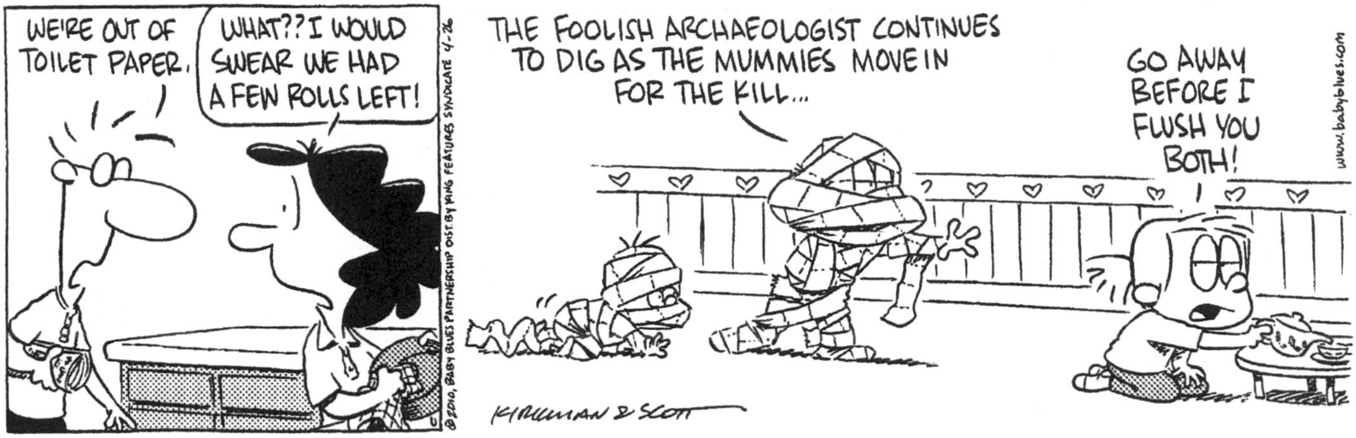
WE'RE OUT OF TOILET PAPER.
WHAT?? I WOULD SWEAR WE HAD A FEW ROLLS LEFT!
©2010, BABY BLUES PARTNERSHIP DIST. BY KING FEATURES SYNDICATE 4-26
THE FOOLISH ARCHAEOLOGIST CONTINUES TO DIG AS THE MUMMIES MOVE IN FOR THE KILL...
GO AWAY BEFORE I FLUSH YOU BOTH!
www.babyblues.com
KIRKMAN & SCOTT

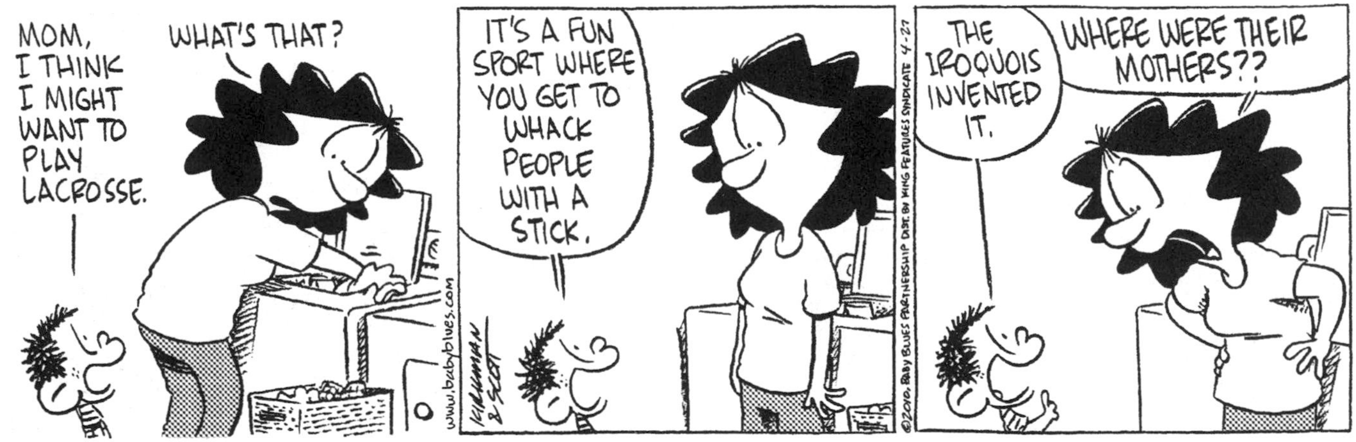
MOM, I THINK I MIGHT WANT TO PLAY LACROSSE.
WHAT'S THAT?
www.babyblues.com
KIRKMAN & SCOTT
IT'S A FUN SPORT WHERE YOU GET TO WHACK PEOPLE WITH A STICK.
©2010, BABY BLUES PARTNERSHIP DIST. BY KING FEATURES SYNDICATE 4-27
THE IROQUOIS INVENTED IT.
WHERE WERE THEIR MOTHERS??

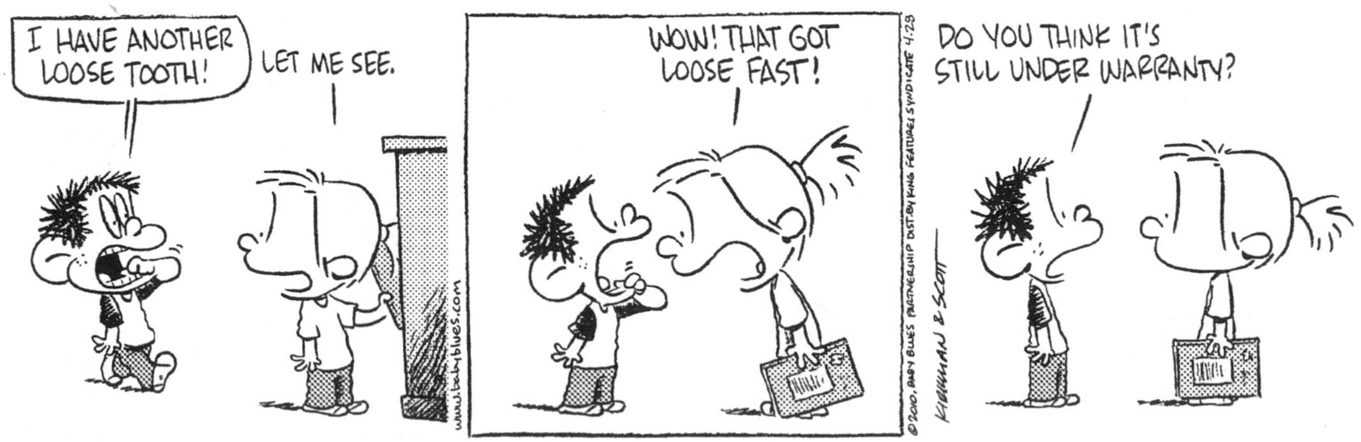
I HAVE ANOTHER LOOSE TOOTH!
LET ME SEE.
www.babyblues.com
WOW! THAT GOT LOOSE FAST!
©2010, BABY BLUES PARTNERSHIP DIST. BY KING FEATURES SYNDICATE 4-28
KIRKMAN & SCOTT
DO YOU THINK IT'S STILL UNDER WARRANTY?

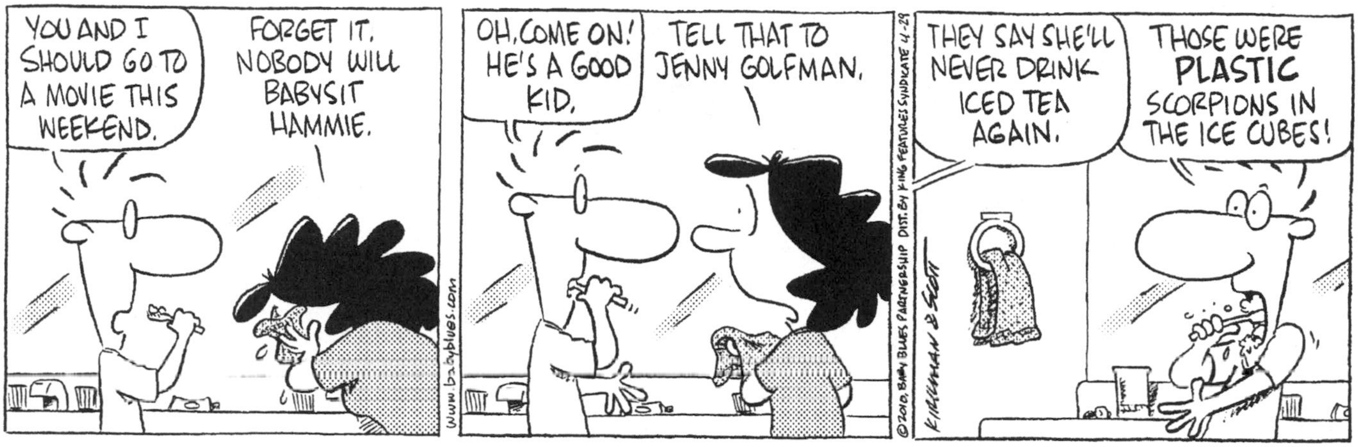
YOU AND I SHOULD GO TO A MOVIE THIS WEEKEND.
FORGET IT. NOBODY WILL BABYSIT HAMMIE.
www.babyblues.com
OH, COME ON! HE'S A GOOD KID.
TELL THAT TO JENNY GOLFMAN.
©2010, BABY BLUES PARTNERSHIP DIST. BY KING FEATURES SYNDICATE 4-29
THEY SAY SHE'LL NEVER DRINK ICED TEA AGAIN.
THOSE WERE **PLASTIC** SCORPIONS IN THE ICE CUBES!
KIRKMAN & SCOTT

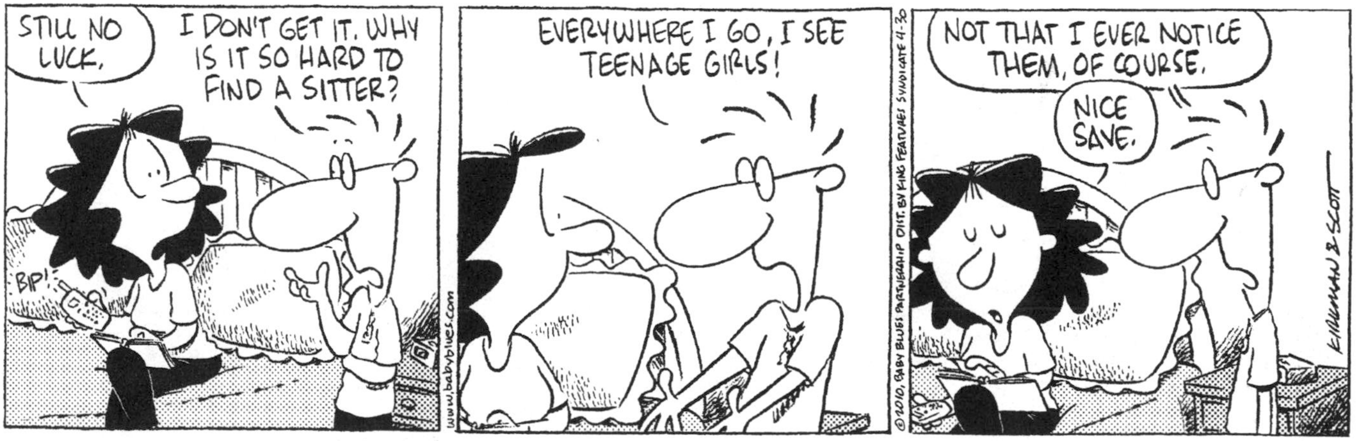
STILL NO LUCK.
I DON'T GET IT. WHY IS IT SO HARD TO FIND A SITTER?
BIP!
www.babyblues.com
EVERYWHERE I GO, I SEE TEENAGE GIRLS!
©2010, BABY BLUES PARTNERSHIP DIST. BY KING FEATURES SYNDICATE 4-30
NOT THAT I EVER NOTICE THEM, OF COURSE.
NICE SAVE.
KIRKMAN & SCOTT

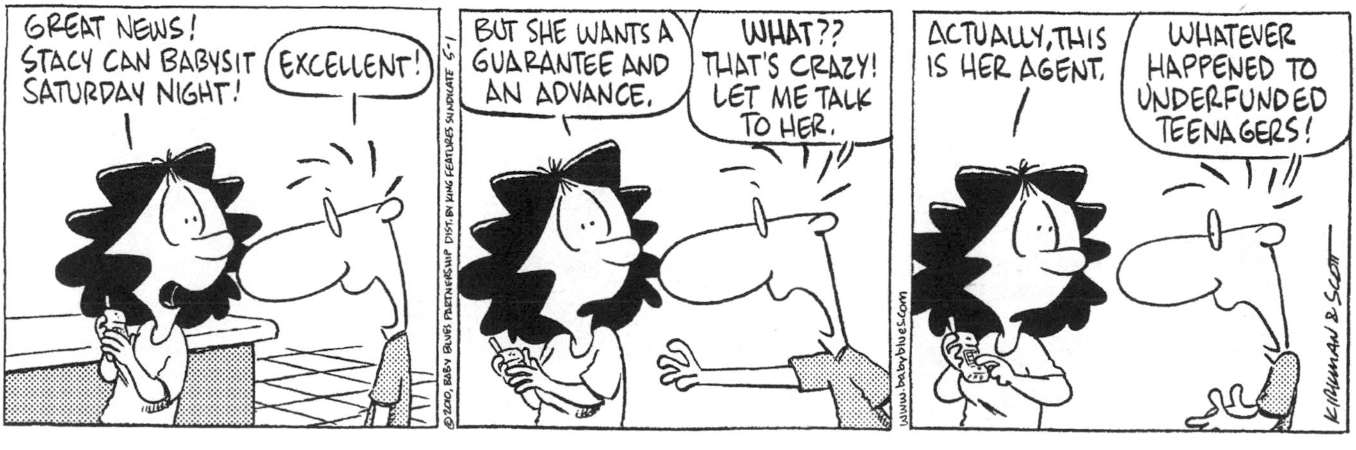
GREAT NEWS! STACY CAN BABYSIT SATURDAY NIGHT!
EXCELLENT!
©2010, BABY BLUES PARTNERSHIP DIST. BY KING FEATURES SYNDICATE 5-1
BUT SHE WANTS A GUARANTEE AND AN ADVANCE.
WHAT?? THAT'S CRAZY! LET ME TALK TO HER.
www.babyblues.com
ACTUALLY, THIS IS HER AGENT.
WHATEVER HAPPENED TO UNDERFUNDED TEENAGERS!
KIRKMAN & SCOTT

BABY BLUES®
BY
RICK KIRKMAN / JERRY SCOTT

I GOT HERE FIRST!
QUIT SHOVING!
DARRYL...?
HAMMIE!
©2003 BABY BLUES PARTNERSHIP DIST. BY KING FEATURES SYNDICATE
GREAT CHICKEN, MOM!
I FINISHED MINE FIRST!
DARRYL...?
HAMMIE...
EXCUSE ME WHILE I GET A FRESH GLASS OF TOILET WATER.
I'LL BEAT YOU TO IT!!
www.babyblues.com
KIRKMAN & SCOTT 5-2
DARRYL!
ACTUALLY, I WANT TO SEE HOW THIS PLAYS OUT.

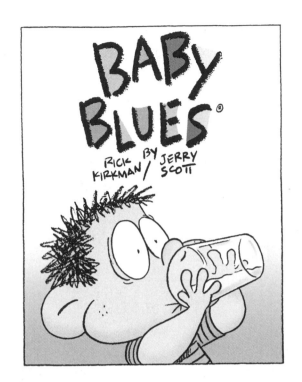

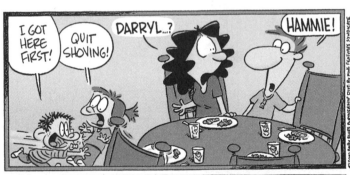

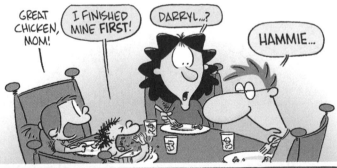

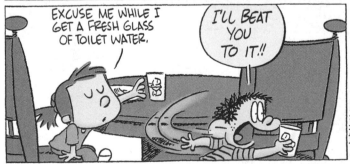

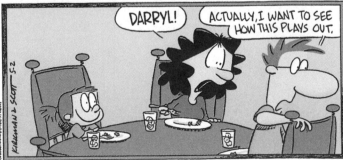

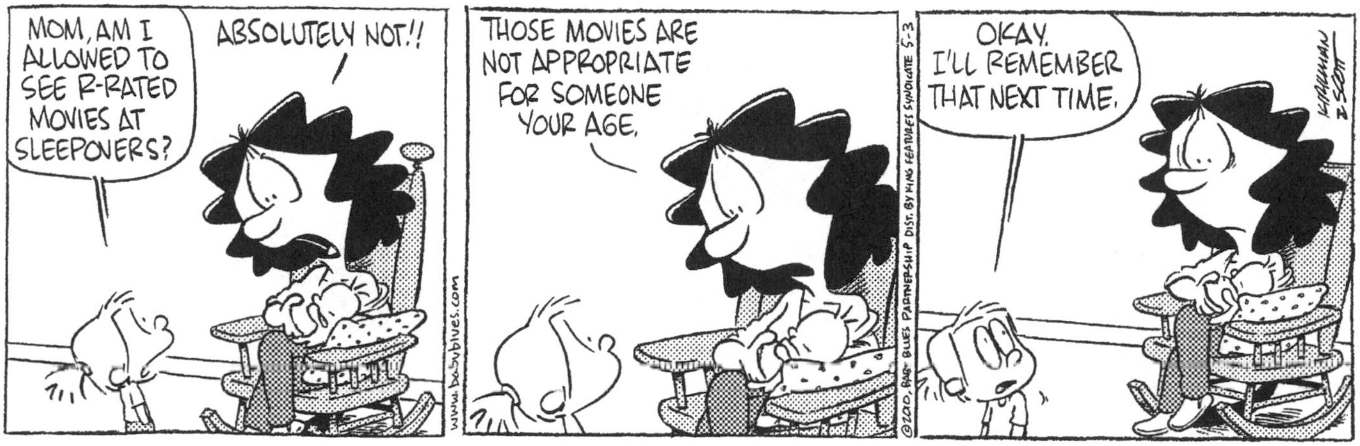
MOM, AM I ALLOWED TO SEE R-RATED MOVIES AT SLEEPOVERS?
ABSOLUTELY NOT!!
www.babyblues.com
THOSE MOVIES ARE NOT APPROPRIATE FOR SOMEONE YOUR AGE.
©2010, BABY BLUES PARTNERSHIP DIST. BY KING FEATURES SYNDICATE 5-3
OKAY. I'LL REMEMBER THAT NEXT TIME.
KIRKMAN & SCOTT

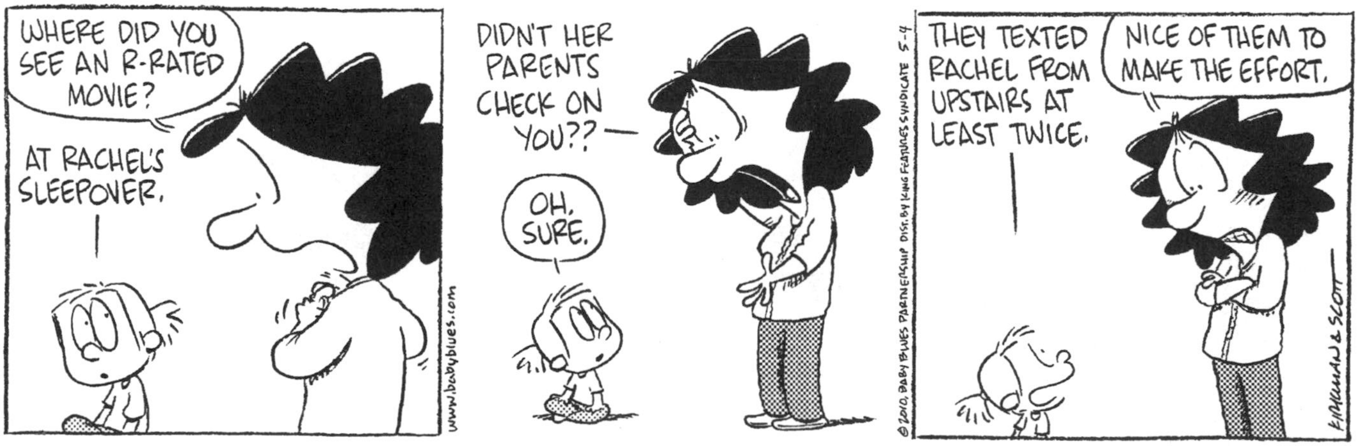
WHERE DID YOU SEE AN R-RATED MOVIE?
AT RACHEL'S SLEEPOVER.
www.babyblues.com
DIDN'T HER PARENTS CHECK ON YOU??
OH, SURE.
©2010, BABY BLUES PARTNERSHIP DIST. BY KING FEATURES SYNDICATE 5-4
THEY TEXTED RACHEL FROM UPSTAIRS AT LEAST TWICE.
NICE OF THEM TO MAKE THE EFFORT.
KIRKMAN & SCOTT

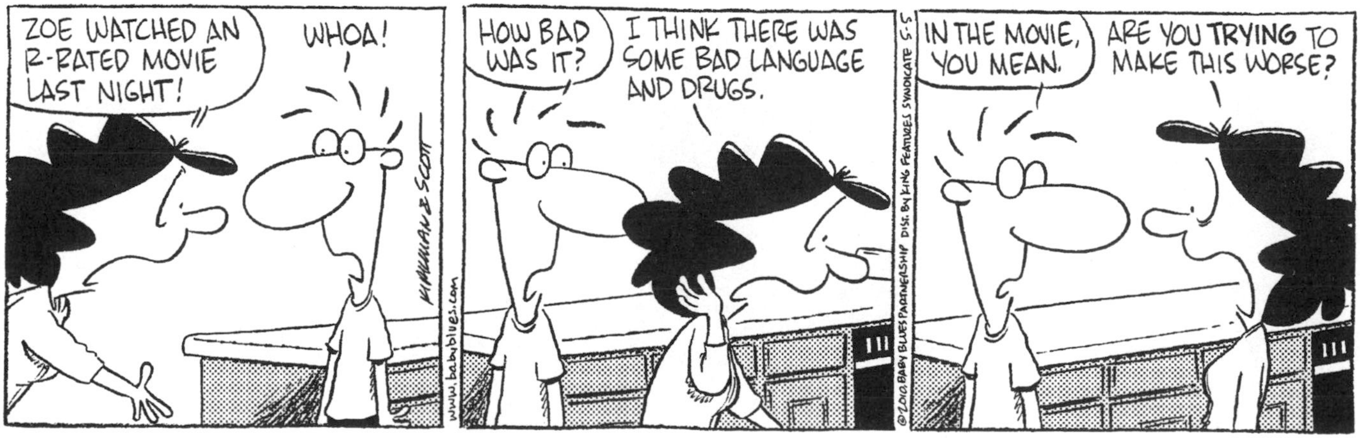
ZOE WATCHED AN R-RATED MOVIE LAST NIGHT!
WHOA!
KIRKMAN & SCOTT
www.babyblues.com
HOW BAD WAS IT?
I THINK THERE WAS SOME BAD LANGUAGE AND DRUGS.
©2010 BABY BLUES PARTNERSHIP DIST. BY KING FEATURES SYNDICATE 5-5
IN THE MOVIE, YOU MEAN.
ARE YOU TRYING TO MAKE THIS WORSE?

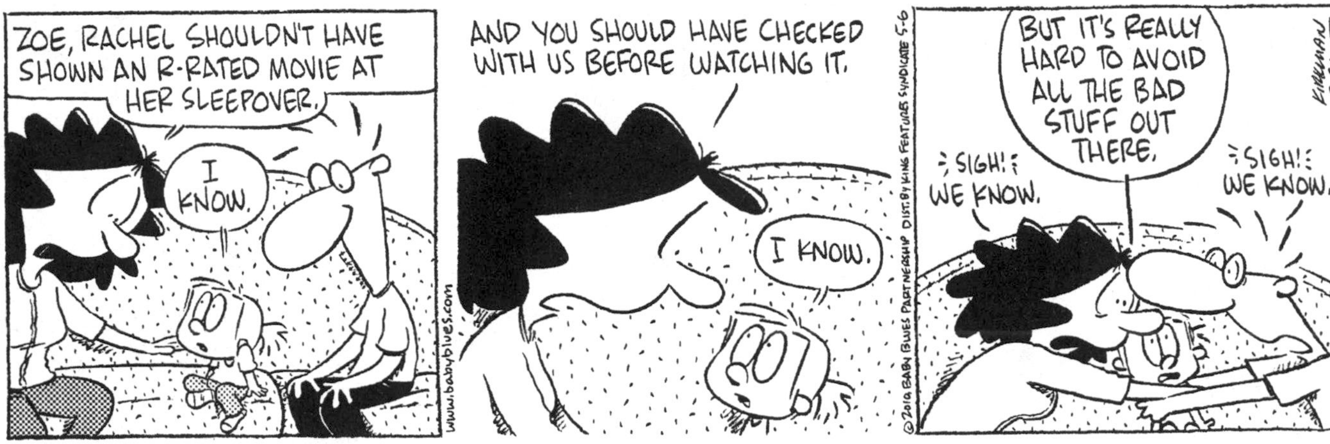
ZOE, RACHEL SHOULDN'T HAVE SHOWN AN R-RATED MOVIE AT HER SLEEPOVER.
I KNOW.
www.babyblues.com
AND YOU SHOULD HAVE CHECKED WITH US BEFORE WATCHING IT.
I KNOW.
© 2010 BABY BLUES PARTNERSHIP DIST. BY KING FEATURES SYNDICATE 5-6
BUT IT'S REALLY HARD TO AVOID ALL THE BAD STUFF OUT THERE.
SIGH! WE KNOW.
SIGH! WE KNOW.
KIRKMAN & SCOTT

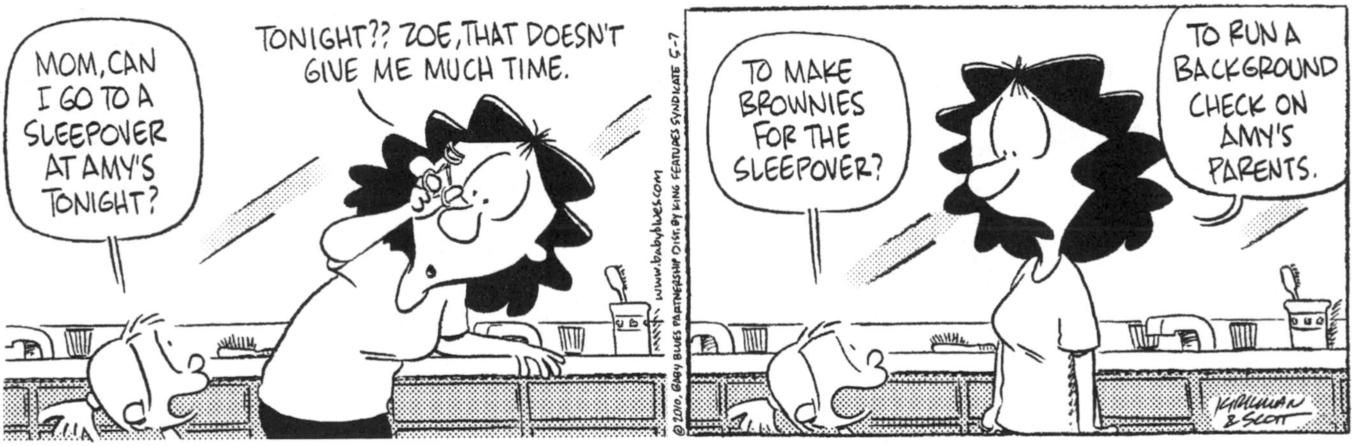
MOM, CAN I GO TO A SLEEPOVER AT AMY'S TONIGHT?
TONIGHT?? ZOE, THAT DOESN'T GIVE ME MUCH TIME.
www.babyblues.com
© 2010, BABY BLUES PARTNERSHIP DIST. BY KING FEATURES SYNDICATE 5-7
TO MAKE BROWNIES FOR THE SLEEPOVER?
TO RUN A BACKGROUND CHECK ON AMY'S PARENTS.
KIRKMAN & SCOTT

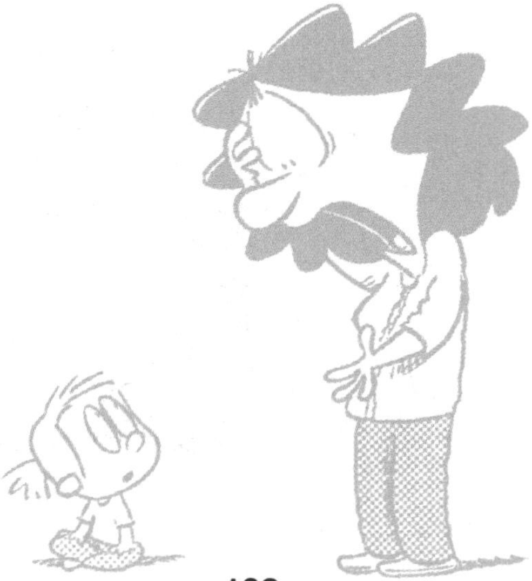

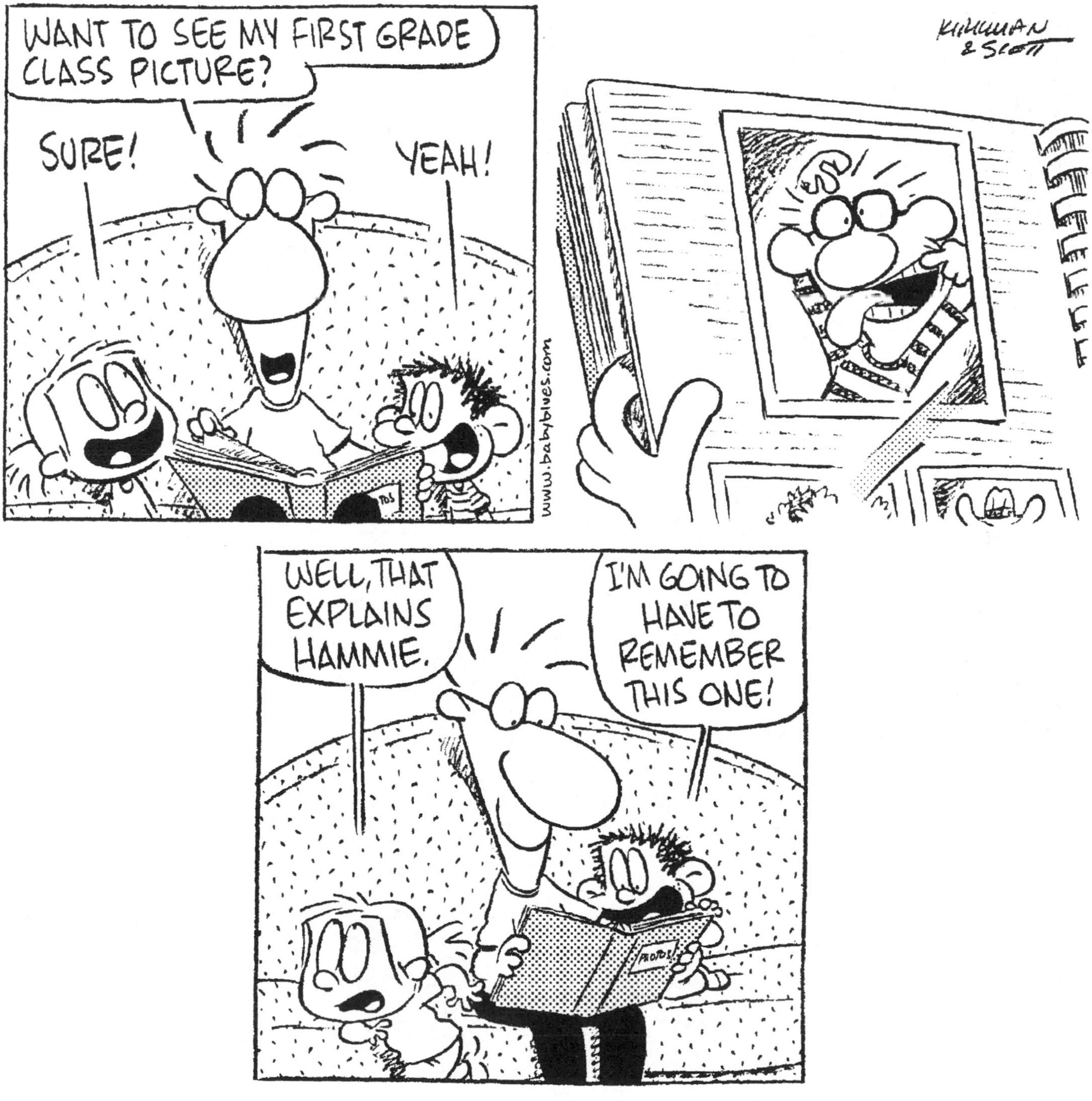
WANT TO SEE MY FIRST GRADE CLASS PICTURE?
SURE!
YEAH!
www.babyblues.com
KIRKMAN & SCOTT
WELL, THAT EXPLAINS HAMMIE.
I'M GOING TO HAVE TO REMEMBER THIS ONE!
PHOTOS!

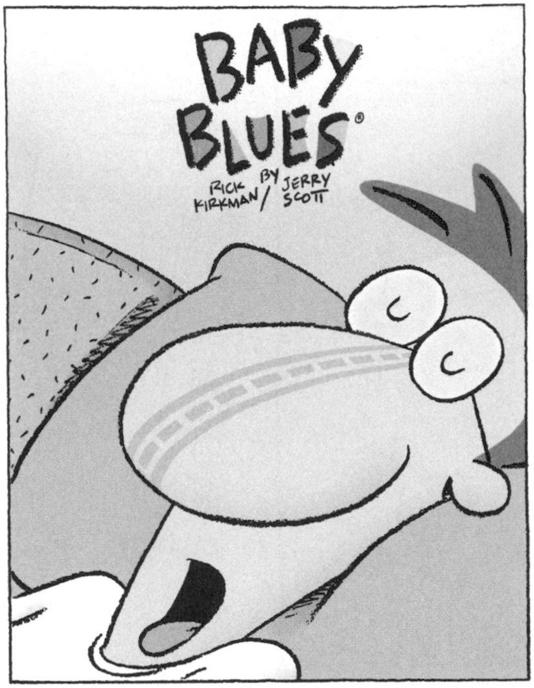
BABY BLUES®
BY RICK KIRKMAN / JERRY SCOTT

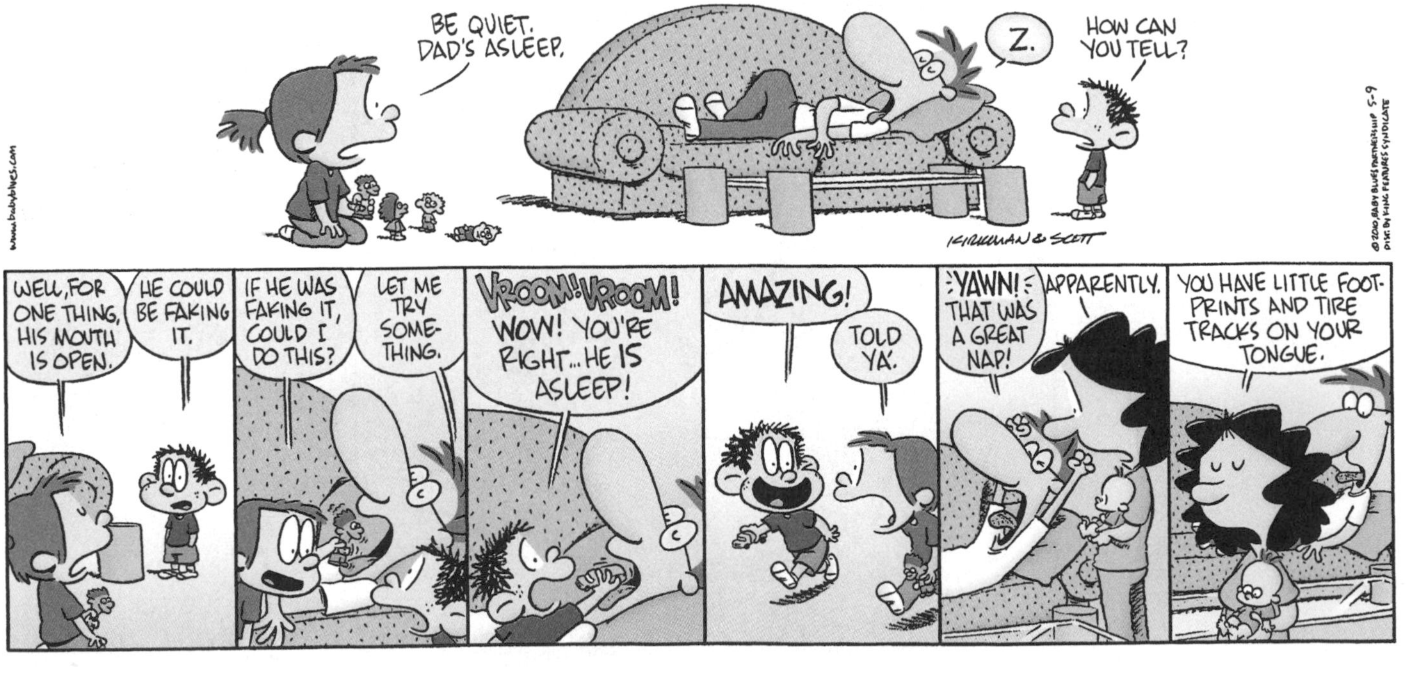
BE QUIET. DAD'S ASLEEP.
Z.
HOW CAN YOU TELL?
www.babyblues.com
KIRKMAN & SCOTT
© 2010 BABY BLUES PARTNERSHIP 5-9
DIST. BY KING FEATURES SYNDICATE
WELL, FOR ONE THING, HIS MOUTH IS OPEN.
HE COULD BE FAKING IT.
IF HE WAS FAKING IT, COULD I DO THIS?
LET ME TRY SOMETHING.
VROOM! VROOM!
WOW! YOU'RE RIGHT... HE IS ASLEEP!
AMAZING!
TOLD YA.
YAWN! THAT WAS A GREAT NAP!
APPARENTLY.
YOU HAVE LITTLE FOOTPRINTS AND TIRE TRACKS ON YOUR TONGUE.

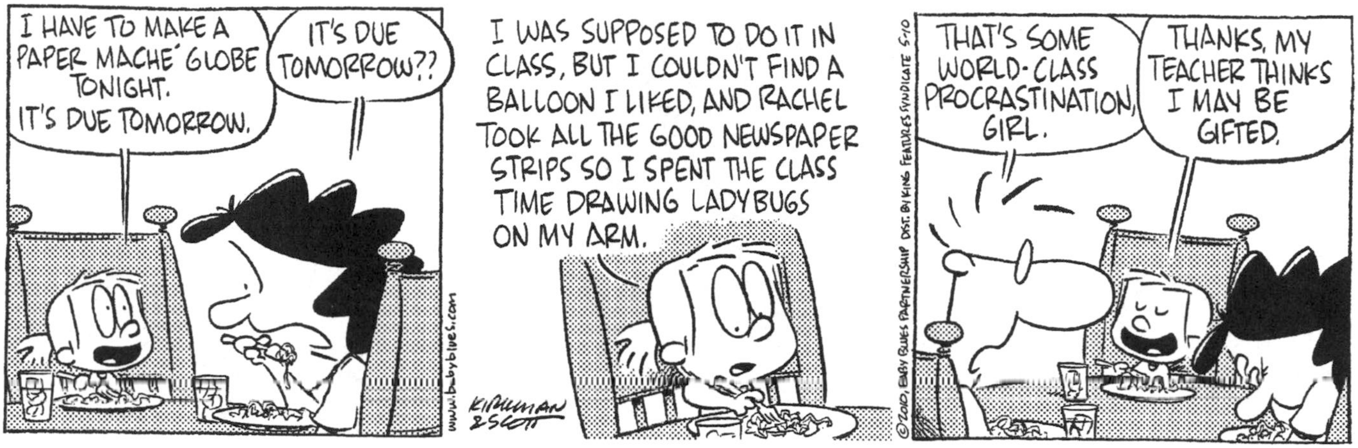
I HAVE TO MAKE A PAPER MACHE' GLOBE TONIGHT. IT'S DUE TOMORROW.
IT'S DUE TOMORROW??
www.babyblues.com
KIRKMAN & SCOTT
I WAS SUPPOSED TO DO IT IN CLASS, BUT I COULDN'T FIND A BALLOON I LIKED, AND RACHEL TOOK ALL THE GOOD NEWSPAPER STRIPS SO I SPENT THE CLASS TIME DRAWING LADYBUGS ON MY ARM.
©2010, BABY BLUES PARTNERSHIP DIST. BY KING FEATURES SYNDICATE 5-10
THAT'S SOME WORLD-CLASS PROCRASTINATION, GIRL.
THANKS, MY TEACHER THINKS I MAY BE GIFTED.

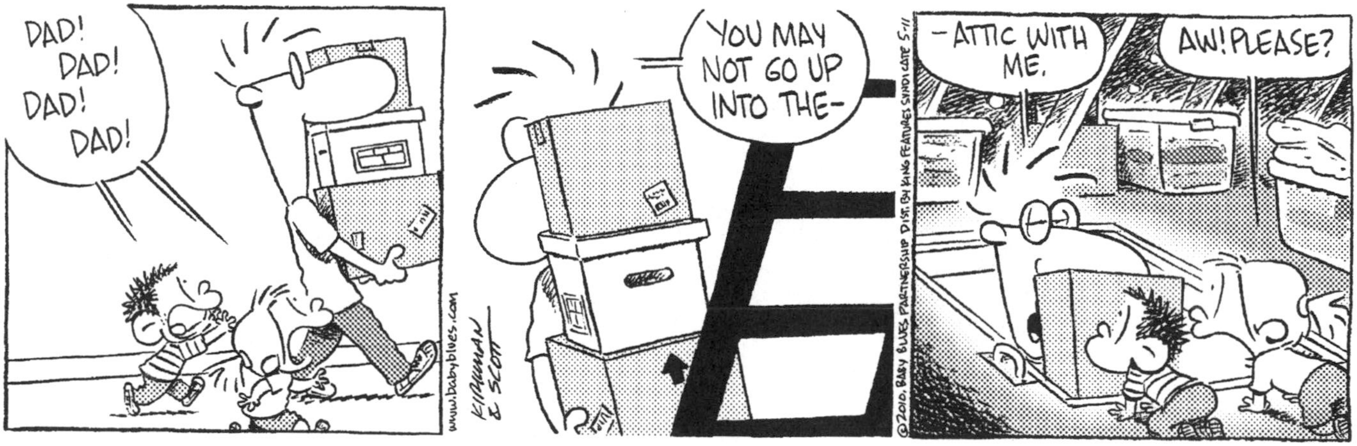
DAD! DAD! DAD! DAD!
www.babyblues.com
KIRKMAN & SCOTT
YOU MAY NOT GO UP INTO THE-
©2010, BABY BLUES PARTNERSHIP DIST. BY KING FEATURES SYNDICATE 5-11
-ATTIC WITH ME.
AW! PLEASE?

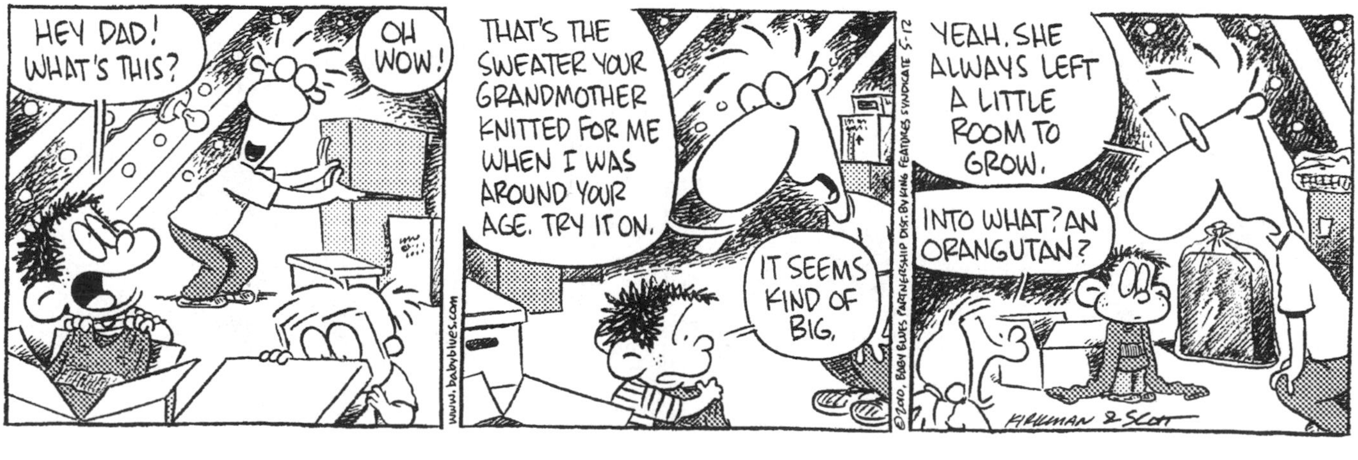
HEY DAD! WHAT'S THIS?
OH WOW!
www.babyblues.com
THAT'S THE SWEATER YOUR GRANDMOTHER KNITTED FOR ME WHEN I WAS AROUND YOUR AGE. TRY IT ON.
IT SEEMS KIND OF BIG.
©2010, BABY BLUES PARTNERSHIP DIST. BY KING FEATURES SYNDICATE 5-12
YEAH. SHE ALWAYS LEFT A LITTLE ROOM TO GROW.
INTO WHAT? AN ORANGUTAN?
KIRKMAN & SCOTT

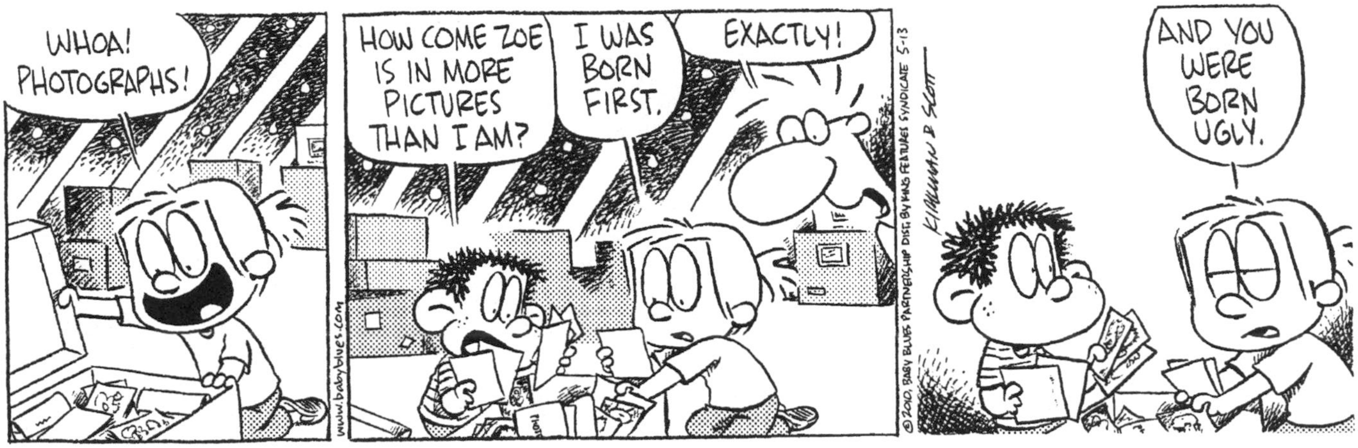
WHOA! PHOTOGRAPHS!
HOW COME ZOE IS IN MORE PICTURES THAN I AM?
I WAS BORN FIRST.
EXACTLY!
AND YOU WERE BORN UGLY.
www.babyblues.com
©2010, BABY BLUES PARTNERSHIP DIST. BY KING FEATURES SYNDICATE 5-13
KIRKMAN & SCOTT

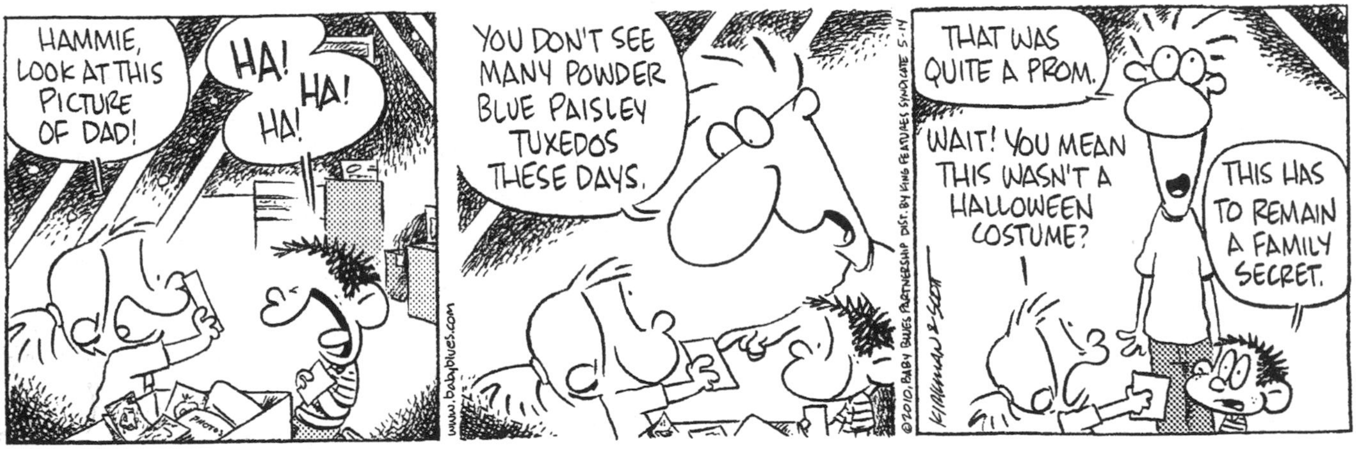
HAMMIE, LOOK AT THIS PICTURE OF DAD!
HA! HA! HA!
YOU DON'T SEE MANY POWDER BLUE PAISLEY TUXEDOS THESE DAYS.
THAT WAS QUITE A PROM.
WAIT! YOU MEAN THIS WASN'T A HALLOWEEN COSTUME?
THIS HAS TO REMAIN A FAMILY SECRET.
www.babyblues.com
©2010, BABY BLUES PARTNERSHIP DIST. BY KING FEATURES SYNDICATE 5-14
KIRKMAN & SCOTT

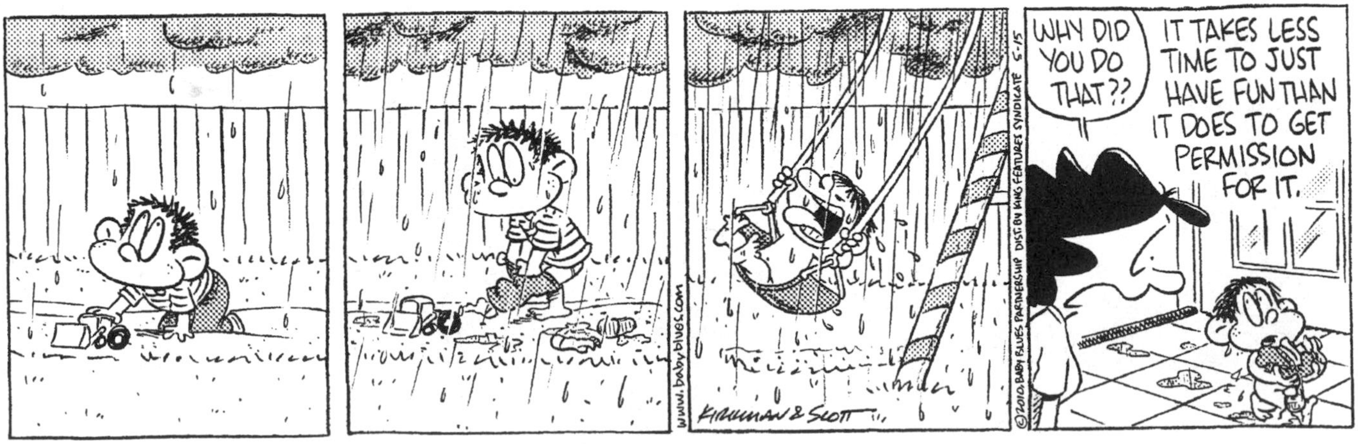
WHY DID YOU DO THAT??
IT TAKES LESS TIME TO JUST HAVE FUN THAN IT DOES TO GET PERMISSION FOR IT.
www.babyblues.com
KIRKMAN & SCOTT
©2010, BABY BLUES PARTNERSHIP DIST. BY KING FEATURES SYNDICATE 5-15

BABY BLUES®
BY RICK KIRKMAN / JERRY SCOTT

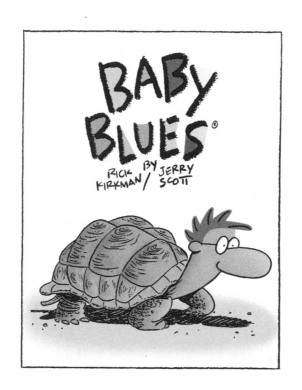

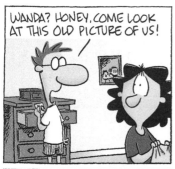

WANDA? HONEY, COME LOOK AT THIS OLD PICTURE OF US!
YOU WERE SO YOUNG AND BEAUTIFUL THEN.
www.babyblues.com
© 2010, BABY BLUES PARTNERSHIP DIST. BY KING FEATURES SYNDICATE
KIRKMAN & SCOTT 5-16
OF COURSE, YOU'RE MUCH MORE BEAUTIFUL NOW.
TOOK YOU LONG ENOUGH!

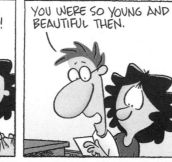

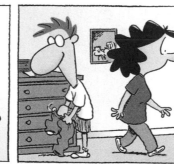

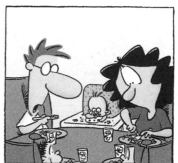

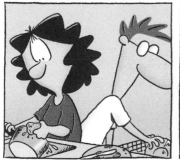

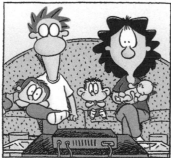

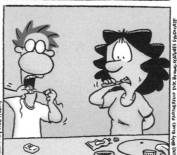

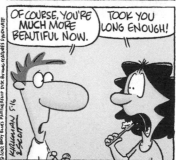

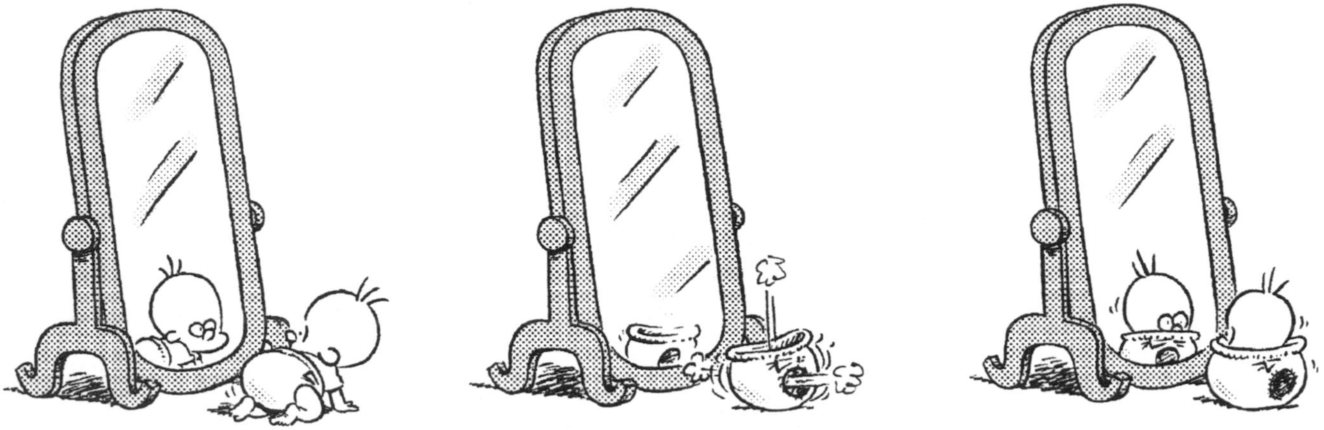

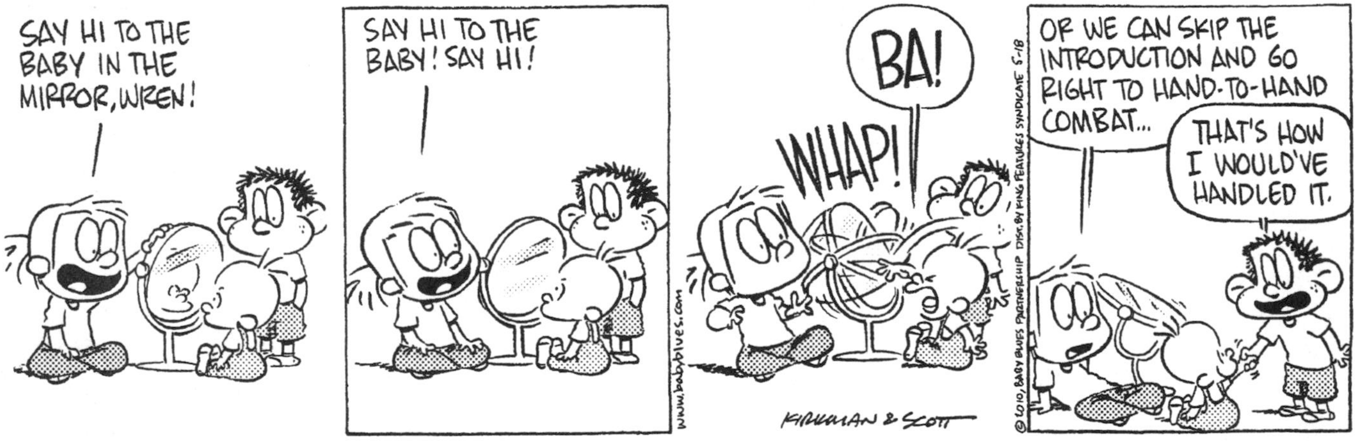
SAY HI TO THE BABY IN THE MIRROR, WREN!
SAY HI TO THE BABY! SAY HI!
BA!
WHAP!
OR WE CAN SKIP THE INTRODUCTION AND GO RIGHT TO HAND-TO-HAND COMBAT...
THAT'S HOW I WOULD'VE HANDLED IT.
www.babyblues.com
KIRKMAN & SCOTT
© 2010, BABY BLUES PARTNERSHIP DIST. BY KING FEATURES SYNDICATE 5-18

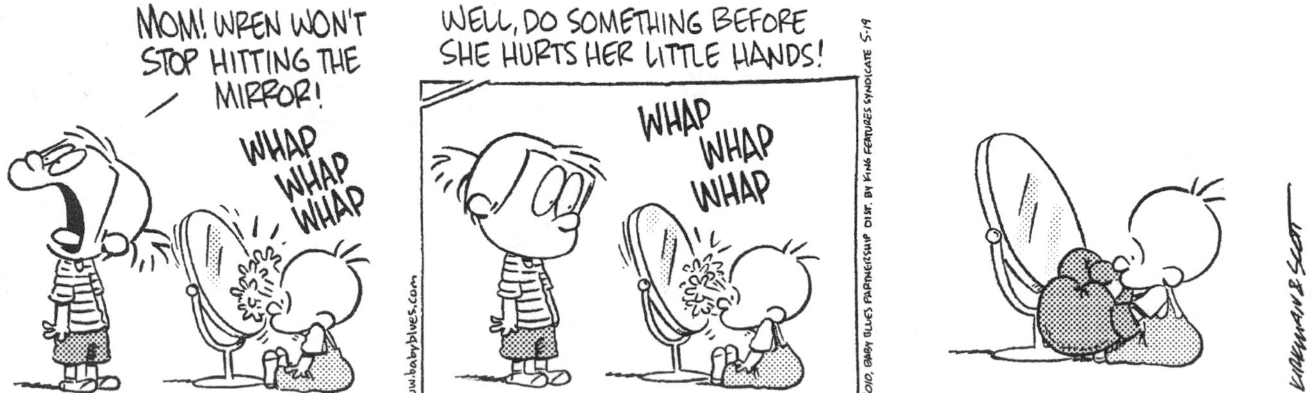
MOM! WREN WON'T STOP HITTING THE MIRROR!
WHAP WHAP WHAP
www.babyblues.com
WELL, DO SOMETHING BEFORE SHE HURTS HER LITTLE HANDS!
WHAP WHAP WHAP
© 2010, BABY BLUES PARTNERSHIP DIST. BY KING FEATURES SYNDICATE 5-19
KIRKMAN & SCOTT

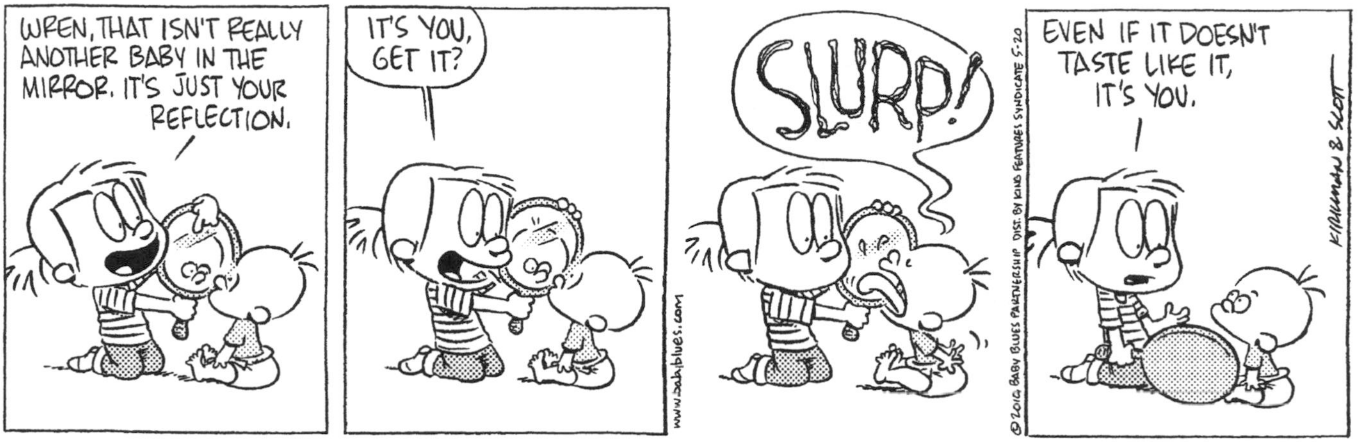
WREN, THAT ISN'T REALLY ANOTHER BABY IN THE MIRROR. IT'S JUST YOUR REFLECTION.
IT'S YOU, GET IT?
www.babyblues.com
SLURP!
© 2010 BABY BLUES PARTNERSHIP DIST. BY KING FEATURES SYNDICATE 5-20
EVEN IF IT DOESN'T TASTE LIKE IT, IT'S YOU.
KIRKMAN & SCOTT

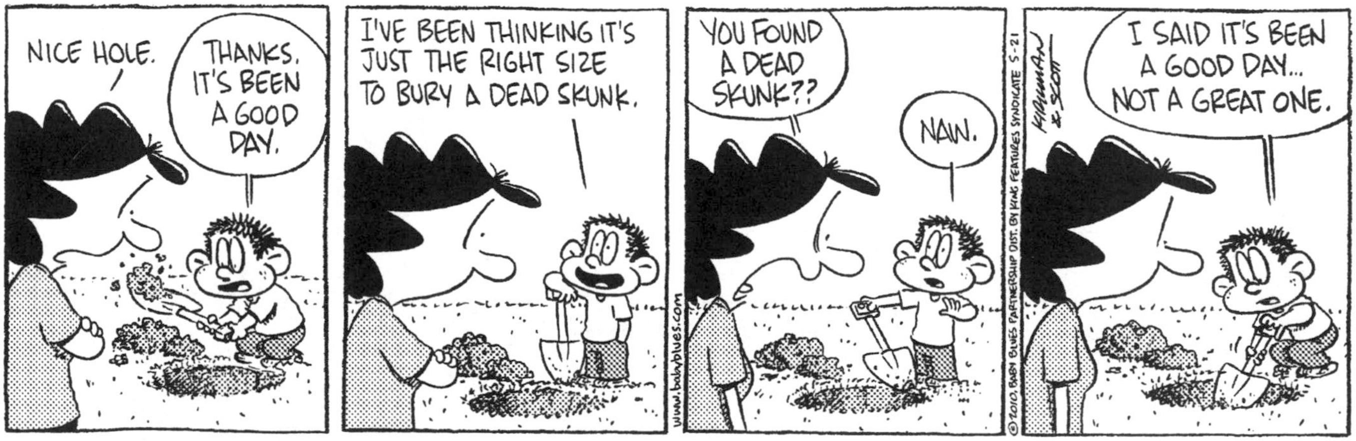
NICE HOLE.
THANKS. IT'S BEEN A GOOD DAY.
I'VE BEEN THINKING IT'S JUST THE RIGHT SIZE TO BURY A DEAD SKUNK.
www.babyblues.com
YOU FOUND A DEAD SKUNK??
NAW.
© 2010 BABY BLUES PARTNERSHIP DIST. BY KING FEATURES SYNDICATE 5-21
KIRKMAN & SCOTT
I SAID IT'S BEEN A GOOD DAY... NOT A GREAT ONE.

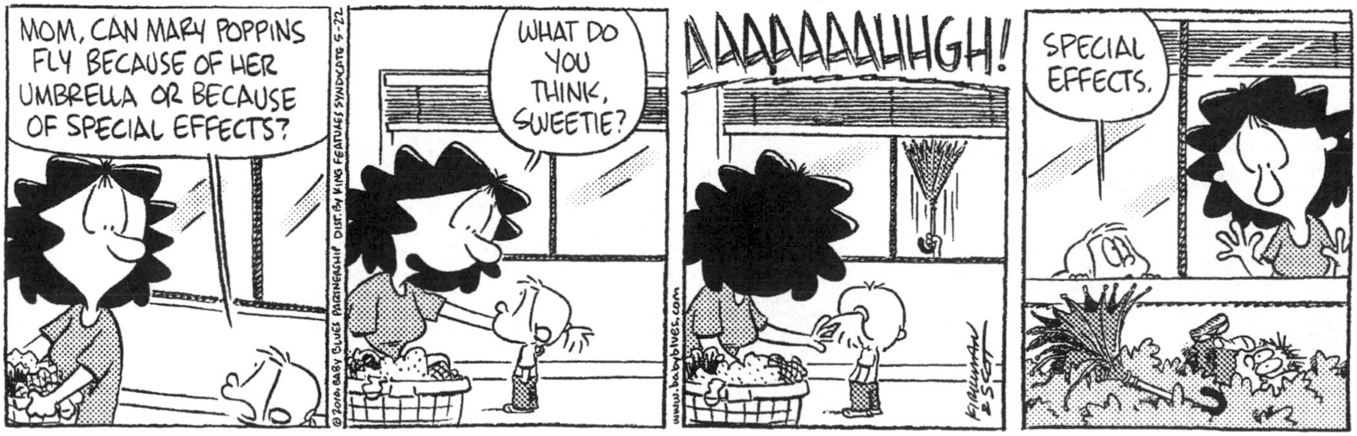
MOM, CAN MARY POPPINS FLY BECAUSE OF HER UMBRELLA OR BECAUSE OF SPECIAL EFFECTS?
© 2010 BABY BLUES PARTNERSHIP DIST. BY KING FEATURES SYNDICATE 5-22
WHAT DO YOU THINK, SWEETIE?
www.babyblues.com
AAAAAAAAHHGH!
KIRKMAN & SCOTT
SPECIAL EFFECTS.

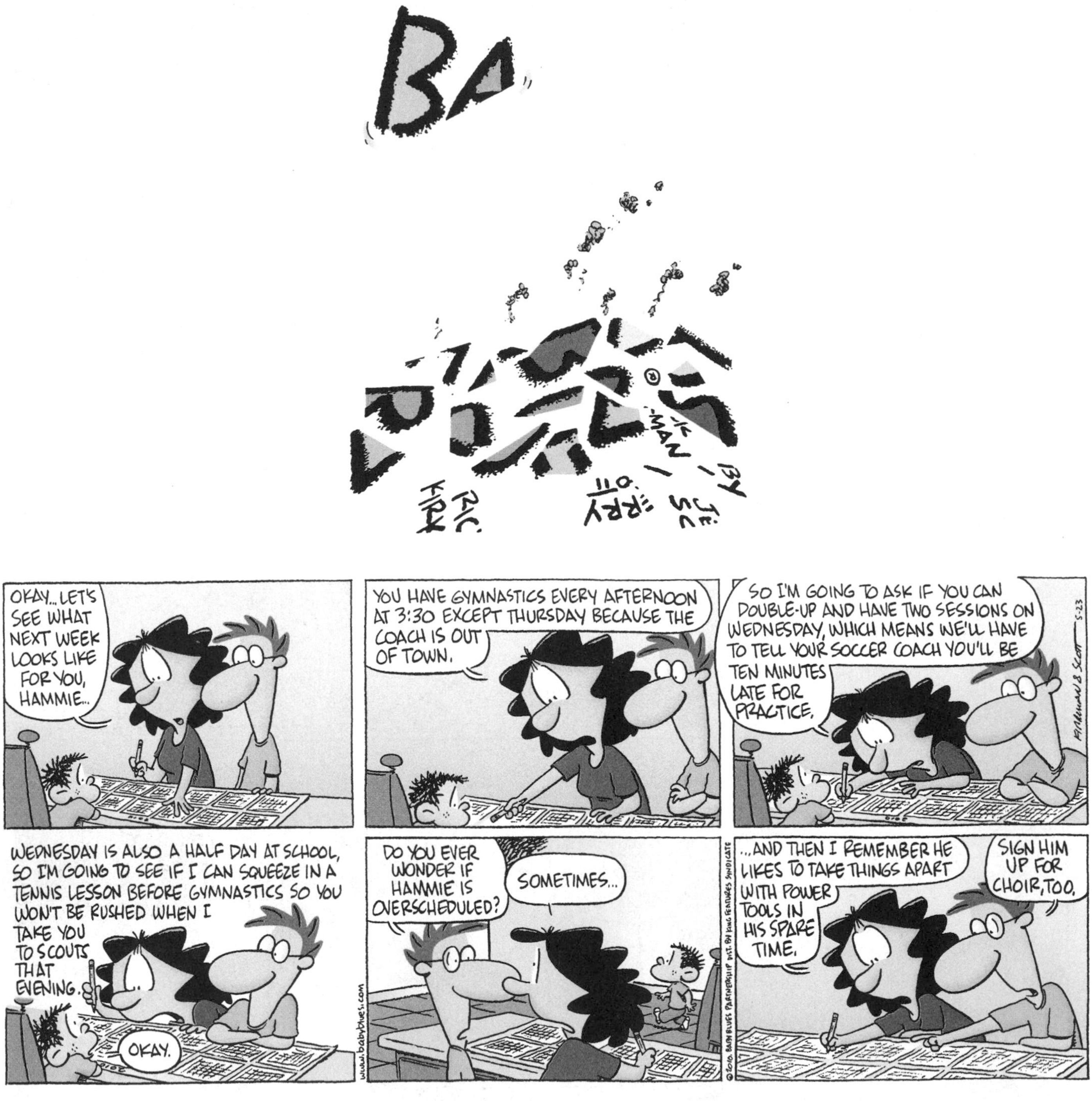
OKAY... LET'S SEE WHAT NEXT WEEK LOOKS LIKE FOR YOU, HAMMIE...
YOU HAVE GYMNASTICS EVERY AFTERNOON AT 3:30 EXCEPT THURSDAY BECAUSE THE COACH IS OUT OF TOWN.
SO I'M GOING TO ASK IF YOU CAN DOUBLE-UP AND HAVE TWO SESSIONS ON WEDNESDAY, WHICH MEANS WE'LL HAVE TO TELL YOUR SOCCER COACH YOU'LL BE TEN MINUTES LATE FOR PRACTICE.
KIRKMAN & SCOTT
5-23
WEDNESDAY IS ALSO A HALF DAY AT SCHOOL, SO I'M GOING TO SEE IF I CAN SQUEEZE IN A TENNIS LESSON BEFORE GYMNASTICS SO YOU WON'T BE RUSHED WHEN I TAKE YOU TO SCOUTS THAT EVENING.
OKAY.
www.babyblues.com
DO YOU EVER WONDER IF HAMMIE IS OVERSCHEDULED?
SOMETIMES...
©2010 BABY BLUES PARTNERSHIP DIST. BY KING FEATURES SYNDICATE
...AND THEN I REMEMBER HE LIKES TO TAKE THINGS APART WITH POWER TOOLS IN HIS SPARE TIME.
SIGN HIM UP FOR CHOIR, TOO.

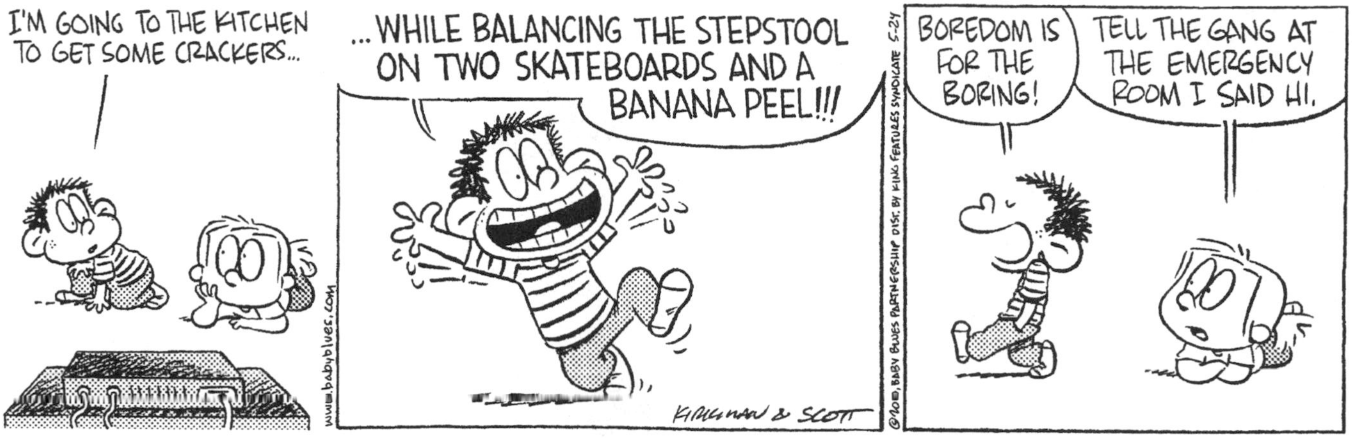
I'M GOING TO THE KITCHEN TO GET SOME CRACKERS...
...WHILE BALANCING THE STEPSTOOL ON TWO SKATEBOARDS AND A BANANA PEEL!!!
BOREDOM IS FOR THE BORING!
TELL THE GANG AT THE EMERGENCY ROOM I SAID HI.
www.babyblues.com
©2010, BABY BLUES PARTNERSHIP DIST. BY KING FEATURES SYNDICATE 5-24
KIRKMAN & SCOTT

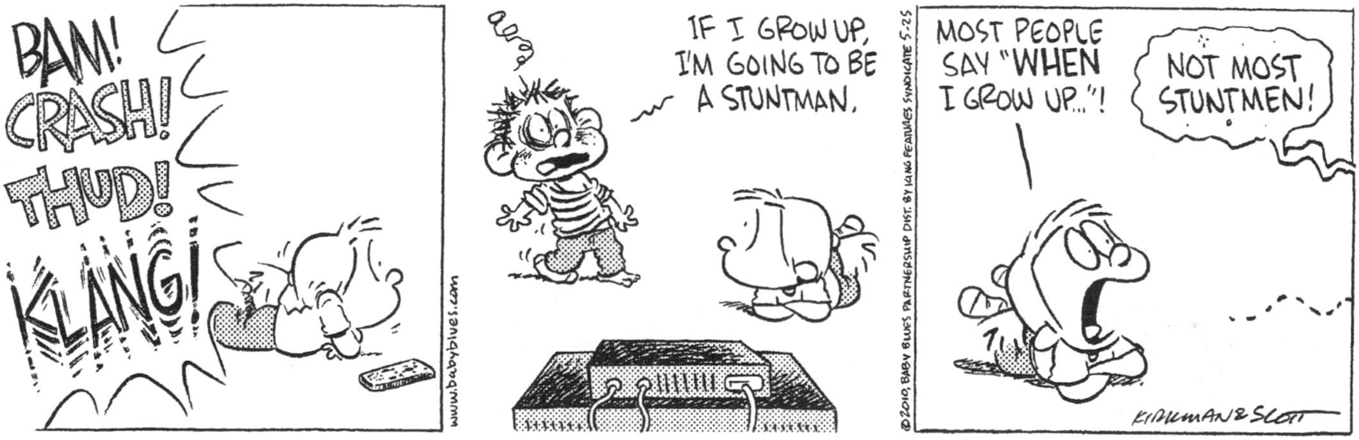
BAM! CRASH! THUD! KLANG!
IF I GROW UP, I'M GOING TO BE A STUNTMAN.
MOST PEOPLE SAY "WHEN I GROW UP..."!
NOT MOST STUNTMEN!
www.babyblues.com
©2010, BABY BLUES PARTNERSHIP DIST. BY KING FEATURES SYNDICATE 5-25
KIRKMAN & SCOTT

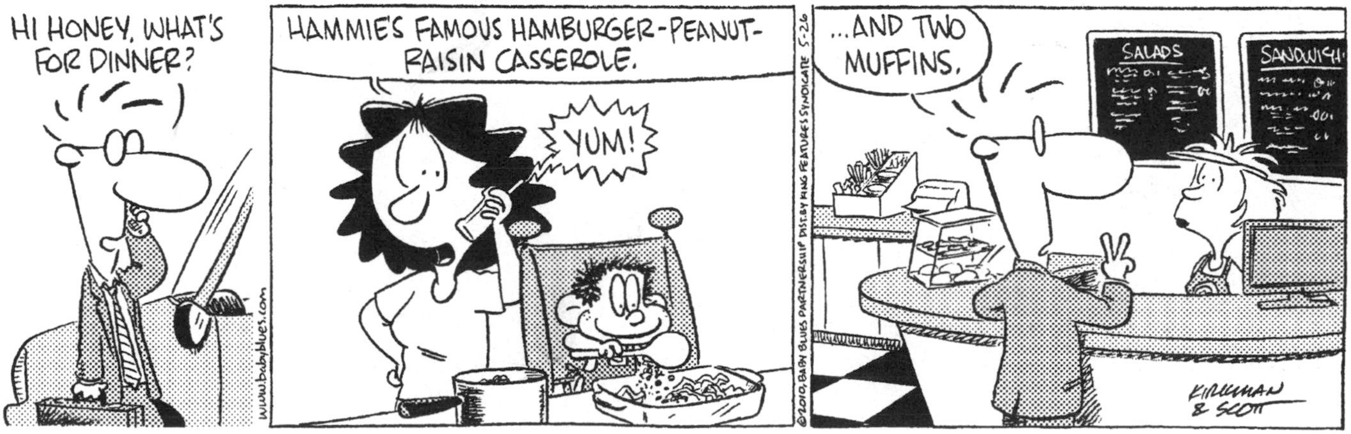
HI HONEY. WHAT'S FOR DINNER?
HAMMIE'S FAMOUS HAMBURGER-PEANUT-RAISIN CASSEROLE.
YUM!
...AND TWO MUFFINS.
SALADS
www.babyblues.com
©2010, BABY BLUES PARTNERSHIP DIST. BY KING FEATURES SYNDICATE 5-26
KIRKMAN & SCOTT

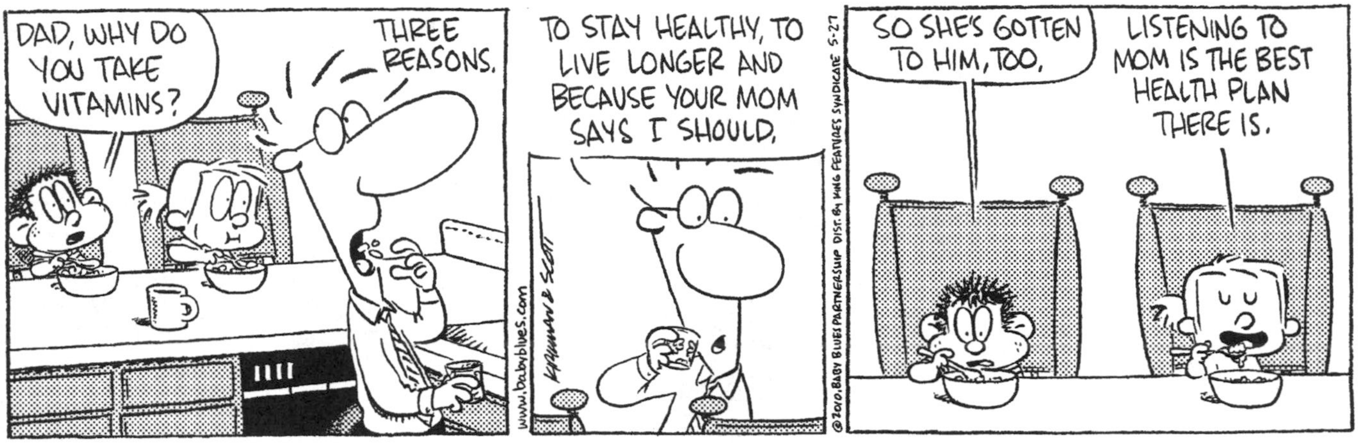
DAD, WHY DO YOU TAKE VITAMINS?
THREE REASONS.
TO STAY HEALTHY, TO LIVE LONGER AND BECAUSE YOUR MOM SAYS I SHOULD.
www.babyblues.com
KIRKMAN & SCOTT
©2010, BABY BLUES PARTNERSHIP DIST. BY KING FEATURES SYNDICATE 5-27
SO SHE'S GOTTEN TO HIM, TOO.
LISTENING TO MOM IS THE BEST HEALTH PLAN THERE IS.

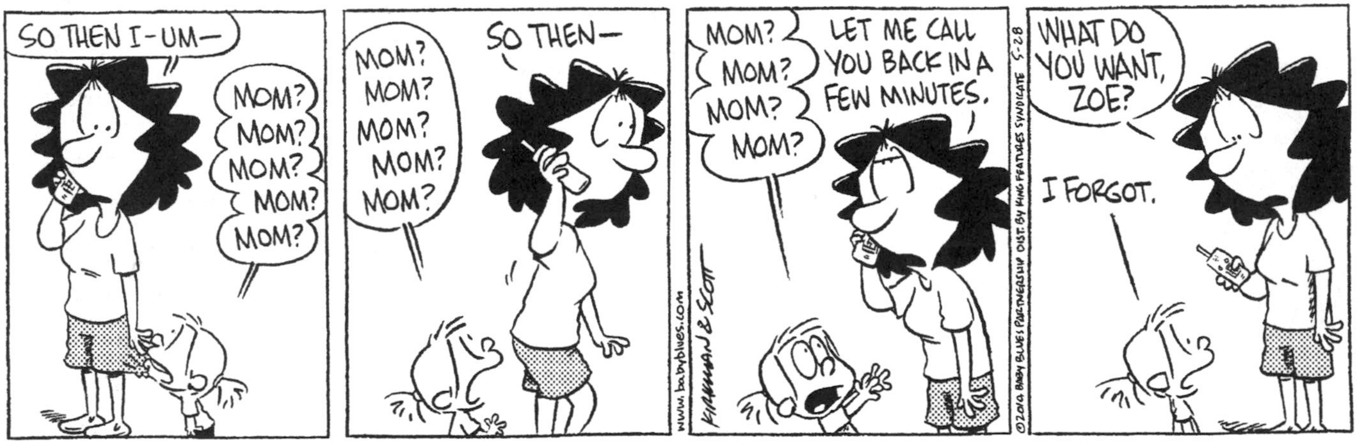
SO THEN I-UM—
MOM? MOM? MOM? MOM? MOM?
MOM? MOM? MOM? MOM? MOM?
SO THEN—
www.babyblues.com
KIRKMAN & SCOTT
MOM? MOM? MOM? MOM?
LET ME CALL YOU BACK IN A FEW MINUTES.
©2010 BABY BLUES PARTNERSHIP DIST. BY KING FEATURES SYNDICATE 5-28
WHAT DO YOU WANT, ZOE?
I FORGOT.

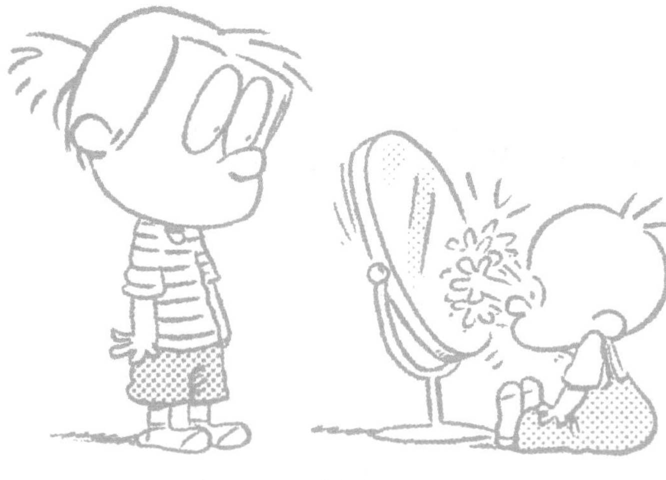

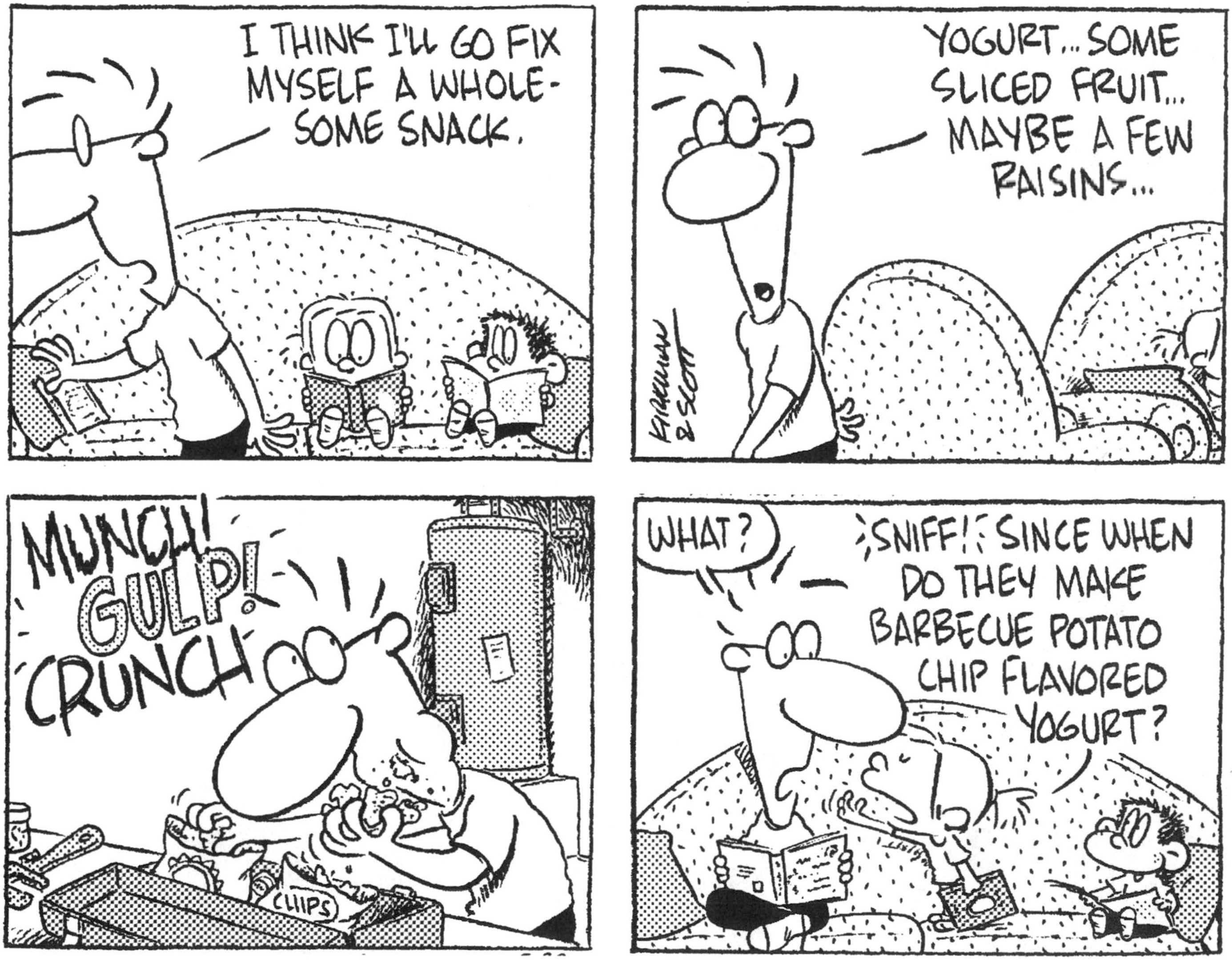
I THINK I'LL GO FIX MYSELF A WHOLESOME SNACK.
YOGURT... SOME SLICED FRUIT... MAYBE A FEW RAISINS...
KIRKMAN & SCOTT
MUNCH! GULP! CRUNCH
CHIPS
WHAT?
SNIFF! SINCE WHEN DO THEY MAKE BARBECUE POTATO CHIP FLAVORED YOGURT?

BABY BLUES®
BY RICK KIRKMAN / JERRY SCOTT
FREE REFILLS

OH! LOOK AT THE PRETTY TOWN, WREN!
SEE THE FIREHOUSE?
AND THERE'S THE SCHOOL.
YOU'RE GOING TO GO TO SCHOOL SOMEDAY, AREN'T YOU?
www.babyblues.com
HERE'S THE POLICE STATION.
HELLO, OFFICER!
SEE THE MAN PAINTING THE COURT-HOUSE?
HE SURE LOOKS BUSY!
KIRKMAN & SCOTT
AND LOOK!
THERE'S THE POST OFFICE AND THE HARDWARE STORE AND THE-
©2010, BABY BLUES PARTNERSHIP DIST. BY KING FEATURES SYNDICATE
THUP! THUP! THUP!
THERE'S A GREAT STORY GOING ON OUT HERE, AND ALL YOU'RE INTERESTED IN IS THE SNACK BAR.
5-30

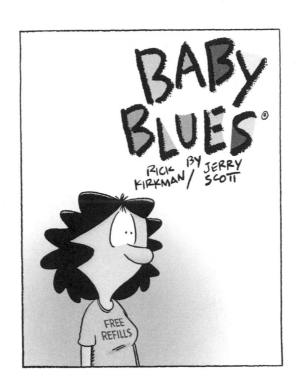

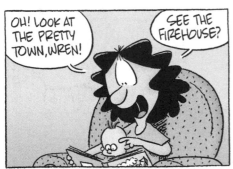

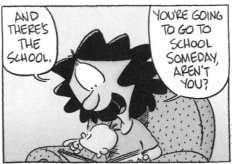

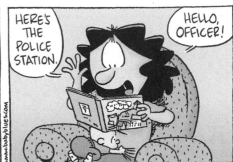

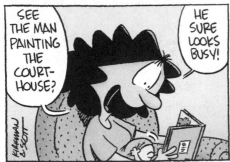

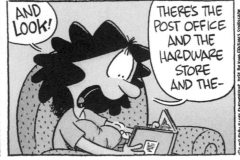

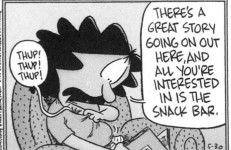

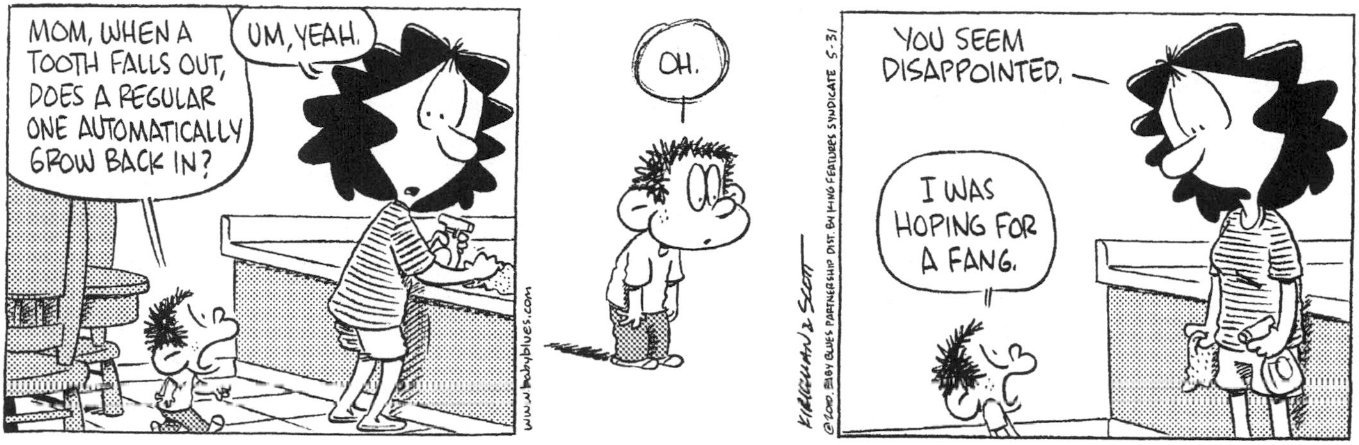
MOM, WHEN A TOOTH FALLS OUT, DOES A REGULAR ONE AUTOMATICALLY GROW BACK IN?
UM, YEAH.
www.babyblues.com
OH.
KIRKMAN & SCOTT
© 2010, BABY BLUES PARTNERSHIP DIST. BY KING FEATURES SYNDICATE 5-31
YOU SEEM DISAPPOINTED.
I WAS HOPING FOR A FANG.

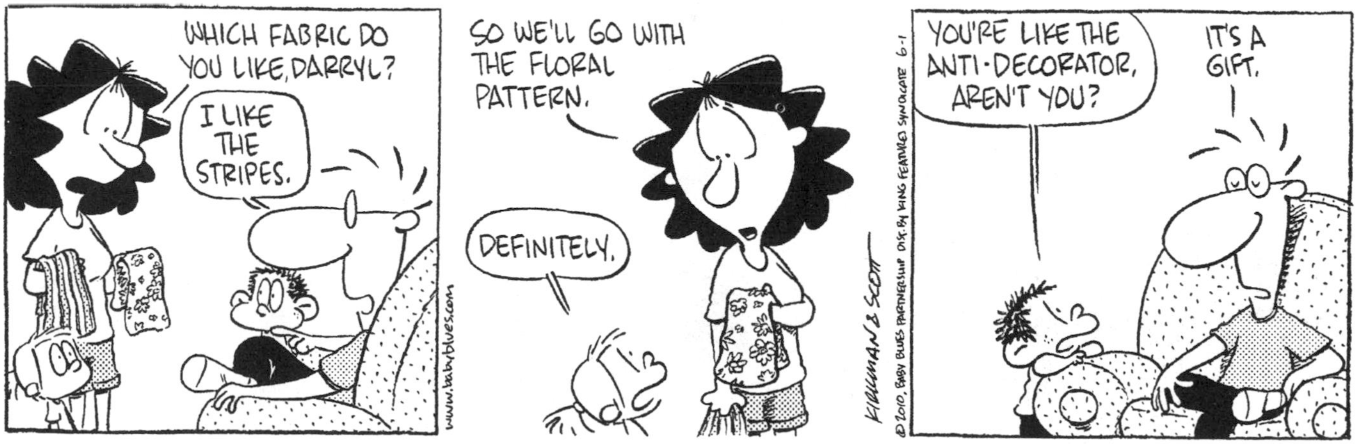
WHICH FABRIC DO YOU LIKE, DARRYL?
I LIKE THE STRIPES.
www.babyblues.com
SO WE'LL GO WITH THE FLORAL PATTERN.
DEFINITELY.
KIRKMAN & SCOTT
© 2010, BABY BLUES PARTNERSHIP DIST. BY KING FEATURES SYNDICATE 6-1
YOU'RE LIKE THE ANTI-DECORATOR, AREN'T YOU?
IT'S A GIFT.

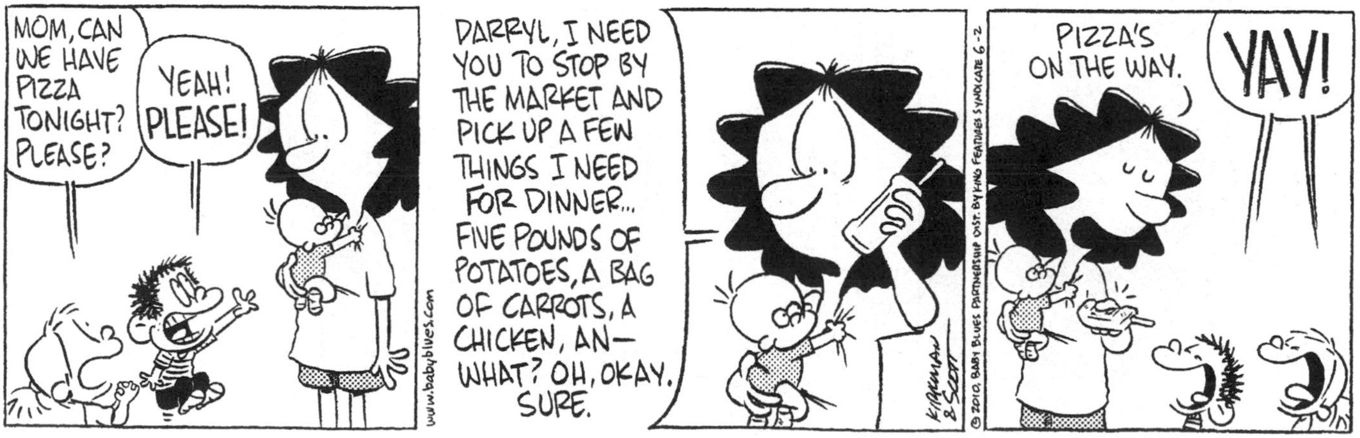
MOM, CAN WE HAVE PIZZA TONIGHT? PLEASE?
YEAH! PLEASE!
www.babyblues.com
DARRYL, I NEED YOU TO STOP BY THE MARKET AND PICK UP A FEW THINGS I NEED FOR DINNER... FIVE POUNDS OF POTATOES, A BAG OF CARROTS, A CHICKEN, AN— WHAT? OH, OKAY. SURE.
KIRKMAN & SCOTT
© 2010, BABY BLUES PARTNERSHIP DIST. BY KING FEATURES SYNDICATE 6-2
PIZZA'S ON THE WAY.
YAY!

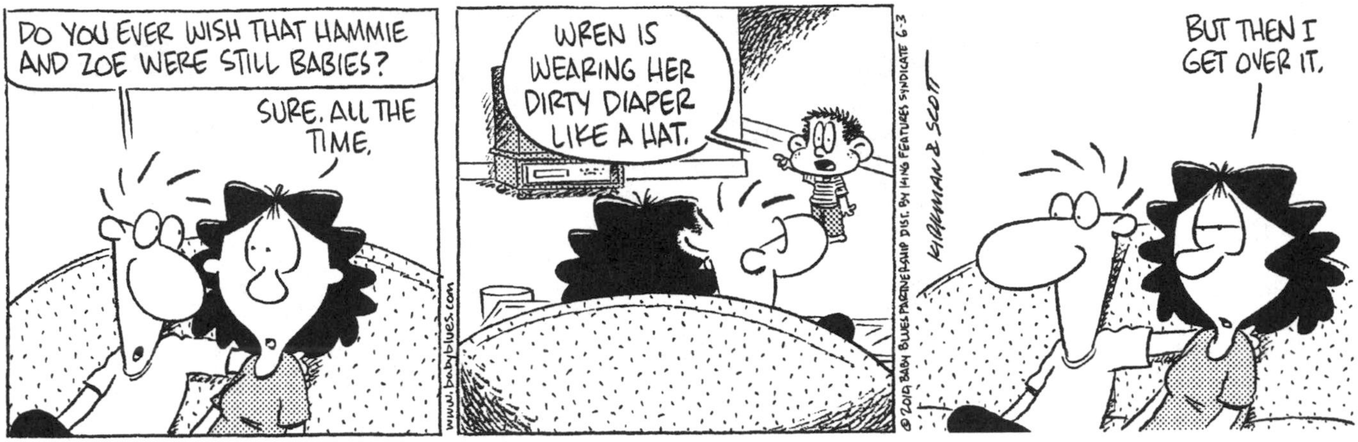
DO YOU EVER WISH THAT HAMMIE AND ZOE WERE STILL BABIES?
SURE. ALL THE TIME.
WREN IS WEARING HER DIRTY DIAPER LIKE A HAT.
BUT THEN I GET OVER IT.
www.babyblues.com
© 2010 BABY BLUES PARTNERSHIP DIST. BY KING FEATURES SYNDICATE 6-3
KIRKMAN & SCOTT

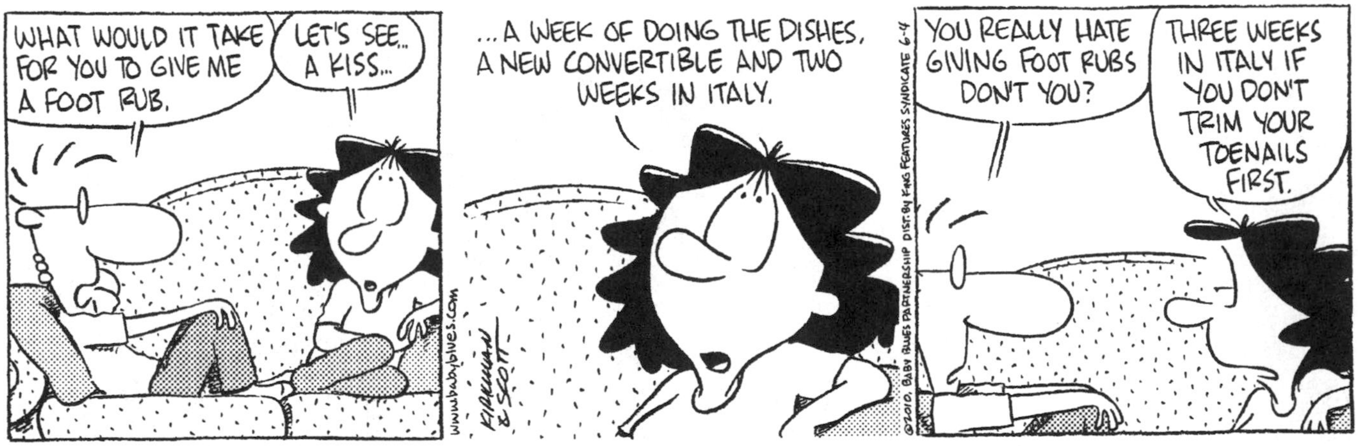
WHAT WOULD IT TAKE FOR YOU TO GIVE ME A FOOT RUB.
LET'S SEE.. A KISS...
...A WEEK OF DOING THE DISHES, A NEW CONVERTIBLE AND TWO WEEKS IN ITALY.
YOU REALLY HATE GIVING FOOT RUBS DON'T YOU?
THREE WEEKS IN ITALY IF YOU DON'T TRIM YOUR TOENAILS FIRST.
www.babyblues.com
KIRKMAN & SCOTT
© 2010, BABY BLUES PARTNERSHIP DIST. BY KING FEATURES SYNDICATE 6-4

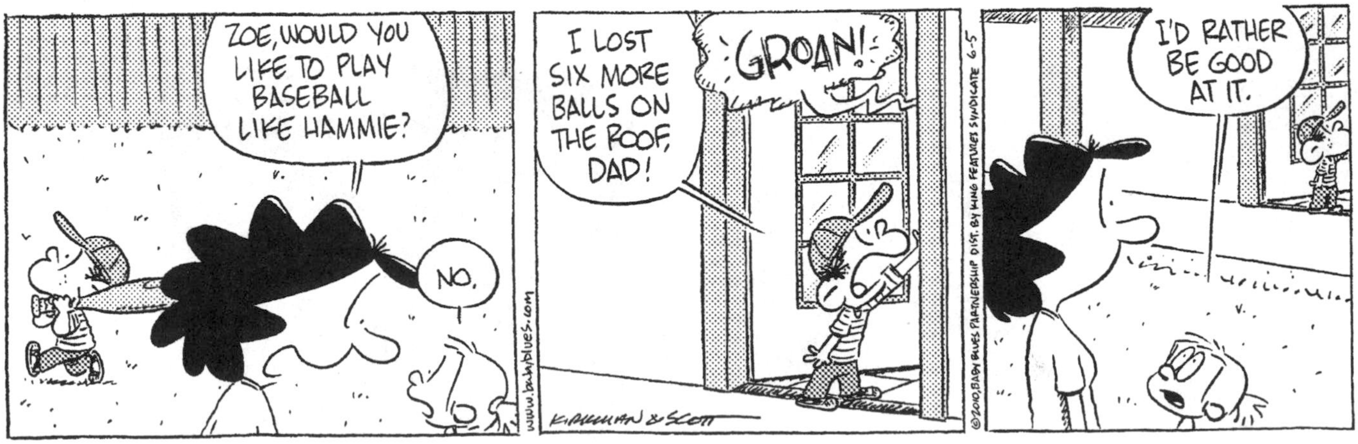
ZOE, WOULD YOU LIKE TO PLAY BASEBALL LIKE HAMMIE?
NO.
I LOST SIX MORE BALLS ON THE ROOF, DAD!
GROAN!
I'D RATHER BE GOOD AT IT.
www.babyblues.com
KIRKMAN & SCOTT
© 2010, BABY BLUES PARTNERSHIP DIST. BY KING FEATURES SYNDICATE 6-5

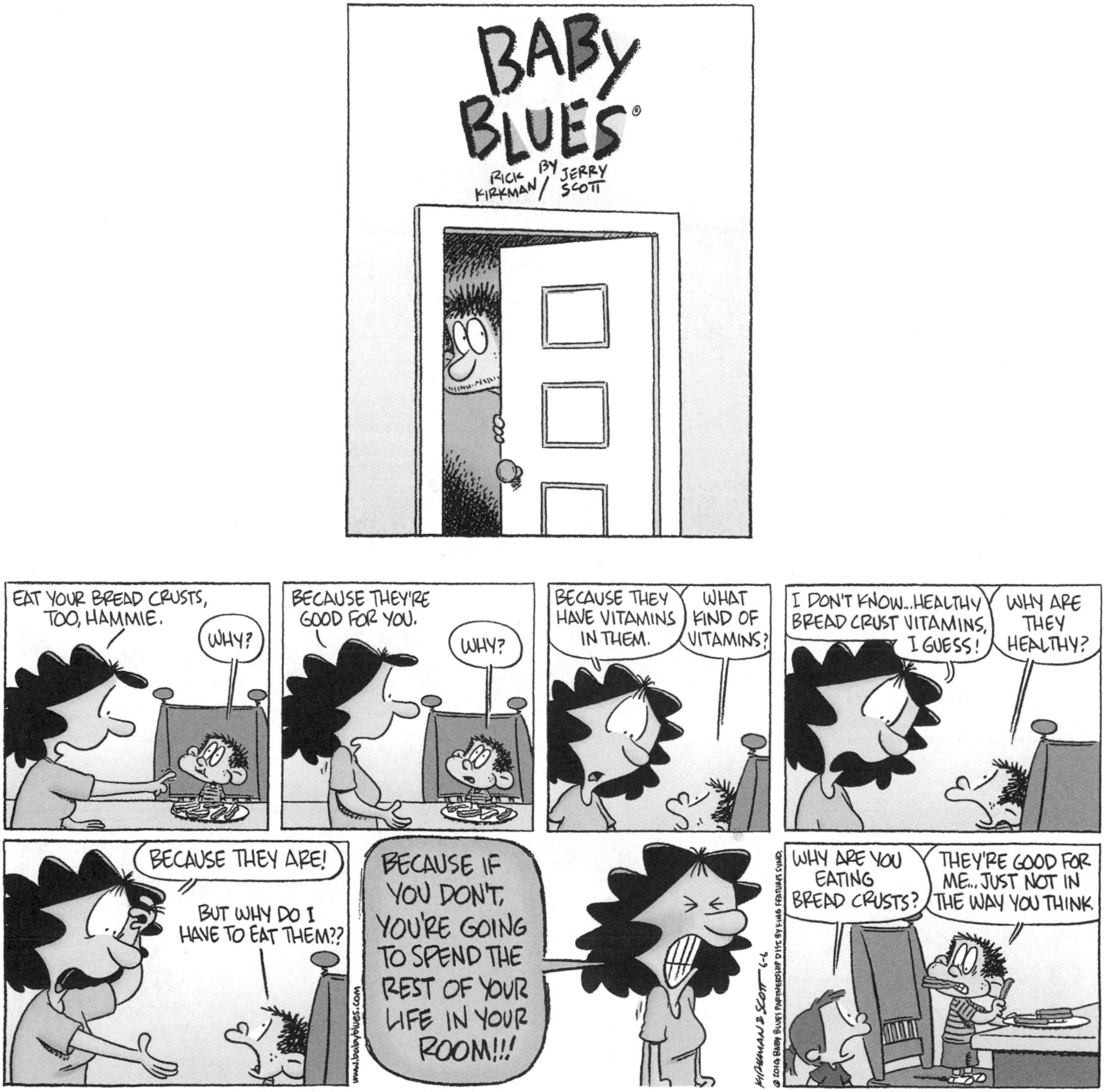
BABY BLUES®
RICK KIRKMAN / BY / JERRY SCOTT
EAT YOUR BREAD CRUSTS, TOO, HAMMIE.
WHY?
BECAUSE THEY'RE GOOD FOR YOU.
WHY?
BECAUSE THEY HAVE VITAMINS IN THEM.
WHAT KIND OF VITAMINS?
I DON'T KNOW...HEALTHY BREAD CRUST VITAMINS, I GUESS!
WHY ARE THEY HEALTHY?
BECAUSE THEY ARE!
BUT WHY DO I HAVE TO EAT THEM??
www.babyblues.com
BECAUSE IF YOU DON'T, YOU'RE GOING TO SPEND THE REST OF YOUR LIFE IN YOUR ROOM!!!
KIRKMAN & SCOTT 6-6
©2010 BABY BLUES PARTNERSHIP DIST. BY KING FEATURES SYND.
WHY ARE YOU EATING BREAD CRUSTS?
THEY'RE GOOD FOR ME... JUST NOT IN THE WAY YOU THINK.

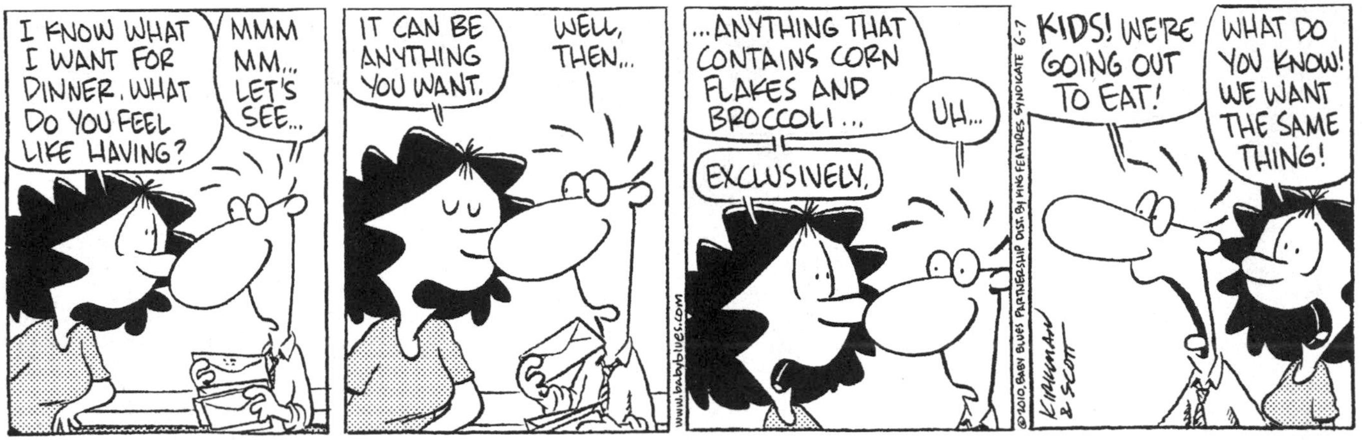
I KNOW WHAT I WANT FOR DINNER. WHAT DO YOU FEEL LIKE HAVING?
MMM MM... LET'S SEE...
IT CAN BE ANYTHING YOU WANT.
WELL, THEN...
...ANYTHING THAT CONTAINS CORN FLAKES AND BROCCOLI...
EXCLUSIVELY.
UH...
KIDS! WE'RE GOING OUT TO EAT!
WHAT DO YOU KNOW! WE WANT THE SAME THING!
www.babyblues.com
©2010, BABY BLUES PARTNERSHIP DIST. BY KING FEATURES SYNDICATE 6-7
KIRKMAN & SCOTT

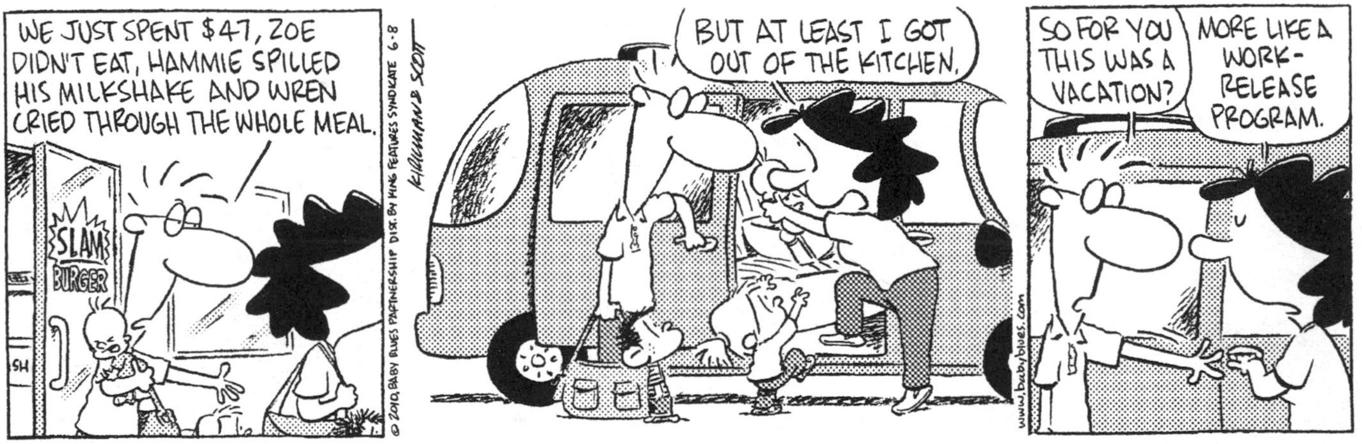
WE JUST SPENT $47, ZOE DIDN'T EAT, HAMMIE SPILLED HIS MILKSHAKE AND WREN CRIED THROUGH THE WHOLE MEAL.
SLAM BURGER
© 2010, BABY BLUES PARTNERSHIP DIST. BY KING FEATURES SYNDICATE 6-8
KIRKMAN & SCOTT
BUT AT LEAST I GOT OUT OF THE KITCHEN.
www.babyblues.com
SO FOR YOU THIS WAS A VACATION?
MORE LIKE A WORK-RELEASE PROGRAM.

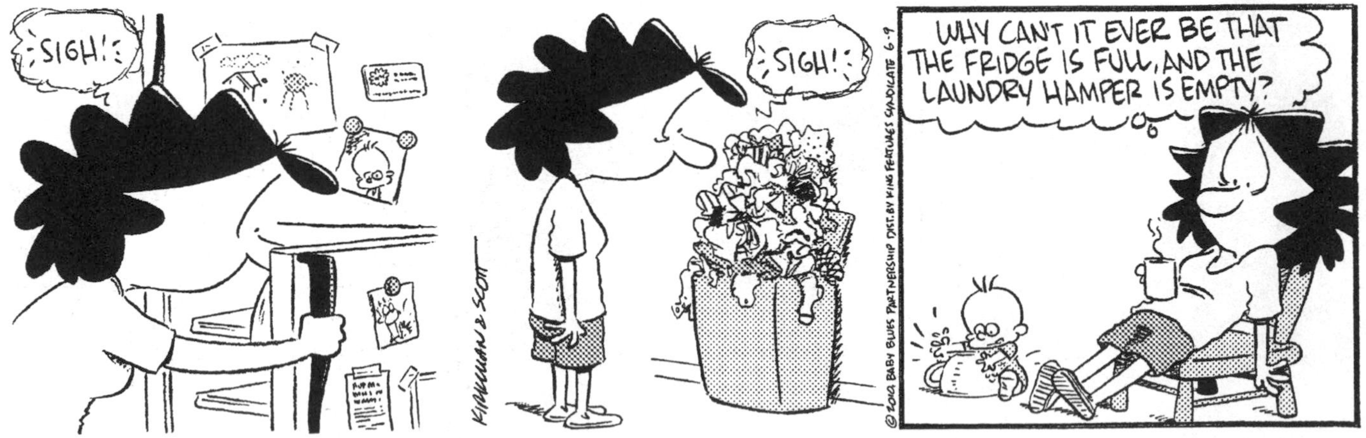
SIGH!
KIRKMAN & SCOTT
SIGH!
©2010 BABY BLUES PARTNERSHIP DIST. BY KING FEATURES SYNDICATE 6-9
WHY CAN'T IT EVER BE THAT THE FRIDGE IS FULL, AND THE LAUNDRY HAMPER IS EMPTY?

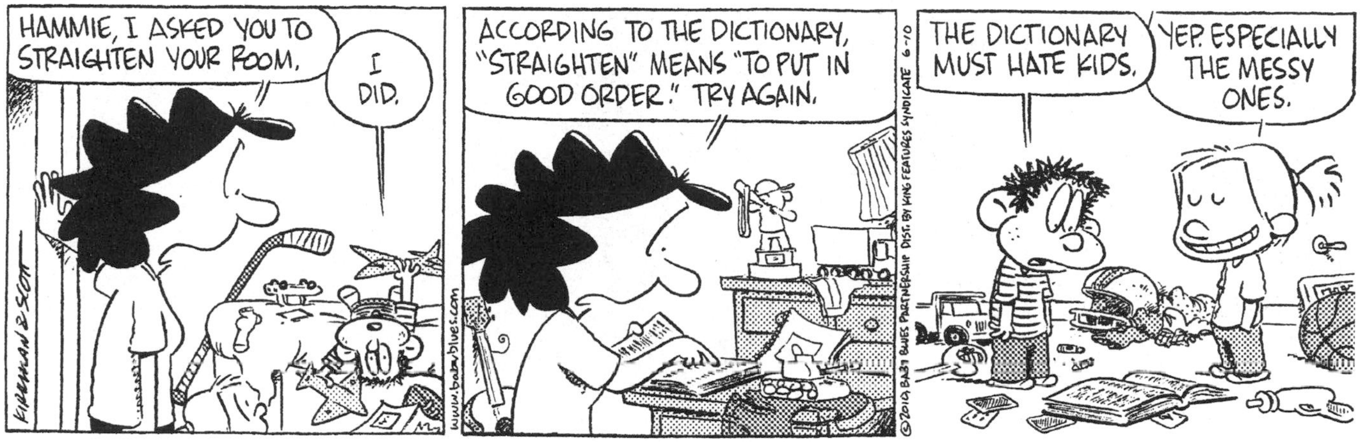
HAMMIE, I ASKED YOU TO STRAIGHTEN YOUR ROOM.
I DID.
ACCORDING TO THE DICTIONARY, "STRAIGHTEN" MEANS "TO PUT IN GOOD ORDER." TRY AGAIN.
THE DICTIONARY MUST HATE KIDS.
YEP. ESPECIALLY THE MESSY ONES.
KIRKMAN & SCOTT
www.babyblues.com
© 2010 BABY BLUES PARTNERSHIP DIST. BY KING FEATURES SYNDICATE 6-10

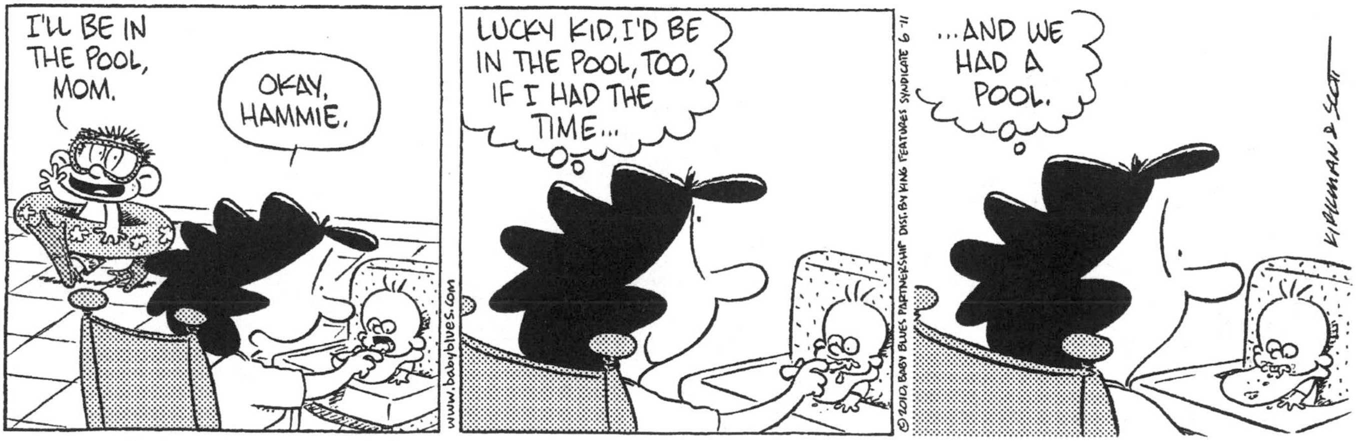
I'LL BE IN THE POOL, MOM.
OKAY, HAMMIE.
LUCKY KID. I'D BE IN THE POOL, TOO, IF I HAD THE TIME...
...AND WE HAD A POOL.
www.babyblues.com
© 2010 BABY BLUES PARTNERSHIP DIST. BY KING FEATURES SYNDICATE 6-11
KIRKMAN & SCOTT

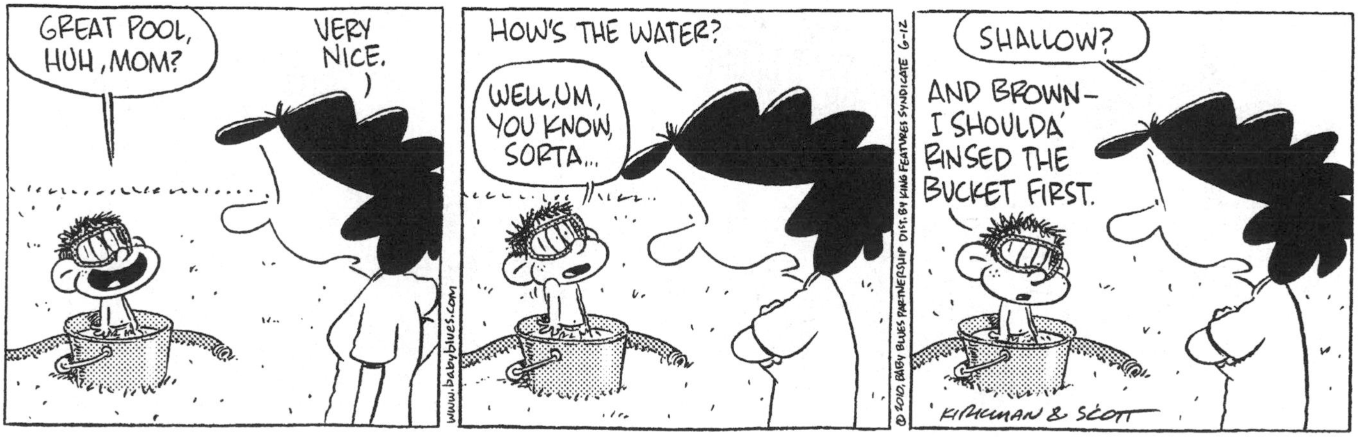
GREAT POOL, HUH, MOM?
VERY NICE.
HOW'S THE WATER?
WELL, UM, YOU KNOW, SORTA...
SHALLOW?
AND BROWN— I SHOULDA' RINSED THE BUCKET FIRST.
www.babyblues.com
© 2010 BABY BLUES PARTNERSHIP DIST. BY KING FEATURES SYNDICATE 6-12
KIRKMAN & SCOTT

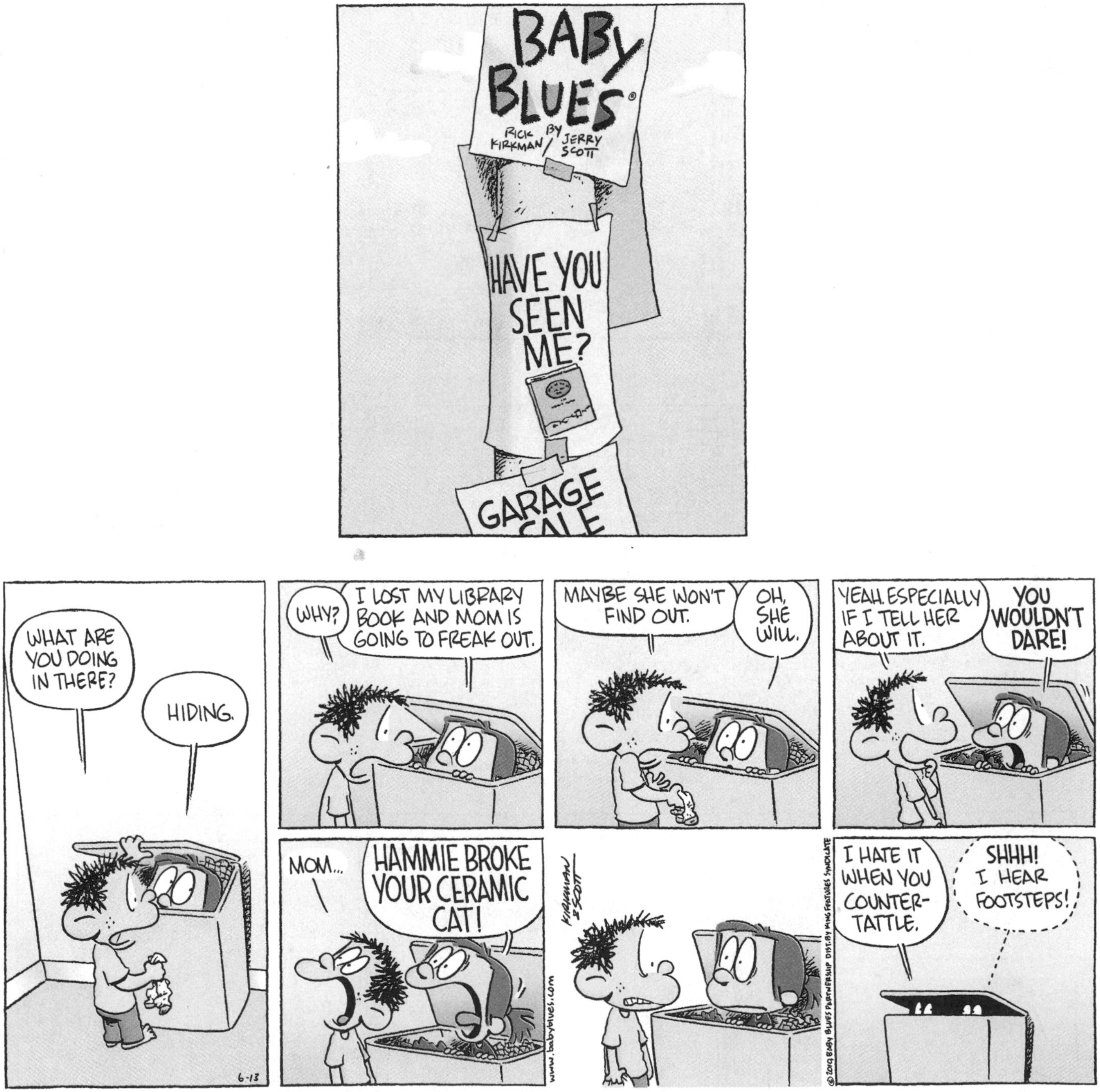
BABY BLUES®
BY RICK KIRKMAN / JERRY SCOTT
HAVE YOU SEEN ME?
GARAGE SALE
WHAT ARE YOU DOING IN THERE?
HIDING.
6-13
WHY?
I LOST MY LIBRARY BOOK AND MOM IS GOING TO FREAK OUT.
MAYBE SHE WON'T FIND OUT.
OH, SHE WILL.
YEAH. ESPECIALLY IF I TELL HER ABOUT IT.
YOU WOULDN'T DARE!
MOM...
HAMMIE BROKE YOUR CERAMIC CAT!
www.babyblues.com
KIRKMAN & SCOTT
©2019 BABY BLUES PARTNERSHIP DIST. BY KING FEATURES SYNDICATE
I HATE IT WHEN YOU COUNTER-TATTLE.
SHHH! I HEAR FOOTSTEPS!

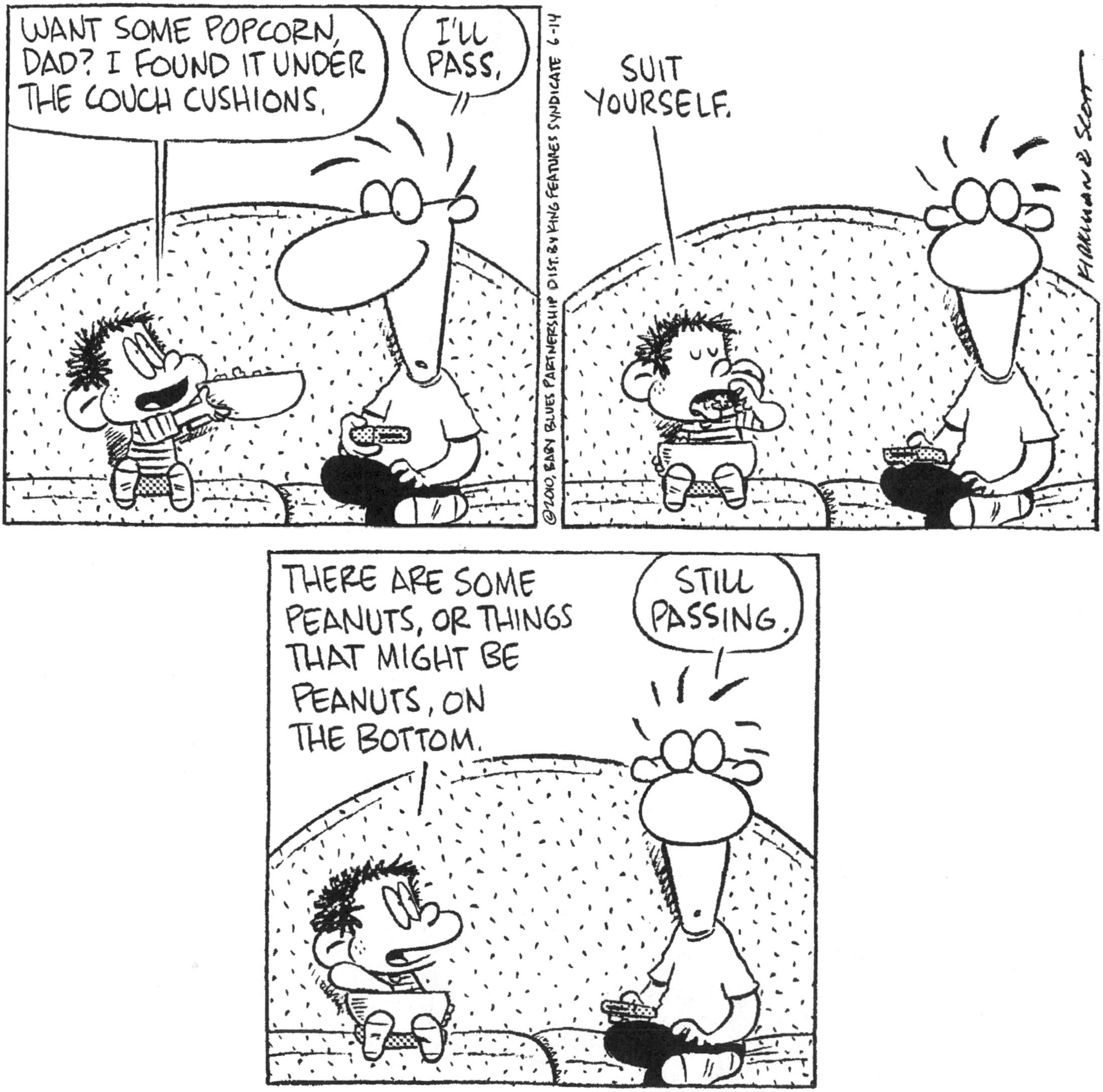
WANT SOME POPCORN, DAD? I FOUND IT UNDER THE COUCH CUSHIONS.
I'LL PASS.
©2010, BABY BLUES PARTNERSHIP DIST. BY KING FEATURES SYNDICATE 6-14
SUIT YOURSELF.
KIRKMAN & SCOTT
THERE ARE SOME PEANUTS, OR THINGS THAT MIGHT BE PEANUTS, ON THE BOTTOM.
STILL PASSING.

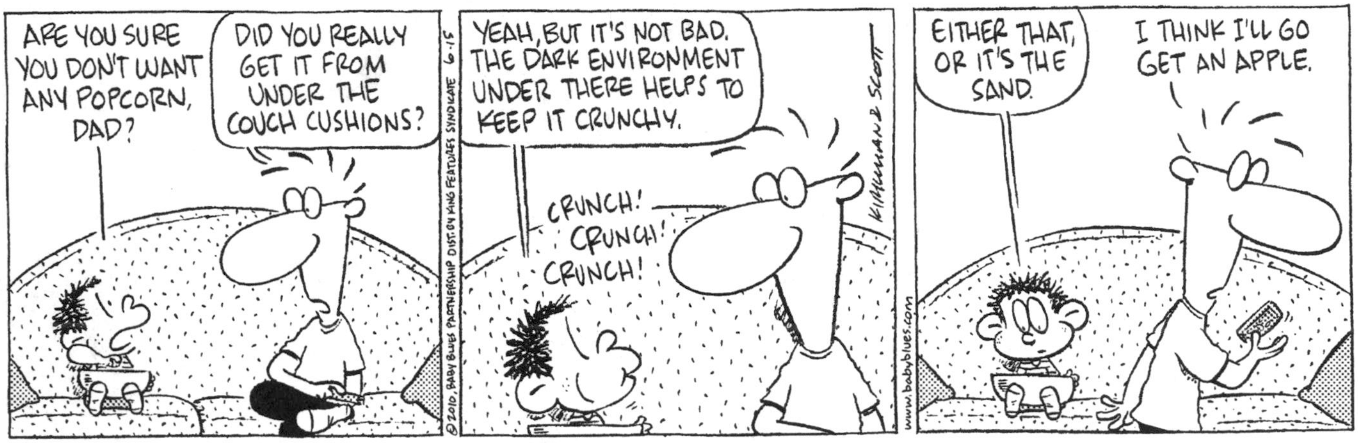
ARE YOU SURE YOU DON'T WANT ANY POPCORN, DAD?
DID YOU REALLY GET IT FROM UNDER THE COUCH CUSHIONS?
© 2010, BABY BLUES PARTNERSHIP DIST. BY KING FEATURES SYNDICATE 6-15
YEAH, BUT IT'S NOT BAD. THE DARK ENVIRONMENT UNDER THERE HELPS TO KEEP IT CRUNCHY.
CRUNCH! CRUNCH! CRUNCH!
KIRKMAN & SCOTT
www.babyblues.com
EITHER THAT, OR IT'S THE SAND.
I THINK I'LL GO GET AN APPLE.

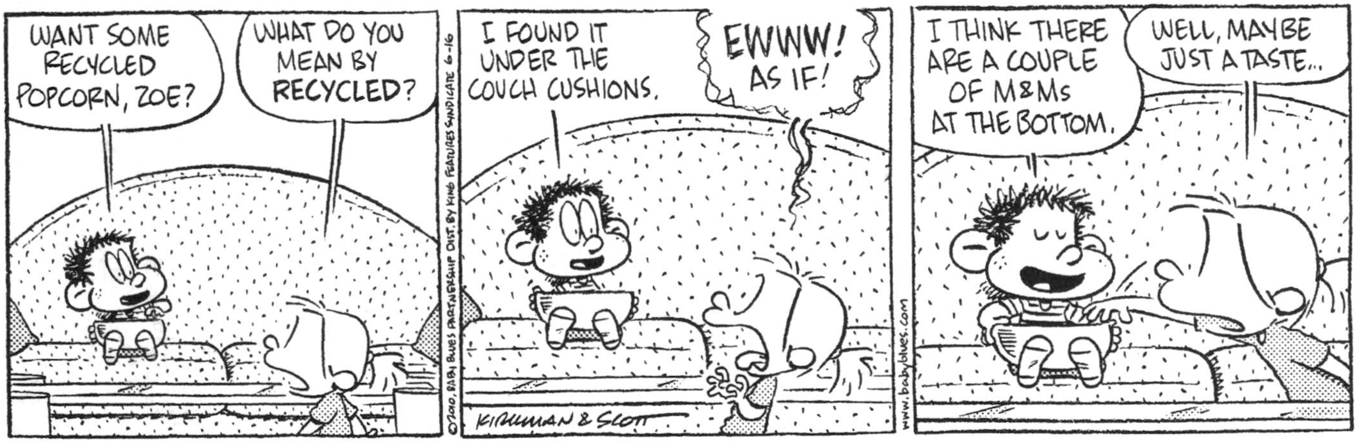
WANT SOME RECYCLED POPCORN, ZOE?
WHAT DO YOU MEAN BY RECYCLED?
© 2010, BABY BLUES PARTNERSHIP DIST. BY KING FEATURES SYNDICATE 6-16
I FOUND IT UNDER THE COUCH CUSHIONS.
EWWW! AS IF!
KIRKMAN & SCOTT
www.babyblues.com
I THINK THERE ARE A COUPLE OF M&Ms AT THE BOTTOM.
WELL, MAYBE JUST A TASTE...

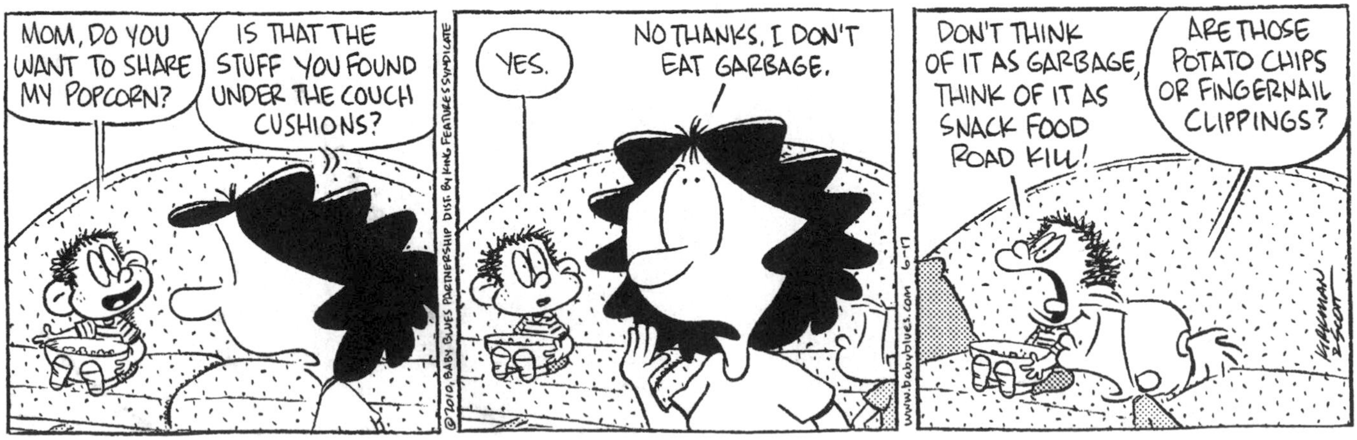
MOM, DO YOU WANT TO SHARE MY POPCORN?
IS THAT THE STUFF YOU FOUND UNDER THE COUCH CUSHIONS?
© 2010, BABY BLUES PARTNERSHIP DIST. BY KING FEATURES SYNDICATE
YES.
NO THANKS. I DON'T EAT GARBAGE.
www.babyblues.com 6-17
DON'T THINK OF IT AS GARBAGE, THINK OF IT AS SNACK FOOD ROAD KILL!
ARE THOSE POTATO CHIPS OR FINGERNAIL CLIPPINGS?
KIRKMAN & SCOTT